British Social Attitudes

Attitudes The 18th REPORT

The *National Centre for Social Research* (NatCen) is an independent, non-profit social research institute. It has a large professional staff together with its own interviewing and coding resources. Some of NatCen's work – such as the survey reported in this book – is initiated by the institute itself and grant-funded by research councils or foundations. Other work is initiated by government departments, local authorities or quasi-government organisations to provide information on aspects of social or economic policy. NatCen also works frequently with other institutes and academics. Founded in 1969 and now Britain's largest social research institute, NatCen has a high reputation for the standard of its work in both qualitative and quantitative research. NatCen has a Survey Methods Centre and, with the Department of Sociology, University of Oxford, houses the Centre for Research into Elections and Social Trends (CREST), which is an ESRC Research Centre. It also houses, with Southampton University, the Centre for Applied Social Surveys (CASS), an ESRC Resource Centre, two main functions of which are to run courses in survey methods and to establish and administer an electronic social survey question bank.

The contributors

John Appleby
Director of the Health Systems Programme at the King's Fund

Ann Barlow
Senior Lecturer in Law at the University of Wales, Aberystwyth

Martin Bobrow
Professor of Medical Genetics at the University of Cambridge

Catherine Bromley
Senior Researcher at NatCen, Scotland and Co-Director of the *British Social Attitudes* survey series

Ian Christie
Associate Director of the consultancy The Local Futures Group

Lynda Clarke
Senior Lecturer at the Centre for Population Studies, London School of Hygiene and Tropical Medicine

John Curtice
Head of Research at NatCen, Scotland, Deputy Director of CREST, and Professor of Politics at Strathclyde University

Simon Duncan
Professor of Comparative Social Policy at the University of Bradford

Geoffrey Evans
Official Fellow in Politics, Nuffield College Oxford and University Reader in the Sociology of Politics

Jonathan Gardner
Research Fellow in the Department of Economics at the University of Warwick

Grace James
Research Fellow in the Law Department at the University of Wales, Aberystwyth

John Hills
Professor of Social Policy and Director of CASE at the London School of Economics

Lindsey Jarvis
Senior Researcher at NatCen and Co-Director of the *British Social Attitudes* survey series

Michael Johnston
Professor of Political Science at Colgate University, New York

Roger Jowell
International Director of NatCen and Visiting Professor at the London School of Economics and Political Science

Theresa Marteau
Professor of Health Psychology at King's College, London

Jo-Ann Mulligan
Research Officer at the King's Fund

Andrew Oswald
Professor of Economics at the University of Warwick

Alison Park
Research Director at NatCen and Co-Director of the *British Social Attitudes* survey series

Ben Seyd
Senior Research Fellow at the Constitution Unit, University College London

Nina Stratford
Senior Researcher at NatCen

Katarina Thomson
Researcher Director at NatCen and Co-Director of the *British Social Attitudes* survey series

British Social Attitudes

Attitudes The 18th REPORT

Public policy, Social ties

EDITORS

Alison Park
John Curtice
Katarina Thomson
Lindsey Jarvis
Catherine Bromley

SAGE Publications
London · Thousand Oaks · New Delhi

National Centre *for*
Social Research

First published 2001

SAGE Publications Ltd
6 Bonhill Street
London EC2A 4PU

SAGE Publications Inc.
2455 Teller Road
Thousand Oaks, California 91320

SAGE Publications India Pvt Ltd
32, M-Block Market
Greater Kailash - I
New Delhi 110 048

British Library Cataloguing in Publication data

A catalogue record for this book is available from the British Library

ISSN 0267 6869
ISBN 0 7619 7453 9

Library of Congress Control Number available

Printed in Great Britain by The Cromwell Press Ltd, Trowbridge, Wiltshire

Contents

List of tables and figures

Chapter 3

Chapter 4

Chapter 7

Chapter 8

Chapter 9

Chapter 10

Chapter 11

Introduction

This volume, like each of its annual predecessors, presents results, analyses and interpretations of the latest *British Social Attitudes* survey – the 18th in the series of reports on the studies designed and carried out by the *National Centre for Social Research*.

Two themes are explored in this year's chapters. The first, addressed in many of the earlier chapters, is the extent to which government policy is (or is not) underpinned by supportive attitudes among the public, and why. Chapter 1, for instance, considers perceptions of poverty and examines views about the role of social security in addressing it. Chapter 6 considers public responses to the many environmental problems of recent years, focusing on the gap between the green ideals expressed by so many, and their often not-so-green behaviour. Other chapters consider marriage and cohabitation, focusing on the gap between law and practice (chapter 2), views about the NHS (chapter 4) and teenage pregnancies (chapter 3), and attitudes towards genetic testing and research (chapter 5). Our finding are mixed; in some areas (such as cohabitation) we find a gulf between public attitudes and government policy – in others (such as the funding of the health service, and policy on teenage pregnancy) there is a much closer fit. And on topics such as social security and environment, questions are raised as to the relationship between policy and opinion, and the role that government does, or could, play in shaping public beliefs and values.

A second theme unites the chapters towards the end of the book. These focus upon the ways in which individuals engage with society as a whole; the ties that bind them to others and the ways in which they participate in social and political life. Chapter 8, for instance, examines 'social capital', examining people's membership of different organisations and the extent to which they trust one another. This theme is explored further in Chapter 7, which examines social capital in the internet age. Chapter 9 considers confidence in government, both the role that this can play in shaping behaviour (such as voting) and the factors that might in turn shape it. And chapter 10 examines responses in England and Scotland to devolution. These chapters reveal that levels of social trust and participation in Britain are not in the perilous state that is sometimes assumed, although confidence in government remains at a low level indeed. Nor is there any evidence that devolution has so far led to an increased likelihood of ties between England and Scotland being severed.

The *British Social Attitudes* series has a widely acknowledged reputation as the authoritative map of contemporary British values. Its reputation owes a great deal to its many generous funders. We are particularly grateful to our core funders – the Gatsby Charitable Foundation (one of the Sainsbury Family Charitable Trusts) – whose continuous support of the series from the start has given it security and independence. But other funders have made long-term commitments to supporting particular modules and we are ever grateful to them too – notably the Department of Health; the Departments for Education and Employment and of Social Security (now combined to form the Department for Work and Pensions); and the Department of the Environment, Transport and the Regions (now the Department of Transport, Local Government and the Regions). In addition, a grant from the Health Education Authority (now the Health Development Agency) provided support for a thought-provoking series of questions on teenage pregnancy.

The series also receives support for particular modules of questions from a number of funding agencies – among them the Economic and Social Research Council (ESRC), the Leverhulme Trust, the Wellcome Trust and the Nuffield Foundation. All of these supported modules being reported in this volume.

In collaboration with a number of eminent academics in Scotland, we launched a new *Scottish Social Attitudes* survey series in 1999, supported in the first instance by the ESRC, and now funded from a range of sources along the lines of *British Social Attitudes*. This new survey is closely associated with its British counterpart and incorporates many of the same questions to enable comparison north and south of the border, while also providing a detailed examination of attitudes to particular issues within Scotland. The first book in this series was published by Edinburgh University Press (Paterson *et al.*, 2000) and the second report, carrying a number of chapters in parallel with this volume, is being published at the end of 2001 (Curtice *et al.*, 2001, forthcoming).

The ESRC also continues to finance two other pieces of the jigsaw. First, it supports the National Centre's participation in the *International Social Survey Programme* (ISSP), which now comprises 38 nations, each of whom help to design and then field a set of equivalent questions every year on a rotating set of issues. Findings from the British part of this survey on attitudes to the environment are included in this volume in chapter 6.

Secondly, the ESRC continues to fund the *Centre for Research into Elections and Social Trends* (*CREST*) – an ESRC Research Centre that links the *National Centre* with the Department of Sociology at Oxford University – whose purpose is to uncover and investigate long-run changes in Britain's social and political complexion. *CREST*'s key activity over the past few years has been the 1997-2001 *British Election Panel Study*, a venture that followed-up respondents to the 1997 *British Election Study* at least annually until the 2001 general election. Some of the first findings from this study are being reported in this volume, in chapter 11.

This year the *British Social Attitudes* team has bid farewell to Nina Stratford, now working on the *National Travel Survey*, and Roger Jowell. The series owes an immeasurable debt to Roger as, without him, the first survey in 1983 would never have taken place and we all miss his enthusiasm, innovation and rigorous approach to design and reporting. Roger has not moved far and is now co-ordinating a new *European Social Survey*, designed to measure and explain the relationship between Europe's changing institutions and the attitudes, values and behaviours of its population. The survey will cover at least 17 nations and its co-ordination is funded through the European Commission's 5th Framework Programme (with supplementary funds from the European Science Foundation).

The *British Social Attitudes* series is, of course, a team effort. The researchers who design, direct and report on the study are supported by complementary teams who implement the sampling strategy and carry out data processing. They in turn depend on fieldwork controllers, area managers and field interviewers who are responsible for getting all the interviewing done, and on administrative staff to compile, organise and distribute the survey's extensive documentation. In this respect, particular thanks are due to Pauline Burge and her colleagues in *National Centre*'s administrative office in Brentwood. Other thanks are due to Sue Corbett and her colleagues in our computing department who expertly translate our questions into a computer-assisted questionnaire. Meanwhile, the raw data have to be transformed into a workable SPSS system file – a task that has for many years been performed with great care and efficiency by Ann Mair at the Social Statistics Laboratory in the University of Strathclyde. Finally, the various chapters of the book have to be organised and formatted, notoriously difficult tasks that Sheila Vioche, as always, performs with consummate ease and serenity.

We are now in our second year with new publishers, Sage, and many thanks are due to Lucy Robinson and Vanessa Harwood for managing the smooth changeover.

As always, however, our warmest praise is reserved for the anonymous respondents across Britain who gave their time to take part in our 2000 survey. Like the 43,000 or so respondents who have participated before them, they are the cornerstone of this enterprise. We hope that some of them will one day come across this volume and read about themselves with interest.

The Editors

References

Paterson, L., Brown, A., Curtice, J., Hinds, K., McCrone, D., Park, A., Sproston, K. and Surridge, P. (2000), *New Scotland, New Politics?*, Edinburgh: Edinburgh University Press.

Curtice, J., McCrone, D., Park, A. and Paterson, L. (eds.) (2001, forthcoming), *New Scotland, New Society? Are social and political ties fragmenting?*, Edinburgh: Edinburgh University Press.

1 Poverty and social security: What rights? Whose responsibilities?

John Hills[*]

In March 1999 Tony Blair surprised the audience to his Beveridge lecture by pledging to eliminate child poverty in Britain over the next 20 years (Walker, 1999). Subsequently, the Labour government extended this to a shorter-term target of halving it in ten years. In addition, as part of the Spending Review in 2000, the Treasury adopted a specific target to reduce by a quarter the proportion of children in families with incomes below 60 per cent of the median income by 2004 (HM Treasury, 2000).

These high profile commitments raise two issues. First, what is meant by 'poverty'? Tony Blair's original pledge gave no specific definition against which progress towards his target could be measured. But definitions of what is meant by poverty can vary greatly. An *absolute* measure uses a fixed measuring rod, adjusted only for inflation, to set the poverty line. For instance, how many people are unable to afford a particular basket of goods which remains the same over time? Achieving poverty reductions against this kind of line (such as the official US poverty line) is a great deal easier than if the poverty line is a moving target which rises with contemporary living standards. This latter kind of *relative* poverty definition is more widely used in continental Europe. Such a relative definition has been implicit in Labour's statements condemning the trebling of child poverty under their Conservative predecessors (as measured using a *relative* cut-off of less than half contemporary mean income). It is now also explicit in the Treasury's own performance indicator. Questions in the 2000 *British Social Attitudes* survey shed light on how the public in general define poverty.

The second issue is how government should go about tackling poverty. Specifically, what is the role of the social security system in achieving this? Labour's policy towards the welfare state in their first term in office was based on the idea of a balance between the 'rights and responsibilities' of citizens and government (Department of Social Security, 1998). Where do people see the balance of such responsibilities as lying, and what then are the implications for

[*] John Hills is Professor of Social Policy and Director of the ESRC Research Centre for Analysis of Social Exclusion (CASE) at the London School of Economics.

the structure and level of social security benefits? Have Labour's changes in the social security benefits system in their first three years of government, coupled with their anti-poverty commitments, affected the popularity and acceptability of social security?

On the first issue of what constitutes poverty, there is a huge and contentious academic literature (for a review, see Alcock, 1997). Definitions used in academic attempts to measure poverty over the last century have included: "living in obvious want and squalor" (Rowntree's secondary poverty line – Rowntree, 1901); having incomes too low to afford a "scientifically" determined basket of goods (Rowntree's primary poverty line); having incomes too low to meet the "human needs of labour" (Rowntree in his survey of York in the 1930s); having incomes (or spending) below 140 per cent of national assistance rates (now Income Support) (Abel-Smith and Townsend, 1965); having incomes too low to allow participation in normal activities and consumption (Townsend, 1979); being unable to afford items which the majority of the population regards as "necessities" (the *Breadline Britain* approach used by Mack and Lansley, 1985); and measures based on the shape of the income distribution, such as having incomes below half of the average, which are published in the Department for Work and Pensions' (formerly Department of Social Security) *Households Below Average Income* series (Department of Social Security, 1997, 1999, 2000, 2001).

Different kinds of poverty measure do not only produce varying figures for the extent of poverty at any one time; they also suggest different trends over time. Let us look at three examples.

First, if we use an *absolute* measure, the numbers in poverty fell slowly in the late 1980s and rapidly in the 1990s. For instance, using a line of 40 per cent of mean income in 1994-1995 adjusted only for inflation, about 12 per cent of the population were in poverty in 1984, 11 per cent in 1990, eight per cent in 1994-1995, and six per cent in 1999-2000 (Department of Social Security, 2001, interpolating figures for 1984).

Secondly, if we use a purely *relative* measure, adjusted in line with growth in general living standards, numbers in poverty in Britain rose rapidly in the second half of the 1980s and then stabilised in the 1990s. For instance, against a line of half of contemporary mean income, nine per cent were in poverty in 1984, 21 per cent in 1990, 18 per cent in 1994-1995 and 19 per cent in 1999-2000.[1]

Thirdly, if we use the *Breadline Britain* measure of being unable to afford three or more items identified by the majority of the population at the time as necessities, poverty rose substantially in the 1980s *and* 1990s. It was 14 per cent in 1983 rising to 21 per cent in 1990, and then again to 24 per cent by 1999 (Gordon *et al.*, 2000).

We shall use the *British Social Attitudes* survey to see whether public beliefs about poverty are consistent with any of these three measures.

On the question of *how* poverty is to be reduced, there is an apparent contradiction within the Labour government's policies. On the one hand, government statements have branded parts of the social security budget as 'spending on failure' and Labour continued the Conservative's general policy of linking the values of benefits to prices (rather than increasing them faster as living standards rose). At the start of their time in office, Labour ministers were sent to "think the unthinkable" on the system's future – cuts in benefits for lone parents and some disabled people were carried through, and failings of the system in terms of disincentives and fraud were highlighted. The responsibilities of claimants, particularly those able to work, were emphasised. And those in work were also expected to do more to provide for their own pensions if able to afford it.

However, at the same time, the government made selective but significant increases above inflation in benefits and tax credits, and introduced a number of benefit and tax changes to "make work pay". As with other aspects of the welfare state, spending was increased in certain areas, but only alongside reform of the structure. Analysis of how government policies between 1997 and 2001 are expected to meet the promise to raise a million children out of poverty shows that the larger part of this is down to increases in benefits and tax credits, including large increases in the allowances for children built into the means-tested Income Support rates (Piachaud and Sutherland, 2001).

Previous analysis of the *British Social Attitudes* suggested that the emphasis the government put on particular parts of its policies matched public opinion. While favouring government action to reduce inequalities, the public was selective in which benefits they think should be increased, favouring increases for pensioners, disabled people, carers and low-paid families but not for unemployed people, who they tended instead to think should be offered jobs in preference to benefits (Hills and Lelkes, 1999).

After three years of the new Labour policies, different things may have happened to public attitudes to poverty and social security:

- The emphasis on reform and the responsibilities of claimants may have made social security benefits more acceptable and popular by bringing them more into line with existing attitudes.
- Alternatively, the emphasis on the conditional nature of benefits may have reinforced their social unacceptability and rendered them less popular.
- Another possibility is that Labour underestimated the popularity of (at least some) benefits and their failure to be more generous has generated an increased demand for spending on them.
- Finally, people may believe that what has been done has been enough, and no more is needed.

This chapter starts with an examination of what the general public understands by 'poverty', their own experience of it, how widespread they believe it to be and whether it has been increasing. We then discuss who or what they blame for poverty, what the government should do about it, and where the rights and responsibilities of the public lie. We conclude by examining the dramatic shifts in opinion on one of the most contentious issues: what should happen to benefits for the unemployed?

What is poverty?

A first check on which definition of poverty best matches public attitudes is shown in the table below. We asked whether people in Britain would be "in poverty" in certain circumstances. Clearly for most people, being unable to afford the things most people have and take for granted does not constitute poverty. But nor is poverty solely a question of not having enough to "eat and live". For most people poverty is also about whether you can afford "other things" that people "need". These results have changed little from when the same questions were asked in earlier years of the *British Social Attitudes* survey, suggesting that people's definitions of poverty are very stable.

Table 1.1 Definitions of poverty, 1986-2000

% who say in poverty if someone had ...	1986	1989	1994	2000
... enough to buy the things they really needed, but not enough to buy the things most people take for granted	25	25	28	27
... enough to eat and live, but not enough to buy other things they needed	55	60	60	59
... not enough to eat and live without getting into debt	95	95	90	93
Base	*1548*	*1516*	*1167*	*3426*

Poverty as being unable to afford necessities is almost a tautology. Such a definition does not by itself tell us what these "things people need" are, whether they change over time, or how many people lack them. However, the results do suggest that most people would have sympathy for something like the *Breadline Britain* approach of measuring poverty – first asking the population what they think of as 'necessities' and then finding out how many people are unable to afford them.

Ours is a rather different conclusion from that reached by Peter Taylor-Gooby (1995), who interpreted the kind of responses shown in the previous table as meaning that only a small number think of poverty in relative terms. The key question is whether views of what constitute the "things people need" change over time with rising general living standards. The other evidence surveyed here and revealed by the various *Breadline Britain* surveys (Gordon *et al.*, 2000) suggests that they do.

A second indication of what people mean by poverty and how widespread they think it is, comes from what they say about their own experiences. When asked to look back over their lives, judging by the standards of that time, only half (51 per cent) say they had never lived in poverty, with a further one in six (17 per cent) saying they had done so only rarely. A third of respondents said they had lived in poverty more frequently: 23 per cent "occasionally", seven per cent "often" and three per cent "most of the time". A quarter said they had experienced poverty as a child, and 37 per cent as an adult (both of these figures including 13 per cent who said "both"). The overlap between the two categories suggests that half of those who had experienced poverty as a child had also done so as an adult by the time of the survey, compared to a third of those who did not report poverty in their childhood.

These numbers closely mirror newly emerging findings on movements in and out of low income from the *British Household Panel Study* in the 1990s. For instance, looking at the first seven years of this survey, only 55 per cent never had incomes in the poorest fifth, but 12 per cent did so for five or more of the years, with four per cent doing so for all seven years (Department of Social Security, 1999). The reported experiences of 'poverty' from the *British Social Attitudes* suggest that this pattern matches public perceptions of their own experience. The results support poverty definitions that would include around a fifth of the population in the 1990s.

Beliefs about what constitutes 'poverty' vary to some extent with people's own experience and other factors, such as political identification, as can be seen in the next table. Conservative identifiers are the least likely and Labour identifiers the most likely to take the most generous definition of poverty, but for all three political groupings a majority favours the needs-based definition. There is more variation by people's own reported experience of poverty and their own assessment of their current income. Two-fifths of those "finding it very difficult" on their current income favour the most generous interpretation, compared with only a quarter of those "living comfortably" on their current income. There is almost as big a gap between those saying they have never been in poverty and those who say they have experienced it "often" or "most of the time".

Of course, causality can go both ways here. Those closest to poverty may have the most generous (or realistic) view of what is needed to avoid it. Alternatively, the people with the most generous interpretation of poverty – that people are poor if they do not have the things most people take for granted – may also be those who are most likely to count themselves as poor at any given level of income, or find it as being too little to manage on. Either of these could generate the pattern seen in the last two sections of the table. However, those finding it "difficult" or "very difficult" on their current income are also much more likely to report low cash incomes than others, suggesting that their difficulties are not just the result of overly high expectations of what they should be able to afford.

Table 1.2 Definitions of poverty, by party identification, own experience of poverty and assessment of current income

% who agree that someone is in poverty if they have ...	... enough for needs, not things most take for granted	... enough to eat and live, not other needs	... not enough to eat and live without debt	Base
All	27	59	93	3426
By party identification				
Conservative	22	55	93	937
Liberal Democrat	23	65	97	341
Labour	30	63	92	1394
By own experience of poverty				
Never	22	54	92	1646
Rarely/occasionally	30	65	93	1381
Often/most of the time	38	67	94	393
By assessment of current income				
Living comfortably	23	59	93	900
Coping	27	58	93	998
Finding it difficult	33	62	92	276
Finding it very difficult	40	67	95	114

Trends in the extent of poverty

We also investigated perceptions of the extent of poverty. We asked:

> *Some people say there is very little **real** poverty in Britain today. Others say there is quite a lot. Which comes closest to your view?*

In 1994, a quarter of respondents (28 per cent) said that "very little real poverty" came closest to their view, but almost three-quarters (71 per cent) preferred the statement that there was "quite a lot". It is difficult to know how to interpret someone saying that there is "quite a lot" of poverty, but it seems fair to say that it is at least not inconsistent with measures of poverty which suggest that around a fifth of the population were poor in the 1990s (as do those based on a line of half of average income or the *Breadline Britain* approach). More to the point, the proportion saying that there was "quite a lot of real poverty" had risen from 55 per cent in 1986 and 63 per cent in 1989. This is certainly inconsistent with a widespread belief in an absolute poverty line, which implies falling numbers in poverty by the mid-1990s

By 2000, there had been a small shift back, with a third (35 per cent) now saying there is "very little real poverty", and a reduced number, but still a majority, 62 per cent, suggesting that there is "quite a lot". This suggests there may have been some decline in public perceptions of the extent of poverty in the second half of the 1990s (or in views of what constitutes "quite a lot"). Again, however, this is not consistent with the *rapid* fall in poverty levels indicated by absolute measures.

Beliefs about the extent of poverty also vary by political identification and personal experience. The next table shows that nearly half of Conservative identifiers, but only a third or fewer of Liberal Democrat and Labour identifiers, think that there is "very little real poverty" in Britain today – no doubt, in part, reflecting the varying personal experiences of voters for different parties. Meanwhile, three-quarters of those who count themselves as having experienced poverty "often" or "most of the time", or who are finding it difficult to manage on their current incomes say that there is "quite a lot". Again, it is not possible to distinguish just from this whether it is experience which is driving a realistic assessment, or a generous assessment which leads to the gloomy view of their own experience.

Table 1.3 Perceptions of level of poverty in Britain, by party identification, own experience of poverty and assessment of current income

		Very little real poverty	Quite a lot of poverty	Base
All	%	35	62	3426
By party identification				
Conservative	%	46	51	937
Liberal Democrat	%	34	65	341
Labour	%	30	69	1394
By own experience of poverty				
Never	%	41	56	1646
Rarely/occasionally	%	30	68	1381
Often/most of the time	%	26	73	393
By assessment of current income				
Living comfortably	%	39	58	900
Coping	%	35	62	998
Finding it difficult	%	24	74	276
Finding it very difficult	%	20	80	114

Interestingly, however, this kind of gradient is not apparent when people's responses are divided according to their reported gross household income. There is little difference between those with incomes in the top and bottom quarters of the population in how much poverty they think there is. This suggests that variations in these views are not simply a matter of social segregation, with those who are themselves poor being more likely to live near and interact with others who are poor, and so be more likely to think that poverty is widespread.

Two further sets of questions give more clues about people's views of trends in poverty. As the next table shows, in both the 1986 and 1989 surveys, half of respondents said that they thought poverty had increased over the previous ten years. By 1994, this figure had risen to more than two-thirds, but by 2000 this had halved: only just over a third thought poverty had increased since 1990, with a similar number thinking it had remained the same. A growing number, but still only a fifth, now thought that it had actually fallen.

Table 1.4 Trends in poverty in Britain over past ten years, 1986-2000

	1986	1989	1994	2000
	%	%	%	%
Increasing	51	50	68	37
Staying at same level	30	31	24	38
Decreasing	15	16	6	20
Base	*1548*	*1516*	*1167*	*3426*

This suggests that most people do not have an absolute poverty line in mind. If they had, they would have been reporting constant poverty in the 1980s and falling poverty in the 1990s. Rather, they do seem to have in mind a poverty line which rises in real terms in some way over time. There is also a feeling that poverty increased less rapidly in the 1990s than it had from the mid-1980s. Neither contradicts the pictures painted by purely relative and the *Breadline Britain* measures, but the data do not allow us to choose between them.

These beliefs – that there is a significant amount of poverty and that it was increasing up until the mid-1990s, if not since – are also consistent with people's views of the income gap between rich and poor. Figure 1.1 shows the trend in *British Social Attitudes* respondents saying that the gap between those with high incomes and those with low incomes is too large. It is plotted alongside the proportion of the population with less than half average contemporary income, the relative measure used in the official *Households Below Average Income* statistics. A very large proportion says the gap is too large – peaking at a level of 87 per cent in 1995, but remaining at more than 80 per cent since then (measured against the right-hand scale). The movements in this series seem to lag behind those for the official measure by about three years

– coinciding (but perhaps no more than that) with the time lag in the availability of these kinds of data.

Figure 1.1 Relative poverty and attitudes to gap between rich and poor, 1983-2000

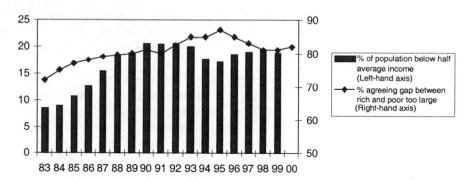

Source: Goodman and Webb (1994); Department of Social Security (2001) and earlier equivalents; *British Social Attitudes* surveys.

However, another series of responses, shown in the next table gives a rather different picture. One might expect notions of 'poverty' to be closely related to whether people can manage on their incomes. But when asked about their feelings about their own household's *current* income in 1986, a quarter of respondents said that they were finding it "difficult" or "very difficult". By 1989 this had barely changed, but by the end of the 1990s fewer than one in six gave this response. If "finding it difficult" on one's own income is an approximation to what constitutes poverty, this suggests a somewhat faster decline in the 1990s than do the purely relative measures, although probably not as fast as that implied by an absolute line. They would not be consistent with the upward trend over the 1990s in the *Breadline Britain* measure.

Table 1.5 Feelings about household's present income, 1986-2000

	1986	1989	1994	1998	1999	2000
	%	%	%	%	%	%
Finding it very difficult	8	6	6	4	4	4
Finding it difficult	18	17	16	12	12	11
Coping	49	49	49	46	47	42
Living comfortably	24	27	29	37	37	43
Base	*3100*	*3029*	*1167*	*3146*	*2091*	*2292*

The different pieces of evidence reviewed in this and the previous section generally suggest that the public do have some form of relative definition of poverty in mind, such as those that implied by looking at those with less than half contemporary average incomes or the *Breadline Britain* measure of being unable to afford "necessities". In summary:

- The majority of the population is more generous in their assessment of what poverty means than a pure subsistence line. Consistently, most people see poverty as being unable to afford necessities which go beyond just being able to eat and live.
- When asked about their own experience of repeated poverty in the past, the responses are remarkably similar to the patterns of low income over time in the 1990s as measured by being in the poorest fifth of the population and reported by the *British Household Panel Study*.
- Many more people say that there is "quite a lot" of real poverty in Britain today than say there is "very little", and trends in responses are inconsistent with widespread belief in an absolute poverty line.
- Similarly, beliefs about trends in the extent of poverty in the 1980s and 1990s are consistent with relative measures, including the view that the growth in poverty levelled off in the 1990s.
- Concerns about the income gap between rich and poor have also been greater in the 1990s than in the 1980s, although they appear to have peaked in the mid-1990s, a few years after the peak in official measures of relative poverty.
- However, during the 1990s there was a sharp fall in the number of people who said that they themselves found it "difficult to manage" on their current income. If this is related to feelings about poverty, it gives a more optimistic picture than the relative measures.

Whose responsibility is poverty?

In general then, people share the government's concerns about poverty, believe that there is quite a lot of it, and that it has grown since the 1980s. The rest of this chapter examines some of the things that might be done about it. Believing that poverty exists and has grown does not necessarily mean that people see it as the government's responsibility to do something about it – or within its capabilities. After all, it might be people's own fault that they are poor. However, data from the 1999 *British Social Attitudes* survey suggest this is not the case: over half of respondents (58 per cent) agreed that "inequality continues to exist because it benefits the rich and powerful", with only one in seven (14 per cent) disagreeing. At the same time almost as many, 55 per cent, rejected the idea that "large differences in income are necessary for Britain's prosperity", with only 17 per cent agreeing. As for the government's responsibility, only a quarter (28 per cent) of respondents in 1994 said that "British governments nowadays can do very little to reduce poverty" compared with over two-thirds (70 per cent) who said that they can do "quite a bit" (proportions that were little changed from 1986).

The next table shows that ascribing "living in need" simply to "laziness or lack of willpower" on the part of the poor is the view of a minority, but one which grew from 15 to 23 per cent during the economic recovery between 1994 and 2000 – a higher level than it had been in the mid and late 1980s. At the same time, the proportion blaming "injustice in our society" for poverty fell from 30 to 21 per cent, its lowest point in the time series so far. This could either reflect a belief that there is now a fairer society as a result of policy changes in the second half of the 1990s, or that, with a better economy, those left behind are more likely to have themselves to blame. A third of the population sees poverty as an inevitable part of modern life, although this is slightly less than the numbers doing so in 1986.

Table 1.6 Reasons why people live in need, 1986-2000

	1986	1989	1994	2000
It's an inevitable part of modern life	37	34	33	34
Because of laziness or lack of willpower	19	19	15	23
Because of injustice in our society	25	29	30	21
Because they have been unlucky	11	11	15	15
None of these/don't know	8	7	8	7
Base	*1548*	*1516*	*1167*	*3426*

This fatalism is reflected in views about future trends: in 2000, two-fifths (41 per cent) said that they thought poverty would increase over the next ten years, a third (35 per cent) that it would stay the same, and one-fifth (18 per cent) that it would fall. This suggests that the public either has no great faith in the government's anti-poverty strategy or are not aware of it, but the picture is at least more optimistic than it was in 1994, when over half (54 per cent) thought poverty would rise over the following ten years and few (10 per cent) that it would fall.

It is instructive to investigate some of these views by political identification and people's own experience of poverty. As seen in the next table, some of the biggest contrasts come in the proportions blaming injustice in our society. For instance, nearly twice as many Labour and Liberal Democrat identifiers (25 per cent) as Conservatives (13 per cent) do so. By contrast, those who say they have never experienced poverty and those currently living comfortably or coping on their incomes are more likely to blame laziness or lack of willpower for poverty than are those who have often been in poverty and those who find living on their present income very difficult. There is much less variation when it comes to seeing poverty as inevitable or a matter of bad luck – across all the groups about half blame one or other of these.

Table 1.7 Reasons why people live in need, by party identification, own experience of poverty and assessment of current income

		Inevitable part of modern life	Laziness/ lack of willpower	Injustice in our society	Unlucky	Base
All	%	34	23	21	15	3426
By party identification						
Conservative	%	38	28	13	14	937
Liberal Democrat	%	35	18	25	14	341
Labour	%	34	20	25	15	1394
By own experience of poverty						
Never	%	35	25	18	15	1646
Rarely/occasionally	%	35	22	22	15	1381
Often/most of the time	%	29	18	29	19	393
By assessment of current income						
Living comfortably	%	35	24	17	15	900
Coping	%	33	25	21	13	998
Finding it difficult	%	31	19	31	15	276
Finding it very difficult	%	31	12	31	22	114

Of key relevance for the role of social security in anti-poverty strategies is how people perceive the adequacy of benefits to keep people out of poverty. As previous years of the *British Social Attitudes* have shown, there are important differences between what people think of the adequacy of social security benefits when asked about them in abstract, and what they think when they are told the specific amounts. This is confirmed in the findings for 2000 shown in the next table. When asked simply about a 25 year old unemployed woman living alone, whose only income comes from state benefits, just over half describe her as "really poor" or "hard up", while a third say she has "enough" or "more than enough to live on". But when the actual amount of benefit, £52 per week after rent, is specified, the proportion saying this is not enough to live on rises to two-thirds (mostly as a result of a decline in the number who "don't know" when asked just about "state benefits").

Interestingly, the pattern is something of the reverse for the single mother and single pensioner. Two-thirds think a single mother whose only income is from state benefits is "really poor" or "hard up", and around three-quarters think this of a single pensioner. When the actual amounts are specified, these proportions fall to around half.

Table 1.8 Whether benefits are enough to live on

		Really poor	Hard up	Enough to live on	More than enough	Don't know
25 year old unemployed woman on:						
State benefits	%	10	46	31	3	10
£52 after rent	%	13	55	28	3	1
Unemployed single mother, one child, on:						
State benefits	%	17	51	23	2	7
£95 after rent	%	10	43	41	5	1
Pensioner living alone on:						
State pension & other benefits	%	20	57	19	1	3
£82 after rent	%	8	40	48	4	1

Base: 3426

This is in line with findings in previous surveys. In 1998, for instance, the proportion saying that a married couple had enough or more than enough to live on was a third (37 per cent) if they were said to be on "unemployment benefit", but less than a fifth (18 per cent) thought this when the amount (after rent) was given. By contrast the proportion saying incomes were enough for a pensioner couple was a quarter (24 per cent) if "on the state pension" but rose to almost a half (46 per cent) when the amount (after rent) was given (Hills and Lelkes, 1999). It strongly suggests that people have a mental image of benefits for the unemployed as being much more generous than they really are, but that the reverse is true for pensions.

Going back to the notions of poverty discussed above, the figures also suggest something about people's implicit poverty lines. An amount of £52 per week is clearly below what most people think is enough for a young single person to live on. On the other hand, just over half think that the £82 for a single pensioner is enough to live on. The closest we have to an official 'poverty line', on which policy now tends to focus is 60 per cent of median income. This works out at £81 per week for a single person in 2000 (after housing costs) and £107.50 for a single parent with a child aged four.[2] The *British Social Attitudes* findings are consistent with this poverty line as being a reflection of typical views.

These views – and particularly the difference between views of unspecified benefit levels and actual amounts – might have been expected to vary depending on people's own experiences of the benefit system, but the next table gives only partial support to this. Pensioners, whether or not they receive means-tested benefits (MTBs) themselves, are least likely to say that any of the people in the next table are "really poor" or "hard up", except when it comes to the single pensioner with an income of £82 per week, when their views are much the same as the other groups. However, and perhaps surprisingly, the responses for those receiving means-tested benefits or unemployment benefits generally change in the same direction as other groups: more say the unemployed woman is really poor or hard up when the amount is specified, and fewer say this for the single mother and pensioner. The changes are as great as, sometimes more than, those of the other groups, suggesting that current experience of state benefits does not in itself correct misconceptions about the benefit system.

Table 1.9 Whether benefits are enough to live on by own current benefit receipt

% who say someone is "really poor" or "hard up"	Pensioners (no MTBs)	with MTBs	Others with UBs or MTBs	Others with benefits	No benefits
25 year old unemployed woman on:					
State benefits	50	50	61	54	60
£52 after rent	68	60	69	70	68
Unemployed single mother, one child on:					
State benefits	55	56	74	72	70
£95 after rent	44	33	52	60	57
Pensioner living alone on:					
State pension & other benefits	76	66	76	80	77
£82 after rent	53	46	48	50	43
Base	*721*	*244*	*589*	*748*	*1106*

Note: MTBs = means-tested benefits; Ubs = unemployment benefits.

What should government do?

The 1998 survey found that three-quarters (73 per cent) of respondents thought it was "definitely" or "probably" the government's responsibility to reduce income differences between rich and poor, with only 17 per cent thinking it was not. On a slightly differently worded question in 1999, two-thirds (65 per cent) agreed that it was government's responsibility, and only 14 per cent disagreed.

   This does not tell us *what* they think the government should do, however. As the next table shows, by 2000, only two-fifths agreed that "government should *redistribute* income from the better-off to those who are less well off" (emphasis added) and just over a third disagreed. This is a large change from 1994, when half thought that government should redistribute and only a quarter disagreed. Notably, as with some of the other questions discussed previously,

1994 represented something of a peak for this kind of view, with more supporting redistribution and fewer disagreeing with it than at any other time since the question was first asked in 1987.

Table 1.10 Redistribution and welfare spending, 1987-2000

	1987	1989	1991	1993	1994	1996	1998	1999	2000
Government should redistribute income to the less well off	%	%	%	%	%	%	%	%	%
Agree	45	50	49	45	51	44	39	36	39
Neither	20	20	20	21	23	26	28	27	24
Disagree	33	29	29	33	25	28	31	35	36
Government should spend more money on welfare benefits for the poor	%	%	%	%	%	%	%	%	%
Agree	55	61	58	53	50	43	43	40	38
Neither	23	23	23	25	25	29	29	30	31
Disagree	22	15	18	20	23	26	26	28	30
Base	*1281*	*2604*	*2481*	*2567*	*2929*	*3085*	*2531*	*2450*	*2980*

The question on whether the "government should spend more money on welfare benefits for the poor, even if it leads to higher taxes" shows a gradual change dating even further back. In 2000, the largest group, just under two-fifths, agreed, but just under a third disagreed. As the lower panel of the preceding table shows, this is a substantial change from responses a decade ago, when up to 61 per cent agreed that more should be spent, and fewer than a fifth disagreed. The differences in trend between the two panels in the previous table, together with the other evidence discussed earlier, suggests that this may represent declining support for 'welfare benefits', rather than a decline in concern about poverty.

The decline in support for spending on "welfare benefits" also contrasts with the continued public support for increased spending on "health, education and social benefits", even if it means higher taxes, shown by *British Social Attitudes* surveys since the late 1980s as can be seen in Table 4.8 in the chapter by Mulligan and Appleby in this volume. In 2000, exactly half of respondents favoured the higher spending/higher tax option, compared to two-fifths who would prefer to keep taxes and spending as they are now, and the mere five per cent who chose lower taxes and lower spending on these items. This, however, marks a shift since 1998 when nearly two-thirds (63 per cent) favoured higher spending and a third (32 per cent) favoured leaving them at the same level. Perhaps we have here an indication that, for some respondents, the spending

increases promised by Labour's 1998 Spending Review and the 2000 Budget
were enough.

Furthermore, within the different categories of public spending, the priority of
social security – never very prominent – has been slipping. Overwhelmingly,
people pick health as their top priority for extra government spending – 55 per
cent did so in 2000, with 81 per cent giving it as either their first or second
priority. Twenty-six per cent picked education as their top priority, and 64 per
cent as either their first or second priority. A mere two per cent put social
security as their top priority, and seven per cent as their first or second priority –
behind housing, public transport, police and prisons, as well as health and
education.

As discussed in analysis of earlier surveys (Hills and Lelkes, 1999), there is
something of a paradox here. The majority of the population is worried about
the gap between rich and poor, and about poverty, and think that it is
government's responsibility to take action. When presented with figures for
actual benefit levels for, say, unemployed people or single parents, most people
think that these are not enough to live on. However, there is declining support
for higher spending on welfare benefits in general. When asked which would be
the priority for extra spending on "social benefits", more than half (52 per cent)
of 2000 respondents opted for pensions (up from 42 per cent in 1990 and 1993),
and 21 per cent for benefits for disabled people. Nearly two-thirds put one or
other of these as their second choice. Only five per cent put benefits for
unemployed people as their highest priority, down from 16 per cent in 1993 (but
compared to eight per cent in 1990), and only eight per cent put them as their
second highest priority.

Benefits for the unemployed are thus a low priority item for the public, within
a low priority social security budget. And yet the risk of a household with an
unemployed head being poor (income below half average) is high and has been
rising – up from 56 per cent in 1994-1995 to 65 per cent in 1999-2000
(Department of Social Security, 2001).

Rights and responsibilities

Part of the explanation of this paradox may lie in something which has been
heavily emphasised in recent government policy statements on social security:
the balance between the 'rights and responsibilities' of claimants. The 2000
British Social Attitudes survey allows us to look at where people see the balance
as lying between government and individuals.

Pensioners

Looking first at the group most favoured by the public – pensioners – the next
table gives an unequivocal answer: four-fifths of respondents thought that it was
definitely government's responsibility to "provide a decent standard of living for
the old", and nearly all of the rest that it *probably* was. Further, rather more (45

per cent) thought that this was "very" or "fairly easy" to do than thought it was difficult (41 per cent).

Table 1.11 Government's responsibility and ability to ensure a decent standard of living for the elderly

		Definitely	Probably	Probably not	Definitely not
Whether it should be the government's responsibility to provide a decent standard of living for the old	%	80	16	1	*

		Very easy	Fairly easy	Neither	Fairly difficult	Very difficult
Easy or difficult for any government, irrespective of party, to ensure that all old people have a decent standard of living	%	17	28	13	28	10

Base: 2008

However, when retired respondents were asked about the adequacy of the present state pension, half (51 per cent) said it was "very low", a third (32 per cent) that it was "a bit on the low side", and only one in six (16 per cent) that it was "reasonable". Not a single one of the 590 respondents opted to say that it was "on the high side". As tellingly, when asked what they expected their state pension would purchase in a year's time compared to now, 61 per cent said less – despite the formal policy of price indexation of the basic pension and faster increases in recent years in means-tested pensions. Only 28 per cent thought it would purchase about the same, and a mere eight per cent that it would purchase more.

Up until the time of the survey in 2000, although the Labour government had introduced the Minimum Income Guarantee for the poorest pensioners, they had at the same time maintained the policy of increasing the basic pension only in line with inflation (which should, nonetheless, have prevented its value falling). Because of the low rate of inflation, this led to the very small cash increase in the basic pension – only 75 pence per week for a single pensioner in April 2000. The survey preceded the subsequent revolt at the 2000 Labour Party Conference, and the decision to make above-inflation increases in the basic pension in April 2001. At the time of the survey, pensioners thought that the state pension was low and losing purchasing power.

Income in retirement is not only a matter for government, though. Nearly three-quarters of respondents agree that "the government should encourage people to provide something for their own retirement instead of relying only on the state pension" and only one in seven (15 per cent) disagree. These are the same proportions as when the question was asked in 1991, despite the continuing publicity over private pension 'mis-selling'. The only real change is a slight shift towards more people agreeing strongly with the statement (up from 19 to 25 per cent).

Table 1.12 Main (and second) source of income when retired, by household income

	Lowest quarter	Second quarter	Third quarter	Top quarter	All
	%	%	%	%	%
State retirement pension	64 (14)	38 (37)	17 (37)	6 (28)	27 (30)
A company pension	10 (13)	26 (13)	44 (13)	49 (10)	35 (12)
A personal pension	15 (12)	26 (16)	29 (18)	33 (15)	27 (15)
Other	4 (17)	8 (22)	9 (28)	13 (45)	9 (30)
None	- (36)	- (9)	- (2)	- (1)	- (9)
Base	498	565	623	518	2425

Note: question asked of non-retired respondents below retirement age only.

Not surprisingly, expectations among those below retirement age of where their retirement income will come from, vary sharply with household income, as shown in the table above. For those in the top quarter of total household income, only one in twenty thought that the state retirement pension would be their main source of income (and only just over a quarter that it would be the second most important source). Company and personal pensions and income from investments were expected to be much more important. By contrast, nearly two-thirds of the lowest quarter thought that the state pension would be their most important source of income. More than a third of those with low incomes thought that they would have no second source of income at all in retirement.

In many ways these expectations reflect the realities of current pension structures, although expectations for the yield of personal pensions look over-optimistic. Most do expect to provide some kind of additional pension for themselves, but at the same time – as witnessed by Table 1.11 – they expect the state to guarantee some kind of floor to living standards in retirement, and generally regard existing state pensions as inadequate to do this (although, as we saw in Table 1.8, this is more evenly balanced when people are presented with the actual amounts of means-tested pensions).

Welfare and work

Another, and increasingly emphasised, part of what government sees as the responsibility of claimants is to look for work. 'Actively seeking work' has always been seen as the responsibility of those claiming unemployment benefits (King, 1995), but this is now steadily extending to other groups. The experimental 'ONE' one-stop-shops for benefit claims and employment advice, followed by the general fusion of the Employment and Benefits Agencies (to become 'JobCentre Plus'), and the extensions of the 'New Deal' with sanctions for non-compliance are all part of this.

The 2000 *British Social Attitudes* survey indicates support for some aspects of this. For instance, under the original 'New Deal for Lone Parents', attendance at the advice interviews to which lone parents were invited was entirely voluntary. From April 2001 it became compulsory for lone parents whose children are all aged over five to attend such interviews, with penalties (benefits cut by around £10 per week) if they do not, but still no compulsion to take a job. As the next table shows, three-quarters of respondents agree that lone parents failing to attend such an interview "every year or so" should have their benefits cut – in most cases only by "a little", but almost a fifth thought they should be stopped altogether. Just over half also agreed that benefits should be cut for long-term sick or disabled people who did not go, when asked, to a job centre to talk about ways in which they might find work. However, for *carers* on benefits, more than half thought their benefits should be unaffected, and only two-fifths that there should be any sanctions, echoing other *British Social Attitudes* findings (Hills and Lelkes, 1999) that carers are the group people are most sympathetic to amongst social security beneficiaries.

Table 1.13 Benefit sanctions for those failing to visit the job centre, when asked, to talk about ways of finding work

		Benefits not affected	Cut a little	Cut a lot	Benefits stopped
Lone parent	%	22	45	12	18
Long-term sick or disabled	%	43	35	7	9
Carer on benefits	%	56	27	5	9

Base: 3426

The other side of this is the government's responsibility – both to ensure that there are jobs and to make sure that 'work pays'. As the next table shows, three-quarters of respondents say that it should definitely or probably be "the government's responsibility to provide a job for everyone who wants one". Support for this strong statement (in contrast to support for actual policies) has actually increased since the 1998 survey (when 67 per cent agreed). People appear to be taking the government at its word when it said "work for those who can, security for those who cannot", at least as far as the first part of the slogan is concerned. But in contrast to ensuring adequate incomes in retirement, people do not think that achieving this is easy: 66 per cent say that it is difficult "these days for any government, irrespective of party to ensure that everyone who wants a job has one", and only 15 per cent think it easy.

Table 1.14 Government's responsibility and ability to ensure jobs

		Definitely	Probably	Probably not	Definitely not
Whether it should be the government's responsibility to provide a job for everyone who wants one	%	39	37	12	6

		Very easy	Fairly easy	Neither	Fairly difficult	Very difficult
Easy or difficult for any government, irrespective of party, to ensure that everyone who wants a job has one	%	3	12	14	47	20

Base: 2008

As for 'making work pay', people continue to distinguish between those with and without children as to whether government should top up low wages. The Working Families Tax Credit, which does this for those with children, had been phased in at more generous rates than its predecessor, Family Credit, from the autumn before the 2000 *British Social Attitudes* survey. Where working couples find it "hard to make ends meet on low wages", 61 per cent favour government topping up their wages, and only 28 per cent favour leaving it up to the couple "to look after themselves and their children as best they can". For lone parents there is even stronger support, 71 per cent favouring top-ups, and only 19 per cent leaving it to the parent. In principle, the Working Families Tax Credit is a popular policy.

The government has now proposed extending this to low paid workers *without* children, through a new 'Employment Tax Credit'. By contrast, the survey suggests little support for the principle of this: 63 per cent (up from 58 per cent in 1998) say that for a working couple without children finding it hard on low wages, it is up to the couple to look after themselves, and only 27 per cent favour government topping up wages.

Child support

Another key battleground in the balance of responsibility for adequate income is the responsibility of absent parents to pay maintenance for their children. Here, *British Social Attitudes* respondents continue to agree with the principle of absent parents paying maintenance for child support (rather than it just being left to government, for instance). In the 2000 survey, 88 per cent agreed that if an unmarried couple with a primary school child split up the father should *always* be made to pay maintenance to support the child (emphasis added). This rate of support is up slightly from the mid-1990s, despite the trials and tribulations of the Child Support Agency.

As far as the amount is concerned, the majority says that it should depend on *both* his income (88 per cent) *and* the mother's income (74 per cent), with views unchanged since the mid-1990s, again despite the problems of the Child Support Agency in actually running systems which are sensitive to incomes. The only real shift is that half of respondents now say that payments should continue regardless of whether the mother remarries. Only 38 per cent say that it should depend on the stepfather's income, and 11 per cent that it should stop altogether. This reverses the balance from 1994, when 37 per cent said it should continue regardless, 46 per cent that it should depend on stepfather's income, and 15 per cent that it should stop.

Where does this leave benefits for the unemployed?

The next figure illustrates one of the most dramatic shifts in the *British Social Attitudes* series since it started. From the discussion above and earlier surveys, we know that a substantial proportion of people think that benefits for the unemployed are not enough to live on. From other questions, discussed further below, we know that many people believe that the benefit system creates disincentives to work. Since 1984, respondents have been asked to choose between these two positions:

> *Benefits for the unemployed are too low and cause hardship*

> *Or, benefits for unemployed people are too high and discourage them from finding jobs*

Up to the 1996 survey the balance lay clearly with the first of these. Around half favoured the statement that benefits were "too low", compared to less than a third favouring the "too high" option (and around a tenth agreeing with neither). But the 1998 survey gave a dramatically different result, with nearly half now favouring the "too high" option, and only 29 per cent saying they were "too low". The responses to the *British Social Attitudes* survey carried out in early 1997 suggest that most of the switch occurred *after* the 1997 election. The new balance was maintained, but with a narrower gap in 1999, but by 2000 the positions had reversed again, with the "too low" option regaining a narrow lead.

Figure 1.2 Attitudes towards benefits for the unemployed

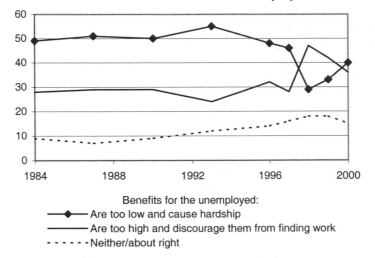

Benefits for the unemployed:
———◆——— Are too low and cause hardship
——————— Are too high and discourage them from finding work
- - - - - - Neither/about right

What are we to make of this? First, the likelihood of someone agreeing with the statement that unemployment benefits are too high will be greater if they believe that the system creates disincentives to work, and also if they believe the system is subject to widespread fraud and abuse. This is confirmed by the responses in the next table which shows the answers to three long-standing questions in this area.

Table 1.15 Level of benefits for unemployed people by related attitudes

Most people on the dole are fiddling in One way or another		Too low and cause hardship	Too high and discourage finding jobs	Base
Agree	%	29	54	1196
Neither	%	40	33	915
Disagree	%	57	17	825
Around here most unemployed people could find a job if they really wanted one				
Agree	%	31	47	1790
Neither	%	51	25	565
Disagree	%	61	16	583
If welfare benefits weren't so generous, people would learn to stand on their own two feet				
Agree	%	21	63	1153
Neither	%	36	32	735
Disagree	%	65	12	1048

Where people *agree* that "most people on the dole are fiddling in one way or another", or that "around here most unemployed people could find a job", or that "if welfare benefits weren't so generous, people would learn to stand on their own two feet", they are much more likely to choose the "benefits for unemployed people are too high" option. By contrast, if they *disagree* with the statements, they are much more likely to favour the "too low" option.

This makes trends in views of fraud and disincentives caused by the welfare system of great importance for attitudes to benefit levels. These trends are illustrated in the next two figures. The belief that fraud is commonplace within the welfare system appears to have increased. In particular, agreement with the statement that "large numbers of people these days falsely claim benefits" rose from 72 per cent in 1994 to 83 per cent in 1998 and 77 per cent in 2000. At the same time agreement that "most people on the dole are fiddling in one way or another" rose from around a third up to 1995 to 39 per cent in 1998 and 40 per cent in 2000 and trends for the statement "many people who get social security don't really deserve any help" track these. Most strikingly, agreement that "around here, most unemployed people could find a job if they really wanted one" moves not just with the economic cycle, but was running at higher levels in the late 1990s than in the boom of the late 1980s. But only one of the series illustrated ("large numbers falsely claim benefits") shows a reversal in growth by 2000, and this is not very large. It is hard to see these changes as explaining the pattern between 1996 and 2000 shown in Figure 1.2.

Figure 1.3 Trends in concerns about fraud in the welfare system (% agreeing with each statement)

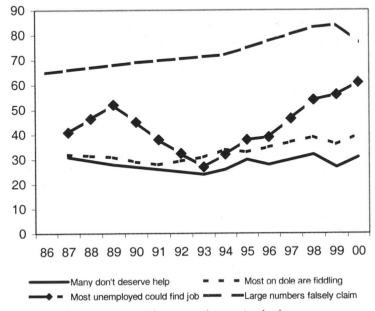

Note: Points interpolated in years when questions not asked.

Trends in statements about disincentives in the system show an even less clear pattern. Agreement with both the statements "the welfare state makes people nowadays less willing to look after themselves", and "if welfare benefits weren't so generous, people would learn to stand on their own two feet" had reached record or near record levels in 1998, but there is no sign of a trend since the mid-1980s. Nor is there any clear trend in agreement with the third statement, that "the welfare state encourages people to stop helping each other".

Figure 1.4 Trends in concerns around disincentives (% agreeing with each statement)

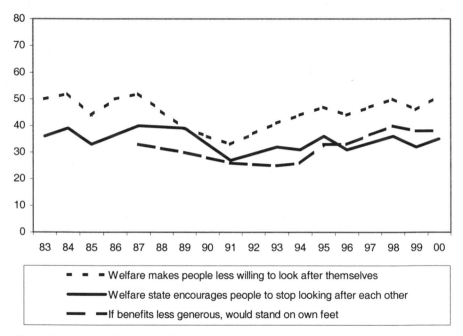

Note: Points interpolated in years when questions not asked.

So, although there is a link between these beliefs and the choice between the two positions on benefit levels, it is hard to see the connection between the gradual trends in Figures 1.3 and 1.4 and the dramatic switches in Figure 1.2 – particularly the switch that we have now seen *back* towards the "too low" position in 2000. That these gradual trends do not explain the picture is confirmed when one examines the equivalents of Table 1.15 for the surveys of 1996 and 1998. They show the same switches (albeit from different starting points) within all nine categories of agreement or disagreement between the three years, first towards the "too high" option, but then back towards the "too low" option.

However, the next table suggests another important part of the story by showing major differences by political identification. At the start, in 1996,

Conservative identifiers favoured the "too high" option, but Liberal Democrat and particularly Labour identifiers, the "too low" option. By 1998 the largest number in all three groups favoured the "too high" option, but by 2000 Liberal Democrat and Labour identifiers had switched back again. What is notable is that the greatest changes in the balances in both directions are for the *Labour* identifiers.

Table 1.16 Level of benefits for unemployed people and political identification, 1996-2000

	Conservative	Liberal Democrat	Labour	All
1996				
Too low	29	47	62	48
Too high	48	30	21	32
Base	*1012*	*391*	*1528*	*3620*
1998				
Too low	15	29	37	29
Too high	61	49	39	47
Base	*818*	*324*	*1398*	*3146*
2000				
Too low	25	38	52	40
Too high	52	36	28	36
Base	*937*	*341*	*1394*	*3426*

It may be no coincidence that the 1998 survey followed a period during which newly-elected Labour ministers, particularly Frank Field, the then Minister for Welfare Reform, had been making a series of speeches highlighting the extent of problems with the system of benefits for the unemployed in the run-up to publication of the welfare reform Green Paper. The Green Paper itself stressed that there were three fundamental problems with the social security system: "increased inequality and social exclusion, despite more spending"; that "people are trapped on benefit rather than helped off"; and that "fraud is diverting resources from genuine claimants" (Department of Social Security, 1998). For some Labour identifiers, hearing these kinds of statements from a Labour, as opposed to a Conservative, government, may have shifted the balance of their opinions from those held up to 1996 and early 1997. By 2000, the political prominence of these issues had declined, and views appear to be reverting to where they were before. This remains a hypothesis,[3] but, if true, has interesting implications for the way in which ministerial rhetoric can still lead, as well as follow, popular beliefs.

Conclusions

In its first term, the Labour government elected in 1997 took a different attitude to social security from its predecessors of the 1960s and 1970s. Parts of social security spending were branded as 'spending on failure' and there was no general increase in benefit levels. The responsibilities of claimants were emphasised, particularly to find work if they were able to work. Those in work were also expected to do more to provide for their pensions. At the same time, the government promised to end child poverty in 20 years, and made selective but significant benefit and tax credit increases above inflation, thus making important progress towards this goal. It made its own task harder by implicitly accepting a relative definition of poverty, and hence a target for the incomes of the poorest which moves upwards with general increases in living standards.

This chapter has examined evidence from the *British Social Attitudes* survey on public attitudes both to the poverty reduction objective and to some of the means being used to achieve it. As far as the objective is concerned, the survey shows that the majority believe that there is a significant amount of poverty, and that government should be doing something to reduce it. In most respects opinions about what constitutes poverty, the income levels people need to avoid it, its extent and recent trends in it, are consistent with the kind of relative poverty definition provided by government statistics.

This chapter also sheds light on the hypotheses advanced in the introduction for what might have happened to public attitudes to poverty and social security over Labour's first three years in office. As far as the first hypothesis is concerned – that the reforms may have made social security benefits more acceptable and popular, by bringing them more into line with existing attitudes – there is little evidence yet of a shift in attitudes on the less popular benefits. Apart from a small recent small fall in the numbers believing that "many people falsely claim benefits", negative perceptions towards welfare benefits, such as many claims being fraudulent, show little sign of reduction since 1996. Indeed the most notable shift is that, in the improved economic climate, more people think that in their area "most unemployed people could find a job if they really wanted to".

Although people do appear to favour spending on certain benefits, even if this means higher taxes, social security remains way down the list of public priorities for spending any additional tax revenues. There is strong – and growing – support, for one of the measures on which the government has put most emphasis: top-ups in income for working families *with children* on low pay, through the Working Families Tax Credit. However, there is little support for extending this to those without children, and the proportion saying that more should be spent on "welfare benefits for the poor" continued to decline in each year from 1996 to 2000.

The discussion in the last section does provide some support for an alternative hypothesis – that the emphasis on the conditional nature of benefits may have reinforced their social unacceptability and rendered them less popular – witnessed by the large swings in opinion when forced to choose between statements about unemployment benefits being too low or too high. The intensity of the government's discussion about problems with the system may have shifted opinions against benefits at around the time of the 1998 survey. In the quieter atmosphere since, opinions have now partly reverted (and have done so without any great change in beliefs about the extent of fraud and disincentives).

The third hypothesis – that Labour underestimated the popularity of (at least some) benefits and its failure to be more generous generated an increased demand for spending on them – is most clearly borne out in the case of pensions. Rather than returning to earnings-linking of pensions, Labour stuck to a policy of price-linking the basic pension, while increasing means-tested pensions more rapidly. The public was not convinced: the 2000 survey clearly shows that people thought that government was failing in its responsibility to provide a decent standard of living in retirement. The, at least temporary, turnaround in policy with real increases in the basic pension in April 2001 was a clear response to this – "Our biggest mistake? 75p on pensions", as Tony Blair put it in the 2001 election campaign.

Finally, is there any evidence that people think that Labour has done enough in reducing poverty? Not according to this survey. The majority continues to be worried about the gap between rich and poor, and has a view of poverty which appears roughly in line with the relative definitions used in government statistics. However, the largest group of respondents in 2000 still thought that poverty would *increase* over the following decade. Few thought it would fall.

What does not follow from this, however, is a widespread demand for higher social security benefits for *all* of the poor – like the government, the public remains selective in what it wants to see done to different parts of the system. However, its knowledge of that system is limited. Many people think that benefits for the unemployed are higher than they are, and say that they are not enough to live on when told the actual amounts.

In both its actions and its choice of which of these to stress, Labour has reacted to the constraints of public opinion. Yet its own rhetoric appears to have the capacity to shift some of those opinions. Giving more prominence to how *low* certain benefits are might help relax some of the constraints on the policies needed to meet its anti-poverty objectives.

Notes

1. Incomes adjusted for the needs of different kinds of households using the official *McClements equivalence scale* and measured before deducting housing costs. Figures from Department of Social Security (2001) for 1994-1995 and 1999-2000 and from Goodman and Webb (1994) for earlier years.
2. Using figures for 1999-2000 at December 2000 prices from Department of Social Security (2001). In recent years, the focus of government statements about the extent of poverty has switched from 50 per cent of mean income to 60 per cent of median income. At present, however, the two figures are virtually the same.
3. I am grateful to participants in seminars at the LSE and Nuffield College, Oxford, for suggesting that this was worth investigating further.

References

Abel-Smith, B. and Townsend, P. (1965), *The Poor and the Poorest*, Occasional Papers on Social Administration No. 17, London: G. Bell and Sons.

Alcock, P. (1997), *Understanding Poverty*, Basingstoke: Macmillan.

Department of Social Security (1997), *Households Below Average Income: A statistical analysis 1979-1994/95*, London: The Stationery Office.

Department of Social Security (1998), *New Ambitions for Our Country: A new contract for welfare*, Cm 3805, London: The Stationery Office.

Department of Social Security (1999), *Households Below Average Income 1994/95-1997/08*, Leeds: Corporate Document Services.

Department of Social Security (2000), *Households Below Average Income 1994/95-1998/99*, Leeds: Corporate Document Services.

Department of Social Security (2001), *Households Below Average Income 1994/95-1999/00*, Leeds: Corporate Document Services.

Goodman, A. and Webb, S. (1994), *For Richer, for Poorer: The changing distribution of income in the United Kingdom 1961/91*, IFS Commentary No 42: London: Institute for Fiscal Studies.

Gordon, D., Adelman, L., Ashworth, K., Bradshaw, J., Levitas, R., Middleton, S., Pantazis, C., Patsios, D., Payne, S., Townsend, P. and Williams, J. (2000), *Poverty and Social Exclusion in Britain*, York: Joseph Rowntree Foundation.

Hills, J. and Lelkes, O. (1999), 'Social security, selective universalism and patchwork redistribution' in Jowell, R., Curtice, J., Park, A. and Thomson, K. (eds.), *British Social Attitudes: the 16th Report - Who shares New Labour values?*, Aldershot: Ashgate.

HM Treasury (2000), *Pre-Budget Report: Building long-term prosperity for all*, Cm 4917, London: The Stationery Office.

King, D. (1995), *Actively Seeking Work?*, Chicago: University of Chicago Press.

Mack, J. and Lansley, S. (1985), *Poor Britain*, London: George Allen and Unwin.

Piachaud, D. and Sutherland, H. (2001), 'Child Poverty in Britain and the New Labour government', *Journal of Social Policy*, **30**: 95-118.

Rowntree, B. S. (1901), *Poverty: A study of town life*, London: Macmillan.

Taylor-Gooby, P. (1995), 'Comfortable, marginal and excluded: Who should pay higher taxes for a better welfare state?' in Jowell, R., Curtice, J., Park, A., Brook, L. and Ahrendt, D. (eds.), *British Social Attitudes: the 12th Report*, Aldershot: Dartmouth.

Townsend, P. (1979), *Poverty in the United Kingdom*, Harmondsworth: Penguin.

Walker, R. (ed.) (1999), *Ending Child Poverty: Popular welfare for the 21st century?*, Bristol: Policy Press.

Acknowledgements

The author is very grateful for helpful suggestions on a previous draft to Tania Burchardt, Orsolya Lelkes, David Piachaud and Jane Waldfogel.

The *National Centre for Social Research* is also grateful to the Department for Work and Pensions for their financial support which enabled us to ask these questions, although the views in the chapter are those of the author alone.

2 Just a piece of paper? Marriage and cohabitation

Anne Barlow, Simon Duncan, Grace James and Alison Park *

Marriages in Britain are now at their lowest level since 1917 and the divorce rate (although now declining slightly) is the highest in the European Union (Eurostat, 2000). Against this backdrop, heterosexual cohabitation (living together as husband and wife without being married) has increased dramatically (from five per cent to 15 per cent of all couples between 1986 and 1999) and is predicted to double by 2021 (Shaw and Haskey, 1999). A quarter of all children are now born to cohabiting families. Lone motherhood has also more than doubled since 1971. Some analysis has suggested that many cohabiting relationships are quite short, usually lasting for a few years before the majority transform into marriage, with most of the rest dissolving. Only a small percentage continue for ten years or more. Similarly, the average duration of lone motherhood is only four years, and most lone mothers enter new partnerships – with many marrying. The popularity of marriage – for some – is also evident from the fact that over 40 per cent of marriages are *re*marriages (see Haskey, 1999, Office for National Statistics, 2001).

So rather than there being any simple 'decline' in marriage, there appears to be a far more complex picture of sequential cohabitations, separations, marriages and divorces. Many of us will experience some or all of these family types at one period or another in our lives.

To some, such statistics demonstrate the decline of the family or, even more ominously, suggest a complete breakdown of family life in Britain. In contrast, others argue that families are simply changing as they always have done, and that family values and relationships are just as healthy as before – but are simply being expressed in different forms. Marriage and cohabitation are often

* Anne Barlow is a Senior Lecturer in Law at the University of Wales, Aberystwyth. Simon Duncan is a Professor of Comparative Social Policy at the University of Bradford. Grace James is a Research Fellow in the Law Department at the University of Wales, Aberystwyth. Alison Park is a Research Director at the *National Centre for Social Research* and Co-Director of the *British Social Attitudes* survey series.

used as key symbols in this debate. Those who argue that the family is breaking down see the two as polar opposites, where marriage leads to 'proper' family behaviour but cohabitation encourages inadequate and even anti-social behaviour (Morgan, 1999). But others maintain that whether people cohabit or are married actually makes little difference to what they *do* as partners and parents (Silva and Smart, 1999).

Certainly the law in England and Wales makes an important distinction between cohabiting and married partners, as we shall discuss in more detail later. Cohabiting partners, unlike married ones, do not enjoy a standard set of legal duties and obligations to one another, and in many cases their legal position is quite inferior or not recognised as a family status at all. As the family is seen, to quote one influential commentator, as "our most precious business: the foundation of social cohesion and economic growth" (Wilkinson, 2000: 5), this places family values – and family law – in sharp political focus. However, the growth in cohabitation has not been recognised through any sort of cohesive legal reform. Although the term 'common law marriage' is often used to describe cohabitation, this concept has not been recognised in law since the Clandestine Marriages Act of 1753. Nonetheless, many people firmly believe that cohabitants have legal rights equivalent to marriage. This 'common law marriage myth' can lull cohabitants into a false sense of security believing they have rights which do not in fact exist. As family lawyers can testify, it leaves them needing expert legal advice when things go wrong, but it is often too late by then.

There are two alternative policy responses to this confusing situation. One is to create supportive policies suitable for a range of family types and behaviours. The other is to plump for some preferred family form, seen as socially superior in some way, and to support this while ignoring or discriminating against others. In practice, this second option is likely to mean focusing family policy on traditional marriage; an option that, given the trends in marriage and cohabitation described above, is vulnerable to the charge of sticking one's head in the sand.

Many other EU governments are tending towards the first option, for example, by giving unmarried cohabitants – and even same sex couples – equal rights in law with married couples. British social policy, in contrast, has veered towards the second, more traditional option. While recognising the increasing diversity of family types and practices, marriage is seen as the best choice and the family form that deserves most support (see, for example, Home Office, 1998). This attempt to preserve marriage as a social norm has left cohabitants in a complex and confusing legal position. They are sometimes treated in law as married (for instance, for social security purposes), sometimes treated as strangers (in terms of property rights in the family home) and sometimes treated as inferior (as illustrated by a cohabiting father's lack of legal status). The alternative would be to extend to cohabiting families the easily understood framework of family law rights and responsibilities available to married couples. Certainly, while there is much political posturing around 'family values', it is not clear that any of the rhetoric reflects a realistic assessment of people's own views and experiences of marriage and cohabitation.

This chapter examines people's attitudes and behaviour in relation to marriage and cohabitation, and then examines the possible policy responses in the light of these. Firstly, we consider briefly how attitudes to marriage and cohabitation have changed over time. Secondly, we focus in detail on views about these forms of relationship and how they vary from one group to another. For instance, do people view cohabitation and marriage differently? Has marriage lost its social significance? Is cohabitation accepted as a substitute for marriage, or just as a prelude to it? Do attitudes differ if there are children involved? Thirdly, we consider the characteristics of cohabitants themselves and their relationships. What sort of people cohabit and how do they compare with married people? Are they younger than average? Do they differ from their married counterparts in terms of class or education? How long do cohabitating relationships last? We also assess whether cohabitation can be usefully seen as a reaction to a bad experience of marriage, or indeed a prelude to marriage itself. Fourthly, we examine beliefs about, and attitudes towards, the law as it stands. Are people aware of the different legal treatment of married and cohabiting couples, or has the common law marriage myth retained its dominance? Finally, we consider the implications of these attitudes and beliefs for social policy and legal reform.

Changing values?

We have seen dramatic changes over the last few decades in people's behaviour in relation to marriage and cohabitation. Our first task is to assess whether these changes have been accompanied by changing attitudes towards marriage and cohabitation and, if so, whether this has affected some groups more than others.

Over the years, the *British Social Attitudes* survey has asked a number of questions about marriage. As shown in the next table, these demonstrate clear changes in people's views particularly in relation to parenthood and sex. In 1989, almost three-quarters of the population subscribed to the view that "people who want children ought to get married". Just five years later, in 1994, this had fallen to 57 per cent and is now down to just over half the population. Similarly, between 1984 and 2000, the proportion of people thinking that there is "nothing wrong" with premarital sex increased from 42 to 62 per cent (and the proportion thinking it to be always wrong shrank from 17 to nine per cent). Opinion about extra-marital sex, however, has barely changed over the last two decades, with over six in ten seeing it as always wrong, suggesting that it is marriage rather than partnership that it is losing its predominant position.

Table 2.1 Attitudes towards marriage, 1984 to 2000

% who agree that:	1984	1989	1994	1998	2000
People who want children ought to get married	n.a.	70	57	n.a.	54
Base		*1516*	*984*		*2980*
% who think that:					
Premarital sex is "not wrong at all"	42	44	n.a.	58	62
Extramarital sex is "always wrong"	59	55	n.a.	52	61
Base	*1675*	*1513*		*1075*	*3426*

n.a. = not asked

The next table shows the widespread acceptability of cohabitation and, indeed, its desirability as a precursor to marriage. Around two-thirds of respondents in 2000 saw cohabitation as perfectly acceptable and just over half actually thought it was "a good idea" for couples who are intending to get married. These attitudes have barely changed since 1994 when we first started asking the question. But, given the pattern in the previous table, we suspect that, if we had had a reading from the 1980s, we might have witnessed a more substantial shift in favour of cohabitation.

Table 2.2 Attitudes towards cohabitation, 1994 to 2000

% who agree that:	1994	1998	2000
It is all right for a couple to live together without intending to get married	64	62	67
It is a good idea for a couple who intend to get married to live together first	58	61	56
Base	*984*	*807*	*2980*

We turn now to the views of different groups and how these have changed over time. Dramatic differences on attitudes to marriage continue to exist, the starkest relating to age. As the next table shows, over eight in ten of people aged 65 or above think that marriage and parenthood should go hand in hand, compared with just over a third of 18-24 year olds. But all age groups have become more liberal in their views over the last decade, the most notable shifts taking place among 35 to 54 year olds. Attitudes towards premarital sex follow a very similar pattern.

Table 2.3 "People who want children ought to get married", by age, 1989 and 2000

% who agree	1989	Base	2000	Base	Change 2000/1989
By age					
18-24	41	167	33	225	-8
25-34	51	254	38	541	-13
35-44	65	248	36	632	-29
45-54	80	207	50	470	-30
55-64	90	180	76	452	-14
65+	93	248	85	656	-8

Overall there is little difference between men and women, both in terms of their views on whether marriage should precede parenthood and in the extent of the change in their attitudes over time. However, young women have notably more liberal attitudes than young men in this respect, with only 29 per cent of 18-24 year old women agreeing (compared with 39 per cent of men). On the matter of premarital sex, men are slightly more liberal in their views than women, but both have become substantially more accepting of it over time.

Other marked differences in view are associated with religion and marital status – as shown in the next table. The religious and married people have more traditional views on these matters than average. There are also differences according to educational background, with those who have no qualifications holding more traditional views than those with them. Curiously, the outlook of those with higher educational qualifications is more traditional than those with qualifications at a lower level, this going against the general tendency for those with higher qualifications to be more liberal than average.

However, if we focus on the change between 1989 and 2000, the important point is that views about the necessity of marriage preceding parenthood have changed *across the board*, even among the most traditional groups. For instance, among those belonging to the Church of England the proportion thinking people should get married if they want children has fallen from three-quarters in 1989 to two-thirds in 2000, a drop of 13 percentage points. Among Catholics the drop has been greater still, from three-quarters in agreement in 1989 to just over half in 2000.

Table 2.4 Per cent who agree that "people who want children ought to get married", by sex, education, religion and marital status, 1989 and 2000

% who agree	1989	Base	2000	Base	Change 2000/1989
By religion					
Church of England	78	476	65	923	-13
Catholic	73	142	55	274	-18
Other Christian	81	185	66	497	-15
No religion	57	447	38	1181	-19
By marital status					
Married	77	833	62	1426	-15
Cohabiting	43	73	23	240	-20
Separated or divorced	52	64	40	370	-12
Widowed	85	98	80	360	-5
Not married	51	205	38	584	-13
By highest educational qualification					
No qualifications	79	534	62	894	-17
CSE/GCSE or equivalent	61	99	48	281	-13
O level/GCSE or equivalent	58	218	47	618	-11
A level or equivalent	57	141	45	319	-12
Higher education below degree	74	162	57	412	-17
Degree	67	111	52	402	-15

Similar findings exist in relation to changing attitudes towards premarital sex – with all groups showing notable changes in a more liberal direction over time.[1]

We found earlier that attitudes to cohabitation have not changed markedly between 1994 (when we first asked about them) and now. However, this apparent lack of overall change disguises considerable change *within* particular groups. The general pattern appears to be one whereby the greatest change has taken place among those with the most traditional views on the subject. For instance, younger people have not particularly changed their minds on this matter over time. But older groups, previously far less accepting, seem to have gradually become more accepting, perhaps as a consequence of changing social reality. Despite this, there remains a notable gulf in the views of those aged 55 and above and those who are younger, as shown in the next table.

Table 2.5 Per cent who agree that "it is all right for a couple to live together
without intending to get married", by age, 1994 and 2000

% who agree	1994	Base	2000	Base	Change 2000/1989
By age					
18-24	83	78	84	225	1
25-34	82	238	80	541	-2
35-44	81	174	78	632	-3
45-54	62	160	75	470	+13
55-64	45	134	57	452	+12
65+	24	199	35	656	+11

This phenomenon of higher levels of change among groups with more
traditional views and relative stasis among those with more liberal ones is also
evident when looking at how views vary by marital status and religion. Thus,
change has been more pronounced among those who *are* religious than among
those who are not (although the religious remain less accepting of cohabitation
overall). Similarly, the biggest shift in views according to marital status has
taken place among the widowed (from 30 per cent agreeing in 1994 to 43 per
cent in 2000).

So there are considerable differences within society when it comes to attitudes
towards marriage and cohabitation. In relation to marriage and parenthood, at
least, opinion has become markedly more liberal over time, with this liberalism
affecting a wide range of groups. What is less clear, however, is why this has
taken place. Three particular possibilities require exploration: firstly, that the
trend is being driven largely by change among one or two particular groups;
secondly, that it reflects other changes within society (for example, declining
religiosity and the rise of cohabitation); and, thirdly, that it stems from a gulf of
opinion between different generations.

The first of our possible explanations we can already rule out – that changing
attitudes to marriage and cohabitation are been driven by changes among one or
two particular social groups. Rather, as we have seen, change has occurred
across society, although quite noticeable differences of view continue to exist
(despite the fact that those with more traditional views have tended to change
slightly more than those with more liberal ones).

Our second possibility is that these shifts in opinion simply reflect the
changing composition of society – the fact that we are less religious than we
once were, more educated and so on. Because these characteristics are linked to
liberal views, we might expect to find that these sorts of social change will
result in attitudes shifting in a more liberal direction. To investigate this we
need to examine whether significant differences exist between our readings
from different years once we have taken account of other differences between

the years in education, religion and so on. To do this we have to use multivariate techniques which allow us to assess the simultaneous impact of a range of different factors. (These methods are described in more detail in Appendix I to this Report.)

Let us start with attitudes towards marriage and parenthood. We saw earlier that more liberal views are held by groups like the non-religious, cohabitants, and people with educational qualifications. However, although the size of all these groups has certainly increased over time, these increases are not sufficient to explain the change in attitudes we have found. So even when we take into account factors like marital status, religion and education (as well as age and sex), people are *still* less likely in 2000 to agree with the proposition that a person should get married if they want to have children. (More details can be found in model A in the appendix to this chapter.) The same is true when we consider beliefs about the acceptability of cohabitation – even when a variety of other social factors are taken into account, we are now more likely to see cohabitation as acceptable than we were in the past.

Our third avenue is perhaps the most promising explanation for the changes we have found – that these changes reflect *generational* differences. These occur when the distinctive views of different age groups remain with them as they get older (rather than being modified by age and experience). In this case, then, we are looking to see whether there is evidence that more liberal, younger, generations are gradually replacing previous, less liberal ones – the end result being that society as a whole becomes markedly more liberal in its outlook. To assess this, we have to compare change within society as a whole with change among individual age cohorts (that is, people born over the same period). To conclude that generational change is taking place we need to find, firstly, marked age differences in attitudes between these cohorts and, secondly, that these attitudes are relatively stable over time – that is, that people's views do not change particularly as they get older.

We have already seen that there are distinctive age differences in opinion on this matter, but the next table rearranges the data presented in Table 2.3 in order to examine whether people's attitudes change as they get older. The left-hand column shows when each of our cohorts was born, and the next two columns show how old they were in 1989 and 2000, the two years which we want to compare. Each row shows views about marriage for each cohort, starting with the youngest. (The youngest two cohorts, in 2000 aged under 29, were too young to have been included in our 1989 survey, and the oldest cohorts, aged 75 plus in 1989, cannot be compared with precisely the same cohorts in 2000 because of a shortage of those aged 76 plus in our sample.)

As the final row in our next table shows, there has been an overall fall of 16 points between 1989 and 2000 in the proportion who think people should get married if they want children. But there has not been nearly as much change in the attitudes of each of our cohorts. In fact, only in one, born between 1955 and 1964, has there been the same amount of change as we found in society as a whole – the remainder have all changed less (particularly the older cohorts). This points strongly towards some of the overall change we have found being generational in origin, reflecting the dying out of older, more traditional, generations and their replacement by the more liberal generations born after them.[2]

Table 2.6 Per cent who agree that "people who want children ought to get married", by age cohort

Cohort	Age in 1989	Age in 2000	1989	Base	2000	Base	Difference
1976-1982	7-13	18-24	-	-	33	225	n.a.
1972-1975	14-17	25-28	-	-	34	205	n.a.
1965-1971	18-24	29-35	41	167	42	410	1
1955-1964	25-34	36-45	51	254	35	610	-16
1945-1954	35-44	46-55	65	248	54	462	-11
1935-1944	45-54	56-65	80	207	76	459	-4
1925-1934	55-64	66-75	90	180	84	369	-6
1915-1924	65-74	76+	95	167	90	236	-5
Pre 1914	75+		89	81	-	-	n.a.
All			70		54		-16

The same pattern of generational change can be found when looking at attitudes towards premarital sex (Park, 2000).

So, although all groups have changed their views on these matters to some extent, a great deal of the overall change we have found is generational, a reflection of the way in which people's views on these matters are shaped distinctively by the social climate within which they grew up (rather than changing markedly as they get older). Over time, therefore, there is a strong likelihood that society will become more liberal still on these matters, although particular groups, such as the religious, are likely to remain more traditional than the rest.

Beliefs about marriage

In order to tease out beliefs about marriage and cohabitation better we turn now to some more detailed questions, asked for the first time in 2000. As seen in the next table, these paint a complex picture. On the one hand, they confirm other research that shows considerable support for a view of marriage as an 'ideal'

(Barlow and Duncan, 2000). Thus, only a tiny minority (nine per cent) dismiss it as being "only a piece of paper", with nearly three-quarters disagreeing. Moreover, nearly three-fifths think that marriage remains the "best kind of relationship". On the other hand, two-thirds think that too many people "drift into marriage" without giving it sufficient thought beforehand.

There is less clear conviction about some of the more 'practical' aspects of marriage than there is about the principle. Traditionally, two of its most important functions were parenthood and the provision of financial security (particularly for women). Parenthood remains the very sphere where official discourse places most value on marriage (for example, Home Office, 1998). But only around a quarter of our respondents think that married people make better parents than unmarried ones, and over two-fifths disagree. Marriage's role in relation to the provision of financial security continues to be reflected in the law which imposes a duty on a spouse to maintain financially the other spouse, both during the marriage, after marriage breakdown and on death. But is this still viewed as a benefit of marriage, particularly given the increasing participation of women in the workforce? In fact, barely half of respondents agreed with the notion that marriage gives couples "more financial security" than simply living together.

Table 2.7 Attitudes to marriage and cohabitation

		Agree	Neither agree nor disagree	Disagree
Married couples make better parents than unmarried ones	%	27	28	43
Even though it might not work out for some people, marriage is still the best kind of relationship	%	59	20	20
Many people who live together without getting married are just scared of commitment	%	36	28	34
Marriage gives couples more financial security than living together	%	48	22	28
There is no point getting married – it's only a piece of paper	%	9	16	73
Too many people just drift into marriage without really thinking about it	%	69	19	10

Base: 2980

A common stereotype is that those who live together have less commitment to their relationship than those who are married. As the table above shows, views about this are polarised, with similar proportions agreeing and disagreeing with the notion.

To help examine attitudes in more detail, we used responses to these questions to construct a 'scale' to summarise people's responses to the first five questions shown in Table 2.7. Factor analysis (see Appendix 1 of this Report) shows that it is these questions which most accurately tap people's underlying beliefs about marriage and cohabitation.[3] The scale is scored from one to five, with the highest scores indicating more traditional beliefs about marriage and the lowest scores the least traditional ones.[4] For ease of presentation, we have used people's scores to allocate them into three roughly equal groups – those with the most traditional views, those with the least traditional views and those whose views fall somewhere in between.

Table 2.8 Views about marriage, by age, marital status and religion

	% with most traditional views about marriage	Base
All	29	2773
Age		
18-24	16	214
25-34	18	514
35-44	15	601
45-54	23	445
55-64	43	420
65+	61	576
Marital status		
Married	36	1337
Cohabiting	8	228
Separated/divorced	19	348
Widowed	51	320
Never married	17	540
Religion		
Church of England	37	858
Catholic	36	261
Other Christian	42	453
Non-Christian	38	84
No religion	16	1109

The table above shows the proportion of people in a variety of social groups whose views put them at the *traditional* end of our scale. This confirms our earlier finding that age is strongly linked to people's attitudes, with older people being much more likely than younger ones to have a traditional view about marriage. As previously discussed, this relationship with age suggests that society's views on these matters may well change over the next few decades, as older groups with more traditional views are replaced by younger ones.

However, age is not the only characteristic linked to distinctive attitudes towards marriage. Marital status also matters, with married people (perhaps not surprisingly!) being nearly five times more likely than cohabitants to have the most traditional views about marriage. Thus, if we focus on one of the statements included in our scale – that married couples make better parents than non-married ones – we find that a third (31 per cent) of married people agree, compared with one in ten (11 per cent) of cohabitants. Perhaps alarmingly, given the potential financial disadvantage cohabitants could face, they are also much less likely than other groups to agree with another of our scale statements – that marriage gives couples more financial security. Only a third (31 per cent) of cohabitants think this, compared with half (50 per cent) of married people. Finally, the religious have more traditional views than the non-religious (although due to small sample sizes the scores of different religious groups are not significantly different from one another).

Of course, many of these characteristics are themselves related to one another. Younger people are less likely to be married than older ones, for example, or to belong to a religion – making it difficult to assess whether it is age, marital status or religion that is most strongly linked to a person's views about marriage. To compensate for this we have to use multiple regression techniques which allow us to assess the importance of a particular characteristic while taking account of its relationship with other possibly relevant characteristics. This confirmed the key importance of, firstly, age, then marital status and then religion in predicting a person's attitudes towards marriage and cohabitation. Further details can be found in model B in the appendix to this chapter.

Our regression also revealed the importance of four other characteristics. Parents are more likely than non-parents to have a more traditional view about marriage (even when the differing age and marital profiles of these two groups is taken into account). Sex also matters, with men being slightly more traditional in their views than women. This is particularly marked among the young – for instance, 42 per cent of young men (aged between 18 and 25) agree with the view that marriage is "the best kind of relationship", compared with only 34 per cent of young women. And, while 24 per cent of young men think married couples make better parents, only 11 per cent of young women agree. Interestingly, given the traditional view of marriage as a source of financial support for women (Scott et al., 1998), as well as women's overall lower earning power (Rake, 2000), there were no gender-related differences in views about the financial security that marriage provides.

Social class also makes a difference, with non-manual workers having slightly more traditional views than manual ones. Finally, whether or not a person is in work also seems to make a difference, with those in paid work having less traditional views than those who are not. Once again, this holds true even when related factors like age are taken into account.

Table 2.9 Views about marriage, by sex, parenthood, class and current economic activity

	% with most traditional views about marriage	Base
All	29	2773
Sex		
Male	31	1187
Female	28	1586
Parenthood		
Has had/fathered child	35	2009
Has not had/fathered child	23	760
Class		
Non-manual	31	1546
Manual	27	1140
Current economic activity		
In work	21	1476
Unemployed	21	116
Looking after the home	32	305
Retired	56	625

Our findings suggest that, overall, marriage is still widely valued as an ideal but that it is regarded with much more ambivalence when it comes to everyday partnering and (especially) parenting. Meanwhile, cohabitation is widely accepted both as a prelude to marriage and as an alternative, even where there are children involved. This is especially true for younger people (particularly young women). This conclusion has important policy implications, suggesting that supporting marriage above and beyond other arrangements does not chime with people's opinions about the practicalities of everyday life as a partner and a parent.

Who cohabits, and how?

Nine per cent of respondents were cohabiting at the time of our survey, and a further 25 per cent had done so at some point in the past. So, although only a minority have experience of cohabitation, they do make up over a third of the population. We turn now to examine their characteristics, and those of their relationships. Is, for instance, cohabitation confined to certain specific groups?

Do cohabitants differ markedly from married couples? The answers to these questions will help us establish whether policy should be targeted at specific groups or whether more general measures would be the best response to increasing levels of cohabitation. We also examine the nature of their cohabiting relationships. How long do they last – are they more a prelude to marriage or a long-term partnership? Have cohabitants made arrangements to take account of their weaker legal situation?

We begin by examining two common – and related – assumptions about cohabitation: firstly, that it is usually short term in nature; and, secondly, that it is usually a prelude to marriage, particularly once children are involved. But to what extent are these assumptions true?

To assess this we asked current and past cohabitants how long their relationship had lasted, whether or not they had children within it, and – for those who were no longer cohabiting – whether or not they had gone on to marry that partner. To some extent the answers belie the notion that cohabitation is usually a short-term arrangement. The average duration among current cohabitants was six and a half years, with only one in five having been in their relationship for a year or less. Moreover, there is little evidence that cohabitation comes to an end with the advent of children, as two-fifths (42 per cent) of current cohabiting relationships involved a child. There is also some indication that cohabitation can play a role as a refuge for those disillusioned by previous experiences of marriage, with just over a third (36 per cent) of current cohabitants having been married before. The comparable figure among those who are married is one-fifth (19 per cent), just over half this rate.

Not surprisingly, among those whose cohabiting relationship had ended, the average duration was – at four years – slightly shorter. A third (32 per cent) had only cohabited for one year or less and a further third (32 per cent) had cohabited for two or three years. Among these past cohabitants there is clear evidence that for many cohabitation was indeed a prelude to marriage – nearly three-fifths (59 per cent) had gone on to marry that partner. What is clear, however, is that though cohabitation may be a prelude to marriage for some, this does not apply to everybody and, even when it does, the prelude can last rather a long time!

Earlier we saw that people's views about marriage and cohabitation vary according to social and demographic characteristics. So too does their behaviour. The next table shows the proportion of different groups who are either cohabiting or married. The most dramatic variation relates to age, with 25-34 year olds being the most likely to cohabit, over one in five doing so – more than twice the average rate. The very youngest are actually more likely to be cohabiting than to be married (although very few are either).

Table 2.10 Current cohabitation and marriage rates by age, religion and income source

	% cohabiting	% married	Base
All	9	56	3426
Age			
18-24	11	4	277
25-34	22	44	614
35-44	12	64	715
45-54	7	70	521
55-64	2	78	501
65+	1	55	791
Religion			
Church of England	7	63	1039
Catholic	8	55	331
Other Christian	5	59	560
Non-Christian	2	56	132
No religion	14	49	1344
Income source			
Earnings	13	61	1057
Pension	1	60	821
Benefits	7	30	213
Other	1	27	110

Not surprisingly, given its close association with attitudes to marriage, religion also makes a difference, with the non-religious being twice as likely as those belonging to religious groups to cohabit, and less likely to be married. The strength of this relationship is confirmed by multivariate analysis (shown in model C in the appendix to this chapter). This analysis also shows that the source of a household's income is associated with whether or not a person cohabits. In particular, those living in households whose main income source is earnings (as opposed to a pension or benefits) are more likely to cohabit than any other group.

Some commentators, especially those who argue that the family is 'breaking down', have claimed that cohabitation is concentrated among the less educated, less skilled and the unemployed (sometimes conceptualised as being part of a socially excluded 'underclass'). This in turn, it is argued, results in family breakdown and poor parenting (see Murray, 1994, Morgan, 1999). However, our results do not support this thesis. If anything, they contradict it, as we found that those whose income mainly comes from benefits are *less* likely than others to cohabit. Moreover, once we take account of age, religion and income source, there is no significant relationship between cohabitation and social class, education or whether a person is in work or not. Indeed, because of the relationship between age and qualifications, those who cohabit tend to be more highly qualified than those who do not.

Cohabitation, though unusual among some groups, is very common among others – particularly the young. And it is likely to become more common over time as younger generations, more likely to cohabit, replace older ones among whom such behaviour is highly unusual. However, this generational shift will be tempered by a lifecycle process whereby some young cohabitants marry their partner when they get older.

The legal position of cohabitants

Given their confusing and often vulnerable legal situation, it is important to find out whether cohabitants have made their own legal provisions to safeguard their position. Cohabiting partners, unlike married ones, do not enjoy a standard set of legal duties and obligations to one another, and in many cases their legal position is quite inferior or not recognised as a family status at all. To address this, we asked all current, and previous cohabitants about three types of legal provision which can be taken out by cohabitants: written agreements about accommodation; wills; and parental responsibility agreements/orders. Because of small differences in the legal situation in Scotland, we focus now only on cohabitants in England and Wales. A detailed discussion about cohabitation in Scotland can be found in Barlow (2001).

Half of past and present cohabiting relationships involved the ownership of a house, either jointly or by one partner, yet in only nine per cent of these cases did the cohabitant make a written agreement with their partner about their shares in the ownership of the family home. The vast majority do not, or did not, have this legal safeguard. There is no notable difference in this respect between past and present cohabitants.

This means that if their relationship breaks down and the partners separate, or if the sole-owner partner dies, the cohabitant may well not be entitled to any share of the family home, a situation likely to cause serious problems for the cohabitant. While those who *purchase* a home jointly may receive advice on ways of safeguarding the shares each of them have in the property, there is no obvious point at which couples will be forced to consider their legal position if one cohabitant moves into the other's home. For this reason, it is only at a point of crisis – for instance, where a partner dies or the relationship breaks down – that the reality of the legal situation will emerge. And, of course, by this stage it will usually be too late to remedy the position, particularly where a cohabitant has died and the surviving partner find themselves evicted from their home at a time which is already extremely distressing. By contrast, married couples enjoy a legal protection which acknowledges that the social function and economic consequences of this relationship justify state intervention to protect the weaker economic party. Yet even though cohabiting couples may function in exactly the same way and for the same reasons (with one partner remaining at home to care for children, for instance), cohabitants do not have the same legal protection.

Equally, married couples automatically inherit from each other where no will has been left, but this is not the case with cohabitants, no matter how long they have lived together. Since 1996, the law[5] provides that a cohabitant of at least two year's standing may apply for financial provision out of their deceased partner's estate. However, any award made by the court is limited to maintenance and is far less generous than that available to a surviving married spouse. Despite this, very few past or present cohabitants (ten per cent) had made or changed a will as a consequence of their cohabitation. Again the vast majority – 90 per cent –had taken no action as a result of cohabiting. Among current cohabitants, a slightly higher proportion (14 per cent) had taken action, but still the large majority have no legal safeguard through a will.

As the law stands, only unmarried mothers are automatically given parental responsibility for their child on birth.[6] Unmarried fathers, unlike their married counterparts, have no legal relationship with their child(ren) unless they either make a formal parental responsibility agreement with the mother to share parental responsibility or are granted an order by the court.[7] However, few cohabitants seem aware of this; among past and present cohabitants with children only one in ten had signed a parental responsibility agreement or order, or both. Among current cohabitants with children, the figure was even lower with only five per cent having a parental responsibility agreement/order or both.

This strongly suggests that, in the overwhelming majority of cases, cohabitants have not taken out any extra legal safeguards to protect their position with regard to inheritance, property rights, or (for fathers) responsibility for their children. Consequently, they remain in a particularly vulnerable legal situation.

Is there 'a common law marriage myth'?

One possible explanation for cohabitants' apparent lack of concern about their legal situation may be the pervasive acceptance of the 'common law marriage myth'. Although this type of legally recognised informal marriage was abolished in 1753, it seems to have widely survived as a social practice and belief, as the everyday use of the terms 'common law husband', 'common law wife' and indeed 'common law marriage' suggests. Moreover, if cohabitants have ever claimed income-related social security benefits, they will know that in *that* context they are treated by the state as husband and wife. Similarly, for cohabitants with children, absence of marriage is irrelevant for Working Family Tax Credit purposes.

To assess beliefs about common law marriage we asked:

> *As far as you know do unmarried couples who live together for some time have a 'common law marriage' which gives them the same legal rights as married couples.*

Over a half of all respondents (56 per cent) thought that unmarried couples in this situation 'definitely' or 'probably' have the same rights as married people. Only just over a third (37 per cent) correctly believed that they do not.

Younger people were more likely than older ones to believe in the existence of common law marriage. And men were slightly more likely to believe it (60 per cent) than women (54 per cent). Once again, the under 25 age group showed the most stark gender differences; among this group 56 per cent of women and only 45 per cent of men thought such a legal status existed. Levels of belief in common law marriage are roughly the same for all social classes, and for people of all educational backgrounds. Perhaps most importantly, three-fifths (59 per cent) of current cohabitants thought that there was such a thing as common law marriage. Little more than a third (35 per cent) knew that unmarried couples did not have the same rights as married ones.

Of course, maybe this belief in common law marriage explains the inadequate steps taken by cohabitants to compensate for their vulnerable legal status. There is a view that, rather than needing to make changes to the law, cohabitants need only to be better informed about their legal status and will then take the necessary steps to protect their position. Our findings do not support this. Thus, cohabitants who (correctly) did *not* believe in the 'common law marriage myth' were not much more likely to have made appropriate provision for themselves than those who (incorrectly) believed in it. For instance, 15 per cent of the former had made or changed a will as a result of cohabiting, compared with nine per cent of the latter – a difference to be sure, but hardly a profound one. And there was no difference in respect of agreements made about shares in the family home or parental responsibility for children.

Perhaps we should conclude that cohabitants are particularly prone to apathy or wishful thinking, assuming that their partner will not die and that their relationship will survive? This may well be true, but it is unlikely that this state of mind is confined to cohabitants alone. One study of engaged couples found that this group were not only unaware of the legal position of married couples, but positively did not want to know their legal position before marrying (Hibbs *et al.*, 2001)! Arguably, this suggests a more general inclination to trust in the law to provide fair and appropriate remedies for all family situations – a challenge to which it might be thought that legislators should rise.

Is there a demand for social and legal reform?

People make decisions within their own lives, and about their relationships with others, in both moral and social terms. The legal position, if it is considered at all, is seen more as a part of the external environment. Certainly this is the message from family research over the last decade or so (see Barlow and Duncan, 2000). This also means that there can be a substantial gap between what people believe is right, and what the law says is right. As we have seen, this is likely to be particularly pertinent for cohabitation and marriage, where the law in Britain treats cohabitants in a confusing and inconsistent way, and leaves them in a weak legal position.

To assess people's views about cohabitation we described three 'scenarios' in which cohabitants would be in a legally vulnerable position compared with a similar married couple. For each we then asked respondents what they think *would* happen at the moment and what they think *should* happen.

The first scenario related to financial support on relationship breakdown, a situation where there is currently no legal right for a cohabitant to claim support. We asked:

> *I'd now like you to imagine an unmarried couple with no children who have been living together for ten years. Say their relationship ends. Do you think the woman should or should not have the same rights to claim for financial support from the man as she would if they had been married? And do you think she does in fact have the same rights as a married woman to claim financial support from the man, or, does she have fewer rights?*

As the next table shows, a narrow majority of all respondents correctly thought that a woman in this situation would have fewer rights than a married woman, with a large minority (over a third) believing that she had the same rights, and around one in ten saying they did not know. However, when we asked what the law *should* be, the situation more than reversed with almost two-thirds thinking that she should have the same rights to financial support, just over a third that she should not, and only a tiny group saying they did not know.

Table 2.11 Whether a cohabitant does and should have same rights as a married person in relation to financial support, property inheritance and parental consent

	Woman's right to financial support after breakdown of relationship	Right to family home after death of partner	Father's right to consent to child's medical treatment
Current law	%	%	%
Does have	38	37	50
Does not have	54	53	38
Don't know	8	10	12
What should happen	%	%	%
Should have	61	93	97
Should not have	37	6	2
Don't know	2	1	1
Base: 3101			

Note: England and Wales only.

The second scenario examines property inheritance, an area where existing law treats cohabitants very much as individuals. While it is the case that a cohabitant who can show they have contributed to the purchase price of the home will normally be able to claim some sort of a share, this is not a right and remains a technical area of law where there is little concession to the way in which families arrange their financial affairs in practice. For example, one cohabitant might pay all the bills and the other the mortgage, and both will see this as contributing equally to the home; legally, however, the payment of bills cannot give a share in the home unless such a share has been legally agreed. One classic example of the hardship this can cause is the case of *Burns v Burns* [1984] Ch 317. Here a cohabitant of 19 years' standing failed to prove she had a share in the home, despite raising two children full-time and then working part-time, but never contributing directly to the mortgage or purchase price. To assess beliefs about, and attitudes towards, this issue we asked:

> *Imagine another unmarried couple without children who have been living together for ten years and live in a house bought in the man's name. Say he dies without making a will. Do you think the woman should or should not have the same rights to remain in this home as she would if she had been married to the man? And do you think she does in fact have the same rights as a married woman to remain in this home, or, does she have fewer rights?*

When it came to what currently happens, the responses were very similar to those obtained when asking about financial support, with just over a third thinking (incorrectly) that the woman would have the same rights as a married woman and about half that she would not. However a resounding 93 per cent of respondents thought that she *should* have such rights, and only six per cent were against this.

Our last scenario asked about the rights of fathers:

> *Now imagine another unmarried couple who have been living together for ten years. They have a child who needs medical treatment. Do you think the father should or should not have the same rights to make decisions about his child's medical treatment as he would if he was married to the child's mother? And do you think he does in fact have the same rights as a married man to make decisions about this medical treatment, or, does he have fewer rights?*

Half of respondents thought (incorrectly) that the father did have the same rights as a married father, even though in reality unmarried fathers have no authority to consent to such treatment unless they have taken out a parental responsibility agreement or order (which, as we saw earlier, is very unusual). When asked whether such an unmarried father *should* have the same rights as a married one, a massive 97 per cent thought that he should, with only two per cent disagreeing.

In fact, the government had agreed to amend the law to enable all fathers who jointly register their child's birth with the mother to automatically acquire parental responsibility. These measures formed part of the Adoption and Children Bill 2001, but this was lost as a result of the general election and has not as yet been reintroduced. Consequently, this proposal has still not become law, despite clear public support for such a change.

One of the reasons given against reforming the law to give cohabitants the same rights as married couples is that it would be oppressive (Bailey-Harris, 1996; Freeman, 1984; Deech, 1980). Perhaps cohabitants are deliberately avoiding marriage-like regulation? If this is true, we would expect to find that cohabitants are *less* favourable than others of changes to the law. This is far from the case. In relation to financial support on marital breakdown and property inheritance, cohabitants were actually keener than others that cohabitants have the same rights as married people. For example, 70 per cent of current cohabitants thought that a cohabiting woman should have the same rights to financial support on relationship breakdown as a married woman, compared with 61 per cent of people overall. And a near unanimous 97 per cent of cohabitants thought that the woman living in the situation described in our second scenario should have the right to stay in the family home. There were no significant differences in the responses of men and women. Thus the wishes of cohabitants cannot be used as a particular obstacle to legal reform.

These findings show clearly that massive majorities believe the law should treat long-standing cohabitants in the same way as married couples and that this is particularly true among people who are themselves cohabiting. Disturbingly, substantial minorities believe the law already does so.

Possible models for reform

In choosing to ignore the legal issues surrounding cohabitation, England and Wales are in a dwindling minority of countries both within Europe and within other Common Law jurisdictions such as Canada and Australia. Closer to home, the Scottish Executive has recently put forward proposals to ameliorate the position of cohabitants, providing for example for joint ownership of household goods acquired during cohabitation and a remedy where one cohabitant has suffered economic disadvantage (Scottish Executive, 2000). If the Westminster government were to decide to legislate, what options are available to them?

Given the support for treating cohabitants in the same manner as spouses, might it not be simpler to extend marriage laws to cohabitants of a certain longstanding, whilst enabling them to contract out if they freely wished to make their own arrangements? This would amount in a way to the reinvention of common law marriage but with the safe-guard of opting out. Such a system now exists in Canada (see Bailey, 2001).

Another possibility is to extend marriage-like rights to those who register their cohabitation relationships and contracts. This model exists in France and the Netherlands, where it is available to same and opposite-sex couples. This effectively creates a new institution not modelled on marriage, in which people agree what should happen on death or relationship breakdown. In return, they get marriage-like tax, insurance and inheritance concessions from the state. It makes it possible for cohabiting couples to gain family law-based legal protection similar to that of married couples – if they so wish. At the very least this approach prompts cohabiting couples to think through these issues. However, given how very few cohabitants make wills, formally agree how their home is to be shared, or take out parental responsibility agreements, it is questionable whether such a registered partnership system would actually work in England and Wales.

Despite engaging in reforms not yet countenanced south of the border, Scotland seems to be heading for the same piecemeal approach enacted in England and Wales, with family law rights remaining almost exclusively triggered by marriage. Interestingly, the broadly similar results of this survey in Scotland (see Barlow, 2001), show that the 'common law marriage myth' is equally alive and well north of the border

Given changing social trends away from marriage, coupled with public support for an extension of marriage-like rights to cohabitants, a better way forward might be to adopt a simpler, more easily understood, framework of family rights, where families are treated by law according to their function rather than form. At the same time, it is important to permit the freedom to contract out of such a framework while leaving a safety net in place. The Family Law Committee of the Law Society (1999) and the Solicitors Family Law Association (2000) have both put forward different proposals to give family law protection to cohabitants. The level of support for reform suggests that these proposals should now be fully considered. Indeed the English Law Commission is expected to publish its long-awaited discussion paper the rights of 'Homesharers' (which include cohabitants) in April 2002. It is to be hoped that the evidence presented here, together with the legal developments elsewhere, will trigger a review of family law and policy as it affects cohabitants in England and Wales. The weight of public opinion suggests that this should ultimately lead to a pluralistic rather than a marriage-centric approach to the legal treatment of families.

Conclusions

Marriage is still widely valued as an ideal, but is regarded with much more ambivalence in terms of its role in partnering and (especially) parenting. Views have changed markedly over time and, for many, marriage is no longer seen as having any advantage over cohabitation in everyday life. Interestingly, women – especially young women – who we might imagine have more at stake (because they are the more practically involved in bringing up children, and are thus more likely to become financially dependent or vulnerable) have the most ambivalent view about marriage as a practical relationship.

Meanwhile, cohabitation is now widely accepted both as a prelude to marriage and as an alternative to it, even where there are children. This is especially so for younger people, and it is likely that this is partly a generational effect which will persist over time (rather than being just a stage that young people go through before getting married and having children). Nor are cohabitants some separate social group or sector of the population. In general, they are similar to married respondents in social and economic terms, except that they are more likely to be non-religious and to be living on earnings rather than a pension or benefits. Britain will probably move towards a Scandinavian pattern, therefore, where long-term cohabitation is widely seen as quite normal, and where marriage is more of a lifestyle choice rather than an expected part of life. In policy terms, therefore, emphasising marriage does not appear to match people's opinions about the practicalities of life as partners and parents.

Despite the widespread social acceptance of cohabitation, the law is confused and confusing. Generally, it treats cohabitants as inferior to married couples but, despite this, very few cohabitants have taken any legal safeguards (such as making a written agreement about property, making a will, or taking out a parental responsibility agreement). Large minorities believe – incorrectly – that the law treats cohabitants in the same way as married couples when it comes to maintenance and property rights, and one in two have an incorrect view about male parental responsibility. This no doubt partly reflects a pervasive 'common law marriage myth', with government bearing some responsibility for the confusion (by, for instance, treating cohabitants as married for social security purposes). What is clear, however, is that massive majorities believe the law *should* treat long-standing cohabitants in exactly the same way as it treats married couples.

Notes

1. Similar liberal shifts in opinion (though of a smaller magnitude) have also occurred in attitudes towards homosexuality.
2. To obtain a rough estimate of how much overall change can be explained by generational replacement we can compare the average within-cohort change (-7 points, the sum of each cohort's change divided by the total number of cohorts) with the overall change (-16 points). If we assume that the within-cohort change is due to period factors (that is, historical changes that take place over time and can be thought of as affecting all individuals alike), and that lifecycle factors have not also been at work, then it follows that what is left must be due to generational replacement. This suggests that over half the change can be explained by generational replacement (nine out of 16 points).
3. The exclusion of the sixth statement from the scale is not surprising as responses to it are not indicative of whether a person is more or less traditional in their views about marriage.
4. The scale was created by, for each item, scoring the most pro-marriage responses as five and the most anti-marriage ones as one. The final score was then divided by five (the total number of items in the scale) to produce a set of scores ranging from one to five. Respondents who did not answer any of the questions, or who responded 'don't know' were excluded from the scale. The Chronbach's alpha for the scale was 0.74.
5. Inheritance (Provision for Family and Dependants) Act 1975 as amended.
6. Section 2 Children Act 1989.
7. Section 4 Children Act 1989.

References

Bailey, M. (2001), 'Canadian and American Approaches to Same-sex cohabitation', paper given to Socio-Legal Studies Association annual conference, April 2001, Bristol.

Bailey-Harris, R. (1996), 'Law and the unmarried couple – oppression or liberation', *Child and Family Law Quarterly*, **8**: 137.

Barlow, A. (2001, forthcoming), 'Cohabitation and Marriage in Scotland: Attitudes, Myths and the Law' in Curtice, J., McCrone, D., Park, A. and Paterson, L. (eds.), *New Scotland; New Society?*, Edinburgh: Edinburgh University Press.

Barlow, A. and Duncan, S. (2000), 'Family law, moral rationalities and New Labour's communitarianism: Part II', *Journal of Social Welfare and Family Law*, **22**: 129-143.

Deech, R. (1980), 'The case against legal recognition of cohabitation', in Eekelaar, J. and Katz, S. (eds.), *Marriage and Cohabitation in Contemporary Societies,* Butterworths: London.

Freeman, M. (1984), 'Legal Ideologies, Patriarchal Precedents and Domestic Violence', in Freeman, M. (ed.), *The State, the Law and the Family: Critical Perspectives,* Sweet and Maxwell: London.

Haskey, J. (1999), 'New estimates and projections of the population cohabiting in England and Wales', *Population Trends,* **95**: 1-17.

Hibbs, M., Barton, C. and Beswisk, J. (2001), 'Why Marry? Perceptions of the Affianced', **31**: *Family Law*, 197-207.

Home Office (1998), *Supporting Families: A Consultative Paper*, London: The Stationery Office.

Law Society Family Law Committee (1999), *Cohabitation – Proposals for Reform of the Law*, London: Law Society.

Morgan, P. (1999), *Marriage-lite: the rise of cohabitation and its consequences,* London: Institute for the Study of Civil Society.

Murray, C. (1994), *Underclass: The Crisis Deepens*, Health and Welfare Unit, Choice in Welfare Series No. 20, London: Institute of Economic Affairs.

Park, A. (2000), 'The generation game' in Jowell, R., Curtice, J., Park, A., Thomson, K., Jarvis, J., Bromley, C. and Stratford, N. (eds.), *British Social Attitudes: the 17th Report – Focusing on diversity*, London: Sage.

Office for National Statistics (2001), *Social Trends*, **31**, London: The Stationery Office.

Rake, K. (ed.) (2000), *Women's incomes over the lifetime,* London: The Stationery Office.

Scott, J., Braun, M. and Alwin, D. (1998), 'Partner, parent, worker: family and gender roles' in Jowell, R., Curtice, J., Park, A., Brook, L., Thomson, K. and Bryson, C. (eds.), *British – and European – Social Attitudes: the 15th Report – How Britain differs*, Aldershot: Ashgate.

Scottish Executive (2000), *Parents and Children: the Scottish Executive's proposals for improving Scottish Family Law*, Edinburgh: Scottish Executive.

Shaw, C. and Haskey, J. (1999), 'New estimates and projections of the population cohabiting in England and Wales', *Population Trends*, **95**: 7.

Silva, E. B. and Smart, C. (eds.) (1999), *The New Family?*, London: Sage.

Solicitor's Family Law Society (2000), *Fairness for Families – Proposal for Reform of the Law on Cohabitation*, Orpington:SFLA.

Wilkinson, H. (ed.) (2000), *Family Business*, Demos Collection 15, London: Demos.

Acknowledgements

The authors are grateful to the Nuffield Foundation for their financial support which enabled us to ask the questions reported in this chapter.

Appendix

Regression analyses

The independent variables used in the following regression analyses were:

Age
1. 18-24
2. 25-34
3. 35-44
4. 45-54
5. 55-64
6. 65+

Sex
1. Men
2. Women

Highest educational qualification
1. Degree
2. Other higher education
3. A level or equivalent
4. O level/GCSE or equivalent
5. CSE or equivalent
6. No qualifications

Marital status
1. Married
2. Cohabiting
3. Separated/divorce
4. Widowed
5. Single

Year
1. 1989
2. 2000

Religion
1. Church of England
2. Catholic
3. Other religion
4. No religion

Main source of household income
1. Earnings
2. Pension
3. Benefits
4. Other income source

Socio-economic group
1. Professional/employers/managers
2. Intermediate non-manual
3. Junior non-manual
4. Skilled manual/supervisor
5. Semi-skilled manual
6. Unskilled manual

Current activity
1. In work
2. Not in work

Parental status
1. Parent
2. Non-parent

In each model, * indicates significance at 0.05 level and ** significance at 0.01 level.

Model A

The logistic regression model referred to in the chapter is detailed here. Data from two survey years (1989 and 2000) was pooled together. The method used is SPSS's Forward Stepwise Method (Conditional).

Dependent variable: Agreement with view that "people who want children ought to get married". Independent variables: age, sex, highest educational qualification, marital status, year of survey, religion.

Category	B	S.E.	Wald	Odds Ratio Exp(B)	Sig
Baseline odds	.507	.065	60.299	1.660	
Age			301.651		
18-24	-.849	.123	47.956	.428	**
25-34	-.753	.079	90.275	.471	**
35-44	-.729	.075	94.852	.482	**
45-54	-.118	.082	2.029	.889	.154
55-64	.873	.099	76.938	2.393	**
65+	1.576	.124	161.830	4.835	**
Highest educational qualification			14.623		
Degree	.209	.089	5.591	1.233	*
Other HE	.204	.089	5.233	1.226	*
A level or equiv.	-.026	.094	.076	.974	.974
O/GSCE or equiv.	-.093	.076	1.493	.912	.912
CSE or equiv.	-.195	.104	3.542	.823	.823
No qualifications	-.099	.075	1.735	.906	.188
Marital status			87.031		
Married	.537	.069	59.646	1.710	**
Cohabiting	-.459	.118	15.118	.632	**
Separated/divorced	-.410	.118	12.161	.663	**
Widowed	.223	.158	1.988	1.249	.159
Not married	.110	.101	1.193	1.116	.275
Religion					
Church of England	.133	.064	4.281	1.142	*
Catholic	-.112	.093	1.453	.894	.228
Other	.480	.075	40.601	1.617	**
No religion	-.502	.058	73.675	.605	**
Year					
1989	.458	.043	114.458	1.580	**
2000	-.458	.043	114.458	.633	**

Base: 4128

Model B

The multiple regression model referred to in the chapter is detailed below. Coefficients are only shown for variables where the model found at least one category to be significantly associated with attitudes to marriage.

Dependent variable: Scores on the attitudes to marriage scale (where high scores indicate a more, and low scores a less, traditional view). Independent variables: age, sex, highest educational qualification, marital status, parental status, socio-economic group, current activity, main source of household income, religion.

	Standardised Beta coefficient
Individual characteristics (comparison group in brackets)	
Age (18-24)	
25-34	- .027
35-44	- .004
45-54	.090 **
55-64	.195 **
65+	.316 **
Marital status (married)	
Cohabiting	- .219 **
Separated/divorced	- .126 **
Widowed	- .049 **
Single	- .159 **
Religion (no religion)	
Church of England	.146 **
Catholic	.098 **
Other religion	.202 **
Parental status (parent)	
Non-parent	.079 **
Socio-economic group (manual)	
Non-manual	.069 **
Sex (female)	
Male	.067 **
Current activity (not in work)	
In work	- .055 **

Model C

The logistic regression model referred to in the chapter is detailed here. The method used is SPSS's Forward Stepwise Method (Conditional).

Dependent variable: Whether respondent is currently cohabiting. Independent variables: age, sex, highest educational qualification, religion, socio-economic group, main source of household income, economic activity of respondent.

Category	B	S.E.	Wald	Odds Ratio Exp(B)	Sig
Baseline odds	-3.558	.215	274.726	.028	**
Age			82.373		
18-24	.844	.217	15.144	2.325	**
25-34	1.426	.181	62.000	4.163	**
35-44	.690	.185	13.970	1.994	**
45-54	.076	.206	.135	1.079	.713
55-64	-1.258	.322	15.271	.284	**
65+	-1.778	.565	9.909	.169	*
Religion			23.949		
Church of England	.145	.128	1.280	1.156	.258
Catholic	-.023	.181	.017	.977	.897
Other	-.551	.158	.12.107	.576	**
No religion	.429	.104	16.648	1.536	**
Main household income source			16.648		
Earnings	.783	.236	11.008	2.189	**
Pension	.355	.452	.617	1.426	.432
Benefits	.044	.287	.024	1.045	.877
Other	-1.182	.538	4.834	.307	*
Sex					
Male	-.134	.065	4.242	.874	*
Female	.134	.065	4.242	1.144	.039

Base: 3213

3 Teenage mums

Lynda Clarke and Katarina Thomson *

Few groups excite as much public concern as 'teenage mothers', a common image being one of a growing army of feckless single young women who deliberately become pregnant in order to obtain council housing and social security. Certainly, the UK has the highest rate of births to teenage mothers in western Europe and, despite a number of government initiatives, rates have remained fairly constant since the early 1980s (Clarke, 1999). This is despite a significant fall in teenage birth rates in most other countries in north and south Europe (particularly in the Netherlands and Scandinavian countries). Meanwhile, research shows that teenage parenthood can have negative social, economic and health consequences for both mother and child (Botting *et al.*, 1998). Teenage mothers are less likely to complete their education or obtain a good job, and more likely to bring up their children in poverty (Kiernan, 1995).

Government has long sought to reduce teenage pregnancy. The major interventions of the last 30 years started in 1974 when free contraception was first introduced and the government recommended free informal sessions offering advice on contraception to young people. Earlier, in 1967, the Abortion Act had made abortion legal and the Family Planning Act had allowed local authorities to give contraceptive advice to women – including unmarried women. The debate gathered new impetus when, in 1983, a report was published by the Royal College of Obstetricians and Gynaecologists recommending that youth advisory centres should be set up to help to prevent late abortions among teenagers. Two years later these developments were halted when Victoria Gillick obtained a court ruling (subsequently reversed) which revoked the right for girls aged under 16 to receive confidential medical services. No subsequent major measures were introduced until the early 1990s, since when there has been a flurry of activity. In 1992, the Department of

* Lynda Clarke is a Senior Lecturer at the *Centre for Population Studies, London School of Hygiene and Tropical Medicine*. Katarina Thomson is a Research Director at the *National Centre for Social Research* and Co-Director of the *British Social Attitudes* survey series.

Health's *Health of the Nation* set a target to reduce the rate of under-age pregnancy by at least 50 per cent by the year 2000. Instead it rose in the mid-1990s, with a subsequent fall back to the levels of the early 1990s. The report also wanted to reduce the rate of sexually transmitted diseases and to consult young people on issues surrounding sexual health. The Education Act in 1993 made the biological aspects of sex education compulsory in all secondary schools. Then, when the Labour government was elected in 1997, they set up four Task Force Groups to examine the problem of unintended teenage pregnancy. These Task Force Groups were originally under the remit of the Department of Health but were succeeded by the Social Exclusion Unit (SEU) a year later.

The SEU published their report in 1999 (Social Exclusion Unit, 1999). This identified three possible reasons for Britain's higher teenage birth rates. These were: *low expectations* – more young people in the UK think they have no prospect of getting a job and so see no reason to avoid pregnancy; *ignorance* – a higher proportion of teenagers in Britain do not use contraception when they start having sex and the reality of bringing up a child alone on a low income is rarely brought home to them; and *mixed messages* – young people receive sexually-explicit messages from the adult world and an implicit message that sexual activity is the norm, but often witness silence and embarrassment about sex from their parents and public institutions.

The government has set itself the goal of halving the rate of conceptions among under 18 year-old girls by 2010. Its four-part Action Plan involves a *national campaign* in order to improve understanding and change behaviour; *better prevention* of teenage pregnancy (including better sex education and access to contraception, with a new focus on reaching young men); *better support* for pregnant teenagers and teenage parents (with a new emphasis on their return to education with child care to help, avoiding lone tenancy and pilot schemes around the country to provide intensive support for teenage parents and their children); and *joined-up action* across government departments and local partnerships to co-ordinate the strategy at national and local levels respectively.

The SEU's report is an excellent policy document developed from the research evidence that also develops a strategy for action. But we know very little about the extent to which general attitudes in the population concur with the government's concern about teenage pregnancy, let alone the extent to which public views about the causes of teenage pregnancy mirror those expressed in policy. Consequently, it is hard to judge the level of support that different government policies might attract. In order to rectify this, the 2000 *British Social Attitudes* survey carried a group of questions about the factors encouraging teenage pregnancies and attitudes towards possible policies to reduce them. The survey was carried out before the national strategy was in force and so can be seen as a measure of public perceptions of teenage pregnancy before the government's campaign, meaning that repetition later on will allow us to measure any changes after the initiatives have been implemented.

Is teenage pregnancy a problem?

Before looking at attitudes towards the *causes* of teenage pregnancies, we need first to establish whether the public actually consider teenage pregnancies to be a major problem at all. To assess this, we asked our respondents to agree or disagree with the view that "teenage pregnancy isn't really that much of a problem in Britain today".

As the next table shows, this permissive sentiment did not meet with much approval; over four out of five disagree. However, there is not quite such unanimity when we ask more detailed questions about the situation. True, the majority agree that people are "far too tolerant" of teenage pregnancies, but a fifth disagree and a quarter neither agree nor disagree. Similarly, although the majority (58 per cent) think it wrong for a teenage couple in a stable relationship to have a child, a substantial minority were not so restrictive in their views. But there is clear support for the view that television and advertisements put young people under too much pressure to have sex before they are ready. Government concern about the mixed messages sent out by the media clearly hits a public nerve.

Table 3.1 General attitudes to teenage pregnancies

		Agree strongly	Agree	Neither	Disagree	Disagree strongly
Teenage pregnancy isn't really that much of a problem in Britain today	%	1	4	11	56	26
People in Britain are far too tolerant of teenage pregnancies	%	13	41	25	17	2
Television and advertising put teenagers under too much pressure to have sex before they are ready	%	16	46	18	17	2
If a teenage couple aged 16 or older are in a stable relationship, there's nothing wrong with them having a child	%	2	18	20	46	12

Base: 2980

Of course, the perception that teenage parents represent a 'problem' might reflect a number of concerns, the most obvious being their age. To examine this we asked whether a teenager could be "just as good a parent" as an older person. This demonstrates a fair amount of support for teenage parents, with those who agree outnumbering those who disagree.

Table 3.2 Teenagers can be just as good a parent as older people

		Agree strongly	Agree	Neither	Disagree	Disagree strongly
A teenager can be just as good a parent as someone who is older	%	3	36	24	29	6

Base: 2980

Perhaps not surprisingly, attitudes of women varied considerably according to their own experience of motherhood. So, agreement that a teenager can be just as good a parent as anyone else rises from 31 per cent among women who have never had children and 34 per cent among those who had their first child in their thirties or later, to 40 per cent among those who had their first child in their twenties and 55 per cent among those who were themselves teenage mothers. There is no similar variation in attitudes among men.

We wanted to probe this issue a little more deeply to find out whether it is youth in itself that is seen as the main problem, or whether it is the common association between teenage and *lone* mothers that underpins adverse public opinion. To do this we asked whether it is "simply too hard", firstly, for a teenager to bring up a child alone and, secondly, for a woman of any age to do this. As the next table shows, while over eight in ten think that parenthood is too hard for most single teenagers, less than half take this view about single women more generally.

Table 3.3 Bringing up a child is too hard for a teenager/any woman alone

		Agree strongly	Agree	Neither	Disagree	Disagree strongly
Bringing up a child is simply too hard for most teenagers to do alone	%	20	63	10	5	1
Bringing up a child is simply too hard for a woman of any age to do alone	%	6	36	24	30	3

Base: 2980

If we focus only on those who think it is too hard for a woman of *any* age to bring up a child alone we find, not surprisingly, that practically all this group (97 per cent) also think it is too hard for a teenager to bring up a child alone. But even among those who *disagree* that it is too hard for a woman of any age to bring up a child alone, three-quarters (74 per cent) still think this is too hard for a teenager. So it is concern about the parenting abilities of teenage mothers that appears to underpin concern about teenage pregnancies more generally – and this is not just because they are often lone mothers, but also because of their relative youth.

The perceived causes of teenage pregnancies

Having established that the public share the government's concern about the level of teenage pregnancies in Britain, we turn now to consider whether there is similar agreement as to the causes of teenage pregnancy and the possible policies that might deal with the problem.

Moral failings among the young

The view held by some 'traditional' family advocates, including some faith groups and individual campaigners, is that premarital and early sexual experience is totally wrong and should be condemned. According to these views, teenage pregnancy can be attributed to the loose morals evident in modern society. There is certainly majority support for this view that teenage pregnancies can arise from a "lack of morals" among the young, with just over half agreeing. But, on the other hand, a quarter disagree and a further fifth opt for the "neither agree nor disagree" option.

Table 3.4 Main cause of teenage pregnancies is lack of morals

		Agree strongly	Agree	Neither	Disagree	Disagree strongly
One of the main causes of teenage pregnancy is the lack of morals among young people	%	13	43	19	21	3

Base: 2980

The tendency to blame teenage pregnancy on a lack of morals among young people increases as we move up the age range. As the next table shows, among those under 55 just under a half take this view, but this rises to around three-quarters among those aged 55 or over. A belief in the role played by morality is also closely related to religiosity as measured by church attendance, and is more prevalent among those with lower levels of education. These differences in attitudes by age are similar to the pattern on many other issues of traditional morality observed elsewhere in the *British Social Attitudes Report* series (see, for example, Park, 2000).

Table 3.5 "One of the main causes of teenage pregnancy is lack of morals among young people", by age, church attendance and education

Age	18-24	25-34	35-44	45-54	55-64	65+
Per cent who agree	43	42	46	48	71	78
Base	225	541	632	470	452	656
Church attendance	**Once a week**		**Less often**		**Never**	
Per cent who agree	73		56		51	
Base	358		810		1798	
Education	**Degree**		**O level or above but below degree**		**Below O level**	
Per cent who agree	36		51		68	
Base	402		1349		1229	

The differences by age, religiosity and education may not, of course, be independent of each other, as it is the case that older people tend to be more religious and also to have less educational qualifications. We can test this by using multivariate analysis, which can take all these factors into account at the same time. The full results are shown in models A to C in the appendix to this chapter. They show that, unsurprisingly, religiosity and education both have a strong and consistent effect in the expected direction – those with higher levels of education and those who are less religious tend towards the permissive end of the spectrum. And, as it happens, the more restrictive views of those aged over 55 do, in fact, persist even when their education and religious profile are taken into account.

Various other socio-demographic factors also emerge as being important for women's views (but not for men's). So, women in the salariat (the professional and managerial class) are the most permissive. And – interestingly – women who live with a child are more permissive than other women. We shall return to the significance of these observations shortly.

Pinpointing the reason behind these age-related differences in attitudes is important if we are to assess prospects for future change.[1] An age difference of the sort seen in Table 3.5 could arise by at least three different processes. It may be that the old, who came of age at a time governed by particular moral codes, have kept these values with them as they have aged. Meanwhile, younger generations, growing up in more 'permissive' times, will hold different values (and, again, tend to keep these as they age). This type of age-related difference is known as a *cohort effect* and implies that general public attitudes will become more permissive as younger cohorts replace older ones. If this is the case here, it would suggest that in the future people would become less inclined to blame teenage pregnancy on a lack of moral values. This would in turn, presumably, make people more open to government policies based less on morality and more on active intervention in the form of sex education in schools and making contraception more readily available.

Alternatively, an age difference of the sort seen in Table 3.5 could arise through people's attitudes changing as they grow older, perhaps in response to particular age-bound events such as having children. Such a *lifecycle effect* does not necessary imply any overall change over time in public attitudes as each change in one cohort's views will tend to be counterbalanced by changes in the views of other cohorts.

There is also the possibility of a *period effect* where a certain event or time-period has a lasting impact, either on the population as a whole or on certain groups who were particularly receptive to it. If it had an equal effect on the whole population, then this would not give rise to any particular differences in views between different age groups (just a shift in overall attitudes from one point in time to another). But if it had a disproportionate effect on one group (for instance, those who were young at the time), then there would be an effect on the age distribution of attitudes. This differs from the cohort effect described earlier in which younger cohorts with ever more permissive views (in this case) replace older cohorts. Rather, a period effect that had a disproportionate impact on those who were young at a certain point in time will travel with them as they get older, rather like a lump caused by a piece of food passing through a snake. Younger cohorts (behind the lump), not subject to the period effect, will revert to views more similar to older cohorts (in front of the lump).

As our questions were asked for the first time in 2000, we can only speculate about which of these three effects is evident in our findings. Nonetheless, some clues exist. In particular, the more restrictive views of the cohort aged 55 and over, which persist when education and religiosity are taken into account, are similar to public views on many other moral issues where a cohort effect has been shown to exist (see, for example, Park, 2000 and Hill and Thomson, 2000). We would expect this sort of cohort effect to lead, gradually, to more permissive attitudes among the public as a whole, as older people with their more restrictive views are replaced by younger cohorts with more permissive ones.

However, there is also the possibility of a period effect. The multivariate analysis suggests a slight tendency for women aged between 35 and 54 to be more permissive than younger women. These women were teenagers in the sixties and seventies when the so-called 'permissive society' was the slogan of the day. They may well have been disproportionately affected by this and carried their views with them into adult life. Younger women, on the other hand, would have had the bulk of their teenage years in the eighties and nineties with the advent of Thatcherism and other subsequent 'back to basics' philosophies. If this is the case, the tendency for overall public attitudes to become more permissive will attenuate slightly, although it should not stop altogether since the young are still more permissive than the over 55s.

However, there is another possible explanation for the distinctive views of women aged between 35 and 54. This is that their views are shaped by the stage they have reached in their lifecycle. A clue here is the fact that those who live with children (most of whom will be mothers) hold more permissive attitudes than those who do not. However, these sorts of age-related difference have little implication for future changes in public attitudes as the lifecycle effects they reflect will probably affect each cohort of women in a similar way.

Deprivation, social exclusion and low expectations

In contrast to the emphasis some place on individual 'morality', the Labour government has sought to argue that a major cause of teenage pregnancy lies in structural factors such as deprivation and social exclusion, and in the resulting low expectations among young people. Research has certainly identified particular social factors as being associated with becoming a teenage mother, including coming from a lower socio-economic background, from a large family and having parents who show little interest in education (Kiernan, 1995). There is also an association between deprived areas and high teenage pregnancy rates. Thus, in the most deprived local authorities 12 per cent of all live births between 1994 and 1996 were to teenagers, compared with two per cent in the least deprived areas (Smith, 1999). Pregnancy rates among teenage girls living in the most deprived areas are six times higher than among their counterparts in the most affluent areas (Botting *et al.*, 1998).

Table 3.6 Teenage pregnancy as a result of deprivation, social exclusion and low expectations

		Agree strongly	Agree	Neither	Disagree	Disagree strongly
Teenage girls living in run down areas are more likely than others to become teenage mothers	%	11	51	17	16	2
Teenage girls who want to get on in life don't usually become teenage mothers	%	17	54	15	10	1

Base: 2980

As the previous table shows, substantial majorities agreed that girls who live in run down areas are more likely to become teenage mothers and, conversely, that girls who want to "get on in life" are less likely to become teenage mums.

However, it would be simplistic to divide people neatly into two camps: those who blame teenage pregnancy on some kind of moral failing among the young; and those who hold societal inequalities to account. People are quite capable of holding both views at the same time. (They might, for example, quite logically think that deprivation and social exclusion *cause,* or – at least – are influential in promoting, a lack of morals.) In fact, those who blame teenage pregnancy on a lack of morals are *more* likely than those who do not to agree that living in run down areas is also associated with a higher than average likelihood of teenage parenthood.

Table 3.7 Lack of moral values, and run down areas as explanations for teenage pregnancies

	People who ...	
	... agree that lack of morals cause teenage pregnancies	... disagree that lack of morals cause teenage pregnancies
Teenage girls living in run down areas are more likely than others to become teenage mothers	%	%
Agree	68	53
Neither agree nor disagree	15	15
Disagree	14	30
Base	*1671*	*696*

We found considerable differences in opinion between particular groups when it came to the possible link between teenage pregnancy and morality. Similar differences exist in relation to the importance of the sorts of 'structural' factors discussed above. Again, we used the technique of multivariate analysis to take a variety of factors into account at the same time (details are shown in models D to F in the appendix to the chapter). This shows that women were less likely than men to see a link between rundown areas and teenage mothers. Moreover, some women were much less likely than others to perceive such a link, this applying particularly to groups who are themselves vulnerable to teenage motherhood (for instance, the young and those living in council housing) and indeed to those who had themselves been teenage mothers. Meanwhile, women with more than basic education (and especially those with degrees) were more likely to agree with structural arguments, perhaps because they are more aware of the findings of the sort of research reported above. These differences were not present among men, although those who were not themselves parents were more likely to see a link between teenage pregnancy and rundown areas than the typical father.

The welfare system

It could be argued that high teenage motherhood rates are promoted by a generous welfare system. The Social Exclusion Unit's report pointed out that there is some association between countries with low levels of teenage parenthood and benefit systems that require lone parents to be available for work before their children have reached their teens (Social Exclusion Unit, 1999). For example, in the Netherlands a mother is required to be available for work when her youngest child is five years old, whereas in the UK it is not until the youngest child is 16. However, despite the stereotypes, there is no solid evidence that teenage mothers in Britain deliberately get pregnant in order to get housing or additional social security benefits. In fact, a recent study found that most young mothers simply had not planned to get pregnant at all (Allen and Bourke Dowling, 1998).

When we asked about these matters we found that just over a half of people agreed that the welfare system rewarded teenage mothers, but this fell slightly – to just under half – when we presented people with the concrete example of a teenage girl deliberately getting pregnant to avoid the housing queue.

Table 3.8 The effect of the welfare system on teenage pregnancies

		Agree strongly	Agree	Neither	Disagree	Disagree strongly
All too often Britain's welfare system rewards teenage mothers	%	12	43	25	14	2
Teenage girls who have children often do so to jump the housing queue	%	10	35	26	22	3

Base: 2980

Not surprisingly, these attitudes are related to general views about the welfare system. The *British Social Attitudes* survey contains a welfare scale which measures this (see Appendix I to the book). Scores on the scale range from one (which indicates the most pro-welfare outlook) to five (most anti-welfare one). Those who agree strongly that the welfare system rewards teenage mothers have a much more anti-welfare outlook (getting a mean score of 3.6 on the welfare scale) than those who disagree that the system rewards such mothers (who only score 2.3 on the scale). Although this may not seem like a very large difference, the fact that the scale only runs from one to five makes it quite significant.

Attitudes to sex education as a policy response

The Labour government has placed some considerable weight on the link between high levels of teenage pregnancy and inadequate information and knowledge about sex and contraception. Consequently, policies aiming to educate and increase access to contraception form a particularly important plank in the government's strategy to reduce teenage pregnancy by 2010. But do the public concur with the view that inadequate information and education *are* linked to high rates of teenage pregnancy? If they do not, these sorts of policies are likely to prove highly controversial, particularly if there is any widespread support for the view that they might actually be counterproductive.

We begin with sex education at school. Fortunately for the government, only about one in five agree that sex education at school "encourages" teenagers to have sex too early while just over half agree that more sex education would cut the number of teenage pregnancies. However, substantial minorities disagree. One in five, for instance, do think that giving teenagers sex education encourages them to have sex when they are too young.

Table 3.9 Sex education, contraception and teenage pregnancies

		Agree strongly	Agree	Neither	Disagree	Disagree strongly
There would be fewer teenage pregnancies if sex education at school gave more advice about sex, relationships and contraception	%	14	40	19	21	4
Giving teenagers lessons at school about sex and contraception encourages them to have sex too early	%	4	18	26	44	6
There would be fewer teenage pregnancies if more parents talked to their children about sex, relationships and contraception	%	18	57	14	9	*
Contraception should be more easily available to teenagers, even if they are under 16	%	13	51	12	18	4

Base: 2980

Views are more clear cut when it comes to the impact of *parents* discussing these matters with their children. Three-quarters think this would cut teenage pregnancy and fewer than one in ten (9 per cent) disagree. This suggests that concern about sex education at school is more likely to reflect worries about the precise content of the classes rather than complete opposition to the notion of sex education *per se*.

Of course, our questions do not specify the content of these 'discussions' about sex, relationships and contraception. After all, some no doubt will think that teenagers should simply be told to 'just say no', while others may feel that the aim should be to make sure that teenagers who have sex do so safely. However, the balance of opinion appears to lie on the latter side, as nearly two-thirds of people agree with the view that "contraception should be more easily available to teenagers, even if they are under 16". Only one in five disagree.

As might be expected, there is an inverse relationship between blaming the morality of the young for teenage pregnancies and supporting sex education and contraception. In other words, those who blame teenage motherhood on a lack of moral values tend to be *less* likely to agree that sex education reduces pregnancies, more likely to think that sex education encourages the young to experiment with sex, and less likely to support contraception. However, it should be noted that there is majority support (59 per cent) for making contraception more easily available to teenagers, even among those who tend to blame teenage pregnancy on a lack of moral values.

Table 3.10 Lack of moral values, and attitudes to sex education and contraception

	People who ...	
	... agree that lack of morals cause teenage pregnancies	... disagree that lack of morals cause teenage pregnancies
% who agree that:		
Sex education at school reduces teenage pregnancies	53	62
Sex education at school encourages teenagers to have sex	34	6
Contraception should be more easily available	59	81
Base	*1671*	*696*

In the light of this, it is unsurprising that, when we look at the views held by different groups within the population, we get a similar, but inverse, picture to that we saw earlier when considering views about the role of moral values (see models G to M in the appendix to the chapter). So, the young are more in favour of a wider availability of contraception. Young women (although not young men) are also more supportive of sex education in schools. Religion plays a role, with those who are more religious being less in favour of contraception and, among men, less in favour of sex education.

However, there are also some differences when compared to our earlier analysis of attitudes to moral values. Interestingly, education bears much less of a relationship to attitudes on sex education and contraception. And owner occupiers are less supportive of sex education and contraception – indicating that there is a socio-economic dimension to attitudes in this area. Intriguingly, having a child in the household, which might on the basis of our previous discussions have been expected to make women *more* supportive of contraception, in fact, makes them less so. But – for the purposes of anticipating changes in public attitudes – the important point is that, once again, age is clearly related to attitudes (especially on contraception but also among women on sex education), even once all the other factors have been taken into account.

Conclusions

The government has stated that:

> Government cannot reduce rates of teenage conception and pregnancy on its own. To achieve the goals set out ... there needs to be nothing less than a common national effort to change the culture surrounding teenage pregnancy ... (Social Exclusion Unit, 1999).

How far this will be achieved, only time – and repetition of these questions – will tell. But our findings suggest that the existing 'common culture' which surrounds teenage pregnancy is one of both concern about the phenomenon and support for many of the main strands of current government policy.

It is *youth* rather than *lone* motherhood which appears to underpin concern about young parenthood. Individual attributes such as lack of morals are commonly blamed for its prevalence, but so too are the same structural factors, such as deprivation and social exclusion, that government policy tends to emphasise. And, while the majority of people feel that the British welfare system is too generous towards teenage mothers, these views are not as strongly held as other possible explanations for young parenthood.

The more traditional views about morality that are held by people aged over 55 are consistent with other similar issues previously analysed in the *British Social Attitudes Report* series. The suggestion from the data is that this is – at least in part – a cohort effect, and the expectation must be that public attitudes will gradually grow more permissive as younger cohorts replace older ones. If so, current interventions stressing sex education and, especially, contraceptive provision should become even more widely acceptable. One of the more surprising findings is, in fact, the generally high level of support for the provision of contraception to teenagers, even those under 16.

The role of television and advertising in promoting sex is roundly condemned, which might discourage the government from relaxing the current legislation and guidelines for broadcasting.

An approach to teenage pregnancy that stresses morality is not necessarily in opposition to the more structural explanations favoured by the government. People who think that a lack of morals are responsible for high teenage pregnancy rates are also likely to think that other structural reasons are at fault as well (such as the effect of living on run down estates). It is these sorts of areas which are being targeted in current measures to educate and employ young people and young mothers. But there it is notable that there is less sympathy with the view that deprivation and teenage pregnancy are linked among those who actually live in some of the areas being targeted – such as those living on housing estates. This should act as a warning sign to the policy makers and practitioners who are involved with designing or delivering such services.

The main interpretation of these results is the striking resemblance between the government's and the public's perceptions of teenage pregnancy. Whether this is due to politicians being effective in getting their message across or to a correct reading of the research and the mood of the public is not clear. It will be interesting to see how the debate and public opinion develop in the light of the government's initiatives.

Note

1. For a full discussion of cohort and lifecycle effects, see Park (2000).

References

Allen, I. and Bourke Dowling, S. (1998), *Teenage Mothers: Decisions and Outcomes*, London: Policy Studies Institute.

Botting, B., Rosato, M. and Wood, R. (1998), 'Teenage mothers and the health of their children', *Population Trends*, **93**, London: The Stationery Office.

Clarke, L. (1999), 'Young mothers and their families: Trends and associated factors and consequences' in *Promoting the Health of Teenage Lone Mothers: Setting the Research and Policy Agenda*, A report of a Health Education Authority Expert Working Group chaired by K. Wellings, London: Health Education Authority.

Kiernan, K. (1995), *Transition to Parenthood: Young mothers, Young fathers – Associated factors and later life experiences*, Welfare Discussion Paper 113, London: London School of Economics.

Hill, A. and Thomson, K. (2000), 'Sex and the media: shifting landscape' in Jowell, R., Curtice, J., Park, A., Thomson, K., Jarvis, L., Bromley, C. and Stratford, N. (eds.), *British Social Attitudes: the 17th Report – Focusing on diversity*, London: Sage.

Park, A. (2000), 'The generation game' in Jowell, R., Curtice, J., Park, A., Thomson, K., Jarvis, L., Bromley, C. and Stratford, N. (eds.), *British Social Attitudes: the 17th Report – Focusing on diversity*, London: Sage.

Social Exclusion Unit (1999), *Teenage Pregnancy*, London: The Stationery Office.

Smith, J. (1999), 'Influence of social economic factors on attaining targets for reducing teenage pregnancy', *British Medical Journal*, **306**.

Acknowledgements

We are indebted to Katherine Hill who carried out preliminary analysis of these results.

The *National Centre for Social Research* is grateful to the Health Education Authority and the Department of Health for their financial support which enabled us to ask the questions reported in this chapter.

Appendix

The multivariate analysis reported in the chapter was produced using logistic regression.

The dependent variables are as follows:

	Predicting agree/agree strongly with ...
Models A-C	One of the main causes of teenage pregnancy is the lack of morals among young people
Models D-F	Teenage girls living in run down areas are more likely than others to become teenage mothers
Models G-I	There would be fewer teenage pregnancies if sex education at school gave more advice about sex, relationships and contraception
Models H-K	Contraception should be more easily available to teenagers, even if they are under 16

The tables show logs odds ratios and significance. A log odds ratio above 1 implies positive correlation with agreeing with the statement. A log odds ratio of less than 1 implies a negative correlation. The significance is shown as follows:

**	Significant at the 1 per cent level
*	Significant at the 5 per cent level

The independent variables are as follows:

Variable	Categories	Men	Base Women	All
Age	18-24	94	131	225
	25-34	218	323	541
	35-44	273	359	632
	45-54	202	268	470
	55-64	212	240	452
reference:	65+	262	394	656
Sex	Women	-	-	1718
reference:	Men	-	-	1262
Education	Degree	192	210	402
	O/A level, HE below degree	598	751	1349
reference:	CSE/None/DK/NA	472	757	1229
Household tenure	Owner occupier	890	1152	2042
	Private renter/other/DK/NA	137	169	306
	Social housing – not estate	51	87	138
reference:	Social housing – estate	184	310	494
Class	Salariat	468	465	933
(where no info on	Routine non-manual	85	589	674
respondent's class,	Petty bourgeoisie	116	75	191
spouse/partner used)	Manual foremen & supervisors	163	80	243
reference:	Working class	406	456	862
Church attendance	Once a week	121	237	358
	Less than once a week	275	535	810
reference:	Never/not religious	858	940	1798
Child <13 in h/hold	Yes	233	411	644
Reference:	No	1029	1307	2336
Teenager in h/hold	Yes	155	248	403
reference:	No	1107	1407	2577
Age at having	Teenager	44	220	264
first child	Thirties/forties	243	200	443
	Not parent	414	406	820
reference:	Twenties	557	890	14

Agree that lack of moral values is a main cause of teenage pregnancy

	Model A Men		Model B Women		Model C All	
Age (ref: 65+)						
18-24	0.197	**	0.439	**	0.316	**
25-34	0.233	**	0.428	**	0.330	**
35-44	0.377	**	0.328	**	0.348	**
45-54	0.297	**	0.341	**	0.329	**
55-64	0.757		0.688		0.745	
Sex (ref: men)						
Women	-		-		0.890	
Education (ref: < O level)						
Degree	0.421	**	0.396	**	0.407	**
O level+ below degree	0.706	*	0.670	**	0.680	**
Tenure (ref: Social housing						
Owner occupier	0.773		1.091		0.952	
Private rental/other	0.759		1.194		0.995	
Social housing, not estate	0.868		0.899		0.898	
Class (ref: working class)						
Salariat	0.721		0.606	**	0.663	**
Routine non-manual	0.950		0.945		0.972	
Petty bourgeoisie	0.895		0.891		0.916	
Manual foremen/supervisors	0.952		0.994		0.956	
Church attendance (ref: never)						
Once a week	3.451	**	2.271	**	2.597	**
Less often	0.952		1.561	**	1.280	**
Child in household (ref: not)						
Child (0-12) in household	0.805		0.721	*	0.793	
Teenager in household (ref: not)						
Teenager in household	1.283		0.818		0.969	
Age having first child (ref: 20s)						
Teenager	0.785		0.844		0.840	
Thirties or older	0.992		1.080		1.031	
Not a parent	1.097		0.836		0.941	
Constant	1.594	**	1.130		1.338	**
-2 log likelihood	1582.998		1968.604		3583.304	
Base	*1223*		*1644*		*2867*	

Agree that girls on run down estates are more likely to become teenage mums

	Model D Men		Model E Women		Model F All	
Age (ref: 65+)						
18-24	0.962		0.392	**	0.572	**
25-34	0.822		0.740		0.799	
35-44	1.146		0.563	**	0.801	
45-54	1.385		0.522	**	0.811	
55-64	1.150		0.946		1.041	
Sex (ref: men)						
Women	-		-		0.686	**
Education (ref: < O level)						
Degree	0.971		3.055	**	1.851	**
O level+ below degree	0.844		1.830	**	1.314	**
Tenure (ref: Social housing						
Owner occupier	1.234		1.663	**	1.498	**
Private rental/other	1.416		1.711	*	1.605	**
Social housing, not estate	0.971		1.370		1.269	
Class (ref: working class)						
Salariat	0.942		0.980		0.908	
Routine non-manual	2.173	**	1.085		1.156	
Petty bourgeoisie	0.923		0.995		0.923	
Manual foremen/supervisors	0.946		0.880		0.943	
Church attendance (ref: never)						
Once a week	1.017		0.819		0.925	
Less often	1.218		1.150		1.171	
Child in household (ref: not)						
Child (0-12) in household	1.288		0.764		0.997	
Teenager in household (ref: not)						
Teenager in household	0.914		1.299		1.126	
Age having first child (ref: 20s)						
Teenager	1.696		0.704	*	0.801	
Thirties or older	1.021		1.186		1.068	
Not a parent	1.768	**	0.789		1.193	
Constant	2.573	**	1.379	*	1.675	**
-2 log likelihood	1601.143		2038.632		3715.149	
Base	*1222*		*1644*		*2866*	

Agree that sex education leads to fewer teenage pregnancies

	Model G Men		Model H Women		Model I All	
Age (ref: 65+)						
18-24	1.282		1.787	*	1.523	*
25-34	1.503		1.969	**	1.696	**
35-44	1.412		1.300		1.315	
45-54	1.114		0.802		0.919	
55-64	1.375		0.937		1.133	
Sex (ref: men)						
Women	-		-		0.931	
Education (ref: < O level)						
Degree	0.970		0.888		0.946	
O level+ below degree	0.904		0.957		0.957	
Tenure (ref: Social housing						
Owner occupier	0.569	**	0.764		0.676	**
Private rental/other	0.707		0.849		0.794	
Social housing, not estate	0.680		1.006		0.905	
Class (ref: working class)						
Salariat	0.941		1.168		1.035	
Routine non-manual	1.139		0.992		0.976	
Petty bourgeoisie	0.997		1.101		1.052	
Manual foremen/supervisors	0.988		1.283	*	1.105	
Church attendance (ref: never)						
Once a week	0.568	**	0.803		0.691	**
Less often	0.807		1.201		1.020	
Child in household (ref: not)						
Child (0-12) in household	1.024		0.864		0.967	
Teenager in household (ref: not)						
Teenager in household	0.862		0.974		0.930	
Age having first child (ref: 20s)						
Teenager	0.635		1.138		0.988	
Thirties or older	1.383	*	1.079		1.235	
Not a parent	1.182		1.132		1.175	
Constant	1.165		1.261		1.300	
-2 log likelihood	1737.624		2142.538		3901.003	**
Base	*1220*		*1649*		*2869*	

Agree that contraception should be more available for teenagers

	Model J Men		Model K Women		Model L All	
Age (ref: 65+)						
18-24	5.500	**	4.933	**	4.911	**
25-34	3.560	**	4.221	**	3.800	**
35-44	2.108	**	2.770	**	2.475	**
45-54	2.158	**	2.509	**	2.407	**
55-64	1.211		1.721	**	1.456	**
Sex (ref: men)						
Women	-		-		1.121	
Education (ref: < O level)						
Degree	0.891		0.938		0.898	
O level+ below degree	0.765		0.889		0.817	*
Tenure (ref: Social housing						
Owner occupier	0.621	*	0.653	*	0.655	**
Private rental/other	0.615		0.883		0.749	
Social housing, not estate	0.763		0.418	**	0.517	**
Class (ref: working class)						
Salariat	1.182		1.147		1.149	
Routine non-manual	0.705		0.807		0.787	
Petty bourgeoisie	0.983		0.782		0.871	
Manual foremen/supervisors	0.976		0.971		0.971	
Church attendance (ref: never)						
Once a week	0.303	**	0.360	**	0.338	**
Less often	0.924		0.741	*	0.810	*
Child in household (ref: not)						
Child (0-12) in household	1.018		0.566	**	0.737	*
Teenager in household (ref: not)						
Teenager in household	0.905		1.133		1.018	
Age having first child (ref: 20s)						
Teenager	0.934		0.942		0.958	
Thirties or older	0.894		0.821		0.870	
Not a parent	0.997		0.769		0.887	
Constant	1.591	*	1.428	*	1.455	**
-2 log likelihood	1567.315		1894.863		3479.277	
Base	*1224*		*1645*		*2869*	

4 The NHS and Labour's battle for public opinion

Jo-Ann Mulligan and John Appleby [*]

The public's attitudes towards the NHS have always been an important measure not only of the (perceived) state of the NHS itself, but of the government too. Last year's *British Social Attitudes* was particularly pertinent in that it was the last round of the survey series before a general election, and also completed a run of three years' surveys covering the first Labour government to be elected for nearly a quarter of a century.

Ascertaining – and understanding – the public's views about the state of the NHS is no mere academic exercise. When the public were asked two days prior to this year's general election, which issues would be most important in determining their voting intentions, the top issue, cited by 73 per cent of the sample, was 'health care'.[1] The latest set of *British Social Attitudes* data provides an important opportunity to examine the extent to which public attitudes towards the NHS have changed under the Labour government, and how recent years compare with longer-term trends.

When we last visited this subject four years ago in *The 14th Report* (Judge *et al.*, 1997), the authors identified a long-term trend of growing dissatisfaction with the health service, but at the same time a reluctance to accept alternative means of delivering health care. In order to understand subsequent changes in public opinion, we need first to examine the way in which the political environment and resource allocation for the NHS have been transformed by the election of the Labour government and its subsequent policies.

The public policy background for the NHS

On the eve of the 1997 general election, voters were told by the Labour Party that they had 24 hours to save the NHS – by voting for the Labour Party. The commitment to cut NHS waiting lists by treating an extra 100,00 patients was

---

[*] Jo-Ann Mulligan is a Research Officer and John Appleby is a Director of the Health Systems Programme at the King's Fund.

included on Labour's 'credit card' of key pledges. Then, as now, Labour were seen by the public as the party most trusted to run the NHS effectively. However, once in power, and as previous governments had found, events conspired to make Labour more vulnerable on health than seemed possible when they took office. Labour decided to pursue a cautious policy on public expenditure which meant sticking – more or less – to the previous Conservative government's spending plans for two years. This precluded a quick injection of large amounts of extra funds into the NHS. Expectations of rapid improvements were not to be fulfilled.

In the winter of 1999-2000, a higher than average number of people with influenza and 'flu-like symptoms put considerable pressure on the NHS. Newspapers and other media ran with the traditional winter crisis story of delays, cancellations and excessive trolley waits. The case of Mavis Skeet personified an impression of a health service stretched to breaking point. The 73 year-old grandmother from Wakefield had had her operation for throat cancer cancelled four times in five weeks in late 1999 because of bed shortages. Finally, her doctors said the delays had made her condition inoperable, and sadly she later died.

In the context of the overall workload of the NHS such personal stories, while tragic, could be seen as comparatively insignificant; after all, every year the NHS treats over 11 million cases in hospital, and many more millions are seen in outpatient and accident and emergency departments. Nevertheless, such stories are important. Not only is the media the public's main source of information about the NHS (Mulligan, 2001), but personal stories can provide a reference point against which to assess their own NHS experience. Making judgements about the quality of a service, such as health care, which is consumed only infrequently can be difficult without such references or comparisons.

The media also encouraged comparisons between Britain's relatively meagre health spending and that of her European partners. The apparently low numbers of doctors and allegedly poor survival statistics all added to the *Daily Mail*'s headlines of 'Britain's Third World wards'. The final blow came when the Labour peer Lord Winston, one of the country's best-known doctors, called the NHS the worst health service in Europe. The pressure to spend more and to be *seen* to be spending more became too much. In January 2000, Blair promised that British health-care spending, measured as a proportion of GDP, would rise towards the EU average by 2006. This meant that the NHS would need to grow by a third in real terms: 7.4 per cent for 2000 and over five per cent a year for the next three years. While the claim to match European spending turned out to be more of an 'aspiration' than a firm commitment, Gordon Brown's March 2000 budget finally confirmed that spending on the NHS would grow by around six per cent in real terms over the next five years. The fieldwork of the 2000 *British Social Attitudes* survey was carried out some three months later, after this news ought to have sunk in, but before the new money had actually been spent.

On the organisational front, the previous decade under the Tories had been one of unparalleled turbulence for the NHS. Any expectation that the pace of change might slow under Labour was soon to be dismissed. The publication in 1997 of the Labour government's White Paper for the NHS in England, the *New NHS* (Department of Health, 1997), announced the supposed demise of the Conservatives' internal market. Labour also introduced a whole battery of other structures including NHS Direct, a telephone advice service. There were to be national service standards, and national performance indicators to measure progress towards them. Given Labour's election pledge on hospital waiting lists, considerable efforts have naturally been devoted on that particular front. The overall effect of this hands-on approach has been to ensure that if things go wrong, blame will be certain to fall on the Blair government.

Finally in July 2000 (during fieldwork for the survey), as a follow-up to the promise of extra money, came a National Plan for the NHS (Department of Health, 2000). The NHS Plan, in effect, is a shopping list of how the extra money will be spent and it has tied Ministers to some very specific targets. There is to be maximum waits for operations, outpatient appointments, accident and emergency attendances and GP visits. By 2005, all hospital waiting lists are to be abolished as everyone will be given a definite booked admission date. In addition, there are to be more doctors and nurses and an ambitious hospital-building programme. There are other more controversial aspects to the plan – in particular, Labour's high profile concordat with the private sector marked a symbolic end to half a century's worth of hostility between the Labour Party and private hospitals.

But what has been the public's assessment of Labour's handling of the NHS? In answering this we compare trends in attitudes since 1998 with the previous administration's period in office. We also examine the public's attitudes to a key target chosen by Labour for their second term, specifically, reducing waiting *times* (as opposed to the earlier emphasis on waiting *lists*). To what extent is this the public's priority? Finally, we look to the future of the NHS, and examine to what extent the public still support the general *idea* of the NHS or whether there are signs that – despite additional money for the NHS – alternative systems are gaining support.

Satisfaction with the NHS

We start by looking at satisfaction with the NHS overall during the period after Labour were elected, compared to the previous Major government. We asked respondents how satisfied or dissatisfied they were with the overall running of the NHS. The purpose of this question is not to provide a definitive account of the public's experience of the NHS but rather to examine trends in the overall mood of the public towards the NHS. Looking back over the 1990s, it is *dissatisfaction* rather than *satisfaction* that appears to fluctuate more widely. The next table shows that *dis*satisfaction with the overall running of the NHS fell from an all-time high of 50 per cent in 1996 to 36 per cent in 1998, a year into the Labour government. Dissatisfaction continued to fall to 33 per cent in 1999 – a level not seen since 1984 – before rising slightly in 2000 to 39 per cent, still well below the level of the latter years of the Major government.

Table 4.1 Satisfaction with the NHS, 1993-2000

	1993	1994	1995	1996	1998	1999	2000
	%	%	%	%	%	%	%
Very or quite satisfied	44	44	37	36	42	46	42
Neither satisfied nor dissatisfied	18	17	18	14	22	20	19
Very or quite dissatisfied	38	38	45	50	36	33	39
Base	*2945*	*3469*	*3633*	*3620*	*3146*	*3143*	*3426*

Thus, in contrast to the bulk of the Major period, those satisfied with the NHS now again outnumber those who are dissatisfied. In fact, the fall in dissatisfaction is highlighted even further in the next graph which shows the whole of the previous decade and a half of Conservative rule.

In many ways the trend in dissatisfaction mirrors the changing funding of the NHS. Dissatisfaction rose substantially during the 1980s coinciding with historically very low real increases in NHS funding between 1983 and 1989. Then, following the unusually large injection of cash for three years in succession from 1990, dissatisfaction fell. The cycle continued during the mid 1990s, when the Major government entered the 1997 general election following one of the lowest real increases in NHS funding for many years. In fact, when we last visited this subject in *The 14th Report,* the authors expressed surprise at the extent to which the Major government was prepared to enter the general election after such a meagre financial allocation for the NHS in the run up to it, a mere 0.7 per cent. From the graph we see that dissatisfaction rocketed in 1995 and 1996, no doubt playing its part in the Conservatives' election defeat.

Figure 4.1 Dissatisfaction with the NHS, 1983-2000

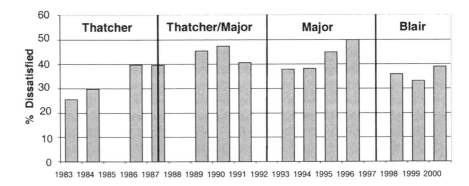

However, since then, the association between funding and satisfaction becomes harder to understand. In spite of the widespread perception that the new Labour government was sticking rigidly to the previous Conservative administration's NHS spending plans for 1997/8 and 1998/9, in fact the outturn figures for these years suggest that gross UK NHS spending increased over these years by 11 per cent compared with the Conservative administration's planned increase of just 4.8 per cent (Department of Health, 1996, Department of Health, 2001). As might be expected given these funding increases, dissatisfaction fell in 1998. However, it is worth noting that the impression in the media and a view promulgated by the government at the time was of a need for relative parsimony in public spending (moreover, the eventual, accurate, outturn spending figures only became available some years later). In 1999, UK NHS spending increased by 10.3 per cent, and again there was a fall in dissatisfaction. However, when the health service received a similarly large increase in 2000/2001, and, importantly, a pledge to provide similar increases in spending for the following three years, dissatisfaction tips upwards to its highest point under Blair. Possibly attitudes lag behind spending decisions, as the money takes some time to take effect. But it might also lead us to ask whether there really was a crisis of public confidence in the NHS in 1996 or whether the survey question was actually tapping levels of satisfaction towards something other than the health service?

One interpretation of the fall in dissatisfaction between the last year of Conservative rule and the first term of New Labour is that it reflects a 'honeymoon' period for Labour voters after the party was elected, regardless of what was actually happening in the NHS. When the results are broken down by political allegiance, it is Labour supporters who account for the greatest decrease in dissatisfaction from 60 per cent in 1996 to 37 per cent in 2000. Dissatisfaction actually went *up* among Conservative voters (although this increase was not statistically significant). Asking people how they feel about the overall running of the NHS turns out to be as much a question about the performance of the government of the day as it is about the performance of the health service.

Table 4.2 Satisfaction with the NHS and party allegiance, 1996 and 2000

	Conservative		**Labour**		**Lib Dem**	
	1996	2000	1996	2000	1996	2000
	%	%	%	%	%	%
Very or quite satisfied	49	44	28	44	33	37
Neither satisfied nor dissatisfied	13	16	12	18	14	20
Very or quite dissatisfied	37	40	60	37	54	43
Base	*1012*	*937*	*1528*	*1394*	*391*	*341*

In order to delve deeper into public attitudes to the NHS, we therefore need to turn to survey questions dealing with specific aspects of health care. Not only will these enable us to trace the specific hotspots of discontent with the NHS, but they are perhaps also less liable to be seen by respondents as indicators of satisfaction with the government as a whole.

Primary care

Turning first to primary care, we do not see any evidence of the decline in dissatisfaction between 1996 and 1998 that we saw on the general question. Family doctors continue to enjoy widespread support with at least three-quarters of respondents stating that they were satisfied with the service, but this is actually slightly lower than during the early Major years.

Table 4.3 Satisfaction with GPs and dentists, 1993-2000

	1993	1994	1995	1996	1998	1999	2000
	%	%	%	%	%	%	%
GPs							
Very or quite satisfied	83	80	79	77	75	76	76
Neither satisfied nor dissatisfied	7	9	10	9	10	9	8
Very or quite dissatisfied	10	11	11	13	14	14	15
Dentists	%	%	%	%	%	%	%
Very or quite satisfied	58	57	55	52	53	53	62
Neither satisfied nor dissatisfied	19	17	17	16	17	17	15
Very or quite dissatisfied	20	22	23	25	23	24	19
Base	*2945*	*3469*	*3633*	*3620*	*3146*	*3143*	*3426*

The fortunes of NHS dentists appear to have received a boost, but only in the last year. Throughout the 1990s they endured a drop in popularity, very probably due to concerns about access to NHS dental care in general after the introduction of a new contract for dentists. The latest results for 2000, however, show an increase in the proportion of respondents who say they are satisfied with NHS dental services from 53 per cent in 1999 to 62 per cent in 2000, reversing the whole of the decline of the 1990s. The reasons for this are not clear. It could be due to the higher profile dentistry received during 2000 culminating in the publication of a national strategy in the autumn. During the past two years ministers have also claimed that the number of NHS dentists is steadily increasing, as have the numbers of treatments performed. Moreover Tony Blair has said that by the end of this year "Everyone who wants access to

NHS dentistry can have it".[2] The government also announced it was setting up a chain of dental access centres where it will be possible to walk in and consult dentists. It is hard to say whether these high-level changes have had a tangible impact on the quality of dental services locally but at the very least the overall mood of the public appears to have become more favourable.

The hospital service

The proportion who were satisfied with inpatient and outpatient hospital services remained steady between 1996 and 1998 across the election period, although levels of *dis*satisfaction fell somewhat. However, as the next table shows, a few years into the Labour government, satisfaction levels began to rise. By 2000, almost three out of five respondents were satisfied. But *dis*satisfaction remained practically stable between 1996 and 2000, in contrast to overall perceptions of the NHS where it first fell and then rose.

Table 4.4 Satisfaction with inpatient and outpatient services, 1993-2000

	1993 %	1994 %	1995 %	1996 %	1998 %	1999 %	2000 %
Inpatient care							
Very or quite satisfied	64	58	57	53	54	58	59
Neither satisfied nor dissatisfied	18	17	18	17	20	19	15
Very or quite dissatisfied	14	16	17	22	17	17	21
Outpatient care	%	%	%	%	%	%	%
Very or quite satisfied	57	56	55	52	52	56	58
Neither satisfied nor dissatisfied	17	18	17	18	20	19	15
Very or quite dissatisfied	23	21	22	25	22	21	24
Base	*2945*	*3469*	*3633*	*3620*	*3146*	*3143*	*3426*

The survey also asked respondents for views on accident and emergency departments. This attracted the most criticism and appears to be seen as the least satisfactory element of the hospital service with 29 per cent of respondents expressing dissatisfaction in 2000.

We can, in fact, delve further into different aspects of hospital care. In some years since the early 1990s the *British Social Attitudes* survey has asked a number of questions on specific aspects of inpatient and outpatient care. It is now possible to look back over time and compare perceptions under the Conservative and Labour governments. Taking outpatient services first, we ask a set of questions around a hypothetical back problem, which are introduced like this:

> *Suppose you have a back problem and your GP referred you to*
> *a hospital outpatient department ...*

Respondents are asked to answer the following questions "from what you know or have heard".

A number of things stand out from the results in the next table. First, there is little evidence of the fall in dissatisfaction after the Labour election victory that we saw earlier towards the NHS overall. People have, if anything, become more critical of certain aspects of the outpatient service since these questions were introduced in 1993. This could, of course, simply reflect rising expectations of what is expected from the hospital service. Equally it might indicate that the quality of outpatient services has not changed substantially over time. Of course, it might be a bit of both.

Table 4.5 Assessment of specific outpatient services, 1993-2000

% who say it would <u>not</u> happen:	1993	1994	1995	1998	1999	2000
... when you arrived, the doctor would see you within half an hour of your appointment?	66	62	61	65	59	66
... you would get an appointment within three months?	49	48	50	50	50	56
... if you wanted to complain about the treatment you received, you would be able to without fuss or bother?	39	41	38	37	36	44
Base	*2945*	*3469*	*3633*	*3146*	*3143*	*3426*

The complaints system was viewed most favourably of the three items. Interestingly, the views of those who had used the outpatient service in the previous 12 months were similar to those without such experience.

The other two of the statements do, of course, address the controversial area of waiting times and lists and it is these which attract the most criticism. Two in three people did not think that the doctor would see them within 30 minutes of their appointment time and over half did not expect to get an outpatient appointment within three months.

The *British Social Attitudes* survey goes on to ask a series of questions about inpatient care:

Now suppose you had to go into your local NHS for observation and maybe an operation. From what you know or have heard, please tell me whether you think ...

Table 4.6 Assessment of specific inpatient services, 1993-2000

% who say it would <u>not</u> happen ...	1993	1994	1995	1998	2000
... the operation would take place on the day it was booked?	39	36	38	46	50
... you would be allowed home only when you were really well enough to leave?	38	44	45	45	46
... there would be a particular nurse to deal with any problems?	39	41	37	40	40
... the doctors would take seriously any views you may have on the sorts of treatment available?	36	38	37	33	37
... the doctors would tell you all you feel you need to know?	29	29	29	26	28
... the hospital doctors would take seriously any complaints you may have?	19	23	21	24	27
... the nurses would take seriously any complaints you may have?	16	17	14	20	23
Base	*2945*	*3469*	*3633*	*3146*	*3426*

In contrast to outpatient services, views about inpatient services are less pessimistic. Half or less of the sample expressed criticism on any of the services with only around a quarter faulting the complaints system. However, there has been a gradual increase in those unhappy with how nurses and doctors deal with complaints since the question was first asked in 1993. There has also been a rise in concerns over premature discharge from hospital and worries whether an operation would take place on the day it was booked for. Both hint at more general anxieties that the service may be over-stretched. The proportion of people who thought that an operation would not take place on the day it was booked rose from 39 per cent in 1993 to 50 per cent in 2000 and came after press coverage of a particularly bad winter for the NHS – and the Mavis Skeet story. On this question we do find a difference between those with and without recent inpatient experience. Sixty per cent of recent inpatients thought the operation would take place on the booked day compared with 47 per cent of those without such experience. So, here, experience of the health service leaves people with more optimistic impressions of it than those who speculate about the service or who judge it from what they hear from others.

Labour success so far?

So, in 1997 the public, full of high expectations, appear to put their trust in the incoming Labour government. Satisfaction with the NHS in general rose immediately after the election, before Labour had even spent any extra money and without a similar increase in satisfaction with specific aspects of the health service. Subsequently, some of the shine seems to have worn off, as the expected improvements have failed to materialise and the new money announced in 2000 had as yet failed to make an impact at the time of the survey. The picture on various aspects of the health service is mixed, ranging from the greatly improved view of dentists to rising concern about some hospital services and considerable dissatisfaction with waiting times and waiting lists, to which we turn in more detail next.

The war on waiting

The length of waiting lists as a particular indicator of the state of the health service assumed a new level of political significance in 1997 with Labour's election pledge to reduce their size by treating an extra 100,000 patients. Even though many argued that the pledge was misplaced, Tony Blair in his speech to the NHS 50th Anniversary Conference in 1998 claimed:

> I am proud of the pledge we made on waiting lists. People are fed up with waiting lists. They wait for a GP appointment. They wait in the GP surgery. They wait for a prescription. They wait for outpatients. They wait to have tests. They wait for results. They wait for their operation. They sometimes even wait to be discharged.

Although the numbers waiting for hospital treatment rose rapidly after the 1997 election, they began to decline during 1998. That decline continued during 1999, and by the end of March 2000 the Government was able to announce that the target of a reduction of 100,000 in the numbers waiting had been achieved. Within that, total waits over 18 months were virtually eliminated, although there were still around 50,000 waiting for over 12 months when the NHS Plan was announced in July of that year. In terms of outpatient waits, the numbers waiting over three months rose sharply in the period 1997 to the end of 1999. In March 2000, the numbers recorded as waiting over three months fell, only to show an increase by the end of June.

Given these observed changes, how did attitudes towards waiting change during Labour's tenure? What is striking about the results shown in the next table is that dissatisfaction with *all* aspects of waiting was higher in 2000 (albeit to varying extents) than it was in 1996. This is despite Labour hitting its headline target. In particular, waiting times before getting an appointment with a hospital consultant attracted the most criticism from respondents with 86 per cent of people saying they were in need of "a lot" or "some" improvement. Eight out of ten people were also unhappy with hospital waiting lists. Dissatisfaction with GP appointment systems was somewhat lower, attracting criticism from just over a half of respondents. Time spent waiting for an ambulance after a 999 call attracted the least amount of criticism, but that still left two in five respondents who were unhappy with the service.

Table 4.7 Assessment of waiting times, 1996-2000

	1996	1998	1999	2000
% who say the following are in need of a lot or some improvement				
Waiting time before getting appointments with hospital consultant	79	82	81	86
Hospital waiting lists for non-emergency operations	77	78	78	81
Time spent waiting in outpatient departments	68	70	70	78
Time spent waiting in A&E departments	73	76	77	78
GP appointment systems	43	48	45	51
Time spent waiting for an ambulance after a 999 call	36	32	36	43
Base	*3103*	*2531*	*2450*	*2980*

Younger people were more critical on each measure than older people. For instance, 59 per cent of those aged 18-33 would like to see an improvement in GP appointment systems compared with just 33 per cent of those aged 65 and over. Similarly, 84 per cent of those in the youngest age group wanted an improvement in time spent waiting in outpatient departments compared with 69 per cent of those in the oldest age group. Those without recent inpatient or outpatient experience were more likely to say that each of the areas was in need of improvement.

Is waiting an important source of dissatisfaction?

While Labour (albeit belatedly) had made good on its promise to reduce the size of the waiting list numbers, they appear to have made remarkably little headway in changing perceptions. Clearly the media are likely to have played a part in influencing perceptions of government success or otherwise. We know from previous research (see, for example, Judge and Solomon, 1993) that newspaper headlines along the lines of 'NHS in crisis' do have an effect on public opinion. Although, as Kneeshaw argues:

> It would be wrong to conclude that the media have simply 'driven' public opinion ... Almost certainly, the media have reflected the reality of waiting ... The media have also reacted to government initiatives and the agenda set by particular ministers. (Kneeshaw, 1998:147)

In other words, the relationship between the media, public opinion and the political agenda is not straightforward. Media coverage of waiting in the NHS has risen sharply in recent years and this is likely both to reflect and to influence public opinion. But to what extent does waiting influence overall satisfaction towards the NHS? Judge *et al.* (1997) in *The 14th Report* showed that socio-demographic backgrounds and political allegiances are all associated with people's attitudes. Yet relatively little is known about the extent to which overall perceptions of the NHS reflect dissatisfaction or otherwise with the particular parts of the service. Is it possible to disentangle the various sources of overall dissatisfaction with the NHS? For example, we know that grappling with the GP appointment system is often the first contact with the NHS for most people. It is therefore reasonable to suppose that evaluations of this might be particularly important in influencing the public view about the health service in general. Similarly, attitudes towards hospital waiting times or the quality of care may (or may not) influence attitudes towards the NHS overall. It seems likely that some other features of the NHS matter more to people than waiting since overall dissatisfaction with the NHS has not risen in the same way that dissatisfaction with waiting times has.

Using the *British Social Attitudes* data collected in 2000 we used logistic regression techniques to explore these questions further. Briefly, regression models identify the association between each of a number of characteristics with, for example, the level of dissatisfaction, while controlling for all of the characteristics included in the model. Therefore, the separate impact of each characteristic is independently tested. We have used it here to explore associations between various aspects of the service characteristics and levels of dissatisfaction with the NHS overall.

We controlled for age, gender, income, party identification and recent experience of the NHS in the model and then included variables which captured attitudes towards waiting times and areas of the inpatient and outpatient service that are thought in need of improvement (see the appendix to this chapter for more details of the model). The results confirm some of our earlier findings. Attitudes towards waiting for treatment are strongly associated with negative perceptions of the NHS overall, but it is attitudes towards waiting *times* rather than hospital waiting *lists* that is the significant predictor of dissatisfaction. In other words, a rise in dissatisfaction with waiting times prompted a rise in dissatisfaction with the NHS. In fact, waiting times to see a consultant had the strongest association with dissatisfaction of all the variables we considered. Attitudes towards time spent waiting in outpatient departments are also strongly linked to dissatisfaction.

However, other aspects to do with quality of care also appear to be important in influencing overall dissatisfaction. Most notably, thinking that hospital doctors would not take seriously the views that patients had on treatment, was strongly associated with negative perceptions of the NHS, as was the belief that an operation would not take place on the day it was booked for. In addition, the dissatisfaction with the amount of time GPs give to patients was also an important influence on overall dissatisfaction.

So it seems Labour got it half right with the war on waiting. Waiting is important to the public, but our results confirm the claims of many critics that the early emphasis on *numbers* on waiting lists was misplaced: the *time spent waiting* is more important to the public. Needless to say the recent change of government focus from waiting lists to waiting times is a more accurate reflection of respondents' concerns. Our findings also mirror similar work by Kneeshaw who argued that:

> While attitudes towards waiting have seemingly become increasingly important indicators of the public's overall level of satisfaction with the NHS, it is evaluations of time spent waiting that accounts for most of this effect. (Kneeshaw, 1998: 151)

That said, other aspects of the service, particularly around listening to patient views, are also important. This gives added urgency to commitments set out in the NHS Plan to improve patient and public involvement in health care. On the other hand, some features of the hospital service, such as being able to choose which hospital to receive treatment in, do not seem to be especially important determinants of overall dissatisfaction compared to waiting times. So, although a substantial proportion of people do not feel they have control over choosing which hospital to attend (76 per cent said they probably or definitely would not have such a choice), it may be that people are not particularly upset about this and are content to leave such decisions to health professionals.

The future of the NHS

While dissatisfaction with the NHS overall is lower under Labour than under the Tories, there are signs of unhappiness with specific parts of the hospital service. That being so, prioritising the NHS for extra spending remains high on the public's agenda. Each year the *British Social Attitudes* survey presents respondents with a list of ten areas of government spending and they are asked to name their first and second priority for extra spending. As in previous years, in 2000 more people (81 per cent) cited health as one of their top two priorities than any other area of public expenditure.

Support for a universal NHS

If health remains a top priority for extra spending, one would expect views on the principles that underlie the service to also have strong support. The survey asks:

> *It has been suggested that the NHS should be available only to those on lower incomes. This would mean that contributions could be lower and most people would then take out medical insurance or pay for health care.*

Opposition to this proposal remained high throughout the 1990s with over seven in ten opposing a two-tier health service. It is now slightly lower than its peak of 78 per cent seen in 1994 but nevertheless, nearly three-quarters (74 per cent) of respondents want to retain a universal health service. While supporters of the three main opposition political parties were united in their opposition of a selective NHS, there are some variations. Twenty-five per cent of Conservative supporters are in favour of a selective NHS compared with only 19 per cent of Labour supporters.

There were also variations by age, with 30 per cent of 18-33 year olds supporting a more selective health service compared to just 21 per cent of the over 65s. One interpretation is that this is a generational effect indicating that support for a universal NHS might diminish in the future as the younger cohorts replace older ones. However, it is as likely to be a lifecycle effect at work with younger generations more willing to embrace a more selective NHS simply because they are less likely to use health services. Certainly Park (2000) reported in *The 17th Report* that lifecycle effects are to be found in the priorities that different age groups attach to government spending on health: younger age groups are the least supportive but become more in favour of health spending as they age. It therefore seems likely that as the young of today age, so their attitudes towards universal health care might also change.

Taxation versus social spending

The public remains committed to a universal NHS, that much is clear. Moreover, they are keen that the government increases spending on health. But are they willing to pay for it? This time around the Chancellor has achieved the neat trick of avoiding higher income taxes whilst simultaneously boosting health spending. A future Chancellor may not be so (fiscally) fortunate. Each year the *British Social Attitudes* survey asks respondents to choose between lower taxation and higher spending on health, education and social benefits. As the next table shows support for increased taxes and spending has in fact fallen during Labour's tenure from 63 per cent in 1998 to 50 per cent in 2000. The extent to which this represents a long-term trend is uncertain.

Table 4.8 Tax and spending preferences for health, education and social benefits, 1993-2000

	1993 %	1994 %	1995 %	1996 %	1998 %	1999 %	2000 %
Increased taxes and more spending on health, education and social benefits	63	58	61	59	63	58	50
Keeping taxes and spending on these services the same as now	29	33	31	34	32	35	40
Reducing taxes and less spending on these services	4	4	5	4	3	4	5
Base	*2945*	*3469*	*3633*	*3620*	*3146*	*3143*	*2292*

As we might expect, this question exposed substantial party divisions with Labour and Liberal Democrat supporters being more likely to support increases in taxes to fund spending on social services than Conservative identifiers. Sixty-three per cent of Liberal Democrat and 57 per cent of Labour identifiers support the proposal compared to just 41 per cent of Conservative voters.

One way around the dilemma of raising taxes to increase social spending is to spell out in more detail where the extra money would go in the form of hypothecated or 'ear-marked' taxes. This year we also asked respondents whether the government should increase income tax by one penny in the pound and spend the extra money on the NHS – a so-called 'NHS tax'. Respondents were told that this would mean that every taxpayer would pay about £100 a year extra on average. Fifty-six per cent were in favour of such a proposal, a slightly higher proportion than that found towards the more general question of taxation and social spending. Of course, as Brook *et al.* (1998) have argued, it is not at all certain that people are as likely to advocate large increases in public expenditure when the tax consequences to them themselves are spelled out, rather than to the mythical 'average taxpayer'.

Private health care

We have found that although a substantial proportion of the public are dissatisfied with specific components of the NHS, and waiting lists in particular, they still appear firmly committed to the concept of a universal service. The growth of the private sector is often seen as a kind of barometer of dissatisfaction with the NHS, as those who are unhappy with the NHS can choose to go elsewhere (if they can afford it). However, the private sector currently forms a relatively small part of the British health care system. As the next table shows, the trend for private health insurance reached a plateau of around 15 per cent during the early 1990s before creeping up slightly towards the end of the decade to 19 per cent in 2000.

Table 4.9 Private medical insurance, 1993-2000

	1993	1994	1995	1996	1998	1999	2000
Per cent covered by private medical insurance	15	15	15	17	17	19	19
Per cent covered by private medical insurance paid by employer	8	8	8	8	9	9	11
Base	2945	3469	3633	3620	3146	3143	2292

The overall trend broadly agrees with other sources who argue that the individual private subscriber market has stagnated, in part because many procedures (hip replacements, cataracts, hernias, etc.) can be funded out of savings more cheaply than buying insurance for the rare occasion when such care is needed (Maynard, 2001). Linked to this is the rapid rise in the price of premiums as insurers concentrate on the more lucrative employer market. This is reflected in the steady rise in the proportion of people whose medical insurance is paid for by their employer, now around 56 per cent.

As we might expect, certain population groups are much more likely than others to have private cover. There is no doubt that private health care insurance tends to be the preserve of the relatively well-off. More than four in ten (45 per cent) of those in the highest income quartile have access to private health insurance, compared with just four per cent of those in the bottom quartile. There are also other subgroup differences with a higher proportion of men than women having private medical insurance (22 per cent and 15 per cent respectively). Men with medical insurance are also more likely than women to have had it paid for by their employer (60 per cent and 50 per cent respectively).

Since 1998 the *British Social Attitudes* survey has also asked respondents whether they have had *any* private medical treatment, regardless of the payment method. This includes people paying directly out of their own pockets for care. As the next table shows, the total number of people saying that they had had medical treatment as a private patient in the last 12 months has increased from five per cent in 1998 to eight per cent in 2000. Recent research by Laing and Buisson suggests that this figure is rising fast (2001).

Table 4.10 Whether had medical treatment as a private patient in the last 12 months, 1998-2000

	1998	1999	2000
	%	%	%
Yes, just me	4	4	6
Yes, not me but close family member	7	6	7
Yes, both	1	2	2
No, neither	88	85	83
Base	3146	2450	2980

When examining why individuals might choose to go private one obvious reason might be dissatisfaction with the quality of NHS services. Calnan *et al.* (1996) found that those with private medical insurance are more likely to be dissatisfied with the NHS than those without it. We find that such an inverse association between private heath scheme membership and NHS satisfaction has, in fact, opened up over time. In 1996, a similar proportion of people with and without private medical insurance were happy with the NHS overall (35 and 36 per cent respectively). The latest data, however, show a shift whereby 35 per cent of those with private health insurance are satisfied with the service compared to 42 per cent of those who do not have cover.

Table 4.11 Private medical insurance and overall satisfaction with the NHS, 1996 and 2000

	No insurance		Insurance	
	1996	2000	1996	2000
	%	%	%	%
Satisfied	36	42	35	35
Dissatisfied	50	39	50	43
Base	3022	1870	593	417

When we examine attitudes towards specific aspects of the service in 2000 the difference in attitudes between those with and without insurance is even more striking. For instance, just four in ten (45 per cent) of those with private health insurance were satisfied with NHS inpatient services compared to six in ten (61 per cent) of those without.

Table 4.12 Private medical insurance and satisfaction with NHS hospital services

	No insurance	Insurance
Inpatient services		
% satisfied	61	45
% dissatisfied	20	29
	No insurance	**Insurance**
Outpatient services		
% satisfied	59	45
% dissatisfied	23	35
Base	*1870*	*417*

The implications for future trends in the take-up of private medical insurance are important. It may well be a way by which individuals can selectively isolate themselves from parts of the NHS system and appears more likely to be pursued by those who are dissatisfied with specific aspects. These respondents may then come to see themselves as paying twice for health and thus become more likely to resist increases in taxation to fund increases in health spending. However, as Emmerson *et al.* (2001) argue, it is not clear whether their dissatisfaction is purely a cause, or also partly an effect of those individuals being in possession of insurance. Those who are dissatisfied with the quality of NHS provision may be more likely to purchase private medical care, but it is also plausible that some individuals may change their evaluation of the NHS after, for instance, an episode of private health care paid for by their employer.

Equally, the growth in private medical care more generally is just as likely to be influenced by the state of the economy as by the state of the NHS, particularly given the rise in employer-sponsored contributions. In fact, we found that possession of private medical insurance does not seem to preclude support for the principle of universal health care; 71 per cent of those with private medical insurance are still opposed to the idea of the NHS being kept only for emergencies and the poor, compared with 74 per cent of those without medical insurance. Similarly, as the next table shows, there were no substantial differences in attitudes towards increasing taxes to fund increases in health or social spending. And those with private medical insurance were, if anything, slightly more likely to support an NHS tax of a penny in the pound. So, while the impact of any future increases in insurance coverage on NHS dissatisfaction remain uncertain, there are few signs that people with insurance are any more willing to abandon the NHS in favour of private health provision.

Table 4.13 Support for increased taxation by private medical insurance

	No insurance	Insurance
% who support increased taxes to fund increases in social spending	49	50
Base	*1870*	*417*
% who support NHS tax of 1p in the pound	60	57
Base	*1613*	*373*

Conclusions

While the public registered their broad assessment of Labour's time in office over the last four years by re-electing Labour in the May 2001 general election, the results presented in this chapter can be viewed as a more detailed evaluation by the public of the last government's record concerning the NHS. Overall dissatisfaction with the NHS dropped substantially at the start of Labour's first term perhaps reflecting a honeymoon period for the government. However, the same could not be said of attitudes towards particular parts of the service. Waiting times in particular continued to attract criticism from the vast majority of respondents and this seems to be an important component of dissatisfaction more generally. The fact that the Labour government has done little to change perceptions of specific aspects of the service will prove worrying to ministers, as will the (small) rise in overall dissatisfaction in the most recent survey. As Labour begins its second term, some will wonder whether its ambitious 10-year plan for the NHS should have started at least three years earlier.

So what of the future? The demise of the NHS was predicted many times during the 1990s and a string of alternatives have been suggested. These radical visions have failed to materialise and the public seems as committed as ever to a universal NHS. Labour have accordingly come forward with the perhaps more mundane solution of pumping more money into the health service. What is more, for the first time in the history of the NHS, a government has promised that its share of the nation's resources will continue to rise in the long term. While this may be in tune with public opinion, it is by no means certain that the mere knowledge of money being spent without a visible recovery in the state of the health service will suffice. What matters at the end of the day is what the service delivers – not how much cash it absorbs. And, inevitably, both the bumper cash injection and the NHS Plan will raise public expectations of what Labour (and the NHS) can produce over its second term.

Notes

1. Times 2001 Campaign Polls Wave 5 carried out by MORI, 7 June 2001.
2. This promise was made on 17 May 2000 in response to a parliamentary question.

References

Brook, L., Preston, I. and Hall, J. (1998), 'What drives support for higher public spending' in Taylor-Gooby, P. (ed.), *Choice and Public Policy: The limits to welfare markets*, Basingstoke: Macmillan Press.

Calnan, M., Cant, S. and Gabe, J. (1996), *Going Private: Why People Pay for their Health Care*, Oxford: Oxford University Press.

Department of Health (1996), *The Government's Expenditure Plans 1996-7 to 1998/9, Departmental Report*, Cm 3212, London: The Stationery Office.

Department of Health (1997), *The New NHS*, White Paper Cm 3807, London: The Stationery Office.

Department of Health (2000), *The NHS Plan*, White Paper Cm 4818-I, London: The Stationery Office.

Department of Health (2001), *The Government's Expenditure Plans 2001/2 to 2003/2004, Departmental Report*, Cm 5103, London: The Stationery Office.

Emmerson, C., Frayne, C. and Goodman, A. (2001), 'Should private medical insurance be subsidised?' in Appleby, J. and Harrison, A. (eds.), *Health Care UK Spring 2001*, London: King's Fund.

Judge, K. and Solomon, M. (1993), 'Public opinion and National Health Service: patterns and perspectives in consumer satisfaction', *Journal of Social Policy*, **22**: 299-327.

Judge, K., Mulligan, J. and New, B. (1997), 'The NHS: new prescriptions needed?' in Jowell, R., Curtice, J., Park, A., Brook, L., Thomson, K. and Bryson, C., (eds.), *British Social Attitudes: the 14th Report – The end of Conservative values?*, Aldershot: Dartmouth.

Kneeshaw, J. (1998), 'Does the public mind having to wait?' in Harrison, A. (ed.), *Health Care UK 1997/98*, London: King's Fund.

Laing and Buisson (2001), *Laing's Healthcare Market Review - 13th Edition 2000-2001*, London: Laing and Buisson.

Maynard, A. (2001), 'W(h)ither the private sector?', *British Journal of Health Care Management*, **7**: 214.

Mulligan, J. (2001), *What do Londoners think of Health Care?*, London: King's Fund.

Park, A. (2000), 'The generation game' in Jowell, R., Curtice, J., Park, A., Thomson, K., Jarvis, L., Bromley, C. and Stratford, N. (eds.), *British Social Attitudes: the 17th Report – Focusing on diversity*, London: Sage.

Acknowledgements

The *National Centre for Social Research* is grateful to the Department of Health for their financial support which enabled us to ask the questions in this chapter.

Appendix

Multivariate analysis

The logistic regression model referred to in the chapter follows. Logistic regression is explained in more detail in Appendix I to this Report.

The model reports the *coefficients* (or parameter estimates) for each of the characteristics specified on the left side of the table. Each coefficient shows whether that particular characteristic differs significantly from its 'comparison group' in its association with the 'dependent variable', that is, the variable under investigation. Only those where the coefficient is shown were included in the relevant model. In each case, the comparison group will be all those not included in the model (for example, in looking at age, as we have included the age groups 30-44, 45-65 and 65+ the comparison group is those aged 18-30).

The derivation and meaning of most variables in the models should be clear. The only one requiring further explanation is 'high income' which refers to household income greater than £32,000 per annum.

Logistic regression model on dissatisfaction with the NHS overall

Variable (comparison group in brackets)	Coefficient	
Age (18-30)		
30-44	0.109	
45-64	0.147	
65+	-0.043	
Income (low income)		
High income	0.122	
Gender (male)		
Female	0.024	
Party identification (not Tory)		
Tory	0.072	
Recent experience of the NHS (no experience)		
Outpatient experience	-0.065	
Inpatient experience	-0.383	**
Areas of waiting in need of improvement (satisfactory or very good)		
GP appointment systems need improving	-0.008	
Amount of time GP gives to patient needs improving	0.394	**
Hospital waiting lists for non-emergency operation needs improving	0.309	
Waiting time to get appointment with consultant needs improving	0.596	**
Time spent waiting in outpatients needs improving	0.549	**
Waiting in A&E needs improving	0.026	
Time spent waiting for an ambulance needs improving	0.126	

Quality of inpatient care (would happen)

Would **not** get to choose hospital for operation	0.194	
Hospital doctors would **not** tell you all you need to know	0.275	
Hospital doctors would **not** take seriously any views you have on treatment	0.467	**
The operation would **not** take place on the booked day	0.389	**
Would **not** be allowed home only when you are well enough to leave	0.353	**
The nurses would **not** take seriously any complaints you may have	0.214	
The doctors would **not** take seriously any complaints you may have	0.270	*
There would **not** be a particular nurse responsible for dealing with any problems	0.134	

Quality of outpatient care (would happen)

Would **not** get a hospital appointment within 3 months	0.362	**
Outpatient doctor would **not** see you within half-hour of arrival	0.202	
Would **not** be able to complain about treatment without fuss or bother	-0.067	
Constant	-3.207	
Base	*2289*	

* = significant at the 5% level

** = significant at the 1% level

5 Genetic research: friend or foe?

Nina Stratford, Theresa Marteau and Martin Bobrow *

It has been a momentous time for genetic research since we last reported on public attitudes in this field in *The 16th Report* (Stratford *et al.*, 1999). The most notable achievement has been the completion of a draft of the human genome sequence, which received a great deal of publicity when it was announced in June 2000. This landmark event was compared to the invention of the wheel and putting a man on the moon, and one scientist spoke of an end to cancer in his lifetime. Francis Collins, one of the leaders of the project, predicted that within 30 years:

> ... [t]he average lifespan in the developed world will be 90, diseases will be diagnosed before symptoms appear, many humans will already be genetically modified and patients with heart disease will be treated with prescriptions tailored to their own genetic makeup.[1]

The social and legal implications of such genetic research are highly controversial and have rarely been out of the media since our last chapter. Much of the controversy stems from the implications for human reproduction. For example, if a genetic test detects a disease in an unborn child, parents may choose to have an abortion. The newer technique of pre-implantation genetic diagnosis (PGD) allows embryos to be screened for genetic disease before being implanted in the womb using IVF treatment. Some argue that these techniques may come to influence human evolution itself by allowing the deliberate selection of human characteristics, such as intelligence and appearance. The use of such technology is currently banned in Britain, other than for preventing serious disease, but the potential is clear to see.

---

* Nina Stratford is a Senior Researcher at the *National Centre for Social Research*. Theresa Marteau is Professor of Health Psychology at King's College, London. Martin Bobrow is Professor of Medical Genetics at the University of Cambridge.

Another genetic technology with implications for human reproduction is gene therapy. This area of research is still in its infancy, but its aim is to treat genetic diseases such as cystic fibrosis by replacing the faulty gene with a working copy. At present it is illegal in Britain to make such changes to reproductive cells where the change would be passed on to future generations (germline gene therapy). Only changes to body cells (somatic gene therapy) are permitted. However, if germline therapy were to prove feasible (and it has already been successfully demonstrated in mice), it could be used to 'enhance' the human genome above and beyond the medical applications, to create so-called 'designer babies'.

Another area of controversy is the question of privacy and access to genetic data. In Britain, people can be pressured to disclose the results of certain genetic tests to insurers. In the United States, the first court cases against companies trying to use genetic information to discriminate against employees have already begun.[2] Many fear that this will lead to the creation of a 'genetic underclass', unable to get insurance or find work.

In this chapter, we look at public opinion on four areas of genetic science with important social or legal implications. We have already discussed in *The 16th Report* why it is important to track public opinion on new genetic technologies and the arguments have not changed. There is still considerable concern about the 'crisis of confidence' in governmental scientific advice and the public lack of trust in science policy and regulation. For example, the House of Lords Science and Technology Committee argues that there is a new mood for dialogue with the public on these issues, both among the government and scientists. Scientists need to understand the impact of their work on society and public opinion, as "science like any other player in the public arena ignores public attitudes and values at its peril" (House of Lords Science and Technology Committee, 2000). The *British Social Attitudes* survey hopes to contribute to this understanding.

We start by looking at how the public perceives genetic causality. Some think that scientific advances will lead us towards a more deterministic view of human characteristics and behaviour (Glover, 1995). If true, this has important implications for how far people can be held responsible for their own actions and how we apportion blame as a society.

Second, we consider issues of access to and privacy of genetic data, and ask why most people are so opposed to the disclosure of such data to insurers or employers. Third, we look at views on prenatal genetic testing and abortion, in comparison with the newer technique of PGD, to see whether views on the former have changed since 1998 and how they compare to views on the latter. Finally, we explore attitudes to human genetic manipulation, both for preventing disease and for the purposes of 'enhancement'.

Nature or nurture?

Hardly a day goes by without an announcement of the discovery of the 'gene for' some trait or illness. The way such findings are reported is often criticised for contributing to an overly simplistic and deterministic view of genetic causality, sometimes referred to as the 'geneticisation' of everyday life. Scientist Steven Rose argues that this view is not based on scientific fact, but rather that it has gained credence because it "suits a society in which we have lost the belief that it is possible to create a more socially just world" (Rose, 2001).

A deterministic view of human characteristics and behaviour raises issues reminiscent of those discussed over the centuries by philosophers who were trying to reconcile the doctrine of free will with that of an omniscient God. In the modern version of the debate, God is replaced by genes as the controlling agent and the question is: how can people be held responsible for their own actions if these are determined in advance by their genetic make-up? The implications of the deterministic view for the criminal justice system could be immense: can you punish someone who was genetically programmed to behave the way they did? On the other hand, some groups, such as some gay rights groups, have seized on genetic explanations of behaviour as a way of combating discrimination. They assume that the public will be more tolerant of homosexuality if it is found to be genetically determined. We shall examine whether they are right to think so.

This debate throws up three key questions. First, are people, in fact, becoming increasingly likely to see human traits as genetically determined, or rather, do they recognise the complex interplay between genetic and environmental factors? Second, do people's causal attributions affect their notions of responsibility and blame? And third, what factors lie behind people's attributions of genetic or environmental causality?

There is, in fact, no evidence that the press coverage of the human genome project has lead the public to become more deterministic over the last two years. As the next table shows, there has been no real change in the proportion who think that height, intelligence, heart disease or aggression are caused by genes, as opposed to lifestyle or upbringing, or a combination of the two. However, a two-year gap is perhaps too short a gap to expect much in the way of change. Genetic science is moving very quickly in this area and public opinion may take some time to catch up.

Even scientists do not agree on the 'correct' answers for many of the traits in the table. With the exception of eye colour (which is unambiguously genetic), it is thought that there is a genetic component to many of these traits, but quantifying it is difficult. The exact balance of genetic and environmental causes will also vary depending on the amount of variation in the environment.[3]

Yet over nine out of ten of our members of the public are prepared to hazard an answer to these questions, though, not surprisingly, views are very split on the origin of many of the traits. Eye colour is the only one where most people, like the scientists, are certain that is completely genetic. And at the other end of the spectrum, few people see genes as playing a substantial role in obesity or aggression and violence. These findings are similar to those of another recent study, which also found that antisocial behaviour is seen as largely dependent on environmental factors (Human Genetics Commission, 2001a).

It seems that we do not have to start worrying just yet about the implications of genetic determinism for the criminal justice system, as very few people think that genes eclipse free will in criminal behaviour.

Table 5.1 Extent to which various traits are perceived as genetically determined, 1998 and 2000

	1998	2000
% saying all or mostly to do with genes ...		
... the colour of a person's eyes	87	-
... height	76	77
... chances of getting cancer	48	-
... intelligence	36	34
... being gay or lesbian	34	-
... chances of getting heart disease	29	29
... chances of being very overweight	15	-
... chances of being aggressive or violent	9	11
Base	*2112*	*2267*

We turn now to our second question: whether genetic determinism, where it does exist, affects notions of responsibility and blame and, specifically, whether genetic determinists are more sympathetic to behaviour that they perceive to be genetically caused. This is, in fact, the case: those who think that homosexuality is all or mostly do to with genes are less likely to think that "sexual relations between two adults of the same sex" is wrong than those who think it is, at least in part, a product of upbringing and lifestyle. A third (33 per cent) of those who think that homosexuality is entirely genetically determined say that it is "not wrong at all", compared to only one in eight (12 per cent) of those who think that it is entirely down to upbringing or lifestyle.[4] Other studies have shown similar results (Tygart, 2000). So it seems that the intuitive reasoning of a section of the gay rights movement may be right in thinking that demonstrating a genetic link to homosexuality may lead to more tolerance.

Are there any important differences between those who espouse genetic determinism and those who do not? Interestingly, younger people are *less* likely to see genes as important than older groups. This is particularly so for views on what determines aggression or violence and intelligence, which again replicates the findings of the Human Genetics Commission (2001a) study. For example, a fifth (20 per cent) of over 65s believe that aggression and violence is all or mostly genetic, compared with less than one in twenty (four per cent) of 18-24 year olds. Nearly two-thirds (63 per cent) of the young believe that aggression and violence is all or mostly down to upbringing or lifestyle, but only one-third (35 per cent) of over 65s agree with this.

Of course, these age differences might simply be due to differences in education: older people are far less likely to have any formal qualifications, or to have studied biology or genetics in school. To address this possibility we used the statistical technique of logistic regression modelling to take a number of factors into account at the same time and calculate their independent impact. In fact, age turns out to be the most important factor linked to views on genetic determinism, once we have taken other factors such as education and social class into account (see models A-D in the appendix to this chapter for more details).

Such age differences may arise either through a generation difference or a life-cycle effect. The former would be caused by the different historical and social conditions that each generation has grown up in. A lifecycle effect, on the other hand, implies that people become more convinced that genetic causes are paramount as they grow older, have children and observe the development of those around them. These alternative explanations cannot be tested with the data currently available to us, and we would need to repeat the module in a few years' time to get to the bottom of this. But genetic science is surely a more prominent feature of life today than it was two or three decades ago and we think that the generation difference is the more likely explanation.

To conclude this section, we have found some evidence that genetic explanations of behaviour are linked to greater sympathy for the perpetrators of the behaviour, which implies that increased genetic determinism in society could indeed lead us to question our notions of responsibility and blame. However, we have also shown that at least over the last couple of years, the public has *not* become more genetically deterministic about the causes of human characteristics, disease and behaviour. Indeed, they overwhelmingly reject such determinism for antisocial behaviour such as violence. And since younger people are the most resistant to genetic explanations, there is no reason to believe that there will be a large shift towards genetic determinism in the near future – unless there are major new scientific discoveries to the contrary.

Privacy and access to genetic data

As genetic testing becomes more widespread, so the issue of who should have access to the results becomes more salient. In this section, we consider how such issues have been dealt with by the regulatory bodies in Britain and whether their approach is in step with public opinion.

In April 1999, the Genetics and Insurance Committee (GAIC) was established to evaluate the scientific and actuarial evidence on the use of genetic test results for insurance purposes. This government advisory body assesses which tests are accurate enough for insurance companies to use, although it has no legal authority. In October 2000, the committee approved the use of genetic test results by insurers for the first time, to assess whether a person will inherit the degenerative Huntingdon's disease. GAIC is also considering the use of tests for early onset of Alzheimer's disease and rare inherited cancers. Britain now stands out as particularly permissive in allowing insurance companies to request the disclosure of a test result. Murthy *et al.* argue that "the GAIC's decision sets the UK apart and opens the way for the expanded use of genetic information by insurers without proper consideration of the ethical and social implications" (Murthy *et al.*, 2001: 60).

At the time the *British Social Attitudes* survey was carried out, the Association of British Insurers (ABI), the industry's self-regulatory body, was looking to licence seven tests, and were insisting on their right to use them before they had been approved by the GAIC. However, as a result of very hostile public and parliamentary comment, the ABI has very recently adopted a more circumspect approach. It has only applied to the GAIC for two more tests to be approved, and has imposed a two-year moratorium on the use of genetic tests by its members. Its voluntary code does not allow insurers to oblige applicants to take a test, and applicants who have already had a test can only be required to disclose the result if the policy is valued over £300,000. Above that level, only tests approved by the GAIC will be taken into account. However, this moratorium is not backed by legislation, as recommended by the Human Genetics Commission (HGC), another government advisory body. The HGC is critical of the regulation of the insurance industry with regard to genetic tests. It argues that "[t]he existing system of self-regulation has failed ... insurance companies are not equally observing the Association of British Insurers' Code of Practice. There currently appears to be no satisfactory means of monitoring and enforcing the code" (Human Genetics Commission, 2001b). Thus the HGC recommended a three-year moratorium to allow time to consider the issues involved.

Critics of the present approach, such as Murthy *et al.* (2001), argue that the current state of play creates a serious disincentive for people to seek tests. Fears of becoming uninsurable may lead some people to forgo a test that would be medically beneficial. Critics also argue that the insurance companies are wrong to try to use test results since genetic testing is as yet too imprecise to be much use in predicting lifespan or chances of developing a disease.

So how have these developments shaped public opinion since we last visited this topic in 1998? Then, we showed that most people were opposed to this use of genetic data, and by 2000, hostility had, in fact, increased further. Some eight out of ten people (79 per cent) believe that insurance companies should "probably" or "definitely" not be allowed to use genetic tests. As shown in the next table, the proportion who feel strongly about it has increased from 48 per cent in 1998 to 56 per cent in 2000, and are thus now in the majority. Four out of five people (79 per cent) are also opposed to employers seeing the results of such tests and even more (88 per cent) object to the idea that employers could compel job applicants to take a genetic test. Moreover, the proportion "definitely" opposing these ideas has also increased between 1998 and 2000.

Table 5.2 Attitudes to the use of genetic data by insurance companies and employers, 1998 and 2000

% saying that it should <u>definitely not</u> be allowed for ...	1998	2000
... insurance companies to use genetic tests to accept or refuse people for life insurance	48	56
... employers to have the right to see the genetic test results of a job applicant	50	57
... employers to make job applicants have a genetic test	66	71
... employers to make job applicants have a test to see if they are sensitive to workplace chemicals	-	9
Base	*2112*	*2267*

Why is the public so opposed to genetic tests being used by insurers and employers? It would be wrong to think that this widespread opposition stems from a general distrust of science. On the contrary, those who trust most in science to do good are the *most* likely to oppose genetic tests: 79 per cent of those who disagree strongly that "overall, modern science does more harm than good" are opposed to employers making applicants take a genetic test, compared to 64 per cent of those who *agree* strongly with this statement.

One hint as to the real reasons behind the opposition is that it is much reduced if the purpose of the test is to *protect* employees. We asked for the first time in 2000 whether employers should "have the right to *make* applicants have a test to see if they are particularly sensitive to chemicals used in the workplace". Only one in six (16 per cent) reject this use of genetic tests, and four-fifths (80 per cent) agree that this should be allowed. The purpose of the test is obviously essential in determining attitudes. If the only beneficiary of the genetic data is the insurer or employer, then public opposition seems inevitable. To reduce opposition, the public would need to be persuaded that they too would benefit from the results of the test.

Related to this, there is strong evidence that a degree of self-interest is at play here: those who would be most affected by these uses of genetic tests are generally the most concerned. For example, those currently in work are more likely to say that employers should definitely *not* have the right to see an applicant's test result (62 per cent) than those who are retired (51 per cent) or looking after the home (49 per cent). As the next table shows, it is those of working age (25-64) who are most opposed to insurance companies and employers having access to such data. This is not surprising as they have most to lose – they are of an age where getting life insurance and mortgages is more important and they are also more likely to be in the labour market.

Table 5.3 Attitudes to the use of genetic data by insurance companies and employers, by age

% saying that it should <u>definitely not</u> be allowed for ...	18-24	25-44	45-64	65+
... insurance companies to use genetic tests to accept or refuse people for life insurance	47	60	60	47
... employers to have the right to see the genetic test results of a job applicant	51	60	61	49
... employers to make job applicants have a genetic test	70	75	75	58
... employers to make job applicants have a test to see if they are sensitive to workplace chemicals	6	10	9	6
Base	181	895	672	516

This self-interest can be seen again among those who say they have a family history of a serious genetic condition (eight per cent of the sample). Two-thirds (66 per cent) of this group are strongly opposed to insurance companies using genetic tests, compared to 56 per cent of those without such a history. However, they are slightly *more* in favour of genetic tests being used by employers to protect vulnerable applicants from exposure to chemicals (87 per cent support, compared to 81 per cent of those with no such family history). This is perhaps also self-interest, such tests perhaps being seen as protecting the genetically vulnerable, such as themselves.

Another reason that the public may be so opposed to insurance companies and employers having access to genetic tests is a belief in equality or collectivism. At the extreme, this belief would require insurance companies to insure everyone who requested it, regardless of any predictive data about relative risks. In this way, individual risks would be shared collectively (in much the same way as the welfare state provides universal health care and a benefits safety net). This view may be gaining ground as successive governments encourage individuals to take out all manner of private sector insurances and pensions rather than rely on state provision. An analysis using the *British Social Attitudes* welfarism scale (see Appendix I to this book) suggests that such sentiments may well play a role. Those who are classified as 'sympathetic' to the welfare state are more likely to be strongly opposed to the use of genetic tests for insurance purposes than those who take the 'middle ground' or who feel that the poor are undeserving of welfare. The next table shows that this difference also applies to the use of such tests by employers.

Table 5.4 Attitudes to the use of genetic data by insurance companies and employers, by welfarism scale

% saying that it should <u>definitely not</u> be allowed for ...	Sympa-thetic	Middle ground	Poor don't deserve
... insurance companies to use genetic tests to accept or refuse people for life insurance	68	57	54
... employers to have the right to see the genetic test results of a job applicant	72	57	52
... employers to make job applicants have a genetic test	82	72	69
... employers to make job applicants have a test to see if they are sensitive to workplace chemicals	13	9	6
Base	*292*	*1060*	*584*

Logistic regression modelling confirms much of the above. The next table shows – in order of importance – the factors which are independently associated with answers to each of the four questions about legitimate uses of genetic tests (see models E-H in the appendix to this chapter for further details). Views on the welfare state, economic activity status and gender are the most important factors linked to attitudes for nearly all of the questions. Women are more opposed to insurers and employers using genetic tests than men; those who are sympathetic towards the welfare state are more opposed than those who are not sympathetic; and those in work are more opposed than all other activity groups. Ethnicity is also a factor in three out of the four scenarios, with whites more likely to oppose these uses of genetic tests than either Asians or blacks.

Finally, views on the causes of illness such as heart disease are linked to attitudes. Generally, those who believe that heart disease is due to a mixture of genetic and lifestyle factors are more likely to oppose insurers and employers using genetic tests than those who believe in genetic determinism. This gives us a clue to another reason underlying such opposition. A belief that illness is influenced by *both* genetic and environmental factors implies that a genetic test alone will be an imperfect predictor of illness. Distrust in the reliability of genetic tests may be another reason for the public's opposition to using them to evaluate insurance or job applications.

Table 5.5 Factors linked to views on the use of genetic data by insurance companies and employers

Insurance companies using genetic tests	Employers having the right to see test results of job applicants	Employers making applicants have a genetic test	Employers making applicants have a test for sensitivity to workplace chemicals
Sex	Welfarism	Economic activity	Welfarism
Welfarism	Economic activity	Sex	Family genetic condition
Social class	Sex	Ethnic background	Religion
Ethnic background	Ethnic background	Welfarism	
Causes of heart disease	Social class	Education	
Economic activity	Causes of heart disease	Causes of heart disease	

But if the public are opposed to the use of genetic information by insurers and employers, they are also resigned to it happening in the near future. Three out of four believe that insurance companies will be using such data within the next 25 years, and over half that employers will do so. Over two-fifths even believe that banks will use such information to decide who to give credit to. Since 1996, people have become even more likely to think that this will happen, as the next table shows.

Table 5.6 Perceived likelihood that insurance companies, banks and employers will use genetic data within the next 25 years, 1996 and 2000

% saying that it is "very" or "quite" likely that genetic information will be used to judge a person's suitability for getting ...	1996	2000
... health or life insurance	72	76
... a job they've applied for	43	58
... credit at the bank	33	42
Base	*2096*	*1963*

So, faced with a perception that the privacy of genetic data is increasingly under threat, the public is becoming even more opposed to this privacy being breached. Any relaxation in the guidelines about the use of genetic tests may lead to greater public hostility, unless the purpose is clearly seen to be to protect individuals rather than to benefit companies.

Prenatal and pre-implantation genetic diagnosis

One application of genetic science that has been in use for some time is genetic testing during pregnancy to identify certain genetic conditions in the unborn child. This method can do nothing to alleviate the genetic condition: if a test is positive, the parents are merely left to choose whether or not to have a termination. Nevertheless, most people support this use of genetic testing – 43 per cent think it should be offered to all pregnant women, 49 per cent think it should be offered if there is a special reason to suspect a problem, and opinions on this have not changed significantly since 1998. Neither have views shifted greatly on which genetic conditions make it acceptable to have an abortion. As in 1998, very few people would condemn an abortion if a serious mental or physical disability is discovered, but a third feel that it is "never right" if the child would live in good health, then die in early adulthood. And nearly half feel the same way about aborting a healthy foetus that would never grow taller than an eight year old.

There is now an alternative to genetic testing and abortion for couples who are at risk of passing on a genetic disease. It is possible to create embryos *in vitro*, genetically test them for the condition the parents want to avoid, and then implant only unaffected embryos into the womb. This is known as pre-implantation genetic diagnosis (PGD), and the first successful PGD procedure took place in the UK in 1990. At the moment it is only used for a small number of fatal diseases caused by single genes, such as Duchenne muscular dystrophy, and its use is still comparatively rare. It hit the headlines in October 2000 when a family not only used PGD to have a second child free of the genetic disease which afflicted their first, but also selected the embryo to be a suitable bone marrow donor to save the life of the first child.

Some people argue that PGD is ethically more acceptable than abortion as the selection takes place at a much earlier stage in the embryo's life. However, as it uses *in vitro* fertilisation, it has the disadvantages that success of conception is not guaranteed and multiple births are more likely. (Its success rate is probably lower than the average of 17 per cent for conventional IVF treatment.) Furthermore, some people view it as just as ethically problematic as abortion since it involves creating and discarding unused embryos. Another objection is that PGD is interfering with human evolution and that it could be used to select characteristics such as intelligence or athletic ability (although at present this is not technologically feasible). King argues that "because abortion is not involved and multiple embryos are available, [pre-implantation diagnosis] is radically more effective as a tool of genetic selection". He sees it as potentially leading to a "full-blown, free-market eugenics" (King, 1999: 176). The Human Fertilisation and Embryology Authority (HFEA), which regulates PGD, has banned its use for selecting the sex or any other social, physical or psychological characteristics of the baby.

As most people will not have heard of PGD it is difficult to ask survey questions about it. We felt we had to provide an explanation of what is involved, which is not easy to do in a couple of sentences. In the end, the question read as follows:

> *There is another way in which couples can try to avoid having a child with a serious medical condition. The woman's eggs are fertilised outside her body with her partner's sperm and genetically tested. Only eggs without the condition are put back, and may then grow into a baby.*
>
> *Suppose it was likely that a couple would have a child with a serious **mental disability**. Do you think it would be right or not right for them to have this sort of treatment?*

To compare attitudes towards abortion and PGD as ways of avoiding genetic disease, we asked about the same conditions for both. The results are shown in the next table and paint a rather curious picture. PGD is seen as *less* acceptable than abortion for serious mental and physical disability, but as *more* acceptable for avoiding having a child that would die early or be short in stature. We suspect that this result may be an artefact of the unfamiliarity of the subject matter and the difficulty of asking about this complex technique. Perhaps when the technique is first explained, people are wary of it as it is something they have not heard of before. Abortion, though not pleasant, is at least familiar. PGD is a difficult concept to absorb, especially when the interviewer is waiting for your answer. However, as the questions progress, perhaps people have had more time to assimilate what PGD actually is and then start to favour it over abortion. This explanation is supported by the fact that it is the first two questions about PGD for which people favour abortion, and the last two questions where they favour PGD (the questions were asked in the order in which they are presented in the next table).

Table 5.7 Acceptability of prenatal testing and abortion, compared to pre-implantation genetic diagnosis (PGD)

% saying "always right" for ...	Prenatal testing & abortion	PGD
... a serious mental disability	49	37
... a serious physical disability	41	35
... a child that would live in good health but then die in its 20s or 30s	16	26
... a child that would never grow taller than an 8 year old	14	24
Base	*2267*	*2267*

In *The 16ᵗʰ Report*, we showed that there was a strong relationship between religion and views on genetic testing and abortion, and this still holds in 2000. Catholics who actively practice their religion by regularly attending church are much more opposed than other groups to offering genetic tests to pregnant women, and to abortion in the event that the test is positive. But do Catholics view PGD as a more ethical alternative to abortion, one which does not involve the destruction of a human life at such an advanced stage? Or do they consider it to be as bad or even worse than abortion as several embryos might have to be discarded to create one unaffected baby?

We can look at this by putting together the answers to the questions on prenatal testing with those on PGD to establish, for each condition, whether the respondent would prefer prenatal testing or PGD, or whether they see both as equally good or bad. In fact, for three of the four conditions, a majority of Catholics do not distinguish between the two – they view both techniques as equally unacceptable. For example, in the case of serious mental disability, over half (56 per cent) feel the same way about both, a quarter (23 per cent) are more positive towards abortion than PGD and one-fifth (21 per cent) feel that PGD is more acceptable than abortion. It is only when it comes to treatment for short stature that Catholics show a clear preference for one technique over the other: a quarter (24 per cent) prefer PGD compared with only one in fifteen (seven per cent) who preferred abortion – but the majority (69 per cent) held the same view about both.

This finding is supported by logistic regression analysis which establishes which factors are independently associated with views on abortion and PGD. The next table shows the results of this analysis, with the factors significantly linked to views listed in order of importance (see models I-P in the appendix to this chapter for further details).

Table 5.8 (a) Factors linked to views on abortion and PGD for serious mental and physical disability

Abortion: serious mental disability	PGD: serious mental disability	Abortion: serious physical disability	PGD: serious physical disability
Religion	Education	Religion	Religion
Sex	Religion	Sex	Attitudes to science
Social class	Age	Age	Education
Ethnic background		Social class	Age
Family genetic condition		Long-standing illness	
Age			

Table 5.8 (b) Factors linked to views on abortion and PGD for premature death and short stature

Abortion: baby healthy but would die in early adulthood	PGD: baby healthy but would die in early adulthood	Abortion: short stature	PGD: short stature
Religion	Religion	Religion	Religion
Sex	Attitudes to science	Age	Attitudes to science
Studied biology/ genetics		Sex	Ethnic background
		Long-standing illness	

Religion is the most important factor for nearly all of the models; Catholics who attend church regularly are more opposed to abortion *and* PGD for all four conditions and this difference is often very large. For example, the odds of a regular Catholic believing that abortion for serious mental disability is "never right" are 22 times greater than for someone who does not regularly follow any religion. Nor do Catholics feel differently about PGD and abortion – they are more opposed to both than other religious and non-religious groups.

Table 5.9 Acceptability of prenatal testing and abortion *versus* PGD, by age

	18-24	25-44	45-64	65+
Serious mental disability	%	%	%	%
Abortion more acceptable than PGD	25	30	32	45
PGD more acceptable than abortion	18	15	15	10
Serious physical disability	%	%	%	%
Abortion more acceptable than PGD	21	26	27	40
PGD more acceptable than abortion	22	17	19	11
Death in early adulthood	%	%	%	%
Abortion more acceptable than PGD	9	14	15	23
PGD more acceptable than abortion	29	30	32	27
Short stature	%	%	%	%
Abortion more acceptable than PGD	8	10	14	20
PGD more acceptable than abortion	37	33	33	24
Base	181	895	672	516

An unexpected finding is that, although age is linked to views on both abortion and PGD, the relationship goes in opposite directions for the two technologies. Where age makes a difference, younger people (usually the 18-24 group) are *more* opposed to abortion than older groups. However, they are *less* opposed to PGD than older people. For example, in the case of serious physical disability, the odds of 18-24 year olds thinking that abortion is "never right" are 4.3 times greater than for over 65s. However, the odds of someone in the youngest group thinking that PGD is "never right" are less than half those of someone in the oldest age group. The previous table shows this in greater detail.

So why should age be linked to views in this way? The finding that the youngest groups are more opposed to abortion replicates what we reported in *The 16th Report*. This is rather puzzling as on most other moral issues, younger people are generally much more liberal than their elders (see, for example, Park, 2000). We suspect that their greater opposition to abortion stems mainly from their relatively limited experience of reproduction and that this will reduce as they grow older. That is, we suspect that this is a lifecycle effect rather than a real generation difference.

The greater enthusiasm of younger people for PGD echoes the finding in *The 16th Report* that teenagers were more likely to favour the use of genetic manipulation for various purposes. This may well stem from a greater enthusiasm for new technology in general and more tolerance of risk. We find a similar pattern in attitudes towards the other new and potentially risky genetic technology we asked about, namely genetically modified (GM) crops. Those who are 18-24 years old are less likely than older groups to see GM crops as extremely or very dangerous to the environment. They are much less likely to think that GM foods should be banned – only a quarter (27 per cent) think so, compared to around half (49-58 per cent) of older groups. They are also much less inclined to agree strongly that we should never interfere with the genes of plants and animals (only 10 per cent compared to 29-35 per cent of older groups).

Gene therapy

In the previous section we considered genetic techniques which enable a reproductive choice from what is already there – that is, genetic screening of an already existing embryo or foetus to determine its genetic make-up and allow a selection to take place. However, it may be possible in the future to determine part of the genetic make-up of an individual directly, through 'gene therapy'. At present, gene therapy trials are focused on trying to cure serious illness. Around a decade ago, the first partly successful treatment took place when a four year old girl born without an immune system received the genes she was lacking. However, despite this early success, progress has been very slow and gene therapy has actually led to the death of one trial participant in the United States in 1999.

Apart from concerns about safety, most of the objections to gene therapy relate to the possibility that it could be used by parents for 'enhancement' of their children – to make them more intelligent, attractive, musical and so on – although the technology for this will not be available in the foreseeable future. Some commentators do not see the possibility of genetic enhancement as a problem. Arthur Caplan, director of the Centre for Bioethics at the University of Pennsylvania, argues that "it is hard to see what is wrong with parents choosing to use genetic knowledge to improve the health and well-being of their offspring".[5] His point is that parents already strive to improve their children's chances in life by environmental means (such as private education, orthodontists, etc.). Adding genetic engineering to their list of options is just a logical extension of this. Such commentators see '21st century eugenics' as a positive opportunity, free of coercion and controlled by parents rather than the state.

However, some envisage a two-tier society emerging from this, with the genetically enhanced elite "GenRich" dominating the non-enhanced "Naturals" (Silver, 1998). There is a tension here between individual freedom and the potential impact on society. Imagine what could happen if parents were allowed to choose the sex of their children. If enough parents preferred, say, boys, this would affect everyone in society, not just those individuals who had exercised this choice.

To tap public attitudes on this, we asked respondents whether it *should* be allowed to change a person's genes, both for medical and enhancement reasons. There has been very little change in attitudes since 1998, as the next table shows. Whereas most people are willing to allow gene therapy for serious illness such as heart disease or breast cancer, they are much more circumspect about enhancing appearance or determining sex or sexuality. People have become slightly less keen on changing someone's genes to make them of average weight, rather than very overweight – down from just under half to a third. The only other change is a small increase in willingness to contemplate genetic manipulation to decide the sex of an unborn baby, although this is still only acceptable to one in six of the population. Moreover, it is a small change and it is not really possible to tell from just these two readings whether it is the start of a trend.

In 2000, we also asked about genetic manipulation for two new items – schizophrenia and baldness. The results for schizophrenia suggest that people are at least as prepared to allow gene alteration for this as for heart disease. Indeed, it is among the three most acceptable uses asked about, second only to breast cancer, which suggests that people view mental illness as of the same order of seriousness. We expected personal or family experience of mental illness to influence answers here, but this was not the case. Baldness is seen as a much less acceptable use of genetic modification, on a par with height and intelligence.

Table 5.10 Attitudes towards genetic manipulation,1998 and 2000

% saying that changing a person's genes should "definitely" or "probably" be allowed to …	1998	2000
… reduce a person's chances of getting breast cancer	72	72
… reduce a person's chances of getting heart disease	68	66
… stop someone having schizophrenia	-	66
… make them less aggressive or violent	59	56
… make them of average weight, rather than very overweight	45	38
… make a person taller or shorter	24	23
… give someone a full head of hair, rather than being bald	-	23
… make a person more intelligent	20	20
… make a person straight, rather than gay or lesbian	18	18
… determine the sex of an unborn baby	12	16
Base	*2112*	*2267*

In our chapter in *The 16ᵗʰ Report*, we developed a 'genetic attitude scale'. This provides a summary measure of attitudes towards genetic manipulation based on a combination of some of the various possible uses we asked about. When we recalculate this scale in 2000, it confirms that very little overall change has occurred. With figures very similar to 1998, about one-fifth of the population (19 per cent) end up being classified as 'enthusiastic', one-half as 'cautious' (48 per cent) and the remaining third as 'restrictive' (33 per cent) about genetic manipulation.

Thus the huge media coverage and the speed of progress being made in genetic science does not seem to have had an impact on attitudes towards gene therapy as yet. This is probably because the promised fruits of genetic research still seem too far off for the recent progress to have made much of an impact on attitudes. Progress in gene therapy, in particular, has been more limited than first expected. Most commentators still talk of most major developments in genetic science being some 20 or 30 years away. This is an area where attitudes need monitoring over the longer term.

In *The 16ᵗʰ Report*, we included a logistic regression model to see what factors were linked to a person's score on the genetic attitude scale. Social class, education and attitudes to science and abortion turned out to be linked to whether someone was 'enthusiastic' towards genetic manipulation. We now repeat this analysis using 2000 data.

As the next table shows, the relationship with attitudes to abortion persists – those who oppose abortion are also less likely to be in favour of gene manipulation. The relationship with education also is replicated – the more highly educated someone is, the *less* likely they are to be 'enthusiastic' about gene manipulation.

There are some differences between 1998 and 2000, however. In 2000, age turns out to be the factor most closely linked to attitudes on gene therapy, whereas it did not feature in 1998. The oldest group (65+) are more 'enthusiastic' than average and those aged 35-44 less so. This is surprising: the oldest group is precisely the one which is most likely to hold a negative attitude towards science in general. So why should they be more willing to allow genetic manipulation? We do not have any definite answers to this. Perhaps they are more lenient as they feel that they are unlikely to live to see the benefits or to bear any of the risks.

Gender also features in 2000, with men more likely to be 'enthusiastic' than women. Several other studies have also shown that women are less enthusiastic about genetic technology than men (MORI, 2000; Eurobarometer, 2000; National Science Board, 2000; Human Genetics Commission, 2001a). Finally, unlike 1998, social class and attitudes to science are not independently related to attitudes on gene therapy in 2000.

Table 5.11 Factors linked to enthusiasm for gene therapy, 1998 and 2000

1998	2000
Social class	Age
Attitudes to abortion	Gender
Attitudes to science in general	Education
Education	Attitudes to abortion

Additional questions asked in 2000 mean that we can now extend the analysis, most importantly to take on board a measure of genetic knowledge – whether the respondent had studied biology or genetics, either at school or later.[6] Many studies have found a link between scientific literacy and attitudes to science and technology, usually that the more highly educated and knowledgeable have more positive attitudes (MORI, 2000; Eurobarometer, 2000; National Science Board, 2000; Human Genetics Commission, 2001a). But others have failed to find this relationship: Priest (2000) found that better-educated and more knowledgeable groups were *not* markedly more positive about encouraging biotechnology. And others still have found that the relationship is ambiguous and that those with more knowledge are both more enthusiastic and more sceptical (Jallinoja and Aro, 2000).

In fact, adding this extra information does not change the results of the model – the same variables turn out to be significant in the same order (see model Q in the appendix to this chapter). Interestingly, this demonstrates that, although general educational level *is* linked to attitudes on gene therapy, having studied biology or genetics in particular are not, which is the opposite of many previous research findings. We suspect that this is due to the fact that the genetic attitude scale is comprised of many non-medical candidates for gene alteration. A recent study found that the relationship between knowledge and attitudes differs for different types of gene therapy (Stratford *et. al.*, forthcoming). Greater knowledge is linked to greater permissiveness about gene therapy for serious illness, but to a more cautious approach towards memory enhancement and germline gene therapy in general. This is confirmed when we look at the results of the *British Social Attitudes* survey for the individual attitude items (see the next table). For the three serious illnesses that gain most support as candidates for gene therapy, there are no significant differences according to education. However, for the rest of the scenarios, which are mostly cosmetic or social changes, those with no qualifications are more in favour of using gene therapy than those with more educational background.

Table 5.12 Acceptability of genetic manipulation for various traits, by education

% saying that changing a person's genes should "definitely" or "probably" be allowed to ...	Degree/ higher education	A level or equivalent	O level or equivalent	No qualifica- tions
... reduce a person's chances of getting breast cancer	72	70	74	73
... reduce a person's chances of getting heart disease	66	64	67	69
... stop someone having schizophrenia	64	68	67	69
... make them less aggressive or violent	51	51	58	62
... make them of average weight, rather than very overweight	36	31	37	44
... make a person taller or shorter	23	17	22	29
... give someone a full head of hair, rather than being bald	19	18	23	30
... make a person more intelligent	15	15	19	27
... make a person straight, rather than gay or lesbian	12	12	18	25
... determine the sex of an unborn baby	11	13	17	20
Base	*576*	*241*	*741*	*698*

Conclusions

The overall message is one of stability in attitudes towards genetic science rather than change. In the light of the immense amount of media coverage over the last couple of years, this may seem surprising. However, despite some progress, most of the concrete medical developments promised are still some way in the future. Much of the reporting has stressed that the deciphering of the human genome is only the first step towards developing new treatments and that it will take decades before we understand which genes are linked to which illness and how to use this information. The lack of change in public opinion may simply reflect this. Public opinion will need to be monitored over a longer period of time as more of the products of genetic research become available.

One area where change might have been expected but has not occurred is in our views on what causes human behaviour and characteristics. We are not yet becoming a nation of genetic determinists – there has been no movement in beliefs on this since 1998, and generally people think that genes are not predominant in determining intelligence, sexuality, weight or aggression. Younger people are even less likely to take a deterministic stance, so, barring startling new scientific discoveries, there seems to be no reason why genetic determinism should gain ground in the future.

The one area where change is evident, is in attitudes to the use of genetic tests by insurers and employers. The public has become even more opposed to giving such institutions access to an individual's genetic data. At the same time, people are more convinced than ever that this is going to happen, sooner or later. Here there has been real change in the regulations as for the first time a genetic test has been approved by a government body for use by insurance companies, which was widely reported in the media. And the public has reacted by opposing such use even more strongly. Our analysis suggests that the reasons behind the hostility are multi-faceted but include a strong degree of self interest, concern that the data will benefit companies at individuals' expense, a belief in the collective sharing of risk, and a lack of trust in the reliability of the tests. If the tests become more reliable, opposition to their use may lessen, but it is difficult to see how the other objections could be easily overcome. This is a challenge for those charged with developing policy in this area.

Notes

1. '30 years on … a brave new genetic world', *The Guardian*, 9 February 2001.
2. 'The politics of genes, America's next ethical war', *The Economist*, 14 April 2001.
3. If the environment is constant, then any variation *must* be genetic and the genetic component will be 100 per cent.
4. We have chosen homosexuality for this analysis as it was the only trait where we had separate questions about its desirability. The figures are for 1998 as the genetic determinism question was not asked about homosexuality in 2000.
5. 'Children of a lesser god', *Financial Times*, 23 December 1999.
6. We also added information on whether the respondent is a parent and on newspaper readership. The interest in newspaper readership was to see whether the different types of coverage and information people have been exposed to are linked to attitudes.

References

Eurobarometer 52.1 (2000), *The Europeans and Biotechnology*, INRA (EUROPE) – ECOSA.

Glover, J. (1995), 'The implications for responsibility of possible genetic factors in the explanation of violence', *Genetics of Criminal and Antisocial Behaviour* (Ciba Foundation Symposium 194, 237-247), Chichester: Wiley.

House of Lords Science and Technology Committee (2000), *3rd Report: Science and Society*, London: The Stationery Office.

Human Genetics Commission (2001a), *Public attitudes to human genetic information*, London: Human Genetics Commission.

Human Genetics Commission (2001b), *Press Release: Human Genetics Commission recommends moratorium on use of genetic test results for life insurance*, 1 May, http://www.abi.org.uk/PoliticalInfo/Weekly/bull125.asp.

Jallinoja, P. and Aro, A. R. (2000), 'Does knowledge make a difference? The association between knowledge about genes and attitudes towards gene tests', *Journal of Health Communication*, **5**: 29-39.

King, D. S. (1999), 'Preimplantation genetic diagnosis and the "new" eugenics', *Journal of Medical Ethics*, **25**: 176-182.

MORI (2000), *Attitudes towards Gene Cloning and Gene Therapy*, http://www.mori.com/.

Murthy A., Dixon A. and Mossialos E. (2001), 'Genetic testing and insurance', *Journal of the Royal Society of Medicine,* **94**: 57-60.

National Science Board (2000), 'Science and Technology: Public attitudes and public understanding', *Science and Engineering Indicators, 2000.*

Park, A. (2000), 'The generation game', in Jowell, R., Curtice, J., Park, A., Thomson, K., Jarvis, L., Bromley, C. and Stratford, N. (eds.), *British Social Attitudes: the 17th Report – Focusing on Diversity*, London: Sage.

Priest, S. H. (2000), 'US public opinion divided over biotechnology?', *Nature Biotechnology*, **18**: September.

Rose, S. (2001), *Darwin, Genes and Determinism*, http://www.bbc.co.uk/education/darwin/leghist/rose.htm.

Silver, L. M. (1998), *Remaking Eden, Cloning and Beyond in a Brave New World*, London: Weidenfeld and Nicolson.

Stratford, N., Marteau, T. and Bobrow, M. (1999), 'Tailoring genes' in Jowell, R., Curtice, J., Park, A., Thomson, K. and Jarvis, L. (eds.), *British Social Attitudes: the 16th Report – Who shares New Labour values?*, Aldershot: Ashgate.

Stratford, N., White, C., Park, A. and Lewis, J. (forthcoming), *Findings from the Consultative Panel on Gene Therapy,* London: The Wellcome Trust.

Tygart, C. E. (2000), 'Genetic causation attribution and public support of gay rights', *International Journal of Public Opinion Research*, **12**: 259-275.

Acknowledgements

The *National Centre for Social Research* and the authors would like to thank the Wellcome Trust for funding both modules of questions in 1998 and 2000. Theresa Marteau is funded by the Wellcome Trust.

Appendix

Logistic regression was used for all of the models detailed below. All figures shown in the tables are odds ratios. Only variables attaining statistical significance are included in the tables. Other variables included in the model are listed below.

Models A-D: Predictors of genetic determinism

The dependent variable was whether people thought each trait was all or mostly due to genes, or whether they thought it was due to upbringing/lifestyle, a mixture of both, just chance or answered that they did not know. The table shows how much more or less likely than average the various groups are to believe that each trait is all or mostly due to genes.

Variables also entered into the models which were shown not to have an independent relationship with any of the dependent variables were: religion, ethnic group, and whether the respondent had a serious genetic condition in their family.

Models E-H: Predictors of attitudes towards insurers and employers using genetic tests

The dependent variable was whether people thought that insurers/employers should definitely not be allowed to use genetic tests in each situation, or whether they thought they definitely/probably should, probably should not, or gave some other answer. The table shows how much more or less likely than average the various groups are to think that each use of genetic testing should definitely not be allowed.

Variables also entered into the models which were shown not to have an independent relationship with any of the dependent variables were: attitudes towards science in general, age, newspaper readership, and whether the respondent had studied biology/genetics.

Models I-L: Predictors of attitudes towards prenatal testing and abortion

The dependent variable was whether people thought that abortion after a positive prenatal test was never right in each situation, or whether they thought it was sometimes or always right or did not know. The table shows how much more or less likely than average the various groups are to think that each type of abortion is never right.

Variables also entered into the models which were shown not to have an independent relationship with any of the dependent variables were: attitudes towards science in general, newspaper readership, level of qualifications, and whether the respondent has children.

Models M-P: Predictors of attitudes towards pre-implantation genetic diagnosis (PGD)

The dependent variable was whether people thought that PGD was never right in each situation, or whether they thought it was sometimes or always right or did not know.

The table shows how much more or less likely than average the various groups are to think that each type of PGD is never right.

Variables also entered into the models which were shown not to have an independent relationship with any of the dependent variables were: social class, gender, newspaper readership, whether the respondent has studied biology/genetics, whether they have children, a long-term health problem or disability, or a serious genetic condition in their family.

Model Q: Predictors of attitudes towards human genetic manipulation

The dependent variable was whether people were 'enthusiastic' on the genetic attitude scale, or whether they were cautious/restrictive or the information was missing. The table shows how much more or less likely than average the various groups are to be 'enthusiastic'.

Variables also entered into the model which were shown not to have an independent relationship with the dependent variable were: attitudes towards science in general, social class, income, ethnic group, religion, newspaper readership, whether the respondent had a serious genetic condition in their family, whether they had children, or had ever studied biology/genetics.

Significance is shown as follows:
*   significant at the 5% level
**   significant at the 1% level

Tabloid readers are those who read *The Mirror/Daily Record*, *Daily Star*, *The Sun* or *Morning Star* three or more times a week. Broadsheet readers take *The Daily Telegraph*, *Financial Times*, *The Guardian*, *The Independent*, or *The Times*. *Daily Express* and *Daily Mail* readers are classified as 'mid market'.

Predictors of genetic determinism

Higher odds ratio = more likely to be genetic determinist

Model	A Height	B Intelligence	C Heart disease	D Violence
Age: 18-24	0.723	0.658 **	0.717 *	0.339 **
25-34	1.102	0.645 **	0.841	0.490 **
35-44	1.155	1.004	0.761 *	0.996
45-54	1.775 **	1.099	0.873	0.959
55-59	1.206	1.569 **	1.162	1.577 *
60-64	0.797	1.089	1.776 **	1.857 **
65+	0.637 **	1.249 *	1.209	2.150 **
Education: Degree/higher education	1.051	ns	ns	0.576 **
A level or equivalent	1.201	ns	ns	0.984
O level or equivalent	1.221 *	ns	ns	1.155
No qualifications	0.648 **	ns	ns	1.527 **
Gender: Male	0.843 **	ns	ns	ns
Female	1.187 **	ns	ns	ns
"Science does more harm than good"				
Agree strongly	0.929	ns	ns	ns
Agree	1.450 *	ns	ns	ns
Neither	0.949	ns	ns	ns
Disagree	1.408 **	ns	ns	ns
Disagree strongly	1.130	ns	ns	ns
Can't choose	0.562 *	ns	ns	ns
Not answered	0.876	ns	ns	ns
Social class: Never had a job	0.792	ns	0.543	ns
I	1.339	ns	0.535 *	ns
II	0.900	ns	1.013	ns
III	1.147	ns	1.342 *	ns
IV	1.365 *	ns	1.696 **	ns
V	0.669	ns	1.495 *	ns
Any children: Yes	0.855 *	ns	ns	ns
No	1.170 *	ns	ns	ns
Studies biology/genetics: Yes	ns	1.211 **	ns	ns
No	ns	0.826 **	ns	ns
Newspaper readership: No daily paper	ns	1.008	0.971	ns
Tabloid	ns	0.952	1.554 **	ns
Mid market	ns	1.055	0.923	ns
Broadsheet	ns	1.472 **	0.829	ns
Regional/other	ns	0.670 *	0.867	ns
Base:	*1932*	*1932*	*1932*	*1932*

ns = not significant.

Predictors of attitudes towards insurers and employers using genetic tests
Higher odds ratio = more likely to think genetic tests by employer/insurer should definitely **not** be allowed

	E Refuse life insurance	F Employer see test	G Make take test	H Sensitivity to chemical
Gender: Male	0.836 **	0.865 **	0.823 **	ns
Female	1.196 **	1.157 **	1.215 **	ns
Welfarism: Sympathetic	1.428 **	1.659 **	1.525 **	1.591 **
Middle ground	0.875	0.851 *	0.874	0.995
Poor don't deserve	0.801 **	0.709 **	0.750 **	0.632 **
Social class: Never had a job	1.020	1.091	ns	ns
I	0.773	1.045	ns	ns
II	1.440 **	1.314 *	ns	ns
III	1.047	0.841	ns	ns
IV	1.065	1.102	ns	ns
V	0.790	0.721	ns	ns
Ethnic group: Black	1.169	0.645	0.836	ns
Asian	0.923	1.328	0.651	ns
White	1.582 **	1.712 **	1.731 **	ns
Other/mixed	0.586	0.682	1.061	ns
Causes of heart disease				
All/mostly genes	1.079	1.082	1.115	ns
All/mostly upbringing/lifestyle	1.143	1.077	1.270 *	ns
Equal mix of both	1.341 **	1.385 **	1.267 *	ns
Just chance	0.756	0.885	0.905	ns
Don't know	0.800	0.701 *	0.616 **	ns
Econ activity: Education/training	0.779	0.895	1.659	ns
In paid work	1.276	1.395 **	1.335 *	ns
Unemployed	1.103	1.175	1.066	ns
Sick/disabled	1.172	0.920	0.673	ns
Retired	0.935	0.944	0.793	ns
Looking after home/family	0.832	0.784	0.794	ns
Education: Degree/ higher educ	ns	ns	1.324 **	ns
A level or equivalent	ns	ns	1.068	ns
O level or equivalent	ns	ns	0.904	ns
No qualifications	ns	ns	0.783 *	ns
Genetic condition in family				
Yes	ns	ns	ns	0.631 *
No	ns	ns	ns	1.585 *
Religion: Regular Catholic	ns	ns	ns	1.542
Regular other religion	ns	ns	ns	0.567 *
Irregular/no religion	ns	ns	ns	1.143
Base	*1842*	*1846*	*1849*	*1854*

ns = not significant.

Predictors of attitudes towards prenatal testing and abortion
Higher odds ratio = more likely to think abortion never right

Model	I	J	K	L
	Mental disability	Physical disability	Die in 20s or 30s	Height of 8 year old
Religion: Regular Catholic	4.828 **	4.547 **	2.042 **	2.357 **
Regular other religion	0.953	0.868	0.903	0.746 *
Irregular/no religion	0.217 **	0.253 **	0.542 **	0.569 **
Gender: Male	1.782 **	1.566 **	1.163 **	1.152 **
Female	0.561 **	0.639 **	0.860 **	0.868 **
Social class: Never had a job	2.320 *	1.661	ns	ns
I	0.756	0.594	ns	ns
II	0.375 **	0.541 **	ns	ns
III	0.738	0.842	ns	ns
IV	1.142	1.218	ns	ns
V	1.802 *	1.824 *	ns	ns
Ethnic group: Black	1.786	ns	ns	ns
Asian	0.464	ns	ns	ns
White	0.559 *	ns	ns	ns
Other/mixed	2.157 *	ns	ns	ns
Genetic condition in family				
Yes	1.378 *	ns	ns	ns
No	0.726 *	ns	ns	ns
Age: 18-24	1.904 **	2.147 **	ns	1.413 *
25-34	1.035	1.289	ns	1.367 **
35-44	0.876	0.770	ns	1.165
45-54	0.839	0.874	*ns*	0.700 **
55-59	0.796	0.767	ns	1.027
60-64	1.502	1.409	ns	0.978
65+	0.578 *	0.497 **	ns	0.631 *
Long-standing health problem/disability				
Yes	ns	1.259 *	ns	1.189 **
No	ns	0.794 *	ns	0.841 *
Studied biology/genetics: Yes	ns	ns	0.874 *	ns
No	ns	ns	1.145 *	ns
Base	*1929*	*1929*	*1929*	*1929*

ns = not significant.

Predictors of attitudes towards pre-implantation genetic diagnosis (PGD)
Higher odds ratio = more likely to think PGD never right

	M Mental disability	N Physical disability	O Die in 20s or 30s	P Height of 8 year old
Educat: Degree/higher education	0.650 **	0.743 **	ns	ns
A level or equivalent	0.990	0.940	ns	ns
O level or equivalent	0.932	1.002	ns	ns
No qualifications	1.668 **	1.429 **	ns	ns
Religion: Regular Catholic	2.041 **	2.217 **	2.294 **	2.096 **
Regular other religion	0.821	0.734 *	0.881	0.812
Irregular/no religion	0.597 **	0.614 **	0.495 **	0.588 **
Age: 18-24	0.633 *	0.603 *	ns	ns
25-34	0.862	0.967	ns	ns
35-44	0.835	0.863	ns	ns
45-54	1.002	1.017	ns	ns
55-59	1.211	1.231	ns	ns
60-64	1.186	1.030	ns	ns
65+	1.522 **	1.543 **	ns	ns
"Science does more harm than good"				
Agree strongly	ns	1.229	1.384	1.556 *
Agree	ns	1.306 *	1.080	1.130
Neither	ns	1.023	1.036	1.026
Disagree	ns	0.653 **	0.831	0.778 *
Disagree strongly	ns	0.675	0.621 *	0.645 *
Can't choose	ns	0.991	1.234	1.194
Not answered	ns	1.393	1.014	0.926
Ethnic group: Black	ns	ns	ns	1.056
Asian	ns	ns	ns	1.196
White	ns	ns	ns	0.663 **
Other/mixed	ns	ns	ns	1.195
Base	*1927*	*1927*	*1927*	*1927*

ns = not significant.

Attitudes towards human genetic manipulation

Higher odds ratio = more likely to be 'enthusiastic' on genetic attitude scale

	Q Genetics scale
Age: 18-24	1.293
25-34	0.867
35-44	0.513 **
45-54	0.974
55-64	1.291
65+	1.362 *
Gender: Male	1.387 **
Female	0.703 **
Education: Degree/higher education	0.790 *
A level or equivalent	0.641 *
O level or equivalent	1.075
No qualifications	1.838 **
Abortion: Not wrong for either reason	1.653 **
Wrong for one reason, not for other	0.947
Wrong for both reasons	0.689 *
Not answered/don't know	0.907
No self-completion	1.022
Base	*1942*

6 How green are our values?

Ian Christie and Lindsey Jarvis [*]

Over the last few years environmental problems have received a great deal of attention in the media and public debate. Concern has increased among campaigning organisations and consumers about the potential risks to health and the environment from genetically modified (GM) crops. The foot and mouth crisis in UK farming, following closely the GM uproar and the BSE scandal, has reinforced concerns that intensive agriculture is environmentally unsustainable and needs profound reform (Pretty, 1998). Meanwhile, the winter of 2000-2001, marked by severe flooding and unprecedented rainfall around the UK, was linked by many observers to climate disruption caused by human activities such as burning fossil fuels. Even if global warming is not to blame, the floods highlighted the risks of changes in land use that make flooding more likely. However, the recent scientific evidence indicates that climate change forced by human action is indeed happening (Environment Agency, 2001), so President Bush's decision to reject the Kyoto Protocol on international cuts in greenhouse gas emissions generated a storm of protest. Regular protests against international leaders at economic summits have received considerable coverage while also drawing attention to the environmental impact of globalisation. More locally, the collapse of British rail services in autumn 2000 drew attention not only to the state of public transport but also to the unsustainable growth in road congestion, exacerbated by problems on the railways. Meanwhile, local campaigners are gearing up for protests against the government's plans for road building and development of more waste incinerators.

This is a formidable list of developments that have a strong environmental policy dimension while also having direct effects on people's lives. Yet there are many signs that the ferment of debate on environmental issues and their connection to food production, health, globalisation and transport is not linked to any *coherent* public response or set of concerns. There is a *disconnection* between awareness of issues and action to tackle them.

[*] Ian Christie is Associate Director of the consultancy The Local Futures Group and an associate of the Centre for Environmental Strategy, University of Surrey. Lindsey Jarvis is a Senior Researcher at the *National Centre for Social Research* and Co-Director of the *British Social Attitudes* survey series.

This gap between environmentally-friendly attitudes and actions is well illustrated by the protests about fuel prices that took place in September 2000. The government was challenged by a series of protests that brought about a near-emergency in the economy as oil refineries were blockaded, and that eventually led to relaxations in fuel taxation. Despite well-attested public concerns about the sustainability of trends in car use, congestion and vehicle pollution (Taylor, 1997; Christie and Jarvis, 1999) there seemed to be widespread sympathy for the aims of the fuel protesters and for the proposition that government should not be making it more expensive for people to drive their cars. As was widely noted at the time, the government, despite its claims to "put the environment at the heart" of its activities, did not respond by making a vigorous case for higher fuel prices by pointing out the connections between fossil fuel use, the threat of climate disruption, and growth in demand for transport. Meanwhile, during the general election campaign of 2001 the big issues that had dominated headlines during the winter – floods, transport, the farming crisis – faded rapidly from the media and political debate, while opinion polls suggested that environmental issues ranked very low among voters' priorities.

The lack of connection between, on the one hand, evidence of impending or actual environmental crisis and, on the other, public attitudes and actions partly reflects the fundamental problems that the political process has when handling the 'green' agenda. Thus, governments operate to timetables that are out of kilter with those of long-term processes at work in the environment (Adam, 1998). There is huge reluctance among politicians to take a lead on environmental policy (for example, to push for increases in taxation or new eco-taxes to constrain environmentally damaging forms of consumption – above all, car use) for fear of the electoral consequences. The 'joined-up' thinking and action required to integrate environmental policy with economic and social strategies are in short supply and hard to do within the fragmented machinery of UK governance (see, for example, Real World Coalition, 2001). Politicians are also deeply resistant to the environmentalist movement's critique of economic growth (Jacobs, 2000).

On this analysis, the lack of commitment and leadership from the political world, and the incoherence with which politicians preach environmental ideals and sustainable development strategies, while continuing to subsidise damaging forms of production and consumption and resisting changes in fiscal and other policy areas to promote truly sustainable industry and lifestyles, is the fundamental constraint on the 'greening' of the UK. But there are many reasons for such political inhibitions and incoherence, and it would be remarkable if these were not reflected in, and reinforced by, similar factors at work in the formation of public attitudes.

The *British Social Attitudes* series has regularly considered the development of attitudes towards environmental problems and possible ways of dealing with them (Dalton and Rohrschneider, 1998; Taylor, 1997; Witherspoon, 1994). Two central conclusions have emerged over the past decade. Firstly, levels of environmental concern are demonstrably lower in Britain than elsewhere in Europe (although concern has increased somewhat). Second, while those who express environmental concern are more willing to support environmental measures or to have done something about the environment themselves, the incidence of environmentally friendly *behaviour* is far lower than the level of environmental *concern*.

Barriers to change

Our previous findings, when considered alongside the political constraints discussed earlier, suggest that environmental concern is likely to continue to lag well behind consciousness of problems, and – for most – personal concern will *not* be matched by commitment to action. A number of factors contribute to this.

First, citizens are now faced by debates on environmental issues that are more complex and confusing than those which surrounded the wave of "Green Consumerism" in the late 1980s. Discussion of the threat of climate change, the problems of car use and the problems of waste and intensive farming are all likely to raise public awareness of the risks we face, but are also likely to lead to uncertainty about the efficacy of any steps an individual might be able to take. Given the enormity of some of the problems discussed in the media and by politicians – above all, global climate disruption – and the lack of strong signals about what can be done about them, many people will feel that they have very little, if any, ability to act even if they do feel some kind of responsibility. A sense of economic and political powerlessness to make any difference is also a major factor here (see, for example, Macnaghten *et al.*, 1995; Clover, 1997).

Second, the most pressing and complex problems we face are those of 'diffuse' impacts on the environment – the polluting emissions from millions of cars, the waste from millions of homes, farms and organisations, the carbon dioxide produced from virtually every sector of the economy. These are 'invisible' and hard to analyse (Adam, 1998), work on timescales that are hard to relate to daily life, and are linked to basic processes of consumption and production in the modern economy. These are much harder to regulate than 'point' emissions from particular factories or other localised sources of pollution that are relatively easy to change or close down. This means that responsibility for dealing with impacts is also very widely diffused (Burke, 1997). In this context, in the absence of strong leadership and signals from the economic system (for example, fuel tax increases) individuals are likely to feel yet more disempowered, even if they do feel concern about the issues.

Third, politicians' reluctance to speak frankly about the probable implications of, for instance, climate policy for personal consumption – such as the need for much more energy saving, restraint in car use, and so on – creates a setting in which public concern is unlikely to be converted into willingness to act or into accurate understanding of the issues. In turn, real or apparent lack of public commitment provides a rationale for politicians' inhibitions about promoting more radical environmental policies and giving the environment a higher priority in campaigning and legislative programmes.

Fourth, previous *British Social Attitudes* data indicate that conventional approaches to awareness-raising and public information are inadequate, relying on an assumption that more knowledge about the problems will produce a change in attitude and behaviour (Witherspoon, 1994). But in the context discussed here, more knowledge could equally well reinforce a sense that nothing an individual can do will make any difference (except possibly make that person worse off in significant respects). A richer model of motivation is needed, reflecting values and emotional dimensions of attitudes to the environment and to people's relationships of trust with political institutions (Macnaghten *et al.,* 1995; Witherspoon, 1994; Clover, 1997; Grove-White *et al.*, 2000).

Finally, the most pressing environmental issues of our time (such as climate disruption) and the policy options to handle them (such as eco-taxes) are highly complex and subject to well-reported disagreement among experts – a situation in which gaining public confidence and translating concern into practical action is very hard to do (Grove-White *et al.*, 2000). Moreover, the complexities, 'invisibility' and the often highly uncertain timetables of environmental threats make regular and comprehensive reporting of 'green' issues in the media hard to achieve, especially given the commercial and editorial pressures faced by journalists (Smith, 2000).

Given all these factors, it seems likely that stable and coherent attitudes towards the environment will be hard to maintain for most citizens. The chapter explores this, focusing upon the extent to which Britain remains a nation that, despite expressing many 'green' concerns, shows much less commitment to acting on them. We do this by focusing upon a number of key areas: namely, people's overall attitudes towards environmental quality, and the relationship between the environment and the economy and our way of life; knowledge about the environment; the extent of specific environmental concerns; the location of responsibility for action to deal with environmental problems; and levels of personal commitment – how far people say they act on their concerns or would be willing to do so. Many of the questions included in the 2000 *British Social Attitudes* survey were earlier asked in 1993, allowing us to look at the extent to which attitudes and behaviour have changed over time. And, where we do find evidence of change, we attempt to account for this.

Views about the environment

To what extent do people think that our way of life is at odds with environmental quality? To assess this, we asked a series of questions about the implications of science and modern life generally for the environment, as shown in the next table. These show some support for the belief that modern life harms the environment, with over six in ten thinking that the world cannot cope with population growth at its current rate. Almost half express an anti-science sentiment, agreeing that "we believe too much in science and not enough in faith and feelings" and that "everything we do in modern life harms the environment". Moreover, only 22 per cent think that science can help us address environmental problems without requiring people to make dramatic changes to their lifestyles. True, the proportion who think science *will* be able to do this has grown slightly since 1993 and the proportion who think that science does "more harm than good", already small in 1993, has shrunk further still, to 21 per cent. But the general message contained in these findings is one of a widespread suspicion that we cannot go on as we are, and that conventional forms of growth are unsustainable in relation to the environment.

Table 6.1 Attitudes towards the environment and science

% who agree	1993	2000
The Earth simply cannot afford to support population growth at its present rate	n.a.	62
We believe too often in science, and not enough in feelings and faith	46	48
Almost everything we do in modern life harms the environment	45	48
Modern science will solve our environmental problems with little change to our way of life	18	22
Overall, modern science does more harm than good	24	21
Base	*1261*	*1963*

Do people then perceive an interdependent pattern between economic growth and the environment? As the next table shows, four in ten agree that Britain needs such growth to "protect the environment" – but a similar proportion think that economic progress will slow down unless we look after the environment better. There has been a *decrease* since 1993 in the proportion agreeing that economic growth is always bad for the environment, from 23 per cent in 1993 to 16 per cent in 2000. This slight move towards seeing economic growth and the environment as potentially reconcilable may reflect the long-standing political use of 'economic growth' as a phrase encapsulating a range of 'feel-good' factors from 'competitiveness' to 'better living standards'. It could also reflect some of the extensive debate – much of it promoted by environmental campaign organisations – around the idea that going 'green' can be good for jobs, technology and business opportunities. Overall, however, few people feel strongly either way, perhaps reflecting a sense of confusion about precisely how weighty the evidence about environmental damage actually is. Given the lack of high-profile and *frequent* public debate and information campaigns that might provide people with a clearer idea of how serious some problems are, how far technology can help and how far lifestyle changes will be needed as well, this is no surprise. This is backed up by the fact that people's responses to the different questions shown in Tables 6.1 and 6.2 are often contradictory, suggesting a high degree of confusion and inconsistency.[1]

Table 6.2 Attitudes towards the environment and the economy

% who agree	1993	2000
In order to protect the environment Britain needs economic growth	41	42
Economic progress in Britain will slow down unless we look after the environment better	n.a.	39
We worry too much about the future of the environment and not enough about prices and jobs today	36	35
People worry too much about human progress harming the environment	30	28
Economic growth always harms the environment	23	16
Base	*1261*	*1963*

Whether or not views on these matters are 'solid' is not clear. Certainly, in the early 1990s the impact of recession tended to drive down levels of concern for the environment and focus attention on economic and social welfare issues (Taylor, 1997). So if there is a similar economic downturn in coming years it will be important to test how far environmental concerns remain a matter of priority for citizens regardless of financial conditions, given the increasing political salience and probable continuation of food scares, 'weird weather' linked to climate change, and so on.

Knowledge

Large proportions of people are unable either to agree *or* disagree with many of the questions we have already considered, a likely reflection of widespread uncertainty in the face of expert disagreements as well as lack of information and understanding. However, we are able to explore levels of environmental knowledge in more detail through answers to an environmental 'quiz' asked both in 1993 and 2000. The percentages of the sample who gave the correct answer to these questions are shown in the next table.

The greatest lack of understanding is displayed in responses to statements about the greenhouse effect: only 21 per cent of respondents know that the greenhouse effect is *not* caused by a hole in the Earth's atmosphere. Set against this, however, is the fact that 80 per cent are (correctly) aware that every time we use coal or oil or gas we contribute to the greenhouse effect. And, aside from the greenhouse effect question, at least half gave correct answers to the remaining statements.

There has been very little change in knowledge over the last seven years. The only notable change relates to antibiotics, with increasing proportions becoming aware that these do not kill viruses. This overall lack of change is hard to account for: possibly it reflects the low coverage of, and attention paid to, complex issues to do with environmental change, as contrasted with people's greater propensity to take an interest in health issues (which, after all, have a more immediate and personal impact than do big environmental questions).

Table 6.3 Environmental knowledge, 1993 and 2000

% who answered correctly ...	1993	2000
Every time we use coal or oil or gas, we contribute to the greenhouse effect *[True]*	79	80
Antibiotics can kill bacteria but not viruses *[True]*	62	79
Human beings developed from earlier species of animals *[True]*	75	74
If someone is exposed to any amount of radioactivity, they are certain to die as a result *[False]*	63	64
All man-made chemicals can cause cancer if you eat enough of them *[False]*	49	53
The greenhouse effect is caused by a hole in the Earth's atmosphere *[False]*	20	21
Base	*1261*	*972*

When we look at people's overall scores on the quiz, we find that eight in ten get at least half of the questions right (with three in ten giving five or six correct answers). So there would appear to be a broad base of environmentally well-informed people in Britain. But how does knowledge relate to attitudes? In particular, does a lack of knowledge about the environment go hand in hand with scepticism about the alleged threats that it faces? We explore this in the next table. This shows responses to two statements that we can use to measure 'environmental cynicism' – that "there are more important things to do in life than protect the environment" (21 per cent agree) and "many of the claims about environmental threats are exaggerated" (24 per cent agree).

The table shows that those with the *least* knowledge about the environment are more likely to have a cynical view of environmental dangers. Among those with the lowest scores on our quiz, for instance, a third take the view that there are "more important" things to do than protect the environment, double the rate found among those with the highest scores. When we combine the two statements together to produce a 'cynicism' measure, we find that 25 per cent of those who were sceptical or cynical about threats to the environment gave fewer than three correct answers in our quiz, compared with nine per cent of those who gave more positive answers about the importance of environmental problems. Moreover, this relationship exists even when other factors such as age, sex and education are taken into account (see model 1 in the appendix to this chapter for more details). Thus, the *least* likely to subscribe to a cynical view about the environment are women, those in work (as opposed to being retired from work), and those with high levels of environmental knowledge.

Table 6.4 Environmental cynicism by knowledge

% who agree ...	0-2 correct	3–4 correct	5-6 correct	Total
There are more important things to do in life than protect the environment				
Agree	34	19	16	21
Neither	21	29	31	28
Disagree	32	50	52	47
Many of the claims about environmental threats are exaggerated				
Agree	33	24	18	24
Neither	29	25	22	25
Disagree	21	46	58	45
Base	*181*	*509*	*282*	*972*

Of course, these analyses cannot tell us the *direction* of this relationship between cynicism and knowledge. So it may be that low knowledge about the environment leads to cynicism about the dangers that it faces – or, alternatively, that cynicism about environmental dangers contributes to a lack of knowledge, or a disinclination to absorb information, about the environment.

So, in summary, general attitudes tend towards the belief that current lifestyles and forms of economic and technical development are *not* compatible with safeguarding the environment. But there is a good deal of agnosticism on the issues – which reflects not only the absence of confident knowledge and judgement among the public but also among experts on many of the problems caused by the interaction of economy, science and the environment. A good summary of this general pattern is provided by responses to the statement "economic progress in Britain will slow down unless we look after the environment better". Just one in ten held a strong view either way and four in ten did not express an opinion. Of the rest, there were almost twice as many likely to agree as disagree.

Perceptions of danger

We turn now to examine the specific environmental problems which people are most concerned about, and how far these have changed in recent years. We begin by considering responses to a set of questions which asks respondents how far they consider different forms of pollution to be serious threats to the environment.

As the table below shows, the pollution of air and water is seen as "very" or "extremely dangerous" to the environment by nearly two-thirds of the population. More indirect environmental threats, such as pesticides getting into the food chain or eco-system, were less likely to be seen as dangers. Comparison with 1993 shows a marked increase in concern about air pollution from industry and, to a lesser extent, from cars.

Table 6.5 Views on specific threats to the environment, 1993 and 2000

% who consider these "very" or "extremely dangerous" to the environment	1993	2000
Air pollution from industry	54	63
Pollution of Britain's rivers, lakes and streams	61	62
Air pollution caused by cars	48	54
A rise in the world's temperature caused by the greenhouse effect	51	50
Pesticides and chemicals used in farming	37	49
Modifying the genes of certain crops	n.a.	39
Base	*1261*	*972*

These results seem to indicate a high degree of acceptance that different types of pollution have serious environmental impacts (although given the complexity of all the issues listed it is probable that many people are simply inclined to assume that "pollution" is always linked to danger in some sense). Around one-third take the 'safe' option in replying "somewhat dangerous" in relation to industrial pollution, watercourse pollution and the greenhouse effect, all of which could be viewed as 'experts-only' issues remote from everyday life.

The most dramatic rise between 1993 and 2000 relates to the view that pesticides and other chemicals used in farming are extremely or very dangerous – no doubt a reflection of intensive media reporting of farming scandals and crises over recent years. But contrary to this, the question as to the dangers of genetically modified (GM) crops, a topic which has also received extensive media coverage, generated strong concern in only four in ten. Given the campaign against GM foods by media outlets and protesters, and the withdrawal of GM products from many supermarket shelves, this might seem surprising. Possibly we see here a slightly more relaxed attitude to what is a *technology* rather than a form of pollution of the same kind as the others listed above (although anti-GM campaigners would argue that GM crops can spread like a contaminant). This said, however, nearly three-quarters of respondents view GM crop modification as dangerous to some extent.

Public concern about GM foods is amply demonstrated by responses to questions asked as part of the 1999 *British Social Attitudes* survey. These were introduced as follows:

> *You may have heard of genetically modified or 'GM' foods. These are made from plants which have had their genes altered. Some people say that growing these plants may damage other plants and wildlife and that food made from them may not be safe to eat. Other people say that growing these plants may mean lower food prices and less use of pesticides and weedkillers.*

As the next table shows, GM foods attract a great deal of criticism. Only one in ten agree with the two pro-GM foods statements that "in order to compete with the rest of the world, Britain should grow genetically modified (GM) foods" and "on balance, the advantages of genetically modified (GM) foods outweigh any dangers". On all four statements, over half opposed GM foods and between 20 and 30 per cent opposed them "strongly".

Table 6.6 Attitudes towards GM foods, 1999

	Agree strongly	Agree	Neither	Disagree	Disagree strongly
To compete with rest of world, Britain should grow GM foods	3	7	18	37	28
Advantages of GM foods outweigh any dangers	2	9	22	34	23
We should never interfere with genes of plants and animals	29	34	18	10	5
GM foods should be banned, even if food prices suffer as a result	21	31	22	14	5

Base: 833

Although seven in ten (73 per cent) believe that "growing genetically modified foods poses a danger to other plants and wildlife" they are less vehement about the dangers of GM foods to the people consuming them. Half (48 per cent) agree that "all GM foods already available in the shops are probably or definitely *not* safe to eat" but three in ten thought they "probably" were safe and four per cent that they were "definitely" safe to eat. Of particular note is the fact that almost one in five (18 per cent) did not know, suggesting a need for additional information about the advantages and disadvantages of GM foods.

Sources of information about pollution

Some of our findings so far have pointed towards a need for greater information about environmental issues. We turn now to consider who might be seen as the most trustworthy source of any such information.

That *trust* is a vital issue for environmental communications and views on risk and responsibility is borne out by a large literature (see, for example, Grove-White *et al.*, 1997; Grove-White *et al.*, 2000; Willis and Rose, 2000; Worcester, 2000). The following table shows the levels of trust that people have in the various different institutions which might supply the public with information about "causes of pollution". The findings confirm that academic research centres and environmental campaign groups are viewed with much more trust by the public than are government departments and, particularly, business and industry.

Table 6.7 Trust in institutions to provide correct information about causes of pollution

		Levels of trust		
		A great deal/ quite a lot	Some	Not much/ hardly any
University research centres	%	64	25	5
Environmental groups	%	54	31	9
Radio or TV programmes	%	28	45	21
Newspapers	%	14	39	41
Government departments	%	13	47	33
Business and industry	%	6	32	55

Base: 972

There is a widespread lack of confidence in business – over half of our sample has little or minimal trust in its communications on the environment, with one in seven expressing "hardly any" trust. The results are also sobering for government and for the press. However, these findings no doubt reflect a generalised lack of respect for and confidence in these institutions rather than a well thought-out view about their environmental communications. However, there is no ringing endorsement of any other groups in society: even environmental groups and university research centres attain just 54 and 64 per cent respectively as sources in which people have "a great deal" or "quite a lot" of trust. Notably, for all the groups we asked about, between a quarter and a half of respondents are bunched into the lukewarm "some trust" camp.

One possible reason for this lack of trust may be the complexity of the issues, perhaps related to the regularity with which expert opinion needs to be revised (or is at least hotly contested by other apparent experts). As for political parties, it would seem that if the public is presented with the spectacle of division and frequent changes of mind by 'experts' – as has been the case, for example, in relation to food scares such as the BSE crisis – then confidence in any information about the risks to the environment and to human health from pollution is undermined.

Who is responsible?

So far we have found that the pattern identified in 1993, one of high levels of concern about the environment, both in a generalised way and in relation to the specific risks posed by pollution of different kinds, continues in our last findings. But, in trying to tease out the relationship between concern and action, it is essential to acknowledge the major problems of 'agency' that exist in relation to the environment. These provide formidable reasons as to why many people feel that there is nothing *they* can do and can encourage the view that other bodies (such as government and business) are better placed to take action. Four questions are of particular importance. First, to what extent do people think *Britain* should be taking a lead in environmental policy, assuming responsibility for a major international role in improving the environment, and moving towards a more environmentally sustainable economy? Second, how much support is there for government regulation of businesses and individuals in order to achieve better environmental outcomes (as opposed to organisations and citizens being free to decide on courses of action for themselves)? Third, to what extent do people feel different actors are currently 'doing their bit' for the environment (to borrow the phrase used in current government information campaigns)? And, fourth, how much are individuals prepared to take personal action and to support measures that could be disadvantageous economically to them for the good of the environment?

Global responsibility

The role of individual countries in global environmental protection has been a major theme of debates over the past two years about climate change, most notably when the USA rejected the Kyoto accord (although the 2000 *British Social Attitudes* survey took place before controversy about this was at its height).

As the findings in the next table suggest, there is strong support for binding international agreements on environmental protection – perhaps reflecting widespread awareness that few of the big ecological problems can be tackled by individual states alone. And there is a very clear view that poorer countries should be expected to shoulder their share of responsibility for environmental protection with three in five *disagreeing* with the view that "poorer countries should be expected to make less effort than richer countries" and only one in five agreeing.

Table 6.8 International action to protect the world environment

		Agree	Neither	Disagree
For environmental problems there should be international agreements that Britain and other countries should be made to follow	%	87	7	2
Poorer countries should be expected to make less effort than richer countries to protect the environment	%	20	15	60

Base: 972

We also asked respondents to assess the environmental contribution Britain was making in comparison to other countries:

> *Some countries are doing more to protect the world environment than other countries are. In general, do you think Britain is doing more than enough, about the right amount or too little?*

Half felt that Britain was not yet doing enough, just over one in three (37 per cent) thought it was about the right amount and only one in twenty that Britain was making an excessive effort.

Overall, the picture is one of public support for a global effort to take responsibility for action, even among poorer countries, with Britain expected to have greater input.

The role of government, business and the individual

Do people see the main role in environmental protection within the UK as falling to government, to business – or does it lie with civil society and individual citizens as a whole?

As the next table shows, over half think that government should legislate to make ordinary people protect the environment, twice as many as agreed that people should be allowed to make their own choices. The difference is even wider in relation to businesses, with eight in ten agreeing that they should be the object of environmental legislation. These results, largely unchanged since 1993, point to a widespread awareness of the problems of individual agency and the need for collective forms of action. They also back up our earlier observations regarding a general lack of trust in business.

Table 6.9 Government legislation *versus* personal or businesses' freedom

% who say ...	1993	2000
	%	%
Governments should let ordinary people decide for themselves how to protect the environment, even if it means they don't always do the right thing	24	27
Governments should pass laws to make ordinary people protect the environment, even if it interferes with people's rights to make their own decisions	57	53
Can't choose	18	19
	%	%
Governments should let businesses decide for themselves how to protect the environment, even if it means they don't always do the right thing	6	8
Governments should pass laws to make businesses protect the environment, even if it interferes with businesses' rights to make their own decisions	84	82
Can't choose	9	9
Base	1261	972

Is everyone 'doing their bit'?

When asked to compare the efforts made to look after the environment by "people in general" with those made by business and industry, only one in seven felt that business was doing the most. By contrast, nearly half (47 per cent) felt that it was people in general who were making more effort. When we asked respondents to compare the efforts made by government with those of the business community, once again just one in seven saw business and industry as doing more for the environment, while about one in three (30 per cent) thought government was doing more. A similar proportion could not choose between the two groups. Finally, we asked respondents to choose between the efforts of government and those of people in general. Once again it was the general public who were thought to be making the most effort. Nearly four in ten (39 per cent) reckoned that they were doing more, compared with just 16 per cent who saw government as making most efforts.

The ranking that emerges from this battery of questions is an odd one. "People in general" are viewed as the most active stewards of the environment; government comes in a poor second; and business and industry are a very poor third. But, as we shall see later when we consider the 'green' actions which respondents themselves carry out, this suggests that many substantially overestimate what their fellow citizens are doing. It also points to considerable ignorance of the welter of environmental legislation, technological investment, business and government initiatives for cleaning up pollution, and other developments over recent years.

Two interpretations suggest themselves. The first is that these replies relate less to the state of the environment and beliefs about the efforts made by business and government, and more to the low levels of trust that people have in companies and policy makers. Where trust is low, willingness to assign credit for effort is likely also to be low. Indeed, when we look at the questions on trust in business and government as environmental sources described earlier, we find this seems to be the case. For example, those with quite a lot of trust in business and industry are four times as likely as those without much trust in it to select business and industry as making a lot of effort over people in general. The same is true for those with trust in government information and support for the effort government makes. The other interpretation is that these results reflect a poor performance by government and business in communicating the extent of the actions they have taken so far: the many environmental reports from major companies and from ministers have not made their mark, it seems. This is no great surprise perhaps, given the technical nature of many of the developments in business and policy, and the tendency of the mass media to report problems much more extensively than any progress or potential solutions in relation to environmental damage (Smith, 2000). More important still, if many environmental problems are known or felt to be *getting worse* (for example, the threat of climate disruption, the reality of traffic congestion, and the experience of frequent food scares), then perhaps awareness of seemingly intractable problems is likely to lead many people to take the view that the efforts of decision makers are inadequate in the face of the challenges, and that they show less good faith than is displayed by many individual citizens and voluntary bodies.

Exploring the role of the individual

There are many reasons why we should not expect environmental concern to translate neatly into the sorts of actions that might help solve or minimise ecological problems. People might think the problems are too big for them to make a difference. They might also have low levels of trust in key sources of collective action (particularly business and government) and feel that there is little point doing one's individual bit if these actors are not delivering results. Moreover, the amount of expert disagreement and uncertainty about some of the big issues means that there is little clear-cut guidance to follow. And, of course, individual action, in the absence of large-scale changes in prices and economic incentives, could well make citizens worse off – or at least feel worse off. Given these factors, and the lack of radical policy changes over the past decade that would begin to tackle them, we might expect to find that personal action still lagged well behind expressions of concern about the environment.

We start by examining the extent to which people believe that what they do for the environment can make a positive difference. Do people feel a diminished sense of agency in relation to the environment? The picture here is mixed. Only a minority (28 per cent) agrees that "it is just too difficult for someone like me to do much about the environment", slightly down from the proportion in 1993 (34 per cent). Four in ten agree that they "do what is right for the environment, even when it costs more money or takes more time" (42 per cent agree, the same proportion as in 1993). And, although four in ten (43 per cent) agree that "there is no point in doing what I can for the environment unless others do the same", the same proportion disagree.

How willing, then, are people to support *collective* action that could hurt them economically for the sake of the environment? We asked if they would be prepared to pay much higher prices, pay higher taxes or accept cuts in living standards. As the following table shows, the message here seems to be that while there is a sizeable minority willing to make sacrifices in economic terms (and over four in ten willing specifically to accept higher prices), there has been a reduction over time in willingness to pay for environmental protection. This may well reflect a much wider sense of mistrust about the quality of the public services secured by taxation, and about the capacity of governments to spend it wisely, rather than specific resistance to higher taxes for the sake of the environment.

Table 6.10 Willingness to make sacrifices to protect the environment

	1993	2000
Pay much higher prices		
Willing	46	43
Unwilling	21	24
Pay much higher taxes		
Willing	37	31
Unwilling	33	40
Accept cuts in your standard of living		
Willing	30	26
Unwilling	43	48
Base	1261	972

These findings suggest that for all the strength of environmental concern, we are far from any kind of breakthrough in public attitudes towards the role of radical economic changes in delivering ecological benefits. Arguably this reflects the failures by successive governments to make a sustained effort to give priority to environmental policy and to communicate the extent of environmental problems and the options for change to the public as a whole.

Being 'green'

We turn now to consider environmentally-friendly behaviour. We found earlier that reduced proportions of people are willing to contemplate making sacrifices for environmental reasons; is this mirrored when we look at people's behaviour? As the next table shows, there is some evidence of reduced environmental action since 1993. Now, three in ten say they have signed a petition about the environment in the last five years, *lower* than the proportion who said they had done this in 1993. The proportion contributing money to 'green' causes has also declined from 29 per cent to under a quarter in 2000.

Another expression of personal concern is membership of an environmental group, whether for protection of the countryside or for campaigning for policy changes. Although membership of groups such as the Royal Society for the Protection of Birds and Friends of the Earth is high – and in some cases far higher than membership of the main political parties – just six per cent of our 2000 sample said that they were members, almost exactly the same proportion as in 1993. And the proportion who said they had taken part in a demonstration or protest about an environmental issue in the previous five years was the same – three per cent – in 1993 and 2000. This form of personal action has therefore remained on a plateau for the best part of a decade despite the best efforts of environmental organisations and a steady or growing awareness of ecological problems.

Table 6.11 Environmental activism, 1993 and 2000

% who have ...	1993	2000
	%	%
... signed a petition about an environmental issue	36	30
... given money to an environmental group	29	23
... membership of any group whose main aim is to preserve or protect the environment	6	6
... taken part in a protest or demonstration about an environmental issue	3	3
Base	*1261*	*972*

However, despite this fall in environmental activism over time, people have become *more* and not less likely to incorporate 'green'-friendly behaviour into their own lives. In 2000, half (51 per cent) "always" or "often" made "a special effort to sort glass or tins or plastic or newspapers and so on for recycling", compared with four in ten (42 per cent) seven years earlier. It seems that the initiatives of some local authorities and environmental organisations to promote recycling are paying dividends. However, although recycling is not an activity that brings economic benefit to individuals (and may be felt to be a time-consuming chore), it is not something likely to cause significant disadvantage to households. By contrast, cutting back on car use for environmental reasons could potentially cause significant problems, especially given the increased extent of travel between work and home and the well-publicised problems of the UK's often shambolic and expensive public transport system. It is perhaps therefore not surprising that although there has been an increase in the proportion of people who "always" or "often" cut back on driving a car for environmental reasons over the last seven years, it has only been from a lowly nine per cent in 1993 to a mere 14 per cent in 2000. Of course, this might not reflect entirely 'green' motivation, but rather a mixture of environmental concern and frustration with the mounting congestion in many towns and cities, and also in some rural areas, that we have seen over the past decade.

Why have some forms of environmentally friendly behaviour (notably recycling) increased while environmentally-inspired political action has fallen? One explanation might be that even if many people have been losing confidence in government and business action on the environment, and in their own ability to influence the political process, they nonetheless wish to make some gesture of commitment where it is relatively easy for them to do so. If this is the case, we might expect to see in future an increase in 'private' environmental behaviour and a further decrease in 'public' action.

Some clues can be gleaned by analysing the characteristics of the different sorts of people who engage in particular forms of environmental activity. To do this we focused upon two particular actions: signing an environmental petition (one of the easiest of what we might call 'public' actions) and recycling. This shows that the characteristics of the people who engage in them are quite different. Education appears to be the most important factor in predicting whether a person has signed an environmental petition, with those who have been through further education having three times the odds of signing as those without any qualifications (see model 2 in the appendix to this chapter for full results). Well-educated working women who have strong political identities are the most likely group to have used this form of environmental protest. The finding that people with a strong political party identification are more likely to have engaged in these sorts of environmental actions will be important to track over time because, as Bromley, Curtice and Seyd explore in their chapter in this Report, strength of political identification is declining.

Although different age groups did not differ markedly in the extent to which they had signed a recent petition, there are dramatic age differences in recycling behaviour. But it is not the young who are most likely to engage in this form of environmentally friendly behaviour; rather, the odds of those in their 60s and above are some seven times higher than the odds of 18-24 year olds recycling (see model 3 in the appendix to this chapter for more details). People with high levels of environmental knowledge and those in intermediate or junior non-manual jobs also have higher odds of recycling than others.

The relationship between age and different forms of environmental behaviour is intriguing and warrants further investigation. In particular, we need to assess the extent to which the characteristics of different age groups have changed over time. Much research has, for instance, suggested that political apathy among the young is growing (for example, Park, 1999). Does this suggest that the young now are less likely to engage in political actions than they have been in the past? To assess this we have to examine the views of different *age cohorts* over time. This will allow us to see whether the decline in environmental activism (as measured by petition signing) has had an equal impact on all age groups or has particularly affected the young.

The results of this analysis are shown in the next table. Its most striking finding is the almost complete eradication of any age gradient in behaviour between 1993 and 2000. Thus, in 1993, a half of those aged 18 to 24 had signed a petition. Older groups were less likely to have done so, with their likelihood declining as we move up the age gradient. Among the oldest groups, only around one in five had signed a petition – half the comparable rate among 18-24 year olds. By 2000, however, only around three in ten of the younger groups and two in ten of the older groups had signed petitions, a far shallower gradient.

The table also shows that as our youngest cohort (aged 18 to 24 in 1993 and 25 to 31 in 2000) got older their likelihood of having signed a petition in the last five years fell dramatically (down 19 points), far more so than for any other group. Moreover, 18-24 year olds in 2000 are significantly less likely than 18 to 24 year olds in 1993 to have done this. On this measure at least, apathy towards environmental political protest has increased substantially among the young.

Table 6.12 Per cent who have signed an environmental petition by age cohort, 1993 and 2000

Cohort	Age in 1993	Age in 2000	1993	*Base*	2000	*Base*	Difference
1976-1982		18-24	-	-	31	*77*	n.a.
1969-1975	18-24	25-31	50	*119*	31	*128*	-19
1962-1968	25-31	32-38	40	*196*	32	*157*	-8
1955-1961	32-38	39-45	39	*174*	33	*134*	-6
1948-1954	39-45	46-52	43	*167*	35	*116*	-8
1941-1947	46-52	53-59	37	*139*	36	*83*	-1
1934-1940	53-59	60-66	31	*102*	23	*101*	-8
1927-1933	60-66	67+	24	*105*	21	*175*	-3
1920-1926	67+	-	19	*256*	-	-	n.a.
All			36	*1261*	30	*972*	-6

We turn now to individual actions taken to protect the environment – in this case, recycling. The next table shows an age cohort analysis of frequent recyclers (defined as those who say that they "always" or "often" recycle). This time, the picture is quite different to that found in our previous analysis, with the most striking finding being the persistence of dramatic age differences in behaviour between 1993 and 2000. It is clear that making this sort of individual effort to help protect the environment is not the realm of the young; those aged 60 to 66, for instance, are twice as likely to recycle as those aged 18 to 24.

There are a number of possible explanations for these differences. In particular, there does appear to be some evidence of a lifecycle effect whereby people's interest in recycling increases as they get older. Thus, if we follow the activities of the cohort born between 1955 and 1961 we can see that their propensity to recycle frequently has increased from 39 to 52 per cent in just seven years (against an average increase of nine points). But there is also a clear period effect, whereby all generations have become keener on recycling over time.

Table 6.13 Per cent who recycle "always" or "often" by age cohort, 1993 and 2000

Cohort	Age in 1993	Age in 2000	1993	Base	2000	Base	Difference
1976-1982		18-24	-	-	32	77	n.a.
1969-1975	18-24	25-31	23	119	30	128	+7
1962-1968	25-31	32-38	35	196	44	157	+9
1955-1961	32-38	39-45	39	174	52	134	+13
1948-1954	39-45	46-52	39	167	52	116	+13
1941-1947	46-52	53-59	42	139	63	83	+21
1934-1940	53-59	60-66	59	102	67	101	+8
1927-1933	60-66	67+	54	105	68	175	+14
1920-1926	67+	-	56	256	-	-	n.a.
All			42	1261	51	972	+9

Conclusions

An earlier *British Social Attitudes* report (Witherspoon, 1994) concluded that:

> *We have shown that many environmental beliefs are rather superficial. Environmental concern is far more widespread than either support for environmental policies or environmental activism. The more specific and costly any proposal to improve the environment seems to be, the more rapidly support dissipates.*

This chapter confirms this general picture. The 'greening' of the public has not been eroded in any significant ways, reflecting the persistence of environmental concern among many and commitment to some forms of personal action (recycling, for example, seems to attract significantly more commitment than in 1993). However, public attitudes have not been dramatically transformed since the early 1990s, despite a range of well-publicised environmental concerns. If anything, there is now slightly *more* resistance to the prospect of fiscal measures to reduce environmental damage. Moreover, there has been a slight fall in propensity to engage in public action such as protests or petition-signing, and this is most marked among the young, raising fears about further falls in the future.

What explains the 'plateauing' of environmental attitudes over the past decade? In the introduction we drew attention to the numerous problems of 'agency' that make it hard for individuals to feel they can take meaningful action, and which also inhibit governments from pursuing radical policy measures. This, in turn, leaves many problems to fester or worsen, further damaging public confidence. Our findings suggest that there is a demand for collective action, and a fairly high level of support for strong legislation to improve the environment even at the cost of higher prices and some curbing of personal choice. However, this goes hand in hand with high levels of mistrust of government and business as agents of collective policy. What can break this pattern? It is hard to resist the conclusion that it will take either a dramatic upsurge in political willpower and courage and/or a breakthrough by the environment itself, with severe crises finally forcing a radical change in attitudes on the part of citizens and policy makers. But it seems safe to assume that we shall have to wait for environmental problems to worsen in order to see a major change in the pattern of values and attitudes that have prevailed over the past decade.

Note

1. Factor analysis of responses identified three groups of statements which were not obviously classifiable. The first factor, for instance, merged a number of contradictory viewpoints, with those who agree with anti-environment statements such as "we worry too much about the future of the environment and not enough about prices and jobs today" also agreeing with pro-environment statements including "economic progress in Britain will slow down unless we look after the environment better".

References

Adam, B. (1998), *Timescapes of Modernity: the environment and invisible hazards*, London: Routledge.

Burke, T. (1997), 'The buck stops everywhere', *New Statesman*, 20 June.

Christie, I. and Jarvis, L. (1999), 'Rural spaces and urban jams' in Jowell, R., Curtice, J., Park, A. and Thomson, K. (eds.), *British Social Attitudes: the 16th report - Who shares New Labour values?*, Aldershot: Ashgate.

Clover, C. (1997), 'Environmental Behaviour', *Agenda 1997/98*, Swindon: Economic and Social Research Council.

Dalton, R. and Rohrschneider, R. (1998), 'The Greening of Europe' in Jowell, R., Curtice, J., Park, A., Brook, L., Thomson, K. and Bryson, C. (eds.), *British – and European – Social Attitudes: How Britain Differs – the 15th BSA Report*, Aldershot: Ashgate.

Environment Agency (2001), *Climate Change, Environment Action* supplement, June, Bristol: Environment Agency.

Grove-White, R., Macnaghten, P., Mayer, S. and Wynne, B. (1997), *Uncertain World: Genetically Modified Organisms, Food and Public Attitudes in Britain*, London: CSEC and Unilever.

Grove-White, R., Macnaghten, P. and Wynne, B. (2000), *Wising Up: The public and new technologies*, Lancaster: IEPPP, Lancaster University.

Jacobs, M. (2000), *Environmental Modernisation*, London: Fabian Society.

Johnston, M. and Jowell, R. (1999), 'Social capital and the social fabric' in Jowell, R., Curtice, J., Park, A. and Thomson, K. (eds.), *British Social Attitudes: the 16th report - Who shares New Labour values?*, Aldershot: Ashgate.

Macnaghten, P., Grove-White, R., Jacobs, M. and Wynne, B. (1995), *Public Perceptions and Sustainability in Lancashire*, Preston: Lancashire County Council

Park, A. (1999), 'The generation game' in Jowell, R., Curtice, J., Park, A. and Thomson, K. (eds.), *British Social Attitudes: the 16th report - Who shares New Labour values?*, Aldershot: Ashgate.

Pretty, J. (1998), *The Living Land*, London: Earthscan.

Real World Coalition (2001), *From Here to Sustainability*, London: Earthscan.

Smith, J. (ed.) (2000), *The Daily Globe: environmental change, the public and the media*, London: Earthscan.

Taylor, B. (1997), 'Green in word' in Jowell, R., Curtice, J., Park, A., Brook, L., Thomson, K. and Bryson, C., (eds.), *British Social Attitudes: the 14th Report – The end of Conservative values?*, Aldershot: Dartmouth.

Willis, R. and Rose, B. (2000), *Steps into Uncertainty: handling risk and uncertainty in environmental policy making*, London: ESRC/Green Alliance.

Witherspoon, S. (1994), 'The Greening of Britain: romance and rationality' in Jowell, R., Curtice, J., Brook, L. and Ahrendt, D. (eds.), *British Social Attitudes: the 11th report,* Aldershot: Ashgate.

Worcester, R (2000), 'Public and "expert" opinion on environmental issues' in Smith, J. (ed.), *The Daily Globe: environmental change, the public and the media*, London: Earthscan.

Acknowledgements

The questions in this chapter were asked as part of the *International Social Survey Programme (ISSP)*. We are grateful to the Economic and Social Research Council for funding our participation in the *International Social Survey Programme* and our ISSP colleagues for the advice and work involved in designing this module.

Appendix

Multivariate analysis

Models referred to in the chapter follow. Two multivariate techniques were used: multiple regression (model 1) and logistic regression (models 2 and 3). These are explained in more detail in Appendix I to this Report.

For the multiple regression models, it is the coefficients (or parameter estimates) that are shown. These show whether a particular characteristic differs significantly from its 'comparison group' in its association with the dependent variable. Details of the comparison group are shown in brackets. A positive coefficient indicates that those with the characteristic score more highly on the dependent variable and a negative coefficient means that they are likely to have a lower score. For the logistic regression models, the figures reported are the odds ratios. An odds ratio of less than one means that the group was less likely than average to be in the group of interest on the dependent variable (the variable we are investigating), and an odds ratio greater than one indicates a greater than average likelihood of being in this group. For both methods, those variables which were selected as significant in predicting this are shown in order of the importance of their contribution.

Two asterisks indicate that the coefficient or odds ratio is statistically significant at a 99 per cent level and one asterisk that it is significant at a 95 per cent level.

Regression analyses

The independent variables used in the following regression analyses were:

Age
1. 18-24
2. 25-31
3. 32-38
4. 39-45
5. 46-52
6. 53-59
7. 60-66
8. 67+

Sex
1. Men
2. Women

Environmental knowledge
Number of statements correct

Highest educational qualification
1. Degree or other higher education
2. 'A' level
3. 'GCSE' level
4. No qualifications

Household income
1. Lowest quartile
2. Second quartile
3. Third quartile
4. Fourth quartile
5. Unknown

Economic activity
1. Paid work
2. Economically inactive
3. Retired

Socio-economic group
1. Professional/employer
2. Intermediate non-manual
3. Junior non-manual
4. Supervisor/skilled manual
5. Semi/unskilled

Religion
1. Church of England
2. Catholic
3. Other Christian or non-Christian
4. No religion

Political identity
1. Strong political identity
2. Some political identity
3. Not very strong political identity
4. None/not disclosed

Children under 16 living in household
1. No children.
2. Children

Model 1: Correlates of holding a cynical view of environmental dangers

Multiple regression
Dependent variable: cynicism about environmental dangers
Independent variables: *Age, sex, environmental knowledge, highest educational qualification, household income, socio-economic group, religion, economic activity, whether have children, strength of political identity.*

Individual characteristics (comparison group in brackets)	Standardised Beta coefficient
No. of environmental knowledge statements correct	.186 **
Sex (Men)	
Women	.139 **
Economic activity (retired)	
Work	.115 **
Inactive	.084 *
Socio-economic group (semi/unskilled)	
Professional/employer	.003
Intermediate non-manual	.108 **
Junior non-manual	.023
Supervisor/skilled manual	-.010
Income (lowest quartile)	
2nd quartile	-.004
3rd quartile	.084 *
Highest quartile	.016
Income unknown	-.039
Religion (no religion)	
Church of England	.018
Catholic	.043
Other religion	.076 *
Age (67+)	
18-24	-.006
25-31	.000
32-38	-.011
39-45	.051
46-52	-.001
53-59	.032
60-66	.069 *

Model 2: Predictors of signing a petition about an environmental issue in the last five years

Logistic regression with dependent variable: Signing an environmental petition in the last five years

Independent variables: *Age, sex, environmental knowledge, highest educational qualification, household income, socio-economic group, religion, economic activity, whether have children, strength of political identity.*

Category	B	S.E.	Wald	Odds ratio (Exp(B))	Sig
Baseline odds	-.805	.124	41.587	.447	**
Highest qualification			36.708		**
Higher education inc. degree	.506	.130	15.113	1.658	**
'A' level or equivalent	.042	.182	.053	1.043	
'GCSE' level or equivalent	.186	.133	1.963	1.205	
Lower than 'GCSE'-level	-.734	.140	27.506	.480	**
Political identity			21.988		**
Strong	.855	.244	12.297	2.352	**
Some	.143	.144	.983	1.153	
Not very strong	-.019	.134	.020	.981	
None/not disclosed	-.979	.220	19.784	.376	**
Men	-.201	.080	6.412	.818	*
Women	.201	.080	6.412	1.223	*
Economic activity			6.474		*
Work	.099	.115	.741	1.104	
Inactive	.283	.133	4.525	1.328	*
Retired	-.382	.154	6.137	.682	*

Number of cases in model: 841.

Model 3: Predictors of recycling

Logistic regression with dependent variable: Making a special effort always or often to sort glass, tins, plastic or newspapers, etc. for recycling

Independent variables: *Age, sex, environmental knowledge, highest educational qualification, household income, socio-economic group, religion, economic activity, whether have children, strength of political identity.*

Category	B	S.E.	Wald	Odds ratio (Exp(B))	Sig
Baseline odds	-.574	.253	5.149	.563	*
Age			71.587		**
18-24	-.874	.237	13.631	.417	**
25-31	-1.020	.198	26.621	.361	**
32-38	-.317	.174	3.311	.728	
39-45	-.086	.182	.225	.918	
46-52	-.166	.183	.827	.847	
53-59	.529	.240	4.861	1.697	*
60-66	.860	.240	12.886	2.364	**
67+					
No. of environmental knowledge statements correct	.230	.064	12.944	1.259	**
Socio-economic group			11.988		*
Professional/employer	-.089	.144	.386	.915	
Intermediate non-manual	.505	.175	8.335	1.657	**
Junior non-manual	.116	.156	.555	1.123	
Supervisor/skilled manual	-.369	.160	5.317	.691	*
Semi-skilled/unskilled	-.162	.144	1.274	.850	

Number of cases in model: 805.

7 Internet use: the digital divide

*Jonathan Gardner and Andrew Oswald**

The internet is changing the world. Each day, more of us are using, and learning from, the giant global library that is the world-wide web. But not everyone in Britain is able or willing to access the internet. This risks creating a new 'digital divide'.

It has been estimated that world-wide use of the internet jumped from 3 million people in 1994 to 377 million in 2000 (Norris, 2001), with predictions that the internet's market penetration will grow from one per cent to 75 per cent in the United States in just seven years – a position which it took the telephone 75 years to achieve (Putnam, 2001). But behind these figures lies a global disparity between those who do, and those who do not, have access to the internet: twice as many people in Sweden log onto the internet as in the whole of sub-Saharan Africa (Norris, 2001). The global gulf between affluent industrialised societies and poorer developing ones demonstrates the relationship between resources and access to technology, but is there a similar digital divide *within* countries that already have highly developed technological infrastructures? Does access to capital, be it financial or intellectual, also determine whether you have access to the internet in Britain?

The impact of the internet on British life is already clear. The number of major corporations and organisations in both the public and private sectors who do *not* have a website could likely be counted on one hand. Many television programmes, and even the commercials between them, sport website addresses, while most national newspapers have launched electronic editions. The Government has set up UKOnline.gov.uk, a website that offers a gateway to government services and information, and has appointed an 'e-Envoy' within the Cabinet Office to oversee and promote the government's digital agenda. Targets have been set to make the UK the best environment in the world for e-commerce by 2002, to ensure that everyone who wants it has access to the

* Jonathan Gardner is a Research Fellow in the Department of Economics at the University of Warwick. Andrew Oswald is Professor of Economics at the University of Warwick.

internet by 2005, and, to make all Government services available electronically by 2005 (Office of the e-Envoy, 2001).

This explosion in references to websites has lead to the common misconception that access to the internet is already near universal. *Coronation Street* – Britain's most popular soap opera – recently provided details of a website address rather than a dedicated telephone helpline when it ran a sensitive story line – and was roundly censured by the Independent Television Commission for doing so.

Does it matter if there is a digital divide? Debate surrounds the potential of the internet to change the way in which humans interact with others, carry out their business transactions and engage and participate in public life. Whether access to the internet at home will ever become as widespread as, say, television or the telephone is open to debate. Some projections suggest that short-term gaps between users and non-users will in time diminish as it becomes a near universal and much needed commodity. A more pessimistic outlook would counter that the internet will simply mirror (and even exaggerate) existing inequalities in access to information and other resources. And therein lies its danger.

This chapter will first build a profile of the typical British internet user in the year 2000 to address the question of whether it is, or is not, appropriate to talk of a 'digital divide' in internet access. We follow this with a more detailed look at internet use more generally. On the one hand, concerns have been voiced about the solitary and socially isolating nature of internet use. Internet 'chat rooms' where groups of individuals can contribute to debates, usually confined to singular topics, facilitate communication between people – but it is a particular kind of communication that often will not result in physical encounters. On the other hand, the internet's ability to bring people together can, it is argued, have the positive impact of strengthening pre-existing social networks. Robert Putnam's influential work on social capital, such as *Bowling Alone* (2001), which argues that the social and community-based interactions between people have positive benefits not only for the individual but also for society at large, seems to deliver an open verdict on the internet's ability to complement or diminish social capital. Our broad aim in the final part of this chapter will therefore be to ask whether the internet is, in the spirit of Putnam's work (Putnam, 1995, 2001, Putnam *et al.*, 1993), a friend or enemy of 'social capital'.

A digital divide?

In the 2000 *British Social Attitudes* survey, we asked respondents whether they themselves "ever use the internet or world-wide web for any reason". For those in work, the question added the tag "other than your work". And for those who said yes, we asked how many hours a week on average they spend using the internet or world-wide web, again other than for their work. The questions were thus designed to measure *personal* internet use, although this could, of course, take place at home, at work, in the library, at an internet café, or anywhere else where there are internet connections.

One-third of British people (33 per cent) report that they use the internet other than for their work, spending an average of three hours per week on it.[1] But this, of course, means that two-thirds do not use it. We turn now to the sources of this digital divide.

Money talks?

As the next table shows, money talks in the digital world. Few poor Britons log on – among those in households earning less than £12,000 per year, little more than one in ten people use the internet. The rich are different: almost two-thirds do so. However, the amount of time that those who have access spend on it does not vary significantly by income, being around 3 hours per week for all groups.

Table 7.1 Internet use, by household income

Household income	% who use the internet	Base
Less than £6,000	14	373
£6,000-11,999	9	427
£12,000-19,999	26	373
£20,000-31,999	43	397
£32,000 or more	61	427

It seems straightforward why money should make a difference. Despite some people being able to use work computers for their own personal needs and the provision of computers in libraries, a home computer remains the most convenient way to gain access to the internet. And buying a computer would be a struggle for those on low incomes. (At the time of writing the computer and auxiliaries costs at least £500). A government initiative to provide households in poorer areas with reconditioned machines is still in its pilot phase. Yet money is not the only thing that matters. Education also has a marked effect – over and above what a person earns.

One of the best single predictors of internet use is having a university degree, as seen in the next table. Almost three-quarters of university graduates log on. At the other extreme, less than one in ten of those with no formal qualifications (who after all make up just under one-third of the population) use the internet.

Table 7.2 Internet use, by highest educational qualification

Highest educational qualification	% who use the internet	Base
Degree	72	300
Higher education	46	328
A level	49	234
O level	30	439
CSE or equivalent	21	303
No qualifications	9	740

Of course, tables 7.1 and 7.2 might be simply telling the same story: those with higher income tend are also more likely to have higher qualifications. But the next table demonstrates that income and education, although interrelated, have separate effects. If you earn less than £15,000 per year, you are five times more likely to use the internet if you have a degree than if you have no qualifications. But you are more than twice as likely again to use it if you have a degree *and* earn over £15,000.

Table 7.3 Internet access, by educational qualification and household income

% who use the internet	Highest educational qualification		
Household income	Degree/HE	Intermediate	No qualifications
£14,999 or under	29	18	6
Base	104	366	475
£15,000 or more	65	41	19
Base	464	466	151

We can take this analysis further by using multivariate techniques which allow us to take a number of different factors into account at the same time. The full details are shown in the appendix to this chapter (see models A and B). We find that income and education retain their separate importance for internet access when other related factors such as age are taken into account, with education perhaps having the slightly stronger effect. Over and above income and education, employers and managers are also more likely to have access to the internet than junior non-manual and manual workers.

In line with the earlier finding, income is not related to the number of hours spent on the internet. Education, however, is. Those with the highest educational qualifications spend the longest on the internet (outside their job), once age and other factors have been taken into account.

Young men glued to their computers?

The common stereotype of an internet user is often a young man, locked away in his bedroom, preferring the internet chat room to real people. It is clear from the data that men are bigger users of the world-wide web: two-fifths of men use it compared with less than a third of women. The men who use it also spend an average of 3.5 hours a week logged on – a full hour more than women. These sex differences remain when other factors (such as income and education) are taken into account (see models A and B in the appendix to this chapter).

Table 7.4 Internet use, by sex

	% who use the internet	Base
Men	40	981
Women	28	1312

Again, the stereotype of the young as the internet users has some validity. As seen in the next table, almost three in five of the 18 to 24 age group use the internet compared with less than one in 20 of the over 65s (despite the alternative stereotype of the e-granny in the library). Among those who do use the internet, the very youngest also spend more time logged on – an average of 4.1 hours, which is twice as long on average as pensioners do. The digital divide between pensioners and the rest is, in fact, a gulf. These differences persist even when other factors are taken into account (see models A and B in the appendix to this chapter).

Table 7.5 Internet use, by age

Age	% who use the internet	Base
18-24	58	176
25-34	51	410
35-44	40	465
45-54	36	339
55-59	23	161
60-64	19	198
65+	5	538

A north/south divide?

Web use is not spread evenly across the country. In London and the South East, around two-fifths of the population have access to the internet, but this falls to less than one-fifth in the north of England. In part, this is, of course, to do with the income and education effects we saw earlier, but the pattern persists even when these are taken into account (see models A and B in the appendix to this chapter), and people in Scotland and the north of England remain significantly less likely to have access to the internet than, for example, those in the South East. Regional variations in internet use were, in fact, highlighted as a matter of concern in the July 2000 monthly joint report from the Government's e-Envoy and e-Minister to the Prime Minister (Hewitt and Pinder, 2000).

Table 7.6 Internet use, by region

Region	% who use the internet	Base
Greater London	42	221
South East (excluding London)	40	427
North West	36	231
South West	35	198
Scotland	30	220
East Midlands	31	199
East Anglia	30	100
Wales	30	145
Yorkshire and Humberside	29	233
West Midlands	27	175
Northern	18	144

In-work and on-line?

Some politicians appear to believe that there might be a connection between job-hunting and web access. This has in part motivated initiatives where poorer households are being given computers. However, as the next table shows the digital divide is, if anything, smaller on this front than on others. True, those in full-time education are by far and away the biggest users of the internet and those who are not in the labour force at all (dominated by the retired) are much less likely to use it. But the difference between the third of the unemployed who use the internet and the just over two-fifths of the employed who do so hardly amounts to a gulf. A further multivariate analysis (not reported in detail in this chapter) found that this difference between the unemployed and those in work is fully accounted for by their difference in educational qualifications and income. Even if we look for a relationship with past experiences of unemployment (having been out of work at least once in the previous five years), there is no reliable pattern. Nor is there any clear difference between the self-employed and employees; 43 and 44 per cent respectively use the internet.

Table 7.7 Internet use, by labour force status

Labour force status	% who use the internet	Base
Education	80	52
Employed	44	1172
Unemployed	31	95
Out of the labour force	13	958

The haves and the have-nots

There is no doubt that there is a digital divide in Britain. On one level the reasons for this are obvious (and arguably remediable): you need money and you need skills to use the internet. The stereotype of internet users being young and male has some validity. Variations between regions appear to exist independently of education and income levels. Custom, habit and confidence with new technology probably provide the explanation why older people are less likely to use the internet. But – looking to the future – the fact that the young are so much more likely to use the internet suggests that the situation will change over time. It is, of course, possible that the young of today will stop using the internet as they grow older. But it is much more likely that, as computers fall in price and those who have grown up with the internet replace older generations, the new technology becomes the norm. This is a slow process, however. In the meanwhile, it would be unwise to assume that shopping, or voting, or even survey research on the web, will reach its full potential until it can reach a larger proportion of the population.

Social capital, citizens and internet use

As we have seen, the stereotypical picture of a young male internet user has some truth to it. But the stereotype often goes further than that to picture a young male loner, cooped up with his computer, preferring internet chat rooms to real people. If that is true, it may have wider implications. A commonly discussed idea is that computers and the internet may be creating a world of worse citizens and worse societies – of humans who are more interested in themselves and their screens than in taking part in group activities.

The decline of social capital in the United States, as charted in Robert Putnam's *Bowling Alone* (2001) and discussed in the chapter by Johnston and Jowell in this volume, is linked to numerous factors, not least the rise of television. In fact, Putnam asserts that no other factor can explain declining civic engagement better than people's increasing reliance on television as their sole form of entertainment. Its private and individualised nature, the relative lack of skill or effort required to watch it, and even the very nature of what people watch, are all indicted. It is no surprise then that questions are being raised about whether the internet could exert these same negative forces. Can our data shed any light on whether social relations, and as a result social capital, are under threat from the world-wide web?

A key determinant of social capital is thought to be trust in other people. But we find that internet users are actually *more* trusting than non-users, implying that they have *more* social capital. Half of our internet users (52 per cent) say that, generally speaking, "most people can be trusted" (rather than "you can't be too careful in dealing with people"). The figure for those who do not use the internet is two-fifths (42 per cent). However, once other factors like age and education are taken into account in a multivariate analysis, there is in fact no difference between internet and non-internet users (see model C in the appendix to this chapter). At any rate, the internet does not seem to have caused its users to become *less* trusting of other people.

As discussed in more detail in the chapter by Johnston and Jowell, membership of social and voluntary organisations are viewed by Robert Putnam as key generators of social capital. Again, those who log onto the internet are, in fact, *more* likely to be members of voluntary organisations than those who do not. Nearly a third (30 per cent) of internet users say they are members of a local community group, whereas just a quarter (23 per cent) of non-users are. This relationship persists also when other factors are taken into account (see model D in the appendix to this chapter). Indeed, given the use that such organisations often make of the internet to advertise their activities, membership may well be driving internet use.

Table 7.8 Internet use, by church attendance

	Internet users	Non-internet users
Frequency of church attendance	%	%
Weekly	11	12
At least once a fortnight	3	2
At least monthly	8	6
Twice a year or less	21	18
Never/No religion	56	61
Base	*684*	*1595*

It is known that in Britain there is a continuing and strong secular decline in church attendance (see, for example, De Graaf and Need, 2000). But it does not appear that the internet is a rival to organised religion. In fact, it appears to be complementary to churchgoing. As the previous table shows, a larger proportion of internet users go to church than non-users, even though internet users tend to be young and churchgoing is greater among the old. Again, this relationship persists when other factors are taken into account (see model E of the appendix to this chapter). To the best of our knowledge, this is the first time that a relationship has been shown to exist between internet use and churchgoing in Britain.

Some commentators worry that computers drive out people's human contact. We can explore this by looking at who people said they would turn to for support if they were feeling a bit down or depressed and wanted to talk to someone about it – a friend, a relative, someone else, or no one.

Contrary to the picture of the internet user as a loner, they are no more likely to say they have no one to turn to than non-users – 7 per cent of internet users say this, compared with 8 per cent of non-internet users. In fact, internet users rely more on friends and less on relatives than non-users, but this may be partly because of their age profile. In further multivariate analysis (not reported in this chapter) we found that this picture persisted once other factors were taken into account. Hence, far from being an isolating force, the evidence suggests that internet use complements – as opposed to displaces – wider social activities and friendships.

Perhaps time spent on the internet is simply replacing time previously spent on other solitary activities such as television watching or reading? We do find some evidence of this. The third of the British population who log onto the web watch less television. Per day, internet users watch an average of 2.4 hours compared to 3.5 hours for non-users. Interestingly, users and non-users of the internet have identical patterns when it comes to reading – both groups read for an average of 3.9 hours per week. Once we take other factors (such as age, education and income) into account, we confirm the finding that internet users watch less television and we find that they actually read *more* books (see models F and G in the appendix to this chapter).

Since people who use the internet engage in above-average levels of civic activity, it would certainly be wrong to view internet users as anti-social loners. Putnam acknowledges that the internet cannot be held responsible for the start of the decline in social capital: "By the time that the internet reached ten per cent of American adults in 1996, the nationwide decline in social connectedness and civic engagement had been under way for at least a quarter of a century" (Putnam, 2001: 170). Our findings suggest that the internet is not contributing to its continuing decline either.

Conclusions

One-third of British people use the internet other than for their work. But there is a wide digital divide between the haves and the have-nots. We find that internet users are younger, more highly educated, and richer than non-users.

If you have a university degree, you are eight times more likely to use the internet than somebody without any educational qualifications. If you earn £32,000 pounds a year or more, you are five times more likely to log on than someone on £10,000 pounds a year. Men use the world-wide web more than women; there is a 'gender' digital divide. Age has an enormous effect. Among people aged 65 or over, only one in twenty ever use the internet. Among adults who are under 25, well over half do. There are also regional differences in web use. The north of England has the lowest internet access while the South East and London come at the top. But holding other influences constant, there is no detectable digital divide between people with jobs and the unemployed. All in all, although internet use may well be set to rise, it is far from universal.

We also find something surprising. Contrary to what many believe, internet users are much more likely to take part in social activity and be good citizens. They attend church more, join voluntary organisations more, are more likely to have friends whom they can rely on in times of trouble, read more books, are not less trusting of other people, and watch fewer hours of television. The image of the world-wide web user as an anti-social loner is simply wrong: internet use and 'social capital' seem to be complementary.

Note

1. Our figures provide a slight update on those in Office of National Statistics (2000).

References

De Graaf, N. D. and Need, A. (2000), 'Losing faith: Is Britain alone?' in Jowell, R., Curtice, J., Park, A., Thomson, K., Jarvis, L., Bromley, C. and Stratford, N. (eds.), *British Social Attitudes: the 17th Report – Focusing on Diversity*, London: Sage.

Hewitt, P, and Pinder, A. (2000), *Office of the e-Envoy Monthly Reports, July 2000*, http://www.e-envoy.gov.uk/publications/reports/pmreports/rep31jul.htm.

Norris, P. (2001), *Digital Divide?*, Cambridge: Cambridge University Press.

Office of the e-Envoy (2001), http://www.e-envoy.gov.uk/aboutus.htm

Office of National Statistics (2000), *Internet Access*, London: ONS.

Putnam, R. D. (1995), 'Tuning in, tuning out: The strange disappearance of social capital in America', *Political Science and Politics*, **28**: 231-248.

Putnam, R. D. (2001), *Bowling Alone – the collapse and revival of American community*, New York: Simon & Schuster.

Putnam, R. D., Leonardi, R. and Nanetti, R. Y. (1993), *Making Democracy Work: Civic Traditions in Modern Italy*, Princeton, NJ: Princeton University Press.

Acknowledgements

The authors would like to thank Bob Putnam and Pippa Norris for their helpful comments on earlier drafts of this chapter.

Appendix

The regression tables in this appendix show coefficients and their significance. Positive coefficients indicate a positive correlation with the dependent variable. Negative coefficients indicate a negative correlation with the dependent variable. Internet use refers to personal internet use throughout.

Significance is shown as follows:
**   Significant at the 1 per cent level
*   Significant at the 5 per cent level

The following independent variables are used in some or all of the regressions:

Variable		Categories
Household income		Less than £6,000
		£6,000-£11,999
		£12,000-19,999
		£20,000-31,999
	reference:	£32,000+
Educational qualification		Degree
		Higher education below degree
		A level
		O level
		CSE
		Foreign
	reference:	No qualifications
Labour force status		In full-time education
		Unemployed
		Out of the labour force
	reference:	In employment
Socio-economic group		Professional
		Employers/managers
		Intermediate non-manual
		Skilled manual
		Semi-skilled manual
		Unskilled manual
	reference:	Junior non-manual
Age		18-24
		25-34
		45-54
		55-59
		60-64
		65+
	reference:	35-44
Sex		Male
	reference:	Female

Independent variables continued

Ethnic origin		Non-white
	reference:	White
Housing tenure		Social renter
		Private renter
	reference:	Owner-occupier
Region		Scotland
		Northern
		North West
		Yorkshire and Humberside
		West Midlands
		East Midlands
		East Anglia
		South West
		Greater London
		Wales
	reference:	South East (excluding London)
Household size		continuous
Internet access		Yes
	reference:	No

Internet access and hours per week by a range of independent variables
(model A: Logit; model B: Ordinary Least Squares)

	Model A Yes / no	Model B Hours per week
Less than £6,000	-0.82 **	-0.32
£6,000-11,999	-1.25 **	-0.43
£12,000-19,999	-0.60 **	-0.34
£20,000-31,999	-0.32	-0.05
Degree	1.80 **	1.09 **
Higher education	1.09 **	0.71 *
A level	0.92 **	0.31
O level	0.45 *	-0.04
CSE	0.25	-0.23
Foreign qualification	-0.49	-0.65 **
Professional	0.53	-0.48
Employers/managers	0.45 *	-0.35
Intermediate non-manual	0.14	-0.61 *
Skilled manual	-0.31	-0.44
Semi-skilled manual	-0.39	-0.59 **
Unskilled manual	-0.47	-0.75 **
Age: 18-24	0.81 **	0.89 **
Age: 25-34	0.42 *	0.43
Age: 45-54	-0.10	-0.33
Age: 55-59	-0.63 *	-0.76 **
Age: 60-64	-0.89 **	-0.76 **
Age: 65+	-2.00 **	-0.79 **
Male	0.51 **	0.63 **
Non-white	-0.05	0.03
Social renter	-0.37	-0.03
Private renter	0.39	0.04
Scotland	-0.53 *	-0.31
Northern	-0.97 **	-0.19
North West	-0.12	-0.10
Yorks and Humberside	-0.29	-0.12
West Midlands	-0.44	-0.47 *
East Midlands	-0.29	-0.28
East Anglia	-0.05	0.01
South West	-0.11	-0.03
Greater London	-0.09	-0.13
Wales	-0.28	-0.17
Household size	0.01	-0.04
Adjusted R^2		0.10
Base	*2220*	*2216*

Attitudes to social trust, membership of voluntary organisations and church attendance by internet access with control variables
(models C and D: Logit; model E: Ordered Logit)

	Model C Social trust	Model D Membership	Model E Church attend
Internet access	0.03	0.51 **	0.45 **
Less than £6,000	-0.64 **	-0.52	0.37
£6,000-11,999	-0.35	-0.34	0.01
£12,000-19,999	-0.24	-0.24	0.17
£20,000-31,999	-0.12	-0.18	0.34 *
Degree	1.11 **	1.13 **	1.04 **
Higher education	0.83 **	0.72 **	0.55 **
A level	0.69 **	0.94 **	0.75 **
O level	0.37 *	0.70 **	0.41 **
CSE	0.07	0.11	-0.12
Foreign	0.47	1.11 **	1.60 **
Education	0.56	0.48	0.32
Unemployed	0.09	-0.39	-0.09
Out of the labour force	0.15	0.54 **	0.42 **
Age: 18-24	-0.62 **	-1.11 **	-0.93 **
Age: 25-34	-0.19	-0.30	-0.54 **
Age: 45-54	0.07	0.76 **	0.50 **
Age: 55-59	0.26	1.22 **	0.84 **
Age: 60-64	0.31	0.83 **	0.82 **
Age: 65+	0.35	0.99 **	0.97 **
Male	0.39 **	-0.18	-0.70 **
Non-white	-0.61 **	-0.49	1.54 **
Social renter	-0.38 **	-0.44 *	-0.13
Private renter	0.13	-0.58 *	-0.10
Scotland	0.43 *	-0.65 **	0.62 **
Northern	-0.13	-0.45	-0.24
North West	-0.26	0.30	0.52 **
Yorks and Humberside	-0.28	-0.15	0.28
West Midlands	-0.24	0.09	0.37 *
East Midlands	-0.34	0.11	0.27
East Anglia	0.05	-0.12	-0.02
South West	-0.04	-0.42	0.03
Greater London	-0.16	0.61 **	0.42 *
Wales	-0.14	-0.63 *	0.34
Household size	-0.00	0.10	0.18 **
Base	*2258*	*2276*	*2259*

Time spent watching TV and time spent reading books by internet access with control variables
(Ordinary Least Square regressions)

	Model F TV hours	Model G Book hours
Internet access	-0.25 *	0.86 **
Less than £6,000	0.66 *	0.21
£6,000-11,999	0.62 **	-0.04
£12,000-19,999	0.15	0.28
£20,000-31,999	0.24	0.12
Degree	-1.12 **	0.88
Higher education	-0.68 **	0.29
A level	-0.57 **	0.79
O level	-0.38 *	0.38
CSE	-0.21	0.43
Foreign	-0.70 *	2.54
Education	-0.35	0.86
Unemployed	1.30 **	-0.20
Out of the labour force	0.63 **	0.69
Age: 18-24	0.38	-0.66
Age: 25-34	-0.01	0.25
Age: 45-54	-0.13	0.51
Age: 55-59	-0.15	0.94
Age: 60-64	0.08	1.90 **
Age: 65+	0.47	1.89 **
Male	-0.02	-1.42 **
Non-white	0.23	-0.36
Social renter	0.17	-0.02
Private renter	0.04	0.49
Scotland	0.29	0.80
Northern	0.31	-0.19
North West	0.07	-0.30
Yorks and Humberside	0.18	0.42
West Midlands	0.02	0.40
East Midlands	0.17	-0.11
East Anglia	-0.24	-0.89
South West	0.14	-0.44
Greater London	0.01	0.13
Wales	0.16	0.75
Household size	0.06	-0.27 *
Adjusted R^2	0.16	0.04
Base	*2274*	*2277*

8 How robust is British civil society?

Michael Johnston and Roger Jowell [*]

In less than a decade the reported decline of 'social capital' has become a popular concern among academics, politicians and social commentators. Broadly defined as "connections among individuals – social networks and the norms of reciprocity and trustworthiness that arise from them" (Putnam, 2000: 19), its decline is often thought to be responsible for a damaging loss in social cohesion and mutual support. In fact, the term 'social capital' is not new; it has existed for a hundred years or so (Putnam, 2000), and the underlying idea – that in any society those who possess or develop close voluntary networks and have frequent interaction with their fellow citizens tend to lead more fulfilling lives and accomplish more – dates back at least to the early 19th century.[1]

Two years ago, we showed that people with stronger links to voluntary organisations tended to be more trusting of others, less estranged from government, more willing to fight perceived injustice and more likely to help their fellow citizens – an impressive array of benefits for British civil society (Johnston and Jowell, 1999). In *Bowling Alone,* Putnam's celebrated treatment of social capital in the United States, even more impressive claims are made. Areas characterised by high social capital are ones where children tend to be healthier and better educated, crime rates are lower, people are "less pugnacious", individuals and families are more affluent, and people generally live healthier, happier lives (Putnam, 2000).

Putnam's study of the United States presents a persuasive picture of declining participation in organisations ranging from bridge clubs and civic groups to professional associations, charities, lodge groups, and even the venerable Parent-Teacher Associations (PTAs). He finds that social trust – the perception that "most people can be trusted" – is both a correlate and a cause of extensive social involvement (Putnam, 2000; Johnston and Jowell, 1999). But he also shows that social trust in the US peaked in the 1960s and has been in decline ever since. Set against this, however, is the fact that small organisations are mushrooming, the Internet is connecting people in new (if disembodied) ways

[*] Michael Johnston is Professor of Political Science at Colgate University, New York. Roger Jowell is the International Director of the *National Centre for Social Research* and a Visiting Professor at City University and the London School of Economics.

and religion continues to be almost as strong a force in US civil society as it always has been.[2]

The erosion of social capital, social trust and civic engagement in the US is attributed to factors as disparate as excessive television-watching, the effects of suburbanisation and a concentration on work and career-building as opposed to leisure (Putnam, 2000). The consequences of these trends are also wide-ranging, including declining political participation, the growing estrangement of people and households from one another, and a gap in community resources.

Most of the research and commentary on social capital has focused disproportionately on the US (Della Porta, 2000). But we are now seeing a broader debate over what some see as a democratic malaise in other advanced democracies. Certainly, many of the correlates of declining social capital identified in the US are present in Britain as well. For instance, turnout in the 2001 British general election was the lowest this century, ethnic and racial tensions are re-surfacing in some cities, crime remains a major problem and many people possess a strong if diffuse sense that civility and social cohesion are in decline.

So one of our major questions in this chapter is whether the gloomy picture painted by Putnam of the US is replicated in Britain. Is there any evidence of a downward trend in organisational participation, for example, or in people's expressed willingness to help, and to seek help from, others? And what does this tell us about social trust in Britain? Have its levels fallen, as they have in the US? And are there any similarities between Britain and the US in the various 'culprits' that Putnam identifies as underlying a decline in social capital?

We also consider the possibility that social capital might have less desirable elements. In particular, as our data in *The 16th Report* suggest, its unequal distribution is a worry. While social capital, like financial capital, certainly has tangible benefits, certain groups are much more likely than others to possess it. Moreover, social capital comes in several forms. Only one sort – what Putnam calls 'bridging social capital' – tends to bring disparate groups together. In contrast, 'bonding social capital' tends to accumulate in more tightly-knit groups, sometimes with the effect of helping others but at other times excluding them (Putnam, 2000). So we need to assess the extent to which social capital can unite or exclude.

In looking at these complex interactions, we have to be very circumspect. After all, causal connections are never certain. It is perfectly plausible that the claimed benefits of engagement with one's fellow citizens, experienced in ways that are as dense and convoluted as the social networks themselves, are attributable to other causes. For instance, people who are more confident of their own abilities to affect the world around them and more willing to help their neighbours may well be just those who are most likely to join or form organisations in the first place. And communities with extensive social capital may well be happier and better off economically to start with; perhaps this is a cause rather than a consequence of their stocks of social capital. Moreover, aggregate statistics on social participation and public opinion may not necessarily reflect changes in individual behaviour or attitudes over time. They may instead be caused by the slow replacement of one generation by another which possesses different attributes and priorities.

Trends in organisational involvement

Social capital comes in many forms, but one of its most important dimensions is the membership of organisations – whether they be 'civic' groups designed to fulfil a public purpose, or social associations whose purpose is just to pursue a particular leisure interest or activity. Thriving organisations are by no means the only vital signs of a healthy civil society (Cohen, 1999), but they do provide the opportunity for fellowship and the formation of reciprocal relationships – a form of 'capital' that can subsequently be drawn upon. There may sometimes be other incentives too, such as group discounts, awards and recognition, or simply 'exclusivity' (Wilson, 1973). Moreover, organisations often give their members administrative and social skills, expand their network of acquaintances and help to build up a system of shared norms and mutual trust.

As we see in the following table, British organisational membership over the 1990s has been relatively stable. In fact, overall participation increased from around one in six to around one in four of the population between 1994 and 1998 and has since settled at that higher level. So, as we noted in *The 16th Report*, although much smaller proportions of the British than of the American population are members of such organisations, their numbers do not seem to be in decline here.

Table 8.1 Membership of community organisations

	1994	1998	2000
	%	%	%
Neighbourhood Watch scheme	13	14	11
Any other local community or voluntary group	7	6	6
Tenants' or residents' association	4	5	5
Political party	3	3	3
Parent-Teacher Association	3	3	2
Local conservation or environmental group	2	2	2
Voluntary group helping sick, elderly, or children	n.a.	2	2
Board of school governors	1	1	1
Neighbourhood council	1	1	1
Parish or town council	1	1	1
	%	%	%
Any one of these groups	17	26	25
None of these groups	83	74	75
Base	*2302*	*3144*	*2293*

A similarly stable pattern exists in relation to membership of sporting and cultural groups. Nearly one in five (18 per cent) belong to some form of sports club, five per cent to a cultural group and two per cent to both a sports club and a cultural group – very similar proportions to those we found in 1998.

Membership of 'green' or 'countryside' organisations also seems to have held its own since 1998. Apart from a few fluctuations, the picture looks stable – with almost one in five adults subscribing to one of these organisations.

Table 8.2 Membership of 'green' or, countryside, organisations

	1998	2000
	%	%
National Trust	9	9
Royal Society for the Protection of Birds	5	4
Other countryside sport or recreation group	2	3
World Wildlife Fund	4	2
Other wildlife or countryside protection group	2	2
Ramblers' Association	1	1
Urban conservation group	1	*
Campaign for Nuclear Disarmament	1	*
Friends of the Earth	1	1
Greenpeace	1	1
Council for Protection of Rural England/Scotland/Wales	*	*
None of these	80	83
Base	*1075*	*2293*

The next table shows *aggregate* memberships of environmental groups, as reported in *Social Trends 31* (Office for National Statistics, 2001), allowing us to trace trends in membership over a longer time period. This shows that almost all environmental groups have actually experienced impressive growth over the last three decades, with the notable exception of Greenpeace in the last ten years or so.[3]

To be sure, for some people 'membership' of these groups may well be rather passive, consisting perhaps of paying dues, receiving literature and enjoying selective discounts (rather than attending meetings and helping organise group events or projects). But for many others it is more active, and for some it may well involve a great deal of interaction with like-minded people, amassing large volumes of social capital in the process. Much of the growth in Britain in membership of green groups reflects the growth of the environmental agenda itself, but by the same token that agenda might not have become so prominent without the participation of these broad-based voluntary organisations. In contrast, membership of national environmental groups in the US grew rapidly through the 1980s and then levelled off during the 1990s. By 1998, membership was back down to about its 1990 level (Putnam, 2000).

Table 8.3 Aggregate trends in 'green' affiliations

	Membership figures (thousands)				
	1971	1981	1991	1997	1999
National Trust[1]	278	1,046	2,152	2,489	2,643
Royal Society for the Protection of Birds	98	441	852	1,007	1,004
Civic Trust	214	n.a.	222	330	n.a.
Wildlife Trusts[2]	64	142	233	310	325
Worldwide Fund for Nature	12	60	227	241	255
National Trust for Scotland	37	105	234	228	236
Woodland Trust	n.a.	20	150	195	200
Greenpeace	n.a.	30	312	215	176
Ramblers' Association	22	37	87	123	129
Friends of the Earth[1]	1	18	111	114	112
Council for the Protection of Rural England	21	29	45	45	49

[1] England, Wales, and Northern Ireland only.
[2] Includes The Royal Society for Nature Conservation.
Sources: Organisations concerned, as reported in *Social Trends* **31** (Office for National Statistics, 2001), Table 11.2, p. 194.

Religious affiliation – whether expressed through identification with a particular religious group or by more active attendance at services and related activities – is also a potentially rich source of social capital. However, the proportion in Britain who profess no religion has grown dramatically over the last two decades, from 31 per cent in 1983 (already very high by international standards) to 40 per cent in 2000. True, among those who *do* profess a religion, attendance at religious services has held fairly steady over time, with 19 per cent attending at least once a week (exactly the same proportion as did so in 1983). But nearly a half of this group attends religious services less often than once a year. So, although there appears to be a steady core of regular church attenders, for many others organised religion plays little or no part in their lives.

Apart from religious affiliation, the only other realm of organisational attachment in Britain which seems clearly to have declined is membership of work-related organisations – trade unions and staff associations. As the next table shows, membership has declined seriously in the last 15 years or so.

Table 8.4 Membership of trade unions and staff associations

% belonging	1984	1987	1991	1994	1998	2000
Trade union	26[1]	24	21	22	19	19
Staff association	n.a.	4	4	4	4	3
Base	*1675*	*2847*	*2918*	*3468*	*3146*	*3335*

[1] The 1984 figure groups trade union and staff association members together.

Of course, joining a trade union is, or was, not always a matter of entirely free choice. So the various changes in legislation (and political atmosphere) during the Thatcher years clearly made it easier than before for reluctant members to leave the movement, as they seemed to do in the late 1980s. By the early 1990s, however, a new lower level of around 20 per cent had begun to establish itself – still a significantly higher proportion than the 13.5 per cent trade union membership in the United States in 2000 (United States Department of Labor, 2001).

In sum, our data so far reveal little variation in membership and participation patterns over the years and, apart from religious identity, nothing approaching the prolonged (and in some cases, drastic) fall-off in memberships reported in the US by Putnam. To the extent that organisational membership is the key source of social capital then, Britain should not have suffered the same depletion that the US has experienced. True, British 'joiners' and grassroots activists seem never to have been as ubiquitous as those found by Tocqueville in his journeys around the young American republic in the 1830s, representing a characteristic that has become central to the American self-image. But we are concerned here with *relative* changes, regardless of the scale of the phenomenon overall. And, despite much vocal suspicion that the same trends are taking place here, we have found little evidence to suggest that British people, like their American counterparts, are abandoning the public square, their interest groups, or even their local sports and recreational clubs.

But before we conclude as a result that Britain's stock of social capital must therefore be safe, we need to consider some of its less tangible forms. The most widely studied of these is *social trust* – that is, the sense we have that most other people can be trusted. Here too, we can look at evidence reaching back at least a generation.

Trends in social trust

By far the largest share of our interactions with our fellow citizens take place outside the framework of a formal organisation and, in democracies at any rate, far beyond the direct reach of the state. Precisely because of this, these interactions – whether with shopkeepers, neighbours or strangers in the street –

have much to do with our overall sense of security, with the familiarity and predictability of society, and with our own place in the larger social fabric. People living in a society with low levels of social trust will tend to be mutually suspicious, lacking in civility and unwilling to join in cooperative activities for the common good. Some commentators also believe that low social trust is associated with low political trust, but the relationship is far from certain (Katzenstein, 2000; Warren, 1999; Inglehart, 1999; Uslaner, 2002, forthcoming). Putnam's data on social trust within the United States are particularly sobering: not only does he find that social trust is declining (see also Inglehart, 1999: 95), but that the trend is primarily generational in origin, with relatively trusting older people slowly being replaced by less trusting younger people. Such a trend suggests that the overall decline in trust will not quickly be reversed (Putnam, 2000).

How much is Britain a socially trusting society? And is there any evidence that we are becoming less trusting over time? We realise of course that social trust is too subtle and complex a phenomenon for a small set of survey items to capture. Even so, following Putnam, we can get a rough and ready idea of trends by examining responses to a naïve question that has been included not only in several *British Social Attitudes* surveys, but also in a variety of other surveys in Britain and abroad. The question asks respondents simply whether, "generally speaking", they think "that most people can be trusted, or whether you can't be too careful in dealing with people".

Responses to this question are shown in the next table. Unfortunately, it is difficult to identify trends over time because many of the readings come from different survey sources and involve different sorts of samples. The possible impact of this is particularly apparent in the two readings taken in 1998. The first (which shows that 30 per cent of people think that "most people can be trusted") comes from the World Values Survey of that year and suggests a fairly sudden and precipitous drop in social trust in Britain. But the second reading (of 44 per cent) comes from the *British Social Attitudes* survey of the same year and suggests relative stasis – when compared both to the same time series a year earlier *and* to all previous World Values Survey measures. However, leaving aside a possible 'real' drop in social trust in the 22 years between 1959 and 1981 (which was incidentally matched by a similar decline in political trust over that period – see Curtice and Jowell, 1995), by far the safest interpretation of this table is one of 'no change'. The fact is that during two decades in which social trust has been in secular decline in the US, we can find no similar pattern in Britain.

Admittedly, the data below tell us only part of the story. All we have shown so far is that there has been no overall change in societal values between the early 1980s and now. But Putnam also discovered generational differences in social trust in the US which he argues will gradually lead to long-term societal changes as older, more trusting cohorts are replaced by younger, less trusting ones. To check whether such a process is evident in Britain we carried out an analysis of age-cohorts using the 1981 and 1990 World Values Surveys and the 2000 *British Social Attitudes* survey (along the lines used by Park, 2000). The results (shown in the appendix to this chapter) demonstrate clearly that generational changes are not eroding social trust in Britain as they appear to be in the US. Any age differences in trust that we found seem to evaporate as people get older and therefore have little impact on societal value change.

Table 8.5 Social trust over time

	1959	1981	1990	1997	1998a	1998b	2000
	%	%	%	%	%	%	%
Most people can be trusted	56	44	44	42	30	44	45
You can't be too careful in dealing with people	n.a.	56	56	57	70	54	54
Base		1190	1440	1355	1073	2071	2293

Sources:
1959: "Some people say that most people can be trusted. Others say you can't be too careful in your dealings with people. How do you feel about it?" Source: Civic Culture/World Values (quoted by Hall, 1999: 431 at note 41 for wording of items, 432 (Table 5) for results); responses of "don't know", "it depends", and "other" were excluded from that analysis.
1981, 1990, 1998a: World Values Surveys, Great Britain (ICPSR study 2790; documentation and data available at http://www.icpsr.umich.edu.
1997, 1998b, 2000: *British Social Attitudes* surveys.

We now turn to the connection between the two major aspects of social capital we have considered so far – involvement in organisations and social trust. As we reported in *The 16th Report* (and as Putnam and others have repeatedly found in other countries), these are indeed closely linked phenomena. They will thus tend to go down in tandem (as in the US) or settle at the same level together (as in Britain) and, if either were to rise, so in all probability would the other.

Our findings suggest that those who are more organisationally-active tend also to be more trusting of others. They also suggest that it is the *fact* of affiliation, rather than the type or extent of activity, that is generally the most decisive factor. To the extent that the connection between social trust and social participation is causally linked, it is likely to be a reciprocal link: so, the more trusting people are, the more likely they are to be joiners, and *vice versa*.

Table 8.6 Social trust, by group membership

	% 'most people can be trusted'	Base
All	45	2293
Membership of community organisation		
None	42	1746
One	52	415
Two or more	57	131
'Green'/countryside group membership		
None	42	1904
One	56	281
Two or more	64	108
Union/staff association membership		
Not a member of either	43	1749
Trade union member	50	411
Staff association member	54	70
Religion and church attendance		
Does not belong to a religion	45	1344
Belongs, attends never, or virtually never	37	580
Belongs, attends once a year or less	44	156
Belongs, attends twice a year	51	206
Belongs, attends once or twice a month	49	174
Belongs, attends once a week or more	50	283
Sports/cultural group membership		
Sports club	49	386
Cultural group	48	110
Neither	43	1756

Of course, the problem with a concept as complex as 'social trust' is that it cannot safely be based on a single survey measure. We cannot be sure, for instance, when different subsets of people respond that they trust "most people", that they are necessarily using the same referent. However, other questions we asked about mutual reliance certainly bolster our impression of stasis over time.

In particular, neighbours, friends and colleagues, and the way they interact with one another, play a critical part in most people's lives. In closely-knit communities people help each other out in many and diverse ways. Those who are able to turn to others for help and support tend to feel more secure and, by the same token, those who help others often find it gratifying. It is not so much the kind of help provided that matters – usually it is rather modest – as much as the networks of mutual dependence and responsibility that it builds up and affirms. To tap feelings about these sorts of relationships we repeated a set of questions, first asked in 1998, which asks people how comfortable they would feel in turning to a neighbour for help in a range of mostly minor difficulties:

> *Suppose that you were in bed ill and needed someone to go to the chemist to collect your prescription while they were doing their shopping. How comfortable would you be asking a neighbour to do this?*

> *Now suppose you found your sink was blocked, but you did not have a plunger to unblock it. How comfortable would you be asking a neighbour to borrow a plunger?*

> *Now suppose the milkman called for payment. The bill was £5 but you had no cash. How comfortable would you be asking a neighbour if you could borrow £5?*

Table 8.7 Feelings about asking neighbours for help in different situations

Asking a neighbour ...		Very comfortable	Fairly comfortable	Fairly un-comfortable	Very un-comfortable
... to collect a prescription	%	54	26	10	11
... to borrow a sink plunger	%	60	26	7	7
... to pay the milkman	%	22	16	17	45

Base: 2293

We also asked how comfortable people would be turning to passers-by for help:

> *Suppose you are in the middle of a town you do not know very well. You are trying to find a particular street and have got a bit lost. How comfortable would you be asking any passer-by for directions?*

> *Again suppose you are in the middle of a town you do not know very well. You need to make an urgent 'phone call from a 'phone box but you only have a £5 note. How comfortable would you be asking any passer-by for the right change?*

Table 8.8 Asking for help in a strange town

Asking passer-by for ...		Very comfortable	Fairly comfortable	Fairly un-comfortable	Very un-comfortable
... directions	%	52	37	8	3
... change for the 'phone	%	21	36	26	17

Base: 2293

Finally, we included a new item asking how likely people would be to intercede on behalf of a vulnerable stranger:

> *Suppose you are walking down a local street. Ahead of you there is a group of teenagers blocking the pavement, forcing an elderly woman to walk out into a busy road. How likely is it that you would help the woman by asking the young people to move?*

Table 8.9 Assisting a vulnerable stranger

	%
Definitely help her myself	54
Probably help her myself	37
Probably not help her, but hope someone else would	6
Definitely not help her, but hope someone else would	2

Base: 2293

So, not only do solid majorities say they would be "very comfortable" asking a neighbour for help either with collecting a prescription or dealing with a plumbing problem, but the proportions who do so have increased significantly since 1998, up from 47 and 54 per cent respectively then to 54 and 60 per cent now. Even on the touchier issue of asking a neighbour for a small loan, the proportion feeling "very comfortable" has increased – from 18 to 22 per cent. And still bigger relative rises have occurred in the proportions who would be "very comfortable" approaching passers-by for directions in a strange town (from 42 to 52 per cent), or for change (from 14 to 21 per cent). Unfortunately, we do not have an earlier reading for our question about helping an elderly woman run a gauntlet of teenagers, but it is notable that a majority believe they would "definitely" help her, even in this rather threatening situation.

These responses (to admittedly hypothetical questions) suggest the existence of a healthy social fabric in Britain, one in which people recognise and believe in their responsibilities to one another. More detailed analysis shows once again that membership of organisations and levels of social trust are indeed linked to an inclination to ask and to give help in these sorts of difficult situations. Although the causal connections are far from clear, it certainly seems likely that, at a minimum, organisational membership reinforces a sense of 'connectedness' to society at large. So these findings certainly confirm Putnam's conclusion that the pay-offs from thriving networks of organisational activity can be considerable, and not just for the individuals who engage in them.

Trust in institutions

A society's social cohesion depends to some extent on the level of confidence its citizens have in its democratic institutions and those who govern them. This may in turn depend on the extent to which ordinary people are integrated into the activities of their communities. An active, well-connected society, it is argued, will feel less vulnerable and therefore be better disposed both to one another and to public agencies and officials. On the other hand, there is some evidence to suggest that this relationship between social and political trust varies significantly across societies (Katzenstein, 2000). To get at these issues we asked the following questions:

> *How much do you trust British governments of any party to place the needs of the nation above the interests of their own political party?*

> *And how much do you trust British police not to bend the rules in trying to get a conviction?*

> *And how much do you trust top civil servants to stand firm against a minister who wants to provide false information to parliament?*

> *And how much do you trust politicians of any party in Britain to tell the truth when they are in a tight corner?*

Responses to these questions are considered in detail in the chapter by Bromley, Curtice and Seyd elsewhere in this volume. So the next table focuses solely on the relationship between *institutional* trust and both organisational membership and social trust. It shows that, by solid margins, social trust is indeed connected to institutional trust in Britain, though on a somewhat selective basis. However, the proposition that those with greater organisational connections will have greater confidence in their democratic institutions is only partially supported. Certainly, membership of community organisations is significantly related to higher levels of trust in government, police, civil servants and MPs. For instance, a quarter of those who belong to two or more community organisations trust government to place the needs of the nation first "just about always" or "most of the time", compared with a sixth of those who do not belong to any such organisation. However, membership of green organisations is less clearly linked to institutional trust. One explanation might be that many green organisations are national and thus more remote, providing less opportunity for the sorts of repeated interpersonal dealings that are said to be critical in building and reinforcing trust (Cooter, 1997; Axelrod, 1984). Another might be that green organisations – unlike most community-based organisations – tend to be lobbies whose very existence arises from a distrust or disapproval of the way in which the public authorities are handling things. Either way, the existence or not of a link between organisational membership and institutional trust seems to depend on what sorts of organisations we have in mind.

Table 8.10 Institutional trust, by organisational membership and social trust

% trust following "just about always" or "most of the time"	Community organisation memberships			Green/countryside memberships			"Most can be trusted"	"Can't be too careful"
	0	1	2+	0	1	2		
... Government	15	19	24	16	18	17	20	13
... Police	57	61	78	57	69	65	68	52
... Civil servants	34	39	46	34	39	48	39	32
... MPs	11	11	16	11	11	7	12	10
Base	1746	415	131	1904	281	108	998	1276

What inhibits the accumulation of social capital?

Putnam attributes the parlous state of American civil society to a number of factors. A key factor is simply a generational change in people's propensity to participate. As noted, however, we cannot find similar evidence of such a trend in Britain. While young people here do tend to be less likely than their elders to be 'joiners' or to express social trust, it seems for the moment that they will revert to type with changes in the lifecycle.

Another prime suspect in the US is the dominance of television, that ready-made culprit for so many societal ills. Those who watch television extensively are found to be less likely to be involved in other activities within their communities, and less likely to trust others. A further factor in the US is residential mobility (much higher there than in Britain), which tends to remove people from communities within which they are well-connected and 'involved' into ones in which they are less so. Two-career households are another culprit, improving standards of living at the expense of closer ties with friends, neighbours and local communities. Finally, the growth of internet usage is increasingly thought to be replacing face-to-face contact within the community by remote and more isolating forms of communication.

Our data do not permit a full longitudinal analysis of whether these factors are increasingly affecting social participation and social trust in Britain too. But in the next table we look at some of these possible culprits for signs that their impact here is as damaging as it appears to have been in the US.

The table confirms that heavy television viewing does appear to work against extensive engagement in community activities. Frequent viewers are significantly less likely to be members of community groups or green and countryside organisations. For instance, over a quarter of those who watch two or less hours of television a day belong to a community organisation, compared with just under a fifth of those who watch five or more hours a day. Moreover, there is a sharp fall off in social trust as television hours increase – an intriguing finding which bears monitoring and closer analysis (for comparative data see Norris, 2000). Again, we cannot pin down causality using these data: does television viewing lead to social isolation, or do less-connected individuals watch more television? Does the decline in social trust reflect the fact that television viewing keeps people from interacting with neighbours, or does the content of what people see encourage or reinforce less-trusting attitudes? We do not know. But in this respect at least, the distribution of social capital in Britain resembles that found in the US.

Residential mobility also appears to have an effect on membership of community organisations, as we would expect from the experience of the US. However, it is not linked to membership of green lobbies, perhaps because these tend to be more national (or international) in character. Surprisingly, however, new arrivals in a neighbourhood seem if anything to approach others with rather *more*, not less, social trust. This might, of course, have something to do with the characteristics of those who relocate. In any event, longer-term residents in a neighbourhood do not differ significantly according to how long they have lived there.

Unlike the US, people in two-career households in Britain do not differ significantly from others in terms either of their organisational memberships or their expressed social trust. While their work may well draw heavily on their time and energy, it might also lead them into networks that they would not otherwise encounter. In any event, our finding here is clearly counter to what the American account would lead us to have expected.

Finally, as is discussed in the chapter by Gardner and Oswald elsewhere in this volume, internet users actually have *higher* levels of social trust than non-users (though this largely reflects their age and educational profile). They are also more rather than less likely to join social and voluntary organisations. There is certainly no evidence to suggest that the internet is an alternative (if rather more brusque) form of social connectedness, but neither does it seem to erode other forms of social participation and thus threaten the vitality of civil society.

Table 8.11 Social capital and social trust, by television viewing, time in neighbourhood and work patterns

| | % belonging to 0/1/2 community organisations | | | % belonging to 0/1/2 green or countryside organisations | | | % think "most can be trusted" | Base |
	0	1	2+	0	1	2+		
All	76	18	6	83	13	5	45	2293
Television viewing								
0-2 hours per day	72	21	7	80	15	5	50	1004
3-4 hours per day	78	17	5	84	12	5	45	809
5+ hours per day	82	15	4	88	9	3	31	471
Time lived in neighbourhood								
Less than 1 year	88	10	2	84	13	3	49	119
1-2 years	81	16	3	86	13	1	42	257
3-5 years	79	16	6	83	11	6	45	312
6-10 years	77	20	3	78	17	5	44	314
11-20 years	69	23	8	84	12	4	46	469
21+ years	76	18	6	82	12	6	44	822
Two-career households	75	20	6	83	13	4	47	581

Strictly speaking, these data cannot either confirm or disprove Putnam's propositions about the factors that might inhibit the accumulation of social capital. However, they persuasively suggest that many of the familiar US concerns about civil disengagement are, for the moment at least, much less apparent (or at any rate far less pronounced) in Britain.

Possible drawbacks of social capital

On two important measures of social capital then, Britain appears to be in a much better state than Putnam's findings suggest for the USA. But there are two cautionary notes we must consider before concluding that we have nothing to worry about here. The first is that a large majority of the population does not belong to any organisation and, moreover, that such membership and social trust vary markedly between different social groups. The second is the possibility that, as a result of this, social capital might have a 'dark side'. It is to these issues that we now turn.

Disparities in membership and trust

How much do different segments of British society share in the fruits of the continuing pool of social capital? We have already ruled out generational differences in Britain as a sign of things to come. But what about other cleavages in society, in particular the usual suspects: gender, race and class?

Without pushing the metaphor of social capital too far, let us adopt the simplifying and plausible assumption that people with links to a local or national organisation are 'better off' than are those without such links, and that 'trusting' people are better off than 'untrusting' ones. Moreover, let us assume that membership of two or more organisations is even better than one, because it implies closer integration into the larger civil society. No organisational links and low trust in contrast indicate a lack of social capital and a degree of social exclusion. In the next table, we look at these different levels of connectedness by gender, race and class.

In virtually all respects the gradient in the next table is in the expected direction, and in most cases rather steep. Social participation and social trust tend to be higher among more powerful segments of society and are thus higher among the middle classes than the working classes, among whites than other races, and among men than women. For instance, the middle classes are significantly more likely than their counterparts to be members of organisations at all (and even more likely to be members of more than one). They also display substantially higher levels of social trust. So too do men have higher levels of social trust than women. And, although men and women are equally likely to be members of community organisations, men are more likely to join green organisations. However, our table somewhat overemphasises gender differences in organisational participation. If we focus on those organisations not shown in the table, men are significantly more likely to participate in sports clubs and trade unions but women are more likely to be members of cultural groups and to attend religious services regularly. In sum, about the same percentages of both genders are not involved in any of the sorts of organisations we asked about.

We must be a little careful of drawing heroic conclusions from the racial differences we have found. In the first place, our sample of 'other' races is small and very heterogeneous, combining not only different national and ethnic groups but also long-settled communities with relatively recent arrivals in Britain. More important, however, is the fact that our lists of organisations almost certainly omitted many kinds of activity that may be particularly important to minority communities. We may therefore be under-counting potentially rich sources of social capital among these groups. Equally, let us not overemphasise methodological issues at the expense of substantive ones. Difficult economic and social conditions will inevitably inhibit and discourage social participation and integration and in turn help to perpetuate social exclusion.

Table 8.12 Social capital and social trust, by gender, ethnic group and class

	% belonging to 0/1/2 community organisations			% belonging to 0/1/2 green or countryside organisations			% think "most can be trusted"	Base
	0	1	2+	0	1	2+		
All	76	18	6	83	13	5	45	2293
Gender								
Men	76	18	6	80	14	6	51	981
Women	76	18	5	85	12	4	40	1312
Ethnic group								
White	76	19	6	82	13	5	46	2140
Other	84	14	2	98	2	-	27	115
Social class								
Professional or employer	68	20	12	70	20	11	55	454
Intermediate non-manual	69	25	7	73	19	7	56	349
Junior non-manual	74	21	5	85	12	4	42	425
Supervisory or skilled manual	81	16	3	90	8	2	43	434
Semi-skilled manual	84	13	3	91	8	1	34	412
Unskilled manual	85	12	4	92	5	3	26	133

As for class differences, the pattern is long-standing and the gradient all too familiar. The higher status one's occupation is, so the more likely one is to be 'connected' to other aspects of civil society, conferring a sort of double benefit. Moreover, when we look behind the table at the detailed answers, we find that the higher social classes are particularly likely to be members of Neighbourhood Watch schemes, political parties, residents' associations and school boards – groups that may serve to protect or buttress their relative economic advantage. They are also more likely to belong to sports and leisure clubs and green lobbies, to which they presumably bring resources and organisational skills and help to influence agendas and strategies. Those in lower-status occupations are consistently less likely to be members of such groups. True, they are a little more likely than their middle-class counterparts to be members of trade unions, but, as noted, unions in Britain are these days considerably less influential than they once were.

Thus, while the overall stock of social capital in Britain seems to be relatively constant, so too is the inequality of its distribution. If a rich organisational life and strong social trust are indeed powerful social and economic assets and, like other forms of capital, embody advantages that accumulate over time, then significant parts of Britain continue to be strikingly asset-poor.

The 'dark side' of social capital

There is little doubt that people who are socially well connected and trusting of their fellow citizens will tend to lead more secure lives than those of their more isolated and less trusting counterparts. They will also have better means at hand to negotiate difficulties in life and to obtain support when they need it. Moreover, as 'joiners', they will be in a better position than that of their counterparts to influence public agendas. In effect, like any other sort of capital, social capital is unarguably a good thing for the people that possess it.

What is less certain, however, is that the accumulation of social capital *per se* is necessarily a good thing for society at large. As Putnam himself notes (Putnam, 2000), certain sorts of 'bonding' social capital may promote or reinforce unhealthy group identities to the detriment of society, uniting certain segments of society and excluding others, creating boundaries rather than building connections and, in the process, fostering indifference and hostility towards outsiders. We have only to look at Northern Ireland – one of the most intensely 'organised' societies in the world – to see these 'dark' and exclusive forms of social capital at work over the years. The fact is that when we refer loosely to social capital as a good thing for society at large, rather than just for its possessors, we are actually referring mainly to 'bridging' social capital – people's connections and activities that cross social divides and help to foster social cohesion.

We will now explore the implications for Britain of these different forms of social capital, identifying in which ways they may be linked to healthier communities and in which ways not. In particular, we will examine the extent to which the unequal distribution of social capital in Britain tends to reinforce rather than mitigate other inequalities and disparities in British society.

We saw earlier that social capital in Britain is disproportionately concentrated among middle-class people – in somewhat different ways from in the US. Not only are working-class people less likely to join in voluntary activities, but they also express strikingly lower levels of social trust. Can we conclude from this that a good deal of the social capital to be found in Britain is of the *bonding* variety – that is, bonding for the middle classes, and not so for others? To the extent that well-connected groups tend to coincide in different guises this could well be the case. To find out, we need to examine in more detail who the joiners of different sorts of organisations are. To the extent that they tend to be those who already possess significant social and economic resources, the advantages that greater organisational connections confer on them might well serve to enlarge and reinforce disparities.

To probe this possibility, we defined a subgroup that might be expected to be particularly well-endowed with social capital – people in middle-class occupations, in the top half of the income distribution and who, for good measure, are aged between 30 and 60. They amounted to 20 per cent of the base sample for this part of the survey. As expected, this relatively 'well-heeled' group comprises a highly organised constituency for its size, accounting for 31 per cent of all community memberships and 35 per cent of the green/countryside memberships in our sample. As the next table shows, this subgroup also has a much higher level of social trust, with six in ten agreeing with the proposition that "most people can be trusted", compared with only four in ten of those who are less well-heeled.

Table 8.13 Levels of social capital among the 'well-heeled'

	% belonging to 0/1/2 community organisations			% belonging to 0/1/2 green or countryside organisations			% think "most can be trusted"	Base
	0	1	2+	0	1	2+		
The 'well-heeled'	65	25	9	71	20	8	59	433
Others	79	16	5	86	11	4	41	1860

More important, perhaps, than the *overall* disparity in participation was the consistency of this difference across a range of organisations which clearly confer advantage on their members. Thus members of the 'well-heeled' group were considerably more likely than others to be members of Neighbourhood Watch schemes, PTAs, boards of school governors, and so on. An impressive 35 per cent of them (compared to 22 per cent of the rest) were members of at least one community organisation.

We have no doubt that this participation is driven by motives of service and obligation towards the broader community. But, as we have shown, membership of organisations has its own considerable rewards in the form of better networks, a greater sense of security and better access to the fruits of civil society. So, to the extent that organised activities tend to 'bond' along class lines rather than 'bridge' across class boundaries, these disparities in participation do matter.

In a more atomistic society such as the United States, this more exclusive form of social capital is more often found within exclusive religious or racial groups. Its negative consequences are manifested in the form of distrust of outsiders and may lead to a kind of localism that hardens into outright prejudice. Fortunately we did not discover such effects in Britain. On the contrary, using several different measures, we found that greater organisational involvement and social trust here inclines people here towards more, not less, engagement with society.

As for the distinction between 'bridging' and 'bonding' social capital, it is very difficult to examine directly from our data, since most organisations offer a range of incentives and attractions to their members (Wilson, 1973). Indeed, they usually *must* do so in order to survive. What is for some members a conscience-driven endeavour is for others a self-serving one and for yet others simply an excuse to get out of the house and socialise on a Tuesday evening. Some members may see their tightly-knit neighbourhood group as a bastion against outsiders, or against change, while others may see it as a building block towards a more caring society. So the characterisation of a group as primarily 'bridging' or 'bonding' requires a set of questions that we did not ask, but that we ought perhaps to ask in future rounds.

What our data do clearly tell us, however, is that the part of the population with most resources also tend to be disproportionately active in organisations which – despite their possibly 'bridging' motives – tend to serve potentially powerful 'bonding' purposes in the process. To the extent that these activities confer further advantage upon those that engage in them through the acquisition of greater social capital, these very skewed patterns of participation both parallel and reinforce other inequalities in Britain.

Conclusions

The well-documented decline of social capital in the United States, and the associated decline in social trust are not mirrored in Britain. Civil society here remains as strong and as active as it was. There is evidence in Britain, as elsewhere, of a gradual decline in electoral turnout, political trust and democratic engagement (Johnston, 1993; Norris, 1999; Curtice and Jowell, 1995, 1997), but for the moment this does not seem to be explained by changing levels of social trust. To a significant – and sustained – extent, British people tend to trust one another, help each other out, and spend portions of their discretionary time in the service of community goals – a situation that many other societies would envy.

But to a significant extent too, this enviable degree of participation remains concentrated within familiar subgroups who start off with many advantages and then bolster those advantages in the course of their voluntary 'joining' activities. In time, as their social capital (in common with other forms of capital) generates increasing returns, these advantages will tend to be reinforced. This matters for those who are left out, restricting their access to important sources of support, influence and confidence. And it matters too for society at large, tending to perpetuate old divisions.

Notes

1. On social capital in contemporary Britain, see Hall (1999); for a classic treatment on the United States, see Tocqueville, (2000).
2. For a critique of Putnam's earlier work, emphasising the vitality of religion, see Greeley (1997).
3. The reduction in Greenpeace's membership over the last decade may be a special case since in that period it has substantially cut back on mass mailing promotions, an important source of development for most mass-membership groups (Putnam, 2000; Bosso, 1995).

References

Axelrod, R. (1984), *The Evolution of Cooperation*, New York: Basic Books.

Bosso, C. J. (1995), 'The Color of Money: Environmental Groups and the Pathologies of Fund Raising' in Cigler, A. J., and Loomis, B. A., *Interest Group Politics, 4th* edition, Washington, DC: Congressional Quarterly Press.

Cohen, J. (1999), 'Trust, Voluntary Association and Workable Democracy: The Contemporary American Discourse of Civil Society' in Warren, M. E. (ed.), *Democracy and Trust*, Cambridge: Cambridge University Press.

Cooter, R. D. (1997), 'The Rule of State Law and the Rule-of-Law State: Economic Analysis of the Legal Foundations of Development', in Bruno, M., and Pleskovic, B. (eds.), *Annual World Bank Conference on Development Economics 1996*, Washington, DC, The World Bank.

Curtice, J. and Jowell, R. (1995), 'The sceptical electorate' in Jowell, R., Curtice, J., Park, A., Brook, L., and Ahrendt, D. (eds.), *British Social Attitudes: the 12th Report*, Aldershot: Dartmouth.

Curtice, J. and Jowell, R. (1997), 'Trust in the political system' in Jowell, R., Curtice, J., Park, A., Brook, L., Thomson, K. and Bryson, C. (eds.), *British Social Attitudes: the 14th Report – The end of Conservative values?*, Aldershot: Ashgate.

Della Porta (2000), 'Social Capital, Beliefs in Government, and Political Corruption' in Pharr, S. J. and Putnam, R. D. (eds.), *Disaffected Democracies: What's Troubling the Trilateral Countries?*, Princeton, NJ: Princeton University Press.

Greeley, A. (1997), 'The Other Civic America: Religion and Social Capital', *The American Prospect*, **32**: 495-510.

Hall, P. (1999), 'Social Capital in Britain', *British Journal of Political Science*, **29**: 417-461.

Inglehart, R. (1999), 'Trust, well-being and democracy' in Warren, M. E. (ed.), *Democracy and Trust*. Cambridge: Cambridge University Press.

Johnston, M. (1993), 'Disengaging from democracy', *International Social Attitudes: the 10th BSA Report*, Aldershot: Dartmouth.

Johnston, M. and Jowell. R. (1999), 'Social capital and the social fabric' in Jowell, R., Curtice, J., Park, A and Thomson, K. (eds.), *British Social Attitudes: the 16th Report - Who shares New Labour values?*, Aldershot: Ashgate

Katzenstein, P. (2000), 'Confidence, Trust, International Relations, and Lessons from Smaller Democracies' in Pharr, S. J. and Putnam, R. D. (eds.), *Disaffected Democracies: What's Troubling the Trilateral Countries?*, Princeton, NJ: Princeton University Press.

Norris, P. (ed.) (1999), *Critical Citizens: Global Support for Democratic Governance*, Oxford: Oxford University Press.

Norris, P. (2000), 'The Impact of Television on Civic Malaise' in Pharr, S. J. and Putnam, R. D. (eds.), *Disaffected Democracies: What's Troubling the Trilateral Countries?*, Princeton, NJ: Princeton University Press.

Office for National Statistics (2001), *Social Trends*, **31**, London: The Stationery Office.

Park, A. (2000), 'The generation game', in Jowell, R., Curtice, J., Park, A., Thomson, K., Jarvis, L., Bromley, C, and Stratford, N. (eds.), *British Social Attitudes: the 17th Report – Focusing on Diversity*, Aldershot: Ashgate.

Putnam, R. D. (2000), *Bowling Alone – the collapse and revival of American community*, New York: Simon & Schuster.

Tocqueville, A. (2000 edn), *Democracy in America* (translated and edited by Mansfield, H. C., and Winthrop, D.), Chicago: University of Chicago Press.

United States Department of Labor, Bureau of Labor Statistics (2001), 'Union Members Summary', http://stats.bls.gov/news.release/union2.nr0.htm

Uslaner, E. M. (2002, forthcoming), *The Moral Foundations of Trust*, Cambridge: Cambridge University Press.

Warren, M. E. (1999), 'Introduction' in Warren, M. E. (ed.), *Democracy and Trust*, Cambridge: Cambridge University Press.

Wilson, J. Q. (1973), *Political Organizations*, New York: Basic Books.

Acknowledgements

The *National Centre for Social Research* would like to thank the Leverhulme Trust for funding the modules of questions on citizenship in the 1998 and 2000 surveys, on which this chapter is largely based.

Appendix

Cohort analysis

Changes in attitudes over time may take the form of *period effects* (a simultaneous change in the same direction among large numbers of individuals, such as a loss of trust over time by all or most people) or might, as Putnam suggests, be *generational effects* (which in the US case are illustrated by older individuals who have trusting attitudes being replaced by younger, less trusting, generations. However, it could also be the case that an individual's level of trust changes at the various stages in his or her lifecycle: as they have children, for example, or acquire property. In relation to social trust, our data for the 1981-2000 time span appears to rule out period effects: there is no real trend to speak of. However, the lack of change over time may mask considerable generational differences which may, in themselves, herald the possibility of future change. In order to investigate this we need to consider the table below.

This table compares levels of social trust for age cohorts over time. These are not the same individuals surveyed at different times; rather, they are instead comparable age groups drawn from the 1981 and 1990 World Values surveys, and from the 2000 *British Social Attitudes* survey. Each result can be compared, with caution, to the one directly to its right: for example, anyone who was aged 18 to 24 in 1981 would be aged 27 to 33 in 1990, and (like it or not!) aged 37 to 43 in 2000. (For reference, a new 18-24 generation is added to the results in both 1990 and 2000, and this 1990 group is represented by the 28-34 year olds in 2000.)

Social trust by age cohorts, 1981, 1990, and 2000

Percentage saying "most people can be trusted"

Age cohort:	1981	Base	1990		Base	2000		Base
			18-24	34	175	18-24	34	176
18-24	39	337	27-33	43	195	28-34	43	304
25-34	41	236	34-43	44	262	37-43	46	326
35-44	50	162	44-53	45	212	44-53	48	350
45-54	52	121	54-63	44	216	54-63	50	349
55-64	44	138	64-73	51	177	64-73	46	312
			74+	49	137	74-83	43	199
						84+	42	67

Sources: For 1981 and 1990, data are drawn from the British section of the World Values Survey dataset (ICPSR Study 2790; data and documentation available at http://www.icpsr.umich.edu). Data for 2000 are from the *British Social Attitudes* survey.

This table shows that although 18-24 year olds were less trusting (judged by responses to this item) in 1990 than the same age group had been in 1981, there is no apparent difference between them and the 18-24 year olds of the year 2000. Moreover, age differences in social trust do not seem that durable: as people get older (at least through the earlier stages of the lifecycle) social trust appears to increase. However, there are less clear-cut indications that this trend levels off (and perhaps reverses) among older citizens.

9 Political engagement, trust and constitutional reform

Catherine Bromley, John Curtice and Ben Seyd *

For many years, critics of Britain's democratic system have argued that it is atrophying. They have claimed that citizens are able to exert only weak control over a system of government that finds it difficult to meet popular needs and demands because of its centralised nature (Barnett, 1993). But in 1997 the Conservative government, whose leader, John Major, had enthused about the traditions and institutions of British life, was replaced by a Labour administration which embraced calls for the reform of many of those same institutions. For example, less than a year before becoming Prime Minister, Tony Blair argued:

> Changing the way we govern, and not just changing our government, is no longer an optional extra for Britain. So low is public esteem for politicians and the system we operate that there is now little authority for us to use unless and until we first succeed in regaining it (Blair, 1996).

One of the main weapons in Labour's attempt to restore public confidence in Britain's political system was a programme of constitutional reform. Indeed the implementation of that programme was arguably the most striking characteristic of Mr Blair's first administration. It included the creation of new devolved institutions in Scotland, Wales, Northern Ireland and London, the strengthening of individual rights through a Human Rights Act, the removal of the bulk of

* Catherine Bromley is a Senior Researcher at the *National Centre for Social Research*, Scotland, and is Co-Director of the *British Social Attitudes* survey series. John Curtice is Head of Research at the *National Centre for Social Research*, Scotland, Deputy Director of the ESRC Centre for Research into Elections and Social Trends, and Professor of Politics and Director of the Social Statistics Laboratory at Strathclyde University. Ben Seyd is a Senior Research Fellow at the Constitution Unit, University College London.

hereditary peers from the House of Lords and the introduction of new proportional voting systems for both devolved and European elections.

Yet for those who hoped that such reforms would rekindle public confidence and involvement in Britain's democracy, the 2001 election held at the end of Labour's first term was a serious disappointment. After already having been lower in 1997 than at any time since 1935, turnout fell by another 12 points to its lowest level since 1918.[1] A little under three in five people in Great Britain (59.1 per cent) voted. Turnout also fell to record low levels in the local and European elections held between 1998 and 2000. It appears that Britain faces a crisis of confidence and participation that is far deeper than any programme of constitutional reform is capable of reversing.

This chapter examines whether this is really the case. We do so in three stages. First, we examine trends in attitudes towards the political system and in political participation in a broad sense – from voting to signing a petition or going on a demonstration. Next, we consider public attitudes towards Labour's programme of constitutional reform and the impact this appears to have had on attitudes towards the political system. Finally, we examine whether long-term changes in British society are undermining confidence in the political system in a way that Labour's programme of constitutional reform could not hope to address.

Is there a 'crisis' of participation in Britain?

Our first question is whether the low turnout at recent elections is symptomatic of a wider public malaise with Britain's political system. This might take one of two forms. On the one hand, people may be losing interest in politics and, consequently, becoming not only less likely to vote but also less likely to take part in other forms of political participation. On the other hand, people may still be interested in politics, but no longer believe that the political system responds to such a conventional activity as voting. As a result, they may have become more inclined to engage in 'unconventional' political activities such as going on protests and demonstrations (Dalton, 1999; Fuchs and Klingemann, 1995; Marsh, 1977). After all, the last few years have been marked by notable examples of these sort of protests, ranging from the anti-globalisation protesters at the 2001 G8 summit in Genoa to the coalition of farmers and lorry drivers who brought many parts of Britain to a near standstill in 2000 in protest against high fuel prices.

There are two ways we can examine whether either of these suppositions is correct. First, we can look at what actions people say they *would* take if parliament were considering a law that they thought was "really unjust and harmful". Second, we can examine the actions that people say they have *ever* taken in response to what they thought was an unjust and harmful government action. The advantage of the former measure is that it gives us an indication of people's *current* reported propensity to engage in politics (and so should be sensitive to any changes in willingness to participate over time). Its disadvantage of course is that it does not measure actual participation. The latter measure does measure this, but as it asks people to report any actions they have taken over their lifetime, the figures that it generates will be less immediately responsive to changes in people's willingness to participate.

The next table shows recent trends in reported willingness to engage in various forms of political activity. Two points stand out. First, there is no evidence at all of a decline in people's reported willingness to engage. The proportion saying now that they would not do anything in response to an unjust law has barely changed at all across the years. In fact, the number of actions that people say they are willing to undertake has actually tended to increase over time. True, at 32 per cent, the proportion who say they would take three or more actions is a little lower now than it was in 1998 (when 37 per cent said they would do this), but both figures are well above the 14 per cent who named this many actions in 1983 or even the 25 per cent who did so in 1986. Second, while the proportion saying they would go on a protest or a demonstration is now twice what it was in 1983, much of that increase had in fact occurred by the beginning of the 1990s. Since then there has been no consistent increase in reported willingness to engage in this sort of activity. Indeed the one and only apparently consistent change in what people say they are prepared to do is to contact the media, a reflection perhaps of the media's greater interest in audience participation (Davis and Curtice, 2000).

Table 9.1 Potential political action, 1983-2000

% saying they would	1983	1986	1989	1991	1994	1998	2000
Sign a petition	55	65	71	78	67	67	68
Contact their MP	46	52	54	48	58	59	50
Contact radio, TV or newspaper	14	15	14	14	21	21	22
Go on a protest or demonstration	8	11	14	14	16	21	16
Speak to an influential person	10	15	15	17	14	18	17
Contact a government department	7	12	12	11	14	17	14
Form a group of like-minded people	6	8	10	7	10	9	7
Raise the issue in an organisation they already belong to	9	10	11	9	7	9	10
None of these	13	10	8	6	7	7	7
Base	*1761*	*1548*	*1516*	*1445*	*1137*	*2030*	*2293*

Looking at what people say they *have* done as opposed to what they say they would do confirms that there has been no decline in overall levels of political participation. In our most recent survey, just over half say that they have undertaken at least one action in response to a government action they considered unjust and harmful. In 1994, when we last asked this question, the figure was a little under a half, as it was in 1986 when we first asked it. Indeed, the proportion who claim to have taken three or more actions has slowly but consistently risen from five per cent in 1986 to nine per cent now.

Nor is there much sign of change in the kinds of political activity in which people engage. Few have ever taken part in significant time-consuming activity, but then it has always been thus. Signing a petition remains by far and away the most common form of non-electoral participation, a relatively undemanding and perhaps fleeting activity. However, we can see that there has been a small but consistent increase over time in the proportion of people who have been on a protest or a demonstration. So perhaps here we do have a sign that there has been some increase at least in more unconventional forms of political activity that might reflect frustration with the conventional workings of democracy.

But one further piece of evidence casts doubt upon this interpretation. For the most part people engage in these unconventional forms of political participation *as well as*, rather than *instead of*, voting. Thus, 87 per cent of those who had ever been on a protest or a demonstration said they voted in the 1997 general election, compared with only 71 per cent of those who had not been on a protest. When it comes to voting in the 1999 European election, the equivalent figures are 50 per cent and 36 per cent respectively. Similar differences are found in relation to all of the other activities in the following table. So there does not appear to be a wholesale shift away from the ballot box to the streets.

Table 9.2 Actual political action, 1986-2000

% saying they had	1986	1989	1991	1994	2000
Signed a petition	34	41	53	39	42
Contacted their MP	11	15	17	14	16
Contacted radio, TV or newspaper	3	4	4	5	6
Gone on a protest or demonstration	6	8	9	9	10
Spoken to an influential person	1	3	5	3	4
Contacted a government department	3	3	4	3	4
Formed a group of like-minded people	2	3	2	3	2
Raised the issue in an organisation they already belong to	5	4	5	4	5
None of these	56	48	37	53	47
Base	*1548*	*1516*	*1445*	*1137*	*2293*

Confidence in the political system

These findings suggest that recent low election turnouts do not appear to be symptomatic of a wider malaise. There is little evidence that other forms of political participation are in decline or that people are resorting to such activities instead of voting.[2] If anything, the opposite is the case. Perhaps, after all, people are reasonably content with the way that their democracy is working?

We can assess this in two ways. First we consider how much trust people have in key political institutions and sets of actors. Then we examine 'political efficacy', that is the confidence that people have in their ability to articulate demands effectively and in the ability of the political system to respond to them. According to Almond and Verba (1963), a democracy requires a balance of efficacy and trust amongst its citizens in order to perform effectively. They need to feel that they can make their views known when necessary, but they should be equally willing to trust their rulers to make the right decisions most of the time.

In truth, we are not (and never have been) very trustful of governments and politicians. As the next table shows, only around one in ten of us trust politicians of any party to tell the truth when they are in a tight corner "just about always" or "most of the time", a figure that has not changed at all in recent years. However there has been a clear change of mood when it comes to our willingness to trust governments to put the needs of the nation above the interests of their own party. Up to (and including) 1991 at least one in three of us trusted governments to do this at least most of the time. But during the 1990s there was a gradual erosion of that trust and now only one in six, a new all time low, take this view of government. True, there appeared to be something of a recovery in the immediate wake of Labour's election victory in 1997 (as registered by our 1998 survey), but this appears to have been only a temporary halt.

Politicians cannot blame this apparently growing cynicism about their motives on any increasing tendency amongst the electorate simply to distrust *all* those in authority. As the following table also shows, there has been no equivalent growing distrust of either the police or civil servants. Indeed we now appear to be more trustful of both of these than we were for much of the 1990s, with the police in particular having apparently been particularly successful at recapturing public confidence. Almost three in five of us now trust them not to bend the rules to try and get a conviction.

Table 9.3 Trends in political trust, 1974-2000

% who trust the following "just about always" or "most of the time"	1974	1987	1991	1994	1996	1998	2000
British governments of any party to place the needs of the nation above the interests of their own political party	39	37	33	24	22	29	16
Politicians of any party to tell the truth when they are in a tight corner	-	-	-	9	9	9	11
British police not to bend the rules in trying to get a conviction	-	52	49	47	51	48	59
Top civil servants to stand firm against a minister who wants to provide false information to parliament	-	46	-	27	28	-	35
Base	*1802*	*1410*	*1445*	*1137*	*1180*	*2071*	*2293*

Source: 1974: Political Action Study. 1987 figure for civil servants: British Election Study 1987 (Base = 3414).

So on our first measure at least it appears that confidence in the workings of our representative democracy has declined, and that far from being reversed during Labour's first term, has eroded even further. But what happens when we look at our second measure, political efficacy? Here we should draw a distinction between two aspects of efficacy. On the one hand, the public will have views about the ability and willingness of the political system to respond to any demands they may make. We refer to this as 'system efficacy'. On the other hand, people will have more or less confidence in their *own* ability to express demands. This we term 'personal efficacy'. While at any one time those who feel personally efficacious also tend to be those who feel that the system is efficacious (Pattie and Johnston, 2001a), this does not necessarily mean that trends in personal and system efficacy should parallel each other over time. Rather, if it is the case that people have lost confidence in the political system then we might well expect to find that system efficacy has declined while personal efficacy has remained the same or even increased.

As in the case of trust, we have to bear in mind that a considerable degree of scepticism has always existed. Clear majorities have always agreed with each of the indicators of system and personal efficacy in the next two tables. So, to identify whether levels of efficacy have declined, we look just at those who *strongly* agree with each of the statements.

Table 9.4 Trends in system efficacy, 1974-2000

% strongly agree	1974	1987	1991	1994	1996	1998	2000
Parties are only interested in people's votes, not in their opinions	19	15	16	25	28	21	26
Generally speaking, those we elect as MPs lose touch with people pretty quickly	19	16	16	25	26	20	23
It doesn't really matter which party is in power, in the end things go on much the same	-	-	11	16	16	17	19
MPs don't care much about what people like me think	-	-	-	-	15	-	14
Base	*1802*	*1410*	*1445*	*1137*	*1180*	*2071*	*2293*

Source: 1974: Political Action Study. In that study respondents were given a four-point scale ranging from "strongly agree" to "strongly disagree". In the subsequent *British Social Attitudes* studies answers were given on a five-point scale with a mid-point labelled "neither agree nor disagree".

The picture revealed by the previous table is clear. As in the case of political trust, levels of system efficacy fell in the 1990s, recovered somewhat in the wake of Labour's election in 1997, but have now fallen back to more or less where they were in the mid-1990s. Thus, for example, in 1987 only around one in six strongly agreed that, "parties are only interested in people's votes, not in their opinions", or that "generally speaking those we elect as MPs lose touch with people pretty quickly". But by 1996 just over one in four subscribed to each of these views, and while these figures fell again to around one in five in 1998, they have now returned to around one in four.

In contrast, for the most part levels of personal efficacy show little or no consistent trend. For instance, the proportion strongly agreeing that "people like me have no say in what the government does" or that politics and government can be too complicated to understand is little different now to what it was when the questions were first asked in the *British Social Attitudes* survey in 1986.

In short, while there seems to have been little long-term change in people's confidence in their own political abilities, confidence in the political system's ability to respond to public demands does appear to have declined. Moreover, that confidence does not appear to have been restored during Labour's first term of office.

Table 9.5 Trends in personal efficacy, 1974-2000

% strongly agree	1974	1987	1991	1994	1996	1998	2000
People like me have no say in what the government does	14	20	16	28	24	17	25
Voting is the only way people like me can have any say about how the government does things	15	-	12	19	15	14	17
Sometimes politics and government seem so complicated that a person like me cannot really understand what is going on	21	-	16	22	22	15	18
Base	1802	1410	1445	1137	1180	2071	2293

Source: 1974: Political Action Study. See also note to table 9.4.

There is one further indication of confidence in government that we can examine. This was first asked by the Kilbrandon Commission on the Constitution in the early 1970s and has been asked periodically by a number of surveys ever since. It reads:

> *Which of these statements best describes your opinion on the present system of governing Britain?*
>
> *It works extremely well and could not be improved*
> *It could be improved in small ways but mainly works well*
> *It could be improved quite a lot*
> *It needs a great deal of improvement*

Thus the question not only asks people to consider how well the political system is performing but also how much could be done to improve it. Responses to it largely confirm the picture painted by our two other measures. Thus, the proportion believing that the system needs little or no improvement reached an all-time low (with just 22 per cent agreeing) in 1995. The advent of the Labour government then saw a significant revival of confidence with nearly half saying that the system needed little or no improvement in 1998, as high as the figure the Kilbrandon Commission itself found in 1973. But now the figure has fallen again. True it remains above the level it reached in the mid-1990s, but our finding that only 35 per cent think that the system needs little or no improvement suggests that Labour's programme of constitutional reform has not had much permanent impact on people's confidence in how they are governed.[3]

Table 9.6 Trends in evaluations of system of government, 1973-2000

% saying system of governing Britain could ...	1973	1977	1991	1995	1996	1998	1999	2000
... not be improved or could be improved only in small ways	48	34	33	22	35	45	48	35
... be improved quite a lot or a great deal	49	62	63	76	63	51	50	63
Base	4892	1410	1034	1758	1180	2071	1060	2293

Sources: 1973: Royal Commission on the Constitution, *Memorandum of Dissent*, 1973; 1977: Opinion Research Centre Survey; 1991/1995: MORI/Rowntree Trust State of the Nation Survey.

The decline in public confidence during the mid-1990s could have reflected the fact that Britain was then being governed by a government, headed by John Major, which was particularly unpopular and was also mired in allegations of 'sleaze'? But if that were the case then its replacement by a new government, let alone one committed to a programme of constitutional reform, should have been sufficient to restore confidence. And according to each of our three measures that evidently has not been the case; the new Labour government has not, as yet at least, restored the bonds between citizens and their political system. It appears instead that there is a more fundamental crisis of confidence in the political system.

Indeed further confirmation that relatively little has changed under Labour comes from the next table which compares levels of efficacy and trust in 1996 (towards the end of John Major's administration) among people who strongly identified with either the Conservative or Labour parties or with no party at all, with the same groups now. Unsurprisingly, we find that levels of trust and efficacy are for the most part higher among strong Labour identifiers now than they were in 1996 when the Conservatives were in power. Meanwhile the opposite pattern is true of Conservative identifiers. But among those with no party political identity levels of efficacy are just as low now as they were in 1996, and their level of trust in government has plummeted.

Table 9.7　Trends in efficacy and trust by party identification, 1996-2000

% strongly agree	1996 Party Identification			2000 Party Identification		
	Labour	Conservative	None	Labour	Conservative	None
Parties are only interested in votes	33	18	35	19	25	35
MPs lose touch too quickly	34	15	30	19	26	30
Doesn't matter who in power	18	7	27	12	15	34
% who trust governments always/most of the time to put nation's interests first	19	34	18	28	19	5
Base	*284*	*186*	*110*	*434*	*304*	*308*

But are we correct in assuming that a decline in levels of trust and efficacy necessarily represents a crisis for the political system? Should we assume that those with low levels of trust are ready to opt out of the political system? Or might a decline simply indicate a public which is less willing to take elected officials' words for granted, and is keener to scrutinise their activities? After all, such scrutiny may be necessary if the public is to ensure that politicians do what they want them to do, especially in a country where general elections may be as much as five years apart (Hardin, 2000). So, far from wanting to withdraw from democracy might those with low levels of trust and efficacy wish instead to see democracy improved (see also Klingemann, 1999)?

　Previous analyses of *British Social Attitudes'* data have themselves cast some doubt on whether those with low level of trust and efficacy are necessarily less likely to participate in elections (Curtice and Jowell, 1995, 1997). However, other research has identified some relationship between abstention and either trust or efficacy (Heath and Taylor, 1999; Pattie and Johnston, 2001b), although other factors (particularly the perceived distance between the parties and the closeness of the contest) appear to be more important. That there is indeed a link between trust, efficacy and turnout is also supported by analysis of data from our most recent survey. So, for example, 78 per cent of those who trust governments to put the interest of the nation first at least most of the time claim to have voted in the 1997 election, compared with only 62 per cent of those who almost never trust governments. The figures for those with high and low levels of political efficacy are almost identical,[4] and there are differences of a similar kind in respect of voting in the 1999 European elections too.

Table 9.8 Political participation by levels of trust and efficacy

| | Trust government to put interests of the nation first ... | | |
	... just about always or most of the time	... only some of the time	... almost never
% voted in 1997 general election	78	76	62
% voted in 1999 Euro election	46	38	29
% ever taken political action	50	54	52
Base	*368*	*1336*	*566*
	Level of system efficacy		
	High	**Medium**	**Low**
% voted in 1997 general election	85	79	69
% voted in 1999 Euro election	60	44	33
% ever taken political action	73	59	49
Base	*99*	*480*	*1345*

This apparent change in the relationship between electoral participation and political trust and efficacy suggests that, even if it were not initially the case, declining levels of trust and efficacy are helping to undermine turnout at the ballot box. Perhaps initial disillusionment with the system has relatively little impact on willingness to vote, but more prolonged disillusionment then begins to have an effect on certain types of voters? But even if this is the case, we should be wary on the basis of the evidence presented here of assuming that falling trust and efficacy explain the large drop in turnout between 1997 and 2001. After all, levels of efficacy are no lower now than they were before the 1997 election. And the drop since 1996 in levels of trust in government is insufficient to be able to account for the 12-point drop in electoral participation between 1997 and 2001.[5]

The above table also helps explain why we could find little evidence earlier of a decline in non-electoral participation despite the apparent decline in trust and efficacy. It shows that, while there is a relationship between system efficacy and ever having done anything in response to a government action that was thought to be unjust and harmful, there is no apparent relationship between engaging in non-electoral forms of political participation and trust in government.

So, the decline in confidence in government that emerged under the last Conservative administration was not reversed during Labour's first term. True, this may have only made a contribution to the decline in turnout at recent elections rather than being principally responsible for it. And there is no evidence of any decline in other forms of political participation. But it does appear that Labour's programme of constitutional reform has, so far at least, failed to reconnect citizens with their politicians. We now turn to addressing why this is the case.

The impact of constitutional change

Reformers believed that constitutional reform would address grievances that the public have about the way that they are governed. And our own previous work also gave reason to believe that it might have a favourable impact. This is because throughout the 1990s those with lower levels of political trust were, for the most part, more likely to have a favourable view of constitutional reform than those with higher levels of trust (Curtice and Jowell, 1995, 1997). We therefore surmised that perhaps their trust would be restored should constitutional reform be implemented.

But of course, implementing constitutional reform could only help restore public confidence in Britain's system of government if people actually welcome its impact in practice. The next table shows what impact people think four examples of constitutional reform have had on the way that Britain is governed. So far at least, the perception appears to be not much. Reform of the House of Lords, freedom of information, and the creation of the Scottish Parliament and the Welsh Assembly are each judged by a majority to have currently made no difference to the way Britain is run. True, in each case more feel that the reform in question has improved matters rather than made them worse, but with the exception of freedom of information the positive balance is only a small one.

Of course, these figures do not directly address the question of whether constitutional reform has increased trust and efficacy among the general public. Moreover, the fact that trust and efficacy have not risen may reflect other influences which have counteracted any beneficial impact that constitutional reform might have had. To assess this, we can conduct two additional analyses. First, we compare the relationship between political trust and attitudes towards constitutional change in 1996 (before reform was implemented) and 2000 (by which time much of Labour's programme was in place). If reform has had a positive impact we would expect to find that trust and efficacy have risen more among those favouring the constitutional reforms that have been implemented than they have among those who are less favourable.

Table 9.9 Evaluations of constitutional reform

		Perceived impact on the way Britain as a whole is governed ...		
		... improved it a lot/a little	... made no difference	... made it a little/ a lot worse
Reforming the House of Lords	%	11	69	8
Introducing freedom of information	%	25	59	3
Creating the Scottish Parliament	%	19	53	13
Creating the Welsh Assembly	%	15	56	12

Base: 2293

The following table undertakes this exercise in relation to freedom of information. It does so by looking at people's views about whether the government should have "the right to keep its defence plans secret" or whether they think "the public has a right to know what they are". Of course, the question we examine here does not address the government's freedom of information legislation directly (as it posits a greater freedom than that legislation has put in place). But we might reasonably assume that the 45 per cent who say that the public has the right to know such plans comprises those who would be most committed to the principle of freedom of information. But, if this is the case, then Labour's legislation seems to have done little to raise their confidence in the political system. Rather, their level of trust has fallen just as much as has the confidence of those who think the government has the right to keep its defence plans secret, while their level of efficacy has actually fallen more.

These findings do not apply only in respect of freedom of information; they equally apply to views about Scottish devolution. Thus, despite the advent of the Scottish Parliament in 1999, levels of trust and efficacy fell by more or less the same amount between 1996 and 2000 among those who favour devolution as they did among those who do not think Scotland should have any kind of parliament at all.

Table 9.10 Changes in trust and efficacy by views about freedom of information, 1996-2000

Attitudes towards defence plans	% trust government just about always/most of the time			% medium/high efficacy		
	1996	2000	Change	1996	2000	Change
Public should normally have right to know	19	13	-6	35	26	-9
Base	*521*	*877*		*521*	*877*	
Government should have right to keep plans secret	26	18	-8	37	33	-4
Base	*614*	*1338*		*614*	*1338*	

Our second way of examining the impact of constitutional reform is to compare what has happened in a part of Great Britain that has experienced high profile constitutional change and another part that has not. The most obvious example is devolution – which has been introduced to a significant extent in Scotland but not in England. If devolution has restored confidence in how Britain is governed we should find more favourable trends in trust and efficacy in Scotland than in England. But, as the next table reveals, trends in both trust and efficacy have almost been identical in Scotland and England over the course of the last three years (for further details see Curtice, 2001, forthcoming).

Table 9.11 Trust and efficacy in England and Scotland, 1997-2000

% strongly agree		1997	2000	Change 97-00
Parties only interested in votes, not in opinions	England	16	26	+10
	Scotland	16	24	+8
It doesn't really matter who's in power, things go on the same	England	8	19	+11
	Scotland	8	20	+12
Base: England		*2187*	*1928*	
Base: Scotland		*756*	*1663*	
% who trust the Government to put nation before party "just about always" or " most of the time"	England	34	17	-17
	Scotland	29	13	-16
Base: England		*2551*	*1928*	
Base: Scotland		*882*	*1663*	

Sources: 1997 England: British Election Study; 1997 Scotland: Scottish Election Study 1997; 2000 Scotland: Scottish Social Attitudes Survey 2000.

So it appears that Labour's programme of constitutional reform has indeed done little or nothing so far to increase people's confidence in how they are governed.

But of course our findings may well not represent the public's final word on Labour's programme of constitutional reform. Certainly, advocates of reform might reasonably argue that it will take time for its benefits to become apparent. Indeed, the UK government's freedom of information legislation had not even come into force by the time of our survey. But, by this argument, it is also clear that constitutional reform has not been an immediate remedy for declining trust and efficacy.

Alternatively, advocates of reform might be tempted to argue that its inability to increase people's confidence in government reflects its failure to go far enough. Indeed in its 2001 General Election handbook, the constitutional reform lobby, Charter88, argue that Britain needs a full blown 'Citizens' Constitution' (Holden, 2001). In particular, some point to the fact that Labour has failed to implement the one piece of its constitutional programme that they see as having the most potential impact on the way Britain is governed – holding a referendum on whether the House of Commons should be elected by an alternative, more proportional, electoral system.

However, as we have previously argued (Curtice and Jowell, 1995), it is far from clear that electoral reform is sufficiently popular for the public to even vote in its favour, let alone respond to its introduction by showing higher levels of trust and efficacy. In our most recent survey, just 35 per cent think that we should "change the voting system for general elections to the House of Commons to allow smaller political parties to get a fairer share of MPs", little different from the readings that have been obtained in response to this question on a number of occasions since 1983. Moreover, if it is the case that the current low level of trust and efficacy reflects a feeling that constitutional reform has not been sufficiently extensive, then we should find that trust and efficacy has fallen more over the last four years amongst the one-third or so who say they are in favour of changing the electoral system than it has amongst those who say they want to keep the system as it is. However, if anything the opposite is the case. For example, the percentage willing to trust governments at least most of the time fell by just three points between 1996 and 2000 among those in favour of electoral reform but by eight points amongst those wanting to keep the existing system.

Perhaps this is to take too narrow a view of the kinds of change to the political system that the public would like to see. After all, all the reforms we have considered so far are ones that still assume a framework of representative democracy in which parties compete at election time for the power to take decisions for the next four or five years. But perhaps what the public wants are *more* opportunities to participate in the process of decision making itself (Dalton, 1999: 74-77). After all, no less than 55 per cent disagreed and only 21 per cent agreed when we put the proposition to them that "even if I had the chance I would not be interested in having more say in government decisions". Moreover, as many as 40 per cent disagreed (although 43 per cent agreed) that, "between elections, the government should get on with running the country rather than bothering about public opinion".

One of the more participatory forms of decision making that has been introduced in recent years by some local councils is the 'citizens' jury'. Information pertinent to a decision that a local council has to make is presented to a small group of residents, sometimes selected at random, which is then invited to consider what decision they would make (Coote and Lenaghan, 1997). In order to tap attitudes towards this rather different kind of approach we asked our respondents how much they would trust the councillors on their local council to come to the "best view" about a proposed "major new building development in their neighbourhood" and how much they would trust "a jury of 12 ordinary local people chosen at random". The jury was clearly the more trusted device; nearly two-thirds said that they would trust this group to come to the best view "just about always" or "most of the time", whereas only one-third said the same of their local councillors.

But what matters for our purposes here is how people's views on these matters vary according to their trust in government or level of political efficacy. And there is some evidence to suggest that differences do exist. Among those who trust governments to put the interests of the nation first at least most of the time, nearly half (48 per cent) also trust local councillors to come to the best view about a planning development at least "most of the time", double the comparable figure among those who do not trust governments in this way (only 26 per cent of whom would trust local councillors in this way). By contrast, these two groups only differ by six percentage points in their views about the ability of a citizens' jury to come to the best view. So those with low levels of trust in government are almost as likely to trust a citizens' jury as are those with high levels of trust, but are much less likely to trust councillors to make the same decision. We find a similar pattern if we compare the attitudes of those with low and high levels of efficacy.

So we have found that Labour's programme of constitutional reform seems to have done little to increase people's confidence in their system of government. So far at least, those reforms have evidently had too little impact upon the public to be able to do so. Maybe over time they might have more success in increasing confidence. And it might be that more radical departures from the norms of representative democracy would be more successful. But, in truth, perhaps changing the way in which Britain is governed is simply not the right antidote to declining public trust and confidence. Perhaps the causes lie elsewhere, reflecting more fundamental and long-term changes in British society and government. It is to these questions that we now turn.

What accounts for declining political trust?

A wide range of explanations has been offered as to why people's confidence in how they are governed is falling, not just in Britain but in much of the developed world. Here we evaluate four of those explanations.[6]

The relative capacity of governments

The first of these explanations is that people no longer think governments can meet public needs and expectations. On the one hand, thanks to rising levels of education and personal affluence, people's expectations of what governments and politicians should achieve have increased. But, on the other hand, thanks to the process of globalisation, governments have lost much of their ability to influence the direction of their country's economy or to pursue distinctive social policies (Giddens, 1994). The resulting gap between what voters expect, and what they think governments can deliver, is held to produce negative attitudes towards political institutions. We might call this explanation the 'relative capacity' argument.

We have available to us two measures of whether people's expectations of politicians and government are rising or not. The first of these comprises what qualities people think it is important for MPs to have. As the next table shows, up to and including 1996 it did appear plausible to argue that expectations of MPs were rising. But now our latest survey has seen expectations fall back again. True, two qualities, "knowing about poverty" and being "independent minded", are still clearly more important to people now than when we first asked this question in 1983. But, so far as most of the other qualities are concerned, the picture now is little different to what it was in 1983.

Table 9.12 Expectations of MPs, 1983-2000

% who think it is important for MPs to ...	1983	1994	1996	2000
... be independent minded	37	48	51	56
... be well educated	50	55	60	54
... be from the local area	48	60	61	54
... be loyal to their party	42	42	44	43
... know about poverty	27	41	45	42
... have business experience	22	30	34	28
... have union experience	14	13	14	14
Base	1761	2302	1180	2293

Our second measure comprises people's views on what responsibilities governments should fulfil. In the following table we show the proportion of people who think that each of four possible responsibilities should "definitely" fall within the remit of government. Here the trends are almost the reverse of what we saw in Table 9.12. Thus, up to and including 1996, expectations of government appeared to be falling rather than rising. In each case the proportion saying the objective in question should definitely be the government's responsibility was lower than it was ten years earlier. But in our most recent survey that trend has been reversed; in all four cases the proportion saying the objective should definitely be the government's responsibility is now either at least as high or higher than it was in 1986.

Table 9.13 Expectations of government, 1986-2000

% who think it definitely should be the government's responsibility to ...	1986	1990	1996	2000
... provide health care for all	84	84	81	87
... provide a decent standard of living for the old	80	77	70	80
... keep prices under control	52	47	40	64
... provide a job for everyone who wants one	30	23	26	39
Base	1321	1197	989	2008

So neither of our measures easily substantiates the claim that there is a gradual, secular increase in people's expectations of politicians and government. Still, it is just about possible to argue that expectations appear to be at least a little higher now than they were in the 1980s. But what about people's perceptions of the ability of governments to deliver? Is there indeed a gap between what people think governments should do and what they think they are actually capable of delivering? Might this account for low levels of trust and efficacy?

In our 2000 survey, for the first time, we followed questions about what governments should do by ones that asked people how easy or difficult they thought it was for government to ensure that each objective was achieved. And indeed, there is a clear recognition that many objectives are not at all easy to deliver. Only 47 per cent think that it is easy for government to ensure that all old people have a decent standard of living (compared with 80 per cent who think that this is definitely government's responsibility), 42 per cent that it is easy to ensure that everyone has good access to adequate health care, and only 31 per cent that it is easy for governments to keep prices under control. Meanwhile, just 16 per cent think it is easy for government to ensure that everyone who wants a job has one.

But is this disjuncture responsible for low trust and efficacy? If it is, we should find lower levels of trust than average among those who believe that a particular objective should be the government's responsibility and who also think it difficult for the government to ensure that it happens. But this is not what we find. In the following table we illustrate this by showing the level of trust and efficacy among those who think that government should be responsible for ensuring that everyone who wants a job has one, broken down by whether they think that objective is easy or difficult for governments to fulfil. And, if anything, those whom it might be thought would be concerned about the relative incapacity of government (that is, who think it difficult for governments to ensure everyone has a job) are very slightly more trustful and efficacious than those who think it is easy. So, in practice then, it is those who think that it is *easy* for governments to deliver who are most likely to be disillusioned by their actual performance. It is thus perhaps good rather than bad news for governments that many people apparently recognise that in a number of respects politicians do not have an easy job.

Table 9.14 The impact of perceptions of government on trust and efficacy

	Believe ensuring everyone who wants a job has one is	
	Easy	**Difficult**
% who trust governments just about always/most of the time	14	18
Base	*308*	*1331*
% with medium or high efficacy	28	30
Base	*308*	*1331*

Table confined to those respondents who say that providing a job for everyone who wants one should "definitely" be the government's responsibility.

Postmaterialism

Our three remaining theories suggest, in different ways, that the decline in people's confidence in government is the result of wider social changes. The first of these theories is postmaterialism. Put forward by Ronald Inglehart (Inglehart, 1977, 1990, 1997; Abramson and Inglehart, 1995) it posits that the post-war experience of rising affluence, and continuous peace in the developed world, means that people have changed their priorities. Rather than seeking material security, which it would appear they can now largely take for granted, people are primarily concerned with developing their opportunities for self-expression and involvement. One consequence of this is that they are less likely to take what governments do on trust and instead seek more opportunities to be involved in, and even to challenge, the decision-making process.

   We included in our survey the most commonly used indicator of postmaterialism:

> *Looking at the list below, please tick a box next to the **one** thing you think should be Britain's **highest priority**, the **most** important thing it should do.*
> *And which **one** do you think should be Britain's **next highest priority**, the **second** most important thing it should do?*

Maintain order in the nation
Give people more say in government decisions
Fight rising prices
Protect freedom of speech
Can't choose

People who say that maintaining order and fighting prices are their two highest priorities are classified as 'materialists' (that is, their primary concern is with economic and physical security). Those who opt for freedom of speech and greater involvement in decision making are 'postmaterialists'. Meanwhile, those who choose any other mixture are regarded as having 'mixed' orientations.

If a rise in postmaterialism is to account for the decline in people's confidence in how they are governed then we need to be able to demonstrate two things: that postmaterialists have lower levels of trust and efficacy than materialists, and that the proportion of postmaterialists in Britain has increased. However, while the first of these is only partly true, the second is not true at all. As the next table shows, postmaterialists are indeed less likely to trust governments to put the interests of the nation first at least most of the time. Just over one in ten postmaterialists falls into this category compared with as many as one in five materialists. But postmaterialists are little different in their level of system efficacy from materialists.[7] And most importantly, only 12 per cent of people in Britain can be classified as postmaterialist, little different from the ten per cent who fell into that category in 1983.[8]

Table 9.15 Trust and efficacy by materialist/postmaterialist orientations, 2000

	% trust government just about always or most of the time	Base	% medium/high efficacy	Base
Materialist	20	*402*	29	*402*
Mixed	15	*1081*	32	*1081*
Postmaterialist	12	*228*	32	*228*

Declining social trust?

An alternative claim as to how social change may be undermining people's confidence in how they are governed is that it reflects a decline in 'social trust'; that is, the degree to which people have trust in one another (Putnam, 1993, 2000). According to Putnam, in America at least, social trust is on the decline. And if we no longer have trust in each other then perhaps we should not be surprised that we do not trust in our politicians either.

Putnam's arguments are addressed more fully in the chapters by Johnston and Jowell and by Gardner and Oswald. Here we simply have to address the same two arguments that we did in respect of postmaterialism: are those with low levels of social trust less likely to trust governments or to have high levels of efficacy, and has social trust declined in Britain in recent years? We also follow the same strategy as we did in respect of postmaterialism by deploying the most commonly used simple indicator of social trust:

> *Generally speaking, would you say that most people can be*
> *trusted, or that you can't be too careful in dealing with people?*

Whether or not there is a link at all between social and political trust is the subject of some dispute. A number of studies have suggested that those who are willing to trust other individuals are no more or less trusting of governments than anyone else (Jackman and Miller, 1998; Newton, 1999; Newton and Norris, 2000). However, this claim is disputed by Hall (1999: 454), while others have suggested that, although such a relationship may exist, it is political trust that helps generate social trust rather than the other way around (Levi and Stoker, 2000).[9] In fact, our latest survey suggests that there is some relationship between social and political trust. Among those who say that "most people can be trusted", one in five trust governments to put the interests of the nation first at least most of the time. But this figure falls to one in eight amongst those who believe that you cannot be too careful in your dealings with other people. And there appears to be an even stronger relationship with political efficacy (see also Johnston and Jowell, 1999). As many as 38 per cent of the trustful have a medium or high level of efficacy on our scale, compared with just 24 per cent of the not so trustful.

However, as in the case of postmaterialism, there is no clear evidence that levels of social trust have declined in Britain over time. As Johnston and Jowell show in Table 8.5, the level of social trust measured by the *British Social Attitudes* survey on three occasions between 1997 and 2000 mirrors that obtained by the World Values Survey in 1981 and 1990 – with around 45 per cent being 'trustful'. Again it appears that British society has simply not changed to the extent that has been claimed.

The decline of party identification

So far we have cast doubt on two of the wider social changes that might be helping to undermine people's confidence in the way they are governed. But there is a further change within British society which remains worthy of exploration. This is the gradual and persistent decline in strength of attachment to political parties (Crewe and Thomson, 1999). According to party identification theory (Budge *et al.*, 1976), those who have a strong attachment to a political party are not only more likely to remain loyal to that party in the polling booth, but are also more likely to support the political system. After all, they identify with a party that plays according to the rules of electoral competition in their country and this should help ensure their own respect for and trust in those rules (Barry, 1970; Crewe *et al.*, 1977). And if this is the case, and if levels of party identification have declined, there would be good reason to expect levels of political trust to decline as well.

The table below confirms that there has indeed been a gradual and persistent decline in attachment to political parties over the last few decades. Whereas in 1987, 46 per cent said they felt "very" or "fairly" strongly attached to the party they supported, now only 32 per cent feel that way. Moreover, as in the case of trust and efficacy, strength of identification weakened notably in the mid-1990s (though equally there was no sign of any recovery in the immediate wake of Labour's election to office in 1997).

Table 9.16 Trends in strength of party identification, 1987-2000

Strength of party identification	1987	1993	1996	1998	2000
Very strong	11	9	9	8	6
Fairly strong	35	33	28	28	26
Not very strong	40	44	47	48	49
No party identification	8	10	10	11	13
Base	2847	2945	3620	3145	3426

Meanwhile, we can also see in the next table that those with a strong party identification are more likely to have high levels of trust both in government and in system efficacy. For example, nearly three in ten of those with a "very strong" party identification trust governments just about always or most of the time, compared with just one in twelve of those who do not identify with a party at all. At last then, we seem to have a plausible explanation as to how long-term changes among the British public have served to undermine confidence in the country's political system.

Table 9.17 Trust and efficacy by strength of party identification, 2000

Strength of party identification	% trust government just about always or most of the time	Base	% medium/high efficacy	Base
Very strong	29	152	45	152
Fairly strong	22	581	40	581
Not very strong	15	1123	28	1120
No party identification	8	308	13	307

However, if this decline in party identification accounts for falling confidence in government we should not expect to find any changes in levels of trust and efficacy among those with a strong party identification; there is no reason these should not be as high now within this group as they ever were. But, as the following table shows, this is not what we find. The proportion of strong identifiers who trust governments at least just about always has fallen from nearly a half in 1987 to under a third now. A similar decline has occurred amongst all of the other levels of identification as well.[10]

Table 9.18 Trends in strength of party identification and trust in government, 1987-2000

Strength of party identification	% trust government just about always/most of the time							
	1987	*Base*	**1996**	*Base*	**1998**	*Base*	**2000**	*Base*
Very strong	48	*188*	25	*106*	34	*153*	29	*152*
Fairly strong	43	*483*	22	*321*	33	*584*	22	*581*
Not very strong	33	*566*	23	*569*	26	*989*	15	*1123*
No party identification	14	*93*	19	*110*	21	*241*	8	*308*
All	37	*1410*	22	*1173*	28	*2071*	16	*2293*

So, at most, falling party identification can only account for part of the decline in trust and efficacy we have seen in recent years. Britain does indeed now have fewer strong party identifiers who are encouraged by their enthusiasm into having confidence in how they are governed. But, even among strong party identifiers, their enthusiasm for their party seems less likely now to translate into trust in how they are governed.

Conclusions

Three key findings have emerged from this study. First, the decline in confidence in how we are governed that emerged during the last Conservative government has not been reversed during Labour's first term of office. In particular, Labour's programme of constitutional reform appears to have done little or nothing to reverse that decline. Second, although that decline in confidence may have depressed turnout at recent elections, its role should not be exaggerated. Moreover, it appears to have had little impact on the public's willingness to engage in other forms of political participation. And third, falling confidence does *not* appear to be primarily the product of irreversible social changes or forces such as globalisation. Labour's attempts to reverse that decline may so far have failed but they cannot be accused of having engaged in a Canute-like attempt to stop an irreversible tide of social change. Britain's democracy may have something of a problem securing the support of its citizens, but it apparently does not face a fundamental crisis.

Constitutional reform might not have been the right remedy for the recent decline in confidence in government, but that does not mean that it is no remedy at all. Equally, while restoring confidence in government might make some contribution to improving electoral turnout, it is unlikely to be a sufficient remedy on its own. Rather, in order to understand recent trends in confidence and participation we probably have to look at other political developments in recent years. Do governments deliver on their promises? Do politicians avoid accusations of sleaze? And does there seem to be much to choose between the parties? Arguably the answers to those questions has been 'no' for too many voters under both the Conservative and Labour administrations in recent years to encourage voters to go to the polls or to have much confidence in how they are governed. If so, the future health of Britain's democracy probably depends on whether or not this must always be so.

Notes

1. Moreover, turnout in 1918 was reduced by the circumstances of war combined with a threefold expansion in the size of the electorate. In practice the level of voluntary abstention was higher in 2001 than at any time since the advent of the mass franchise.
2. We may also note that there is no evidence that reported interest in politics has declined either. One in three say that they have a great deal or quite a lot of interest in politics, a figure that was virtually unchanged from when we first asked this question in 1986.
3. Our latest reading is also confirmed by the latest State of the Nation survey conducted by ICM in autumn 2000. This found just 31 per cent saying that the system could not be improved or could only be improved in small ways (see www.icmresearch.co.uk).
4. Political efficacy is here measured using a Likert scale based on the first three items in Table x.4. In each case the component items are scored from 1 = "Strongly agree" = low efficacy to 5 = "Strongly disagree" = high efficacy. Those classified as having low efficacy are those with an average rounded score across all three items of 1or 2, those as having high efficacy are those with an average score of 4 or 5 while those with an average score of 3 are those deemed to have medium efficacy. The scale has a Cronbach's alpha of 0.66.
5. Moreover, we should note that the proportion who say that "It is everyone's duty to vote", is at 64 per cent no different now from what it was in 1996, and is only four points lower than it was in 1991 and 1994. So there appears so far at least to be little undermining of the sense that voting is a civic duty. See also Electoral Commission (2001).
6. The range of explanations is discussed extensively in Norris (1999), Levi and Stoker (2000) and Pharr and Putnam (2000).
7. The table in fact rather understates the impact of postmaterialism on trust in government. Postmaterialists tend to be highly educated and those with a degree tend to have higher levels of trust. The low level of trust amongst postmaterialists is thus even more remarkable given their educational level. However, multivariate analysis of the relationship between educational attainment, postmaterialism and

system efficacy indicates that the absence of any bivariate association between the last two is not the result of the potentially confounding impact of educational attainment.

8. The latter figure comes from the 1983 British Election Study.
9. Moreover, Newton and Norris (2000) suggest that while there may be no relationship at the individual level, governments are able to perform more effectively in societies with high levels of social trust and as a result are able to secure a higher level of political trust.
10. Equally when the level of trust in government rose in 1998, it rose amongst each group of identifiers.

References

Abramson, P. and Inglehart, R. (1995), *Value Change in Global Perspective*, Ann Arbor: University of Michigan Press.

Almond, G. and Verba, S. (1963), *The Civic Culture; Political Attitudes and Democracy in Five Nations*, Princeton, NJ: Princeton University Press.

Barnett, A. (1993), *Debating the constitution: new perspectives on constitutional reform*, Cambridge: Polity Press.

Barry, B. (1970), *Sociologists, Economists and Democracy*, London: Collier-Macmillan.

Blair, A. (1996), 'Democracy's second age', *The Economist*, 14 September 1996.

Budge, I., Crewe, I. and Farlie, D. (eds.) (1976), *Party Identification and Beyond*, New York: Wiley.

Coote, A. and Lenaghan, J. (1997), *Citizens' Juries: Theory into Practice*, London: IPPR, 129-190.

Crewe, I., Särlvik, B. and Alt, J. (1977), 'Partisan Dealignment in Britain 1964-74', *British Journal of Political Science*, **7**: 129-90.

Crewe, I. and Thomson, K. (1999), 'Party loyalties: dealignment or realignment?' in Evans, G. and Norris. P. (eds.), *Critical Elections – British Parties and Voters in Long-Term Perspective*, London: Sage.

Curtice, J. (2001, forthcoming), 'Devolution and Democracy: New Trust or Old Cynicism' in Curtice, J., McCrone, D., Park, A. and Paterson, L. (eds.), *New Scotland, New Society? Are Social and Political Ties Fragmenting?*, Edinburgh: Edinburgh University Press.

Curtice, J and Jowell, R (1995), 'The sceptical electorate' in Jowell, R., Curtice, J., Park, A., Brook, L., and Ahrendt, D. (eds.), *British Social Attitudes: the 12ᵗʰ Report*, Aldershot: Dartmouth.

Curtice, J. and Jowell, R. (1997), 'Trust in the Political System' in Jowell, R., Curtice, J., Park, A., Brook, L., Thomson., K, and Bryson, C. (eds.), *British Social Attitudes: the 14ᵗʰ Report - The end of Conservative values?*, Aldershot: Ashgate.

Dalton, R. J. (1999), 'Political Support in Advanced Industrial Democracies' in Norris, P., *Critical Citizens: Global Support for Democratic Governance*, Oxford: Oxford University Press.

Davis, R. and Curtice, J. (2000), 'Speaking for the Public: representation and audience participation during the 1997 British general election campaign', *Harvard International Journal of Press/Politics*, **5**: 62-77.

Electoral Commission (2001), *The Official Results*, London: Politicos.

Fuchs, D. and Klingemann, H. D. (1995), 'Citizens and the State: A Changing Relationship?' in Klingemann, H. D., and Fuchs, D., *Citizens and the State*, Oxford: Oxford University Press.

Giddens, A. (1994), *Beyond Left and Right*, Cambridge: Polity Press.

Hall, P. (1999), 'Social Capital in Britain', *British Journal of Political Science*, **29**: 417-461.

Hardin, R. (2000), 'The Public Trust' in Pharr, S. J. and Putnam, R. D. (eds.), *Disaffected Democracies: What's Troubling the Trilateral Countries?*, Princeton, NJ: Princeton University Press.

Heath, A. F. and Taylor, B. (1999), 'New Sources of Abstention?' in Evans, G. and Norris. P (eds.), *Critical Elections – British Parties and Voters in Long-Term Perspective*, London: Sage.

Holden, A. (ed.) (2001), *Unlocking the Policies*, London: Charter88.

Inglehart, R. (1977), *The Silent Revolution: Changing Values and Political Styles*, Princeton, NJ: Princeton University Press.

Inglehart, R. (1990), *Culture Shift in Advanced Industrial Society*, Princeton, NJ: Princeton University Press.

Inglehart, R. (1997), *Modernization and Postmodernization: Cultural, Economic and Political Change in 43 Societies*, Princeton, NJ: Princeton University Press.

Jackman, R. W and Miller, R. A. (1998), 'Social Capital and Politics', *Annual Review of Political Science*, **1**: 47-73.

Johnston, M. and Jowell. R. (1999), 'Social Capital and the Social Fabric' in Jowell, R., Curtice, J., Park., A. and Thomson., K. (eds.), *British Social Attitudes: the 16th Report - Who shares New Labour values?*, Aldershot: Ashgate.

Klingemann, H. D. (1999), 'Mapping political support in the 1990s; a global analysis' in Norris, P., *Critical Citizens: Global Support for Democratic Governance*, Oxford: Oxford University Press.

Levi, M. and Stoker, L. (2000), 'Political Trust and Trustworthiness', *Annual Review of Political Science*, **3**: 475-507.

Marsh, A. (1977), *Protest and Political Consciousness*, Beverley Hills: Sage.

Newton, K. (1999), 'Social and Political Trust in Established Democracies' in Norris, P., *Critical Citizens: Global Support for Democratic Governance*, Oxford: Oxford University Press.

Newton, K. and Norris, P. (2000), 'Confidence in Public Institutions: Faith, Culture or Performance?' in Pharr, S. J. and Putnam, R. D. (eds.), *Disaffected Democracies: What's Troubling the Trilateral Countries?*, Princeton, NJ: Princeton University Press.

Norris, P. (1999), 'Introduction: The Growth of Critical Citizens?' in Norris, P., *Critical Citizens: Global Support for Democratic Governance*, Oxford: Oxford University Press.

Pattie, C. and Johnston, R. (2001a), 'Losing the Voters' Trust: Evaluations of the Political System and Voting at the 1997 British General Election', *British Journal of Politics and International Relations*, **3**: 191-222.

Pattie, C. and Johnston, R. (2001b), 'A Low Turnout Landslide: Abstention at the British General Election of 1997', *Political Studies*, **49**: 286-305.

Pharr, S. J. and Putnam, R. D. (eds.) (2000), *Disaffected Democracies: What's Troubling the Trilateral Countries?*, Princeton, NJ: Princeton University Press.

Putnam, R. D. (2000), *Bowling Alone – the collapse and revival of American community*, New York: Simon & Schuster.

Putnam, R. D. (1993), *Making Democracy Work: Civic Traditions in Modern Italy*, Princeton NJ: Princeton University Press.

Acknowledgements

Most of the questions reported in this chapter were financed by a grant from the Economic and Social Research Council (grant no. L215252032) as part of its Democracy and Participation Programme.

10 Is devolution strengthening or weakening the UK?

John Curtice and Ben Seyd [*]

The recent creation of devolved assemblies in each of Scotland, Wales and Northern Ireland constitutes the most radical change in the government of the United Kingdom since 1922, when the Irish Republic left the Union and Northern Ireland was given its own parliament. For some, their creation will demonstrate the ability of the Union to accommodate the diversity of aspirations and identities that exist within it, and thereby give it a new strength. For others, devolution is the thin end of a wedge (or, alternatively, a stepping stone) that will eventually drive the component territories of the United Kingdom – England, Scotland, Wales and Northern Ireland – apart. And, whichever argument is correct, the introduction of devolution is certainly an attempt to respond to apparent dissatisfaction with and questioning of the Union among many people living outside of England.

Whether devolution does eventually strengthen or weaken the Union will ultimately be determined in the court of public opinion. To strengthen it, the new devolved bodies need to be seen as a success by the people they seek to serve and people's sense of commitment to a sense of Britishness needs to be enhanced, as well as support for keeping Scotland, Wales and Northern Ireland within the UK increased. If the devolved bodies are seen as a failure, or if they come to encourage a separate sense of identity and a taste for national independence, or, indeed, if they create a feeling of resentment in England, then the Union will undoubtedly be weakened.

Of all the recent moves towards devolution, none appears to be more momentous for the future of the Union than the creation of a separate Scottish Parliament in Edinburgh. After all, Northern Ireland has experienced devolution before and the Welsh National Assembly lacks any primary legislative powers. But in Scotland, the second largest component of the United Kingdom, a parliament has been created that can pass laws across a wide range of

---

[*] John Curtice is Head of Research at the *National Centre for Social Research*, Scotland, Deputy Director of the ESRC Centre for Research into Elections and Social Trends, and Professor of Politics at Strathclyde University. Ben Seyd is a Senior Research Fellow at the Constitution Unit, University College London.

responsibilities including health, education and criminal justice. In short, what for nearly 300 years had been considered to the best way of managing the Union between Scotland and England – a single imperial parliament – has simply been overturned.

So, monitoring how people in England and Scotland are reacting to the experience of devolution is essential in forming any assessment of whether this radical constitutional change is delivering its objectives. This is the task that this chapter sets out to tackle. It examines how people both in England and in Scotland have reacted to the initial experience of devolution. What impact if any has it had so far on their national identity and commitment to the Union? What do Scots make of their new devolved institutions? And how has England reacted to the new privileges granted to its neighbour? Is there any hint of an 'English backlash' – for example, greater demand for similar privileges for England?

To address these questions, we have access not only to the *British Social Attitudes* survey, but also to the *Scottish Social Attitudes* survey. This was conducted by the *National Centre for Social Research* alongside its British counterpart and includes many identical or functionally equivalent questions (Curtice *et al.*, 2001, forthcoming). The *Scottish Social Attitudes* survey interviewed no less than 1,663 respondents in Scotland in 2000, thereby giving us a far more accurate and comprehensive picture of opinion north of the border than could be obtained from the 325 people interviewed in Scotland by the *British Social Attitudes* survey. In addition both the British and the Scottish survey repeated key questions that had been asked on previous surveys in England and Scotland, including the first *Scottish Social Attitudes* survey in 1999 (Paterson *et al.*, 2001).

Evaluations of devolution

We begin by asking what people in Scotland and in England have made of devolution so far. If devolution is contributing to a strengthening of the Union, we would anticipate that people would believe that creating the Scottish Parliament and the Welsh National Assembly has improved the way that Britain as a whole is governed. And certainly, so far as the Scottish Parliament is concerned, as the next table shows, over three times as many people in Scotland believe that its creation has improved the way that Britain is governed, as think that it has made things worse.

However, even in Scotland, a plurality believes that creating the Scottish Parliament has made no difference to the way that Britain is governed. Meanwhile, in England, those who think either Scottish or Welsh devolution has improved matters only just outnumber those who think it has made them worse, while a majority think it has made no difference. True, there is little sign of any 'English backlash', but at the same time, even in Scotland, many people are apparently not convinced that their new parliament has made much difference

Table 10.1 Perceptions of devolution, in England and Scotland

The way Britain as a whole is governed has been ...		... improved,	no difference,	made worse
England				
by creating Scottish Parliament	%	18	54	13
by creating Welsh Assembly	%	15	57	12
Base: 1928				
Scotland				
by creating Scottish Parliament	%	35	44	10
by creating Welsh Assembly	%	18	46	4
Base: 1663				

This conclusion is reinforced by other evidence from our Scottish surveys. At the time of the first Scottish election in 1999, we asked respondents whether the Scottish Parliament or the UK government at Westminster would come to have most influence over the way Scotland was run. About the same number of people (41 per cent) thought that the Scottish Parliament would have most influence as thought the UK government at Westminster would (39 per cent). But after their initial experience of devolution, no less than two-thirds of Scots now feel that the UK government has most influence in Scotland, while only one in eight give that accolade to the Scottish Parliament. Moreover, as the next table shows, whereas people in Scotland had a highly optimistic view of what the Scottish Parliament would achieve when they voted for it in the 1997 referendum, their expectations have now come down to earth. Overall, no less than 30 per cent think that the new parliament will *not* achieve any of the four objectives specified in the next table. While such a decline in expectations was perhaps inevitable, it does confirm the impression that many people in Scotland now appear to be wondering whether their new parliament will improve the way they are governed after all (see also Surridge, 2001, forthcoming).

However, few Scots think that the new parliament will do any actual harm. Even on the issue on which they are least optimistic about the new body's ability – improving Scotland's economy – only 13 per cent think that having the parliament is going to make things worse. Rather, on most issues, Scots now simply think their parliament will make no difference either way. But while it might appear from this evidence that devolution is so far doing little to strengthen Scots' commitment to the Union, equally predictions that it would break it apart are not sustained either. At the time of the referendum, no less than 42 per cent thought that creating the Scottish Parliament would make it more likely that Scotland would eventually leave the UK, a figure that had fallen to 37 per cent by the time of the first Scottish election, and is now 27 per cent – just barely above the 25 per cent who now think the new parliament makes it more likely that Scotland will remain in the Union.

Table 10.2 Expectations of the Scottish Parliament, in Scotland, 1997-2000

% saying Scottish parliament will	1997	1999	2000
Give Scotland a stronger voice in the UK	70	70	52
Give ordinary Scottish people more say in how Scotland is governed	79	64	44
Increase standard of education in Scotland	71	56	43
Make Scotland's economy better	64	43	36
Base	*657*	*1482*	*1663*

Source: 1997: Scottish Referendum Study.

Sources of conflict?

So far then, it appears that devolution has neither strengthened nor weakened the Union. Some critics of devolution, however, have not been so much concerned about what the Scottish Parliament might or might not be able to achieve for Scotland, but rather about the danger that it would generate conflict between Scotland and England (Dalyell, 1977). In particular, two potential flashpoints were identified. The first was whether it would be possible to sustain a situation where Scottish MPs at Westminster could vote on health and education in England, while their English colleagues no longer had any say on such matters in Scotland (the so-called West Lothian question). Second, it was argued that the higher level of public spending *per capita* in Scotland would come under closer public scrutiny, once issues of public spending were no longer settled in private around the UK Cabinet table but could be the subject of contention between the two parliaments.

At first glance, it appears from the next table that critics of devolution were correct in believing that the voting rights of English and Scottish MPs could well be a source of tension. Almost two-thirds of people in England agree that "now that Scotland has its own parliament, Scottish MPs should no longer be allowed to vote in the UK House of Commons on laws that only affect England". Yet, on closer examination, this issue is not clearly a source of conflict, for over half of people in Scotland also agree with the proposition. While this may be an issue that MPs themselves find difficult to resolve, especially those on the Labour benches on which most Scottish MPs currently sit, it is not one that seems likely to set the English and Scottish publics at odds with each other. Indeed, although they are more reluctant than others to see Scottish MPs' voting rights limited, even a majority of Labour identifiers north and south of the border agree that this should happen.

Table 10.3 Relations between England and Scotland, in England and Scotland

	England	Scotland
Scottish MPs should no longer be allowed to vote on English legislation	%	%
Strongly agree	18	14
Agree	46	39
Neither agree nor disagree	19	17
Disagree	8	19
Disagree strongly	1	4
Base	*1695*	*1506*
Compared with other parts of the UK, Scotland's share of government spending is ...	%	%
Much more than fair	8	2
Little more than fair	13	8
Pretty much fair	42	27
Little less than fair	10	35
Much less than fair	2	23
Whose economy benefits more from Scotland being part of the UK?	%	%
England's	8	43
Scotland's	37	16
About equal	39	36
Conflict between the Scots and the English is ...	%	%
Very serious	4	10
Fairly serious	16	28
Not very serious	54	53
There is no conflict	21	9
Base	*1928*	*1663*

Equally, there is relatively little potential for disagreement between the two publics over Scotland's share of government spending. True, two in three Scots believe that Scotland gets *less* than its fair share. But only just over one in five people in England believe that Scotland gets *more* than its fair share. Indeed, what is perhaps most striking about public opinion in England on this subject, is the low salience that it has. No less than a quarter of people in England were unable to express a view on it. Perhaps if politicians in England continue to press this issue, public opinion will become less accepting of Scotland's current financial position. But, evidently, the attempts that have been made so far by those English politicians who do feel strongly about the subject, have failed to secure much of an echo among their constituents. Moreover, there is no evidence in our survey that antipathy towards Scotland's share of public expenditure is greater in the North of England, some of whose politicians have perhaps been the most critical of Scotland's more generous provision.

So, neither the status of Scotland's MPs nor its share of public spending seem so far at least to be likely flashpoints between the two countries – at least so far as their publics are concerned. Nor, indeed, do many people on either side of the border regard themselves as in "very serious conflict" with each other. True, only around one in five people in England and one in ten in Scotland believe that there is *no* conflict between the Scots and the English. But, in both cases, over half think that the conflict that does exist is "not very serious". Such a view is perhaps no more than a recognition of differences of tradition and history that may, for example, be played out on the sporting field, but are also largely confined to that arena.

But if Scottish devolution so far shows little sign of generating resentment among people in England and thus conflict between them and people in Scotland, neither has it yet done much to persuade people in Scotland that they get a fair deal out of the Union. We have already seen that two out of three Scots believe that they actually get less than their fair share of UK public spending. Meanwhile, as the previous table showed, they are also inclined to believe that England gets more out of the Union economically than Scotland does – a view not shared in England. Although the proportion of Scots believing that England benefited most declined from 48 per cent at the time of the referendum to 38 per cent on the occasion of the first election to the Scottish Parliament (Paterson *et al.*, 2001), it has, as we can see, now risen once more to 43 per cent. Once again it appears that while devolution has apparently done little harm to the Union, it has not done it much good so far either.[1]

Independence for Scotland?

But, of course, the acid test of whether devolution is pulling the Union apart is whether or not there has been any increase in the proportion who believe that Scotland should become an independent country outside the United Kingdom. Arguably too, the apparent disappointment with the impact so far of the Scottish Parliament only really matters if it is undermining support for the devolution project as a whole.

The next table suggests that neither of these possible developments have, in fact, so far come to pass. Support for Scottish independence did rise in the immediate wake of the referendum that voted in favour of creating the Scottish Parliament. But, at 30 per cent, the proportion of people in Scotland who now favour being an independent country, either inside or outside the EU, is little different from the 28 per cent who took that view at the time of the 1997 general election. It is certainly still a long way from comprising a majority. Similarly, support in England for Scottish independence rose between 1997 and 1999 from 14 per cent to 24 per cent, but has since fallen back somewhat to 20 per cent. At most, the creation of the Scottish Parliament has made it possible for a few more people in England to conceive of the possibility that her neighbour might become independent, rather than caused any groundswell of opinion in favour of ejecting Scotland from the Union. We should note, however, that only a third (36 per cent) of people in England say that they would be sorry to see Scotland become independent and leave the UK. While only 7 per cent would be pleased, a majority (55 per cent) would be neither pleased nor sorry. This suggests that the amount of affective, rather than cognitive, support for the Union within England should not be overstated.

The next table also shows that a majority of people both north and south of the border continue to support the idea of a Scottish Parliament within the UK, with most of them backing the model that currently exists of a parliament with taxation powers. Indeed, in both England and Scotland such opposition as existed to the idea of creating some form of Scottish legislature is even lower now than it was at the time that Labour first came to power. In short, whatever might be thought to be its limitations in practice, devolution continues to be, in the words of the former Labour leader John Smith, the "settled will of the people", not just in Scotland but in England, too.

Table 10.4 Constitutional preferences for Scotland, in England and Scotland, 1997-2000

	May 1997	Sept 1997	1999	2000
England				
Scotland should ...	%		%	%
be independent, separate from UK and EU	6		8	8
be independent, separate from UK but part of EU	8		16	12
remain part of UK with its own elected Parliament which has some taxation powers	38		44	44
remain part of the UK with its own elected Parliament which has no taxation powers	17		10	8
remain part of the UK without an elected parliament	23		13	17
Base	*3150*		*2718*	*1928*
Scotland				
Scotland should ...	%	%	%	%
be independent, separate from UK and EU	8	9	10	11
be independent, separate from UK but part of EU	20	28	18	19
remain part of UK with its own elected Parliament which has some taxation powers	44	32	50	47
remain part of the UK with its own elected Parliament which has no taxation powers	10	9	8	8
remain part of the UK without an elected parliament	18	17	10	12
Base	*882*	*676*	*1482*	*1663*

Source: May 1997: British/Scottish Election Study. Sept. 1997: Scottish Referendum Study.

We should not, however, assume from this that there would not be popular support for changing the *details* of the current devolution settlement. That at least appears to be the case so far as people in Scotland are concerned. We have already noted that no less than two-thirds of people in Scotland believe that the UK government at Westminster has most influence over the way that Scotland is run, not the Scottish Parliament. And, for many people in Scotland, this is a potential source of dissatisfaction. For when asked who *should* have most influence over the way Scotland is run, only one in eight say that the UK government should, while nearly three-quarters say it should be the Scottish Parliament. It will therefore come as no surprise that two in three Scots agree that the Scottish Parliament should have more powers, or indeed that this proportion has increased by ten points since 1999.

But if people in Scotland want a more powerful parliament than the one that they have seen on display so far, there is as yet little sign that people in England are clamouring to share in the experience that Scotland now enjoys. True, as the next table shows, there has been an eight point drop over the last year in the proportion of people in England who believe that there is no need for any constitutional change in England. But this has been matched by only a marginal increase in support for either an English parliament or regional assemblies – more people now simply say they do not know. Even after a year of seeing the Scottish Parliament in action, a majority of people in England were apparently still happy for decisions about their laws and public services to be made by the UK government and parliament at Westminster. Less than one in five back the idea of creating regional assemblies, the long-term policy aim of the current Labour government. Indeed, ironically, it appears that people in Scotland are rather more in favour of the idea of English devolution than people in England are themselves!

As we have already suggested, the demands by politicians and campaigners for England to be treated more equitably have been greater in some regions than others. Undoubtedly the most vociferous campaigning has occurred in the North East of England (Tomaney, 2000). Yet, while this is the one region where less than half of people want England to be governed as it is now, even there only one in four currently support the idea of a regional assembly. Meanwhile, in the southern half of England support for regional assemblies stands at only around one in six. At present, the current Labour government envisages that regional assemblies will be created where a region votes for one in a referendum. It appears that those who favour such assemblies still have much persuasion to do before they can win any such referendums.

Table 10.5 Attitudes towards constitutional reform for England, in England and Scotland, 1999 and 2000

	1999	2000
England	%	%
England should be governed as it is now, with laws made by the UK parliament	62	54
Each region of England to have its own assembly that runs services like health	15	18
England as whole to have its own new parliament with law-making powers	18	19
Base	*2718*	*1928*
Scotland		%
England should be governed as it is now, with laws made by the UK parliament		45
Each region of England to have its own assembly that runs services like health		15
England as whole to have its own new parliament with law-making powers		28
Base		*1663*

National identity

So far we have looked at recent trends in people's constitutional preferences in England and Scotland. But public support for the Union has traditionally been based on more than cognitive preference. It has also been supported by a sense of national identity, that is, a sense of feeling British. To feel British has not necessarily meant that people could not feel English or Scottish as well (Heath and Kellas, 1998). Nevertheless, British identity did provide a sense of attachment to the United Kingdom in which people in all parts of it could share. Creating separate devolved institutions in parts of the United Kingdom might serve to emphasise the differences between them in people's minds, and thus result in an increasing tendency to feel English or Scottish, rather than British. Indeed, previous research conducted at the time of the 1999 Scottish election suggests that this was precisely what was happening both north and south of the border, even before devolution was actually in place (Curtice and Heath, 2000; Paterson *et al.*, 2001).

We have two measures of national identity available to us, with which we can assess what has happened during the early lifetime of devolution. The first is the so-called Moreno scale, named after the political scientist who first used it in comparisons of Scotland and Catalonia (Moreno, 1988). Recognising the possibility that people may feel British as well as Scottish or English, it asks people to state the relative importance of these identities to them. The question runs as follows in Scotland (and similarly in England by substituting 'English' for 'Scottish'):

> *Some people think of themselves first as British. Others may think of themselves first as Scottish. Which, if any, of the following describes how you see yourself?*
>
> *Scottish, not British*
> *More Scottish than British*
> *Equally Scottish and British*
> *More British than Scottish*
> *British, not Scottish*

As the next table shows, the results obtained by this measure suggest that the increase in feeling English or Scottish observed after the first election to the Scottish Parliament has been maintained. One in three people in England now give priority to their Englishness over their Britishness, almost identical to the proportion who did so in 1999, and up on the one in four who felt that way in 1997. Meanwhile, in Scotland, over two-thirds now feel wholly or mostly Scottish, again the same as in 1999 (though with rather more of them now feeling wholly Scottish), but up on the three in five who felt that way in 1992 or 1997.

Table 10.6 Moreno national identity, in England and Scotland, 1992-2000

	1992	1997	1999	2000
England		%	%	%
English not British		7	17	19
More English than British		17	15	14
Equally English and British		45	37	34
More British than English		14	11	14
British not English		9	14	12
Other		5	3	6
Base		*3150*	*2718*	*2887*
Scotland	%	%	%	%
Scottish not British	19	23	32	37
More Scottish than British	40	38	35	31
Equally Scottish and British	33	27	22	21
More British than Scottish	3	4	3	3
British not Scottish	3	4	4	4
Other	1	2	3	4
Base	*957*	*882*	*1482*	*1663*

Sources: 1992: Scottish Election Survey 1992. 1997: British/Scottish Election Surveys 1997.

Our second measure, which is shown in the next table, tells a similar story. Here we asked people to choose which one identity best described the way they thought of themselves.[2] In both England and Scotland we can see a decline in feeling British and an increase in feeling English/Scottish between 1997 and 1999. And, in both cases, that increase has more or less been sustained in our most recent surveys. Moreover, we can also see that in 1979, when Scotland failed to back devolution with sufficient enthusiasm for it to be implemented, three times as many people in Scotland felt British as do so now.

Table 10.7 Forced-choice national identity, in England and Scotland, 1979-2000

	1979	1992	1997	1999	2000
England		%	%	%	%
English		31	34	44	41
British		63	59	44	47
Base		*2442*	*3150*	*2718*	*2887*
Scotland	%	%	%	%	%
Scottish	57	72	72	77	80
British	39	25	20	17	13
Base	*661*	*957*	*882*	*1482*	*1663*

Sources: 1979: Scottish Election Survey 1979. 1992, 1997: British/Scottish Election Surveys 1992 and 1997.

So, there appears to have been some undermining of the sense of Britishness in both England and Scotland in the period since people in both Scotland and Wales decided to vote in favour of devolution.[3] Moreover, in both countries it appears to be a decline that has occurred more or less evenly across all age groups, social classes and religious denominations as well as among both sexes. To that degree at least, devolution appears to have weakened the Union. However, we should bear in mind that Britishness also fell heavily in Scotland during the period after 1979 when Scotland was denied devolution. So we should be very wary indeed of claiming that the sense of Britishness would be significantly stronger now had devolution not happened.

Still, the sense of Britishness is clearly weaker than it once was. And it is also clearly much weaker in Scotland than it is in England. But what consequences flow from these patterns depends at least in part on what difference feeling Scottish, English or British makes to other social and political attitudes. If those who feel English or Scottish are largely similar in their attitudes to those who feel British, then changes and differences in national identity may have few implications for the stability of the Union. It is to an examination of whether or not that is true that we now turn.

National identity and social attitudes

Perhaps the most obvious area where we might expect national identity to make a difference both in England and in Scotland is in respect of constitutional preferences. In the next table we show attitudes towards some of the key constitutional issues we examined earlier, broken down by a collapsed version of Moreno national identity.[4]

We find that, in Scotland, national identity does make a difference to constitutional preferences. Those who feel predominantly Scottish are not only (unsurprisingly) more likely than others to be in favour of Scottish independence, but they are also less likely to be opposed to devolution for England. They are also rather less likely to believe that Scottish MPs should not vote on English laws.

Table 10.8 Constitutional preference by national identity, in England and Scotland

England	Predominantly English	Equally English/British	Predominantly British
% who favour Scottish independence	23	17	14
% who oppose English devolution	54	52	59
% who believe Scottish MPs should not vote on English laws	69	63	66
Base	618	646	499
Scotland	Predominantly Scottish	Equally Scottish/British	Predominantly British
% who favour Scottish independence	37	14	7
% who oppose English devolution	41	54	55
% who believe Scottish MPs should not vote on English laws	52	50	66
Base	1108	350	121

In England, in contrast, the pattern is far more muted – if it exists at all. Those who feel predominantly English are rather more likely to favour Scottish independence, but at nine points the gap between them and the predominantly British is far less than the equivalent 30-point gap in Scotland. Meanwhile, when it comes to English devolution, there is barely any difference at all between the three categories of national identity in our table, let alone on whether Scottish MPs should vote on English laws. In other words national identity makes more difference to attitudes towards English devolution in Scotland than it does in England itself!

The same conclusion also holds for attitudes towards Scotland's share of government spending, who benefits most from the Union, and whether there is conflict between the Scots and the English. In each case, national identity makes a difference to people's views in Scotland but not in England. So while any further decline in Britishness in Scotland might pose some demands on the Union, it is far from clear that any continued rise in Englishness in England need result in any difficulty at all (Curtice and Heath, 2000).

This difference between England and Scotland in the apparent impact of national identity on attitudes is not confined to constitutional preferences. It is also evident when it comes to attitudes towards the role of government and the extent of social inequality in society. In Scotland, those who are predominantly Scottish are more concerned about social inequality and more likely to see the need for government activity to reduce it. In short, they can be characterised as more left-wing. Thus, for example, as we can see from the next table, over half of those who are predominantly Scottish believe that the government should definitely be responsible for ensuring that everyone has a job, whereas only one in three of the predominantly British take that view. In contrast in England, a person's national identity makes little difference to their views on these issues.

Table 10.9 Attitudes to role of government and social inequality by national identity, in England and Scotland

England	Predominantly English	Equally English/British	Predominantly British
% who say the government should definitely be responsible for ensuring everyone has a job	43	37	37
% who agree that the government should redistribute income from the better off to the less well off	41	38	35
% who agree that there is one law for the rich and one law for the poor	70	63	65
Base	*552*	*571*	*439*

Scotland	Predominantly Scottish	Equally Scottish/British	Predominantly British
% who say the government should definitely be responsible for ensuring everyone has a job	53	40	33
% who agree that the government should redistribute income from the better off to the less well off	52	43	43
% who agree that there is one law for the rich and one law for the poor	70	60	44
Base	*1005*	*317*	*109*

Again, we find a different story north and south of the border if we look at attitudes towards Europe and ethnic minorities. We might expect those who adopt an apparently narrower English or Scottish identity, rather than a broader multinational British one, to be less keen on the development of an even larger supranational unit such as the European Union, as well as being less tolerant of ethnic minorities. However, in Scotland at least, as the next table shows, there is no consistent evidence that this is the case. Indeed, if anything, those with a predominantly Scottish national identity are more favourably disposed towards the European Union than those with a predominantly British identity. The nationalist movement in Scotland has long aimed to promote a 'civic nationalism' rather than an ethnically based one, with both membership of the European Union and promotion of the rights of ethnic minorities in Scotland a key part of their platform. It appears that this has indeed helped to ensure that a Scottish national identity is not an exclusive one.

Table 10.10 Attitudes towards the European Union and ethnic minorities by national identity, in England and Scotland

England	Predominantly English	Equally English/British	Predominantly British
% who think the UK should leave the EU or EU powers should be reduced	63	55	60
% who would vote not to join the Euro in a referendum	70	67	65
% who say they are "very" or "a little" racially prejudiced	33	24	27
% who think equal opportunities for blacks and Asians have "gone too far" or "much too far"	48	28	36
Base	552	571	439

Scotland	Predominantly Scottish	Equally Scottish/British	Predominantly British
% who think the UK should leave the EU or EU powers should be reduced	47	52	59
% who would vote not to join the Euro in a referendum	53	56	57
% who say they are "very" or "a little" racially prejudiced	18	19	21
% who think equal opportunities for blacks and Asians have "gone too far" or "much too far"	32	29	26
Base	1005	317	109

In England, in contrast, feeling English is somewhat associated both with less tolerance of ethnic minorities and with opposition to further European integration. In particular, nearly a half of those who feel predominantly English say that equal opportunities for blacks and Asians have gone "too far" compared with only just over a third of the predominantly British. The relationship between Englishness and opposition to Europe is less apparent in our table because opposition is, in fact, concentrated among those who feel "English, not British" rather than among those who are "more English than British" (see also Curtice and Heath, 2000). If we look, for example, at the views of the exclusively English on the Euro, opposition is as high as 73 per cent.[5]

So we have seen that in Scotland national identity is clearly associated with constitutional preferences and also with a more left-wing stance on policy issues. In England, this is either less true or not true at all. Meanwhile there is no consistent evidence that Scottish national identity is particularly associated with a tendency to be less inclusive towards the outside world, whereas there is a hint at least that English national identity is. Evidently national identity has different meanings and implications in the two countries.

There are at least two probably interrelated reasons as to why this is so. First, national identity has been politicised in Scotland, whereas it has not been in England. In England there is little or no relationship between national identity and the party someone supports (Curtice and Heath, 2000). But in Scotland those who feel Scottish are, in particular, more likely to support the SNP and, to a lesser extent, Labour, while the minority who feel British still give significant support to the Conservatives (Brown et al., 1999; Paterson et al., 2001). Meanwhile the SNP is not just a nationalist party in favour of independence, but is also nowadays a left of centre 'social democratic' party and, as we have already noted, pro-European. This helps explain why Scottishness has not just become associated with support for independence but also with more left-wing values, while at the same time has avoided acquiring a particularly exclusive character.

Second, people in Scotland also appear to draw a sharper distinction between what it means to be Scottish and what it means to be British than people in England do between being English and being British. This is revealed by the results to a number of questions designed to measure people's national sentiment, first for England/Scotland and then for Britain as a whole (Heath et al., 1999). For example, we asked people, first whether they thought "People in England/Scotland are too ready to criticise their country", and then whether they thought "People in Britain are too ready to criticise their country". In each case they could respond on a scale ranging from "agree strongly" to "disagree strongly". If people tend to give similar answers to the two questions, this suggests they draw little distinction between what it means to be English/Scottish and what it means to be British. If on the other hand they tend to give different answers, then they would appear to draw a clear distinction.

The next table shows the correlation between the answers given by people in England and those in Scotland to three similarly or identically worded questions about English/Scottish national sentiment and British national sentiment. In each case we can see that although there is a positive correlation in Scotland, it is weaker than in England. Thus, for example, there is a correlation of 0.65 between people's views about whether people in England are too ready to criticise their country and whether people in Britain are too ready to criticise their country. The equivalent correlation in Scotland in contrast is just 0.39.

Although people in Scotland do not have entirely different views about Scotland and about Britain, they do draw more of a distinction than do people in England between England and Britain. And, if people in England can see little difference between England and Britain, we should not be surprised that whether they feel English or whether they feel British makes little difference to their social and political attitudes.

Table 10.11 Relationship between views about England/Scotland and Britain, in England and Scotland

Correlation* between attitudes when nation = England/Scotland and nation = Britain	England	Scotland
People in (nation) are too ready to criticise their country	0.65	0.39
Base	1890	1635
There are some things about (nation) that make me ashamed	0.59	0.29
Base	1898	1642
(Nation) has a lot to learn from (other countries/ rest of Britain) in running its affairs	0.27	0.10
Base	1827	1613

*Kendall's tau-b.

Conclusions

These are early days for devolution. But our analysis suggests that, so far at least, both the hopes and the fears that have been expressed about the implications of devolution for the United Kingdom may well have been exaggerated. Devolution has not led to an increase in support for Scottish independence; nor does there appear to be much potential for conflict between the peoples of England and Scotland over how the relationship between the two countries should be managed, let alone signs of an 'English backlash'. While there was a decline in Britishness both north and south of the border between 1997 and 1999, our latest reading does not provide any consistent evidence of a further movement in that direction. In any event, in England at least, national identity does not appear to have much influence on people's views on the future of the Union or indeed many other topics.

At the same time, the Scottish Parliament has yet to make much impact on people's perceptions of how they are governed. Indeed, many people in Scotland appear to feel that Westminster still has rather more influence north of the border than they had anticipated, and as a result they are hoping for a more powerful Scottish Parliament than they have seen so far. And while national identity may not currently make much difference to people's views in England, and while people in England may indeed still have difficulty in distinguishing between England and Britain, we cannot rule out the possibility that England's politicians will eventually succeed in politicising people's sense of national identity, much as it already is in Scotland. Devolution appears to have set sail on a fair wind so far as public opinion is concerned. But whether it is eventually judged a success depends on the skills and actions of the politicians who have been entrusted by the public with the task of making it work.

Notes

1. We might also note that while the proportion of people in Scotland who think that there is very or fairly serious conflict between the Scottish and the English did fall slightly from 43 per cent to 38 per cent between 1999 and 2000, the level still remains above the 30 per cent level in 1992 just after the Conservatives' fourth election victory, let alone the 15 per cent level in 1979 just after the first attempt to implement devolution failed.
2. In the 1997, 1999 and 2000 surveys, respondents were first invited to state all of the identities that described how they thought of themselves and then asked which single one best described themselves. In the 1979 and 1992 survey, respondents were only invited to name one identity. Respondents were also offered a slightly shorter list of identities in 1992, except that in 1979 the option 'British and Scottish' was offered. However, as the results in 1992 and 1997 are largely similar in each country, it appears unlikely that these methodological differences compromise our substantive conclusions.
3. The 1997 figure in Table 10.7 is from the British/Scottish Election Studies conducted in the late spring and summer of 1997 before the Scottish and Welsh referendums were held. That the Scottish referendum gave a boost to feeling a Scottish rather than a British identity amongst people in Scotland is further attested by the fact that on our forced choice measure no less than 83 per cent of respondents to the Scottish Referendum Study, conducted in the autumn of 1997, said that they were Scottish and just 13 per cent that they were British.
4. Because of the small numbers of people in Scotland who are either mostly or wholly British rather than Scottish we have combined these two categories (labelling them 'predominantly British'). To keep our analysis symmetrical, we have done the same among those who feel mostly or wholly English or Scottish.
5. It is, however, the case that the association between national identity and attitudes towards Europe, found by Curtice and Heath (2000) in 1999, is rather weaker in the 2000 survey.

References

Brown, A., McCrone, D., Paterson, L. and Surridge, P. (1999), *The Scottish Electorate: The 1997 election and beyond*, London: Macmillan.

Curtice, J. and Heath, A. (2000), 'Is the English lion about to roar? National identity after devolution' in Jowell, R., Curtice, J., Park, A., Thomson, K., Jarvis, L., Bromley, C. and Stratford, N. (eds.), *British Social Attitudes: the 17th Report – Focusing on Diversity*, London: Sage.

Curtice, J., McCrone, D., Park, A. and Paterson, L., (eds.) (2001, forthcoming), *New Scotland, New Society? Are social and political ties fragmenting?*, Edinburgh: Edinburgh University Press.

Dalyell, T. (1977), *Devolution: The end of Britain?*, London: Jonathan Cape.

Heath, A., and Kellas, J. (1998), 'Nationalisms and constitutional questions', *Scottish Affairs*, Special Issue on Understanding Constitutional Change, 110-127.

Heath, A., Taylor, B., Brook, L. and Park, A. (1999), 'British national sentiment', *British Journal of Political Science*, **29**: 155-175.

Moreno, L. (1988), 'Scotland and Catalonia: The path to Home Rule' in McCrone, D., and Brown, A. (eds.), *The Scottish Government Yearbook 1988*, Edinburgh: Unit for the Study of Government in Britain.

Paterson, L., Brown,. A., Curtice, J., Hinds, K., McCrone, D., Park, A., Sproston, K. and Surridge, P. (2001), *New Scotland, New Politics?*, Edinburgh: Edinburgh University Press.

Surridge, P. (2001, forthcoming), 'Society and democracy: the new Scotland' in Paterson, L., Curtice, J., McCrone, D. and Park, A. (eds.), *New Scotland, New Society? Are social and political ties fragmenting?*, Edinburgh: Edinburgh University Press.

Tomaney, J. (2000), 'The regional governance of England' in Hazell, R. (ed.), *The State and the Nations: The first year of devolution in the United Kingdom*, Exeter: Imprint Academic.

Acknowledgements

Much of the data for England reported in this chapter was funded by grants made by the Leverhulme Trust to both the Governance of Scotland Forum, University of Edinburgh, and the Constitution Unit, University College, London as a result of its 'Nations and Regions' initiative. The 2000 *Scottish Social Attitudes* survey was funded by the Economic and Social Research Council (grant no. R000238065). We are grateful to both bodies for their financial support. We have also profited from the advice and work of many colleagues who have been working alongside us on these various projects.

11 The Conservatives and Europe: waving or drowning?

Geoffrey Evans [*]

The traditional division between Labour and Conservative supporters in post-war British politics has been between a left that favours interventionist and redistributive policies and a right that stresses the importance of the free market and low taxation (Heath *et al.*, 1994; Evans *et al.*, 1996). However, by the 1997 election, this gap appeared to be narrowing, both among political elites (Budge, 1999; Norris, 1999; Webb and Farrell, 1999) and more widely among the electorate (Sanders, 1999). There was also evidence that Britain's relationship with the European Union had become an issue that provided an alternative basis of party support among at least some of the electorate, though without yet seriously challenging the importance of economic and redistributive concerns (Evans, 1999a). Since 1997, of course, we have seen the continued ascendancy of Labour, with its buoyant popularity culminating in a 'second landslide' (Norris, 2001) in 2001. This raises a question as to whether the basis of support for the main British parties has been significantly transformed, perhaps starting in 1997 but being consolidated in 2001 (Evans and Norris, 1999).

The driving force behind any such change has been Labour's move to the centre on economic and law and order issues over the last decade or so.[1] By moving to the centre on economic issues in particular, Labour has reduced the political significance of differences between the redistributive policies of the different British parties. This means that, for the opposition Conservative Party, the most plausibly effective way of competing with Labour is to appear more competent than them with respect to economic management (see Bara and Budge, 2001 for a recent discussion). But, of course, this is not an easy task; the incumbent government continues to reap the popularity benefits of the healthy state of the British economy and the Conservatives still carry the burden of their perceived mistakes when last in office in the 1990s. In effect, with Labour occupying the centre ground on many economic and redistributive issues (as well as on issues such as law and order) and the economy continuing to function effectively, the options for the Conservatives to win back votes on traditional

---

[*] Geoffrey Evans is Official Fellow in Politics, Nuffield College Oxford and University Reader in the Sociology of Politics.

issues are heavily constrained. So the stage is set for the Conservatives to try to open up new avenues of competition, avenues on which they are closest to the core of public opinion and have a better chance of taking votes from Labour. European monetary integration is just such an issue. Attitudes towards integration are to some degree distinct from views on core 'left-right' issues, meaning that it provides an alternative basis for vote choice. It is also an issue on which the Conservatives are potentially more in tune than Labour with popular opinion (Evans, 1998a). Consequently, and contrary to the assumptions of many journalistic commentators on the 2001 election, a distinctive approach on Europe could potentially *gain* the Conservatives votes rather than lose them.

The historical roots of this re-aligning potential lie in the reversal of the main parties' positions on European integration that took place around the time of Labour's policy review in the late 1980s (George and Rosamund, 1992). From being opposed to European integration, Labour became more positive; while under Mrs Thatcher's leadership the Conservatives moved to a somewhat more hard-line position (Sowemimo, 1996; Berrington and Hague, 1998). In becoming more pro-European, Labour shifted itself away from the views of its traditional supporters, the working class, and towards those of its new target group, the educated middle classes that provided the core of new party members and a basis for the party's eventual electoral success in the 1990s. However, as long as Europe remained a side issue of no great consequence for vote choice this was not a risky strategy. Working-class Eurosceptics were unlikely to shift to the Tories purely over Europe (Evans, 1999a). This was especially true given the other problems that beset the then Major government: its much criticised handling of the ERM fiasco (Sanders, 1996; Evans, 1999b); sleaze-related image problems; clear divisions over Europe (Evans, 1998a); and its failure to deliver in a range of other areas.

However, following the Maastricht meeting of 1991 and the referendums in France and Denmark, European integration has become increasingly salient in domestic politics and in the minds of the electorate (Franklin *et al.*, 1994). European monetary union has become arguably the most significant single public policy issue facing the government and the country as a whole. And the vague and poorly formed public attitudes of earlier days (see Janssen, 1991) have gradually became more consistent and strongly held (Evans, 1995, 1998b). Moreover, many polls have indicated very negative popular reactions to monetary integration, with the most significant opposition lying precisely in Labour's working-class heartlands (Evans, 2000).

Unsurprisingly, therefore, given their rather desperate standing in the polls, the 2001 campaign saw the Conservatives stressing their scepticism about the adoption of the Euro. Indeed, despite being noticeably split in its position over Europe at some points in recent years, the Conservative Party has maintained a far clearer anti-EMU stance than either of the other main parties. Moreover, they have become even more distinctively Eurosceptic since 1997 – at least in terms of the content of their manifesto (Bara and Budge, 2001) – while Labour and the Liberal Democrats have become closer together in their pro-integration stance. So the Conservative position on European integration, and particularly that on the adoption of the Euro, represents a distinct choice that is consistent with the views of Eurosceptic, or at least EMU-sceptic, voters.

Of course, it would be foolish indeed to infer the electorate's concerns from those of the parties. So this chapter examines whether or not Europe has become more important in explaining voters' behaviour, and economic policy less so. Has Labour's move to the centre changed the face of British electoral politics? How important is Europe in shaping how people vote? And what role did Europe play in the Conservative's defeat in the 2001 election?

We begin by examining whether the traditional left-right axis of party competition has become less important for voters. Then we examine whether the Conservatives were more successful than in 1997 in making EMU, and European integration more generally, a source of competition for votes between the parties.

Unlike most of the chapters in this Report, the data we use here largely comes from the *British Election Panel Study* (BEPS) which followed the same group of respondents between 1997 and 2001. Further details of the study can be found in the appendix to this chapter.

Do the parties still differ on traditional 'left-right' matters?

If voters are to respond to the changing ideological positions of the parties they must first of course recognise that changes have occurred. This recognition might take a number of forms, including a narrowing of the perceived gap between the Labour and Conservative parties *and* the replacement of the Liberal Democrats as the centre party on these issues. To assess this we can use responses to a series of 'scale' questions which ask respondents to indicate where they stand on a range of issues, and where they think each of the parties stands. The issues covered include European integration, redistribution, taxation and government spending, and nationalisation and privatisation.

First, redistribution. To assess views about this, respondents are presented with an 11-point scale, the two ends of which are described as follows:

> *The government should make much greater efforts to make people's incomes more equal*
>
> *The government should be much less concerned about how equal people's incomes are*

A higher score indicates a belief that government should be less concerned about people's incomes, and a lower score that government should make greater efforts to equalise incomes. Looking at where people place each of the parties on this scale allows us to check whether they were seen to be closer together or further apart in their positions in 2001 than they were in 1997. The results are illustrated in the next figure which shows that between 1997 and 2001 the perceived positions of the parties on redistribution came much closer to one another. The Conservatives were still the outliers, but less so than in 1997.

Figure 11.1 Redistribution; perceived position of the parties and own position, 1997-2001

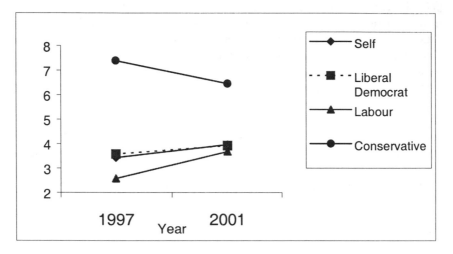

Similar patterns exist in relation to perceptions of the parties' positions on taxation and spending and on nationalisation and privatisation. (The average scores for each scale are shown in model 1 of the appendix to this chapter.) This means that, on each of the three measures of economic policy that are characteristically seen as being critical to left-right politics, there was a substantial and statistically significant narrowing of the perceived distance between Labour and the Conservatives or Liberal Democrats between 1997 and 2001. True, in 2001 Labour were seen to have almost exactly the same stand on redistribution as the average respondent. But their advantage over the Conservatives was none the less reduced by the Conservative's substantial move from the right to the centre.

The next figure carries out the same exercise in relation to Europe. The two contrasting positions presented to respondents were:

> *Britain should do all it can to unite fully with the European Union*

> *Britain should do all it can to protect its independence from the European Union*

This time a higher score indicates a more anti-European stance, and a lower score a more pro-European one. This shows exactly the opposite pattern to that which we observed in relation to redistribution. This time the Conservatives are seen to be *diverging* away from the stance of both Labour and the Liberal Democrats. Moreover, the Conservatives remain the party closest by far to the average respondent's view – with an even bigger advantage in 2001 than they had in 1997 (although they are now perceived to occupy a position slightly to the right of the electorate itself).

Figure 11.2 European integration

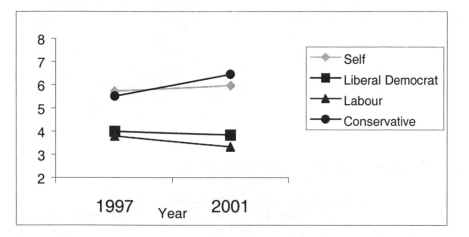

These findings suggest that the contraction of the traditional left-right divide at least provides the *possibility* of a different source of division between the parties. In the minds of the electorate there is now a larger gap between the parties on European integration than there is on redistribution. If this issue is linked to vote choice, then the gap should benefit the Conservatives, whose stance is seen as far closer to the electorate's average position.

But what evidence is there that parties' positions on Europe are linked to the choices that voters make? To assess this we can focus on people who did *not* vote Conservative in 1997 and look at how their vote in 2001 relates to their perceptions about the parties' stance on Europe. This shows that that those who thought Labour had moved further away from European integration between 1997 and 2001 were less likely to switch their vote to the Conservatives in 2001 (under six per cent doing so) than those who did not (nine per cent of whom switched their votes in this way).

Of course, these differences are small and more detailed analysis is required before we can be confident that our findings are not merely artefacts of the many complex relationships that exist between vote choice over time and other factors. To take account of this we use logistic regression (see Appendix I of this volume for a more detailed description of this technique), which allows us to control for changes in many variables simultaneously while predicting the likelihood of a person voting Conservative or Labour in 2001. Our findings are presented in model 2 in the appendix to this chapter. This model predicts a Labour *versus* Conservative vote in 2001 and shows that, once we take account of peoples' perceptions in 1997, perceived changes in party positions on both integration and redistribution *are* related to vote choice in 2001. If we conduct a similar analysis on Labour and Conservative voters in 1997 this pattern becomes even clearer. When the Conservatives are perceived to have become more anti-integration the likelihood of a person switching to them increases, as it does (and to a far stronger degree) when Labour are perceived to have become more pro-integration. On redistribution, the opposite pattern occurs: when Labour are perceived to have moved to the right the likelihood of a Conservative vote increases, whereas when the Conservatives are perceived as having moved to the left the Conservatives' vote increases.

So, perceived changes on both types of issues appear to have affected voting in 2001. But have respondents' views on European integration now begun to rival their views on redistribution as a basis of their party preferences? Has Europe become an issue that governs how people vote? We begin by examining how the issue of European integration has changed in character since 1997.

The importance of Europe in British politics

In some ways, public attitudes towards European integration have not changed greatly since 1997. The next table shows that over this period there was little change in attitudes towards either EMU or Britain's long-term policy on European integration more generally, though more now opt for the centre option on EMU and there are fewer "don't know" responses.

Table 11.1 The single currency and Britain's role in Europe, 1997-2001

% who think Britain should ...	1997	2001
Replace the pound by the single currency	16	16
Use both the pound and a new European currency	23	28
Keep the pound as the only currency	58	54
Don't know	3	2
Leave the European Union	16	13
Stay in the EU and try to reduce the EU's powers	48	48
Leave things as they are	14	23
Stay in the EU and try to increase the EU's powers	10	9
Work for the formation of a single European government	7	5
Don't know	6	2

Base: 1749

Responses to a question about the proposed referendum on adoption of the Euro and the dropping of the pound show a steadfast opposition, with only 30 per cent of the population as a whole endorsing such a change. Even among Labour and Liberal Democrat voters only minorities (42 per cent in each case) say they would vote 'Yes' to such a proposal. So, although it could be argued that Mr Blair has neutralised the issue in some way by insisting on a referendum, at present it is unlikely to lead to the acceptance of the Euro – even among Labour voters.

Not only have attitudes towards Europe remained relatively unchanged, but so too has their relationship with attitudes towards redistribution. Even in 1997 Europe had started to become an issue that cross-cut the traditional left-right dimension in British politics. Negative attitudes towards Europe were widespread among left-wing voters, and positive ones were found among those on the right-wing, meaning that the issue had the potential to form a distinct basis of party support. This was no different in 2001. This is demonstrated by the correlations between the various issues that form the core of left-right politics in Britain – redistribution, taxation and spending, and nationalisation and privatisation – and attitudes towards the EU. Using factor analysis (described in more detail in Appendix I to this Report) we can see that in 2001, as in 1997, these issues remain noticeably distinct from one another, with European issues being part of one dimension or 'factor' (as signified by their high and emboldened scores in the table below) and left-right ones part of another quite distinct factor.

Table 11.2 Left-right and European attitudes

	1997		2001	
	Factor 1	**Factor 2**	**Factor 1**	**Factor 2**
Redistribution scale	.02	**.74**	.04	**.77**
Tax/ Spend	.03	**.70**	.09	**.69**
Nationalisation/ Privatisation	.02	**.71**	.04	**.73**
EU integration scale	**.82**	.20	**.86**	.13
Long-term policy on EU	**.80**	.02	**.75**	.04
Keep pound/ adopt Euro	**.78**	-.07	**.81**	.02

In these respects, therefore, attitudes towards Europe were similar in 1997 and 2001. But, since 1997, there are several ways in which the European issue has changed its political character and which suggest that it may have become more electorally important over time.

The first relates to party competition. One obvious reason for the muted impact of attitudes towards European integration on support for the Conservatives in 1997 was the presence of the Referendum Party, which stood for many seats in that election. The Referendum Party obviously competed with the Conservatives for Eurosceptic votes and probably reduced the benefit to the Conservatives of their position on this issue (McAllister and Studlar, 2000). Without this competition we might expect the Conservatives to obtain more benefit from their Euroscepticism.

A second problem for the party in 1997 was the extent of its division on Europe. A divided party is clearly less likely than a unified one to get across a clear and positive message, and the Conservative divisions no doubt weakened their electoral appeal on this issue (Evans, 1998a, 1999a). Consequently, for the

Conservatives to appeal to Eurosceptics in 2001 they would need to have reduced the public's belief that they are divided over the issue. In this they do appear to have been successful. Most people (63 per cent) now see the Conservatives as clearly Eurosceptic, compared with only 48 per cent in 1997.[2]

A third factor that might lead us to expect that Europe has become more important since 1997 is the changing significance of the European question itself. The whole question of European Monetary Union has moved on considerably during Labour's first term in office, with this issue now giving a sharper focus to concerns about what integration can mean and providing, of course, a symbol to stand behind. If so, we might expect to see a change in the meaning of attitudes towards integration, a shift from a general but unfocused concern with integration, pro- or anti-, to one that reflects the highly politicised EMU issue more directly.

We can explore this idea by examining the patterns of association between EMU, attitudes towards more general aspects of policy on European integration, and positions on the European integration scale discussed earlier (in relation to Figure 11.2). If EMU *is* more central to these attitudes than it used to be, it should have a stronger impact on a person's views about European integration. This indeed proves to be the case. The next table shows the strength of association between a person's position on the scale and their views on, firstly, EMU and, secondly, Britain's long-term policy towards Europe. The higher the coefficient, the stronger the relationship between a person's general stance on European integration and their answers to each of these two related questions. This shows that views on EMU now predict a person's general views on Europe far more strongly than do answers to our general EU policy question, which was not the case in 1997.

Table 11.3 The inter-relationship between views about European integration and European Monetary Union, 1997 and 2001

	1997	2001
Pound/Euro	.32	.47
Long-term policy	.37	.31
R^2	.33	.43

In 2001, therefore, the European issue was one that continued to cut across the left-right dimension within British politics; moreover, the British public remained largely EMU-sceptic. There were, however, some essential differences between 2001 and 1997. Firstly, the Referendum Party was not standing against the Conservatives. Secondly, the Conservatives were perceived to be less split on the issue in 2001 than they had been before. And, thirdly, the highly politicised question of EMU had become more central to the issue of European integration. The stage was set for Europe to become a basis of a new political alignment in British politics and, potentially, a source of votes for the Conservative Party.

Europe and party choice in the 2001 election

If Europe has become an important basis of vote choice we would expect to see it become a stronger predictor of vote in 2001 than it was in 1997, both in absolute terms and in relation to the strength of traditional left-right issues. To assess this, the next table examines the association between attitudes towards Europe and redistribution and patterns of voting in 1997 and 2001. For this purpose we divide responses on the integration scale into pro-European integration (those giving a score between 0 and 4), neutral (5) and anti-European integration (6 to 10), and likewise for our redistribution scale. This shows that the difference between Labour and Conservative voters in attitudes towards integration was somewhat more pronounced in 2001 than in 1997. In contrast, differences between these groups in their views on redistribution were more or less the same as before. As a result, in 2001 the gap between Conservative and Labour supporters in their views on European integration was actually slightly larger than that on redistribution, a quite different picture to that which applied in 1997. Similar changes in emphasis can be seen when comparing the Conservatives and the Liberal Democrats. In this case, however, the gap on European integration in 2001 (39 per cent) is far larger than the gap on redistribution (28 per cent).

Table 11.4 The prevalence of Eurosceptic and anti-redistribution views among party supporters in 1997 and 2001

% who have Eurosceptic views on EU integration	1997	Con-Lab difference	2001	Con-Lab difference
Conservative	64		78	
Labour	35	29	37	41
Liberal Democrat	39		39	
% who oppose redistribution measures				
Conservative	47		54	
Labour	11	36	16	38
Liberal Democrat	22		26	

Base: 1749

Of course, such figures can only give us a limited feel for the robustness of the changes that took place between 1997 and 2001. To obtain a more sophisticated and comprehensive estimate of these changes, one that takes into account the relationships between attitudes towards redistribution and integration, we once again turn to logistic regression techniques. The results can be found in model 3 in the appendix to this chapter. This confirms that a person's views on EU integration are clearly a more important predictor of their vote in 2001 than was the case in 1997. Indeed, when predicting whether or not a person votes Labour or Conservative, the impact of this is of a comparable magnitude to a person's views on redistribution.[3] Even if we include views on other related issues (such as taxation and spending, unemployment versus inflation, and nationalisation versus privatisation), attitudes toward the EU have by far the strongest single effect in 2001, which again was not the case in 1997. The inclusion of further attitude measures such as those on EMU and Britain's EU policy leave the basic conclusions unaltered.

The dynamics of vote switching

The relationship between voting behaviour and issues such as Europe tells us little about *how* the emergence of a new cross-cutting issue leads to change; rather, it simply describes the results of such change. To understand how Europe has had an impact on electoral behaviour, we need to examine whether it has led to changes in the vote choices of individual electors. The panel design of the *British Election Panel Study* enables us to do this with greater confidence than would be the case with a cross-sectional study (like the *British Social Attitudes* survey) in which different samples of people are interviewed each year (see Evans and Andersen, 2001).

To do this, we focus on those who switched either to the Conservatives or to Labour. The next table compares the attitudes towards integration and redistribution of those who shifted their vote to the Conservative or Labour Parties in 2001 with those who did not. It also shows us the views of respondents who voted consistently for Labour or Conservative at both elections.

Table 11.5 Views on Europe and redistribution by vote switching, 1997-2001

	EU integration (%)		Redistribution (%)		Total (%)
	Pro	Anti	Pro	Anti	
Switched to Conservatives	15	80	46	47	7
Did not switch	44	41	67	22	77
Consistent Conservatives	14	77	30	57	16
Switched to Labour	46	40	66	24	7
Did not switch	27	60	52	37	67
Consistent Labour	49	36	77	14	26

Base: 1749

As we can see, people who switched to the Conservatives in 2001 were overwhelmingly opposed to European integration but had mixed views on redistribution. Thus, while 80 per cent oppose EU integration, only 47 per cent express anti-redistributive views. By contrast, those who switched to the Labour Party over the same period were more equally split on Europe (with 40 per cent opposing further integration) and more unequally divided on redistribution (with only 24 per cent falling into our 'anti-redistribution' category). In this they do not differ markedly from people who did not switch to Labour (who were also relatively pro-redistribution).

Further analysis shows that Eurosceptics were five times more likely than pro-EU respondents to have switched to the Conservatives than not to have switched. The differences in vote switching among people with different attitudes towards redistribution were far less pronounced, with right-wing respondents being only three times more likely to have shifted to the Conservatives than not to have switched. Similar though, far more muted differences in the impact of European *versus* redistributive attitudes are found with respect to switches to Labour.

At this point, we may perhaps be left wondering why – if Europe has become a more important source of division – the Conservatives did not win the 2001 election (or at least, why they still did so badly). The answer is simply that most voters did not change their allegiance over this period. Thus, most Conservatives in 2001 had voted Conservative in 1997 (67 per cent), and most Labour voters in 2001 had done the same in 1997 (66 per cent). Consequently, most Conservative and Labour voters in 2001 were drawn from their supporters in 1997 (70 per cent and 78 per cent respectively). So no issues moved that many voters to switch during this electoral cycle. What our analysis does tell us, however, is that amongst those people who *did* shift allegiance, Europe mattered more than redistribution. And this was particularly the case for the Conservatives, who thereby gained support, even if only by a few percentage points, as a result of their relative Euroscepticism compared with the other main parties.

The figures in Table 11.5 are based on attitudes held in 2001. But, by taking account of our 1997 measures of respondents' attitudes, we can also see which changes in the importance of respondents' positions on European integration stem from their *own* changing attitudes and which have occurred without attitude change, presumably instead reflecting the changes in party positions during this period. Model 4 (in the appendix to this chapter) shows that, when prior vote is taken into account, the effects of a person's views on European integration on their voting Conservative are substantially larger than the effects of their views on redistribution. If we examine the models while controlling for 1997 attitudes it unsurprisingly reduces their concurrent effect, with the effects of prior positions on the two scales being comparable. None the less, changes in attitudes towards European integration between 1997 and 2001 are far more strongly connected with changes to Conservative support than is change in attitudes towards redistribution. Models of vote switches to Labour in 2001 display a similar pattern though the magnitudes of effects are smaller, with those for redistribution only marginally statistically significant.

As a final consideration we can estimate the importance of issues whilst taking into account the information we have about respondents' perceptions of party positions (rather than assuming a general position).[4] To do this we subtract scores for self-placement on our scales from those for each of the parties, thus obtaining distance measures. Model 5 in the appendix to this chapter presents models predicting these scores. In general, the results using these measures of distance from the parties are very similar for those obtained using respondents' positions on the two scales. The effect of a person's position on European integration increases substantially over time, both in absolute terms, and relative to that for redistribution. More informatively, however, we can now see that on the question of integration, perceived distance from the Labour Party is far more important than distance from the Conservatives. On redistribution the opposite is the case. The same pattern is true when we take account of past vote (model 6); it is distance from Labour on the EU and from the Conservatives on redistribution that explain vote switching.

Conclusions

Most academic discussions of the impact of Europe on domestic politics in Britain have focused on disputes and divisions among activists and parties. By contrast, this chapter has examined whether Britain's relationship with the European Union has become an issue that is increasingly consequential for electoral behaviour. Two general propositions have been examined. The first is that the traditional left-right axis of party competition in Britain has become less important. The second is that European monetary integration now provides a basis of realignment in British electoral politics. The answer to both questions is yes. Labour's move to the centre on many economic and social policy issues in the 1990s has arguably changed the face of electoral politics in Britain. And, among the many implications of this move are the likely opening of new lines of differentiation between the parties as Labour risks losing support on the left (either to the Liberal Democrats or abstention) and the Conservatives struggle to adapt to an environment where their free market economic policy appeal has been marginalised.

Since the mid-1990s, the issue of European integration has been given undeniable political salience by the ongoing process of European monetary integration and has thus provided a particularly significant opportunity for the hard-pressed Conservatives to open a new 'front'. It is clear that this has become more important in shaping vote choice since 1997. As yet, however, the success of this strategy is limited. True, the Conservatives were closest to public opinion, and – among those who were attracted to the party, and away from Labour – Europe appears to have been an important consideration. But most people remained unmoved and did not change their vote between 1997 and 2001. Moreover, we cannot be sure that the changes we have found reflect the adoption of a positive Eurosceptic strategy by the Conservatives. Rather, there are signs that it is distance from the *Labour Party's* perceived position on Europe that counts for Labour/Conservative voting, not closeness to the

Conservatives' position. Consequently, any benefits that accrue to the Conservatives over Europe may therefore reflect Labour's actions – and particularly the government's endorsement of EMU – rather than their own. It might therefore be more effective for the Conservatives to continue moving to the centre on redistributive issues (given that it is distance on this issue from the Conservatives that is linked with voting for them rather than for Labour). This of course should reduce the prominence of the left-right divide for party competition yet further (unless Labour moves to the left), while the continued harmonisation of European tax and monetary policies should ensure that European integration remains a significant and potentially growing source of party competition. Other things being equal, the process of realignment is likely to continue.

Notes

1. Although the driving force behind that move more than likely derives from Britain's changing social structure and the strategy implications of the growth of the middle class and the contraction of Labour's traditional support base in the manual working classes.
2. An alternative illustration can be seen in model 1 in the appendix to this chapter, which shows that the standard deviations for perceptions of the Conservatives' position on European integration fell significantly between 1997 and 2001 (from 3.05 to 2.73). Indeed, by the last election these perceptions were little *more* heterogeneous than for the other two main parties (Labour = 2.44; Liberal Democrats = 2.28).
3. The overall reduction in model Chi^2 is actually slightly greater for integration than redistribution.
4. The importance of doing this when there are systematic biases in perception has been shown by Evans (1998a).

References

Bara, J. and Budge, I. (2001), 'Party policy and ideology: still new Labour?' in Norris, P. (ed.), *Britain Votes 2001*, special issue of Parliamentary Affairs: Oxford University Press.

Berrington, H. and Hague, R. (1998), 'Europe, Thatcherism and traditionalism: opinion, rebellion and the Maastricht treaty in the backbench Conservative Party, 1992-94' in Berrington. H. (ed.), *Britain in the Nineties: The Politics of Paradox*, London: Frank Cass.

Budge, I. (1999), 'Party policy and ideology: Reversing the 1950s?' in Evans, G. and Norris, P. (eds.), *Critical Elections: British Parties and Voters in Long-term Perspective*, London: Sage.

Evans, G. (1995), 'The state of the Union: attitudes towards Europe' in Jowell, R., Curtice, J., Park, A., Brook, L. and Ahrendt, D. (eds.), *British Social Attitudes: the 12th Report*, Aldershot: Dartmouth.

Evans, G. (1998a), 'Euroscepticism and Conservative electoral support: how an asset became a liability', *British Journal of Political Science*, **28**: 573-90.

Evans, G. (1998b), 'How Britain views the EU' in Jowell, R., Curtice, J., Park, A., Thomson, K. and Bryson, C. (eds.), *British – and European - Social Attitudes: How Britain differs - the 15th Report*. Aldershot: Ashgate.

Evans, G. (1999a), 'Europe: A New Electoral Cleavage?' in Evans, G. and Norris, P. (eds.), *Critical Elections: British Parties and Voters in Long-term Perspective*, London: Sage.

Evans, G. (1999b), 'Economics and Politics Revisited: Explaining the decline in Conservative support, 1992-95', *Political Studies*, **47**: 139-151.

Evans, G. (2000), 'The working class and New Labour: A parting of the ways?' in Jowell, R., Curtice, J., Park, A., Thomson, K., Jarvis, L., Bromley, C. and Stratford, N. (eds.), *British Social Attitudes: the 17th Report - Focusing on Diversity*. London: Sage.

Evans, G. and Andersen, R. (2001), 'Endogenizing the Economy: Political preferences and economic perceptions across the electoral cycle', Paper presented at the 59th annual national meeting of the MidWest Political Science Association, Chicago, 19-22 April.

Evans, G., Heath, A. F. and Lalljee, M. G. (1996), 'Measuring left-right and libertarian-authoritarian values in the British electorate', *British Journal of Sociology*, **47**: 93-112.

Evans, G. and Norris, P. (eds.) (1999), *Critical Elections: British Parties and Voters in Long-term Perspective*, London: Sage.

Franklin, M., Marsh, M. and McLaren, M. (1994), 'Uncorking the bottle: popular opposition to European unification in the wake of Maastricht', *Journal of Common Market Studies*, **32**: 455-472.

George, S. and Rosamund, R. (1992), 'The European Community' in Smith, M. and Spear, J. (eds.), *The Changing Labour Party*, London: Routledge.

Heath, A. F., Evans, G. and Martin, J. (1994), 'The measurement of core beliefs and values: the development of balanced socialist/laissez-faire and libertarian/authoritarian scales', *British Journal of Political Science*, **24**: 115-132.

Janssen, J. (1991), 'Postmaterialism, Cognitive Mobilization and Public Support for European Integration', *British Journal of Political Science*, **21**: 443-468.

McAllister, I. and Studlar, D. T. (2000), 'Conservative Euroscepticism and the Referendum Party in the 1997 British General Election', *Party Politics*, **6**: 359-372.

Norris P. (1999), 'New Politicians? Changes in Party Competition at Westminster' in Evans, G. and Norris, P. (eds.), *Critical Elections: British Parties and Voters in Long-term Perspective*, London: Sage.

Norris, P. (ed.) (2001), *Britain Votes 2001*, special issue of Parliamentary Affairs, Oxford University Press.

Sanders, D. (1996), 'Economic performance, management competence and the outcome of the next general election', *Political Studies*, **44**: 203-231.

Sanders, D. (1999), 'The impact of left-right ideology' in Evans, G. and Norris, P. (eds.), *Critical Elections: British Parties and Voters in Long-term Perspective*, London: Sage.

Sowemimo, M. (1996), 'The Conservative Party and European integration 1989-95', *Party Politics*, **2**: 77-97.

Webb, P. and Farrell, D. M. (1999), 'Party Members and Ideological Change' in Evans, G. and Norris, P. (eds.), *Critical Elections: British Parties and Voters in Long-term Perspective*, London: Sage.

Acknowledgements

We are grateful to the Economic and Social Research Council who funded the *British Election Panel Study*, through its grant to the *Centre for Research into Elections and Social Trends* (*CREST*). We are also indebted to all the members of the panel who agreed to be re-interviewed over the four years between 1997 and 2001.

Appendix

The British Election Panel Study 1997-2001

The first wave of the 1997-2001 *British Election Panel Study* (BEPS II) was formed by the 1997 sample from the *British Election Study*. Respondents to the 1997 survey were followed up on seven further occasions (autumn 1997*, spring 1998, summer 1999, spring 2000, autumn 2000*, spring 2001* – during the election campaign, and finally in the summer of 2001 following the general election). Of the 3,615 respondents to the 1997 Election Study, 2,333 took part in the final wave after the 2001 general election. The panel contains a boosted Scottish sample to enable analysis of trends within Scotland to be analysed separately. This boosted sample is weighted down to enable nationwide analysis leaving 1,749 respondents from both the 1997 and summer 2001 surveys used here. BEPS II was directed by the Centre for Elections and Social Trends (CREST), and fieldwork was conducted by the *National Centre for Social Research*.

*These waves were carried out by telephone (with postal versions for panel members without phones). All other waves were carried out face-to-face using Computer Assisted Personal Interviewing and paper supplements.

Additional Tables and Regression models

Model 1 Perception of parties and self assessment on 11-point scales in 1997 and 2001, mean scores (with standard deviations in brackets)

	EU integration		Redistrib-ution		Tax/Spend		Nationalis-ation/ Privatisation	
Perceptions of ...	**1997**	**2001**	**1997**	**2001**	**1997**	**2001**	**1997**	**2001**
Own position	5.7	6.0	3.4	4.0	2.7	2.9	4.4	4.2
	(3.4)	(3.3)	(3.3)	(2.1)	(2.3)	(2.2)	(2.7)	(2.6)
Conservatives	5.5	6.5	7.4	6.4	6.0	5.2	7.0	6.5
	(3.1)	(2.7)	(2.8)	(2.7)	(3.0)	(2.7)	(3.4)	(2.7)
Labour	3.8	3.3	2.6	3.7	2.6	3.2	3.8	4.5
	(2.6)	(2.4)	(2.2)	(2.3)	(2.2)	(2.0)	(2.5)	(2.3)
Liberal	4.0	3.8	3.6	3.9	2.8	2.7	4.5	4.5
Democrats	(2.4)	(2.3)	(2.1)	(2.0)	(2.2)	(2.1)	(1.9)	(1.8)

Base: 1749

Model 2 Logistic regression of shifts in perceptions of party positions 1997-2001 and Conservative/Labour vote in 2001

Perception of ...	1997		2001	
	B	S.E.	B	S.E.
Conservatives' position on redistribution	-.11	(.03)	-.20	(.04)
Labour's position on redistribution	.13	(.03)	.16	(.05)
Conservatives' position on EU integration	.10	(.03)	.10	(.04)
Labour's position on EU integration	-.14	(.03)	-.24	(.23)
Conservative vote in 1997			3.81	(.23)
Chi^2 (8 df)	178.27		577.8	
Pseudo R^2	.20		.60	

Model 3 Multinominal regression of vote in 2001 on the EU integration and redistribution scales

	1997		2001	
	B	S.E.	B	S.E.
Labour				
Redistribution	-.31	(.02)	-.29	(.02)
Integration	-.18	(.02)	-.28	(.02)
Liberal Democrats				
Redistribution	-.17	(.03)	-.17	(.03)
Integration	-.17	(.03)	-.27	(.03)
Did not vote				
Redistribution	-.15	(.03)	-.19	(.03)
Integration	-.07	(.03)	-.14	(.03)
Redistribution Chi^2	221.5		167.4	
Integration Chi^2	126.0		176.1	

NB: Conservative vote is the reference category.

Model 4 Logistic regression of the effects of views on Europe and redistribution on switching to the Conservatives/Labour between 1997 and 2001

	Effects on Conservative vote in 2001				Effects on Labour vote in 2001			
	B	S.E.	B	S.E.	B	S.E.	B	S.E.
Conservative/Labour vote in 1997	2.71	(.15)	2.61	(.15)	2.55	(.13)	2.48	(.13)
Redistribution 2001	.13	(.02)	.096	(.03)	-.07	(.02)	-.05	(.03)
Integration 2001	.21	(.03)	.184	(.03)	0.13	(.02)	-.10	(.02)
Redistribution 1997			.07	(.03)			-.05	(0.25)[†]
Integration 1997			.07	(.03)			-.07	(.02)
Pseudo R^2	.48		.49		.43		.43	

[†] = Not significant.

Model 5 Logistic regressions predicting Conservative versus Labour vote as a function of distance from the parties on redistribution and EU integration

	1997		2001	
Distance from ...	B	S.E.	B	S.E.
Conservatives on redistribution	.40	(.03)	.41	(.04)
Labour on redistribution	.04	(.03)[†]	-.02	(.03)[†]
Conservatives on EU integration	.02	(.02)	-.08	(.03)
Labour on EU integration	.17	(.03)	.34	(.03)
Pseudo R^2	.50		.50	

[†] = Not significant.

Model 6 Logistic regressions predicting Conservative versus Labour vote as a function of distance from the parties on redistribution and EU integration, controlling for 1997 vote and attitudes

Distance from ...	B	S.E.
Conservatives on redistribution 2001	.29	(.04)
Labour on redistribution 2001	-.11	(.04)
Conservatives on EU 2001	-.06	(.04)
Labour on EU 2001	.32	(.04)
Conservatives on redistribution 1997	.08	(.04)
Labour on redistribution 1997	.13	(.04)
Conservatives on EU 1997	.01	(.04)
Labour on EU 1997	.11	(.03)[†]
Conservative vote 2001	3.12	(.04)
Pseudo R^2	.733	

[†] = Not significant.

Appendix I
Technical details of the survey

British Social Attitudes

In 2000, three versions of the *British Social Attitudes* questionnaire were
fielded. Each 'module' of questions is asked either of the full sample (3,426
respondents) or of a random two-thirds or one-third of the sample. The structure
of the questionnaire (versions A, B and C) is shown at the beginning of
Appendix III.

Sample design

The *British Social Attitudes* survey is designed to yield a representative sample
of adults aged 18 or over. Since 1993, the sampling frame for the survey has
been the Postcode Address File (PAF), a list of addresses (or postal delivery
points) compiled by the Post Office.[1]
  For practical reasons, the sample is confined to those living in private
households. People living in institutions (though not in private households at
such institutions) are excluded, as are households whose addresses were not on
the Postcode Address File.
  The sampling method involved a multi-stage design, with three separate stages
of selection.

Selection of sectors

At the first stage, postcode sectors were selected systematically from a list of all
postal sectors in Great Britain. Before selection, any sectors with fewer than
1,000 addresses were identified and grouped together with an adjacent sector; in
Scotland all sectors north of the Great Glen were excluded (because of the
prohibitive costs of interviewing there). Sectors were then stratified on the basis
of:

- 37 sub-regions
- population density with variable banding used, in order to create three equal-sized strata per sub-region
- ranking by percentage of homes that were owner-occupied in England and Wales and percentage of homes where the head of household was non-manual in Scotland.

Two hundred postcode sectors were selected, with probability proportional to the number of addresses in each sector.

Selection of addresses

Thirty-one addresses were selected in each of the 200 sectors. The sample was therefore 200 x 31 = 6,200 addresses, selected by starting from a random point on the list of addresses for each sector, and choosing each address at a fixed interval. The fixed interval was calculated for each sector in order to generate the correct number of addresses.

The Multiple-Output Indicator (MOI) available through PAF was used when selecting addresses in Scotland. MOI shows the number of accommodation spaces sharing one address. Thus, if the MOI indicates more than one accommodation space at a given address, the chances of the given address being selected from the list of addresses would increase so that it matched the total number of accommodation spaces. MOI is largely irrelevant in England and Wales as separate dwelling units generally appear as separate entries on PAF. In Scotland, tenements with many flats tend to appear as one entry on PAF. However, even in Scotland, the vast majority (87.7 per cent) of MOIs had a value of one. The remainder, which ranged between three and 12, were incorporated into the weighting procedures (described below).

Selection of individuals

Interviewers called at each address selected from PAF and listed all those eligible for inclusion in the sample – that is, all persons currently aged 18 or over and resident at the selected address. The interviewer then selected one respondent using a computer-generated random selection procedure. Where there were two or more households or 'dwelling units' at the selected address, interviewers first had to select one household or dwelling unit using the same random procedure. They then followed the same procedure to select a person for interview.

Weighting

Data were weighted to take account of the fact that not all the units covered in the survey had the same probability of selection. The weighting reflected the relative selection probabilities of the individual at the three main stages of selection: address, household and individual.

First, because addresses in Scotland were selected using the MOI, weights had to be applied to compensate for the greater probability of an address with an MOI of more than one being selected, compared to an address with an MOI of one. (This stage was omitted for the English and Welsh data.) Secondly, data were weighted to compensate for the fact that dwelling units at an address which contained a large number of dwelling units were less likely to be selected for inclusion in the survey than ones which did not share an address. (We use this procedure because in most cases of MOIs greater than one, the two stages will cancel each other out, resulting in more efficient weights.) Thirdly, data were weighted to compensate for the lower selection probabilities of adults living in large households compared with those living in small households. The resulting weight is called 'WtFactor' and the distribution of weights is shown in the next table.

Table A.1: Distribution of unscaled and scaled weights

Unscaled weight	Number	%	Scaled weight
0.1111	2	0.1	0.0611
0.1250	6	0.2	0.0687
0.1667	3	0.1	0.0917
0.2500	5	0.1	0.1375
0.3333	3	0.1	0.1833
0.5000	1	0.0	0.2750
0.5833	1	0.0	0.3208
0.7500	2	0.1	0.4125
0.7778	1	0.0	0.4277
0.8750	1	0.0	0.4812
0.9000	1	0.0	0.4950
1.0000	1187	34.6	0.5500
1.7500	1	0.0	0.9624
2.0000	1790	52.2	1.0999
3.0000	294	8.6	1.6499
4.0000	99	2.9	2.1998
5.0000	14	0.4	2.7498
6.0000	7	0.2	3.2997
7.0000	2	0.1	3.8497
8.0000	6	0.2	4.3996

Base: 3426

All weights fell within a range between 0.1 and 8. The mean weight was 1.82. The weights were then scaled down to make the number of weighted productive cases exactly equal to the number of unweighted productive cases (n = 3,426).

All the percentages presented in this Report are based on weighted data.

Questionnaire versions

Each address in each sector (sampling point) was allocated to either the A, B or C third of the sample. If one serial number was version A, the next was version B and the next after that version C. Thus each interviewer was allocated 10 or 11 cases from each version and each version was assigned to 2,066 or 2,067 addresses.

Fieldwork

Interviewing was mainly carried out between June and September 2000, with a small number of interviews taking place in October and November.

Fieldwork was conducted by interviewers drawn from the *National Centre for Social Research*'s regular panel and conducted using face-to-face computer-assisted interviewing.[2] Interviewers attended a one-day briefing conference to familiarise them with the selection procedures and questionnaires.

The mean interview length was 70 minutes for version A of the questionnaire, 75 minutes for version B and 66 minutes for version C.[3] Interviewers achieved an overall response rate of 62 per cent. Details are shown in the next table.

Table A.2 Response rate on British Social Attitudes 2000

	Number	%
Addresses issued	6,200	
Vacant, derelict and other out of scope	677	
In scope	5,523	100.0
Interview achieved	3,426	62.0
Interview not achieved	2,097	
Refused[1]	1,609	29.1
Non-contacted[2]	207	3.7
Other non-response	281	5.1

1 'Refused' comprises refusals before selection of an individual at the address, refusals to the office, refusal by the selected person, 'proxy' refusals (on behalf of the selected respondent) and broken appointments after which the selected person could not be recontacted.

2 'Non-contacted' comprises households where no one was contacted and those where the selected person could not be contacted.

As in earlier rounds of the series, the respondent was asked to fill in a self-completion questionnaire which, whenever possible, was collected by the interviewer. Otherwise, the respondent was asked to post it to the *National Centre for Social Research*. If necessary, up to three postal reminders were sent to obtain the self-completion supplement.

A total of 458 respondents (13 per cent of those interviewed) did not return their self-completion questionnaire. Version A of the self-completion questionnaire was returned by 87 per cent of respondents to the face-to-face interview, version B by 87 per cent and version C by 86 per cent. As in previous rounds, we judged that it was not necessary to apply additional weights to correct for non-response.

Advance letter

Interviewers were supplied with letters describing the purpose of the survey and the coverage of the questionnaire, which they posted to sampled addresses before making any calls.[4]

Analysis variables

A number of standard analyses have been used in the tables that appear in this report. The analysis groups requiring further definition are set out below. For further details see Thomson *et al.* (2001).

Region

The ten Standard Statistical Regions have been used, except that we generally distinguish between Greater London and the remainder of the South East. Sometimes these have been grouped into what we have termed 'compressed region': 'Northern' includes the North, North West, Yorkshire and Humberside. East Anglia is included in the 'South', as is the South West.

Standard Occupational Classification

Respondents are classified according to their own occupation, not that of the 'head of household'. Each respondent was asked about their current or last job, so that all respondents except those who had never worked were coded. Additionally, if the respondent was not working but their spouse or partner *was* working, their spouse or partner is similarly classified. The main Social Class variables used in the analyses in this report are Registrar General's Social Class, Socio-economic Group and the Goldthorpe schema.

   Since 1991, the *Standard Occupational Classification 1990* (SOC 90) has been used for the occupation coding on the BSA survey series.[5] SOC has a hierarchical structure, consisting of 371 Unit Groups which can be aggregated into 77 Minor Groups, 22 Sub-major Groups and nine Major Groups.

Registrar General's Social Class

The combination of SOC with employment status for current or last job generates the following six Social Classes:

I	Professional etc. occupations	
II	Managerial and technical occupations	'Non-manual'
III (Non-manual)	Skilled occupations	
III (Manual)	Skilled occupations	
IV	Partly skilled occupations	'Manual'
V	Unskilled occupations	

They are usually collapsed into four groups: I & II, III Non-manual, III Manual, and IV & V.

   The remaining respondents are grouped as "never had a job" or "not classifiable". For some analyses, it may be more appropriate to classify respondents according to their current social class, which takes into account only their present economic position. In this case, in addition to the six social classes listed above, the remaining respondents not currently in paid work fall into one of the following categories: "not classifiable", "retired", "looking after the home", "unemployed" or "others not in paid occupations".

Socio-economic Group

As with Social Class, each respondent's Socio-economic Group (SEG) is based on his or her current or last occupation. SEG aims to bring together people with jobs of similar social and economic status, and is derived from a combination of employment status and occupation. The full SEG classification identifies 18 categories, but these are usually condensed into six groups:

- Professionals, employers and managers
- Intermediate non-manual workers
- Junior non-manual workers
- Skilled manual workers
- Semi-skilled manual workers
- Unskilled manual workers

As with Social Class, the remaining respondents are grouped as "never had a job" or "not classifiable".

Goldthorpe schema

The Goldthorpe schema classifies occupations by their 'general comparability', considering such factors as sources and levels of income, economic security, promotion prospects, and level of job autonomy and authority. The Goldthorpe schema was derived from the SOC unit groups combined with employment status. Two versions of the schema are coded: the full schema has 11 categories; the 'compressed schema' combines these into the five classes shown below.

- Salariat (professional and managerial)
- Routine non-manual workers (office and sales)
- Petty bourgeoisie (the self-employed, including farmers, with and without employees)
- Manual foremen and supervisors
- Working class (skilled, semi-skilled and unskilled manual workers, personal service and agricultural workers)

There is a residual category comprising those who have never had a job or who gave insufficient information for classification purposes.

Industry

All respondents whose occupation could be coded were allocated a *Standard Industrial Classification 1992* (SIC 92). Two-digit class codes are used. As with Social Class, SIC may be generated on the basis of the respondent's current occupation only, or on his or her most recently classifiable occupation.

Party identification

Respondents can be classified as identifying with a particular political party on one of three counts: if they consider themselves supporters of that party, as closer to it than to others, or as more likely to support it in the event of a general election (responses are derived from Qs.140-148). The three groups are generally described respectively as *partisans, sympathisers* and *residual identifiers*. In combination, the three groups are referred to as 'identifiers'.

Attitude scales

Since 1986, the *British Social Attitudes* surveys have included two attitude scales which aim to measure where respondents stand on certain underlying value dimensions – left-right and libertarian-authoritarian. Since 1987 (except 1990), a similar scale on 'welfarism' has been asked.[6]

A useful way of summarising the information from a number of questions of this sort is to construct an additive index (DeVellis, 1991; Spector, 1992). This approach rests on the assumption that there is an underlying – 'latent' – attitudinal dimension which characterises the answers to all the questions within each scale. If so, scores on the index are likely to be a more reliable indication of the underlying attitude than the answers to any one question.

Each of these scales consists of a number of statements to which the respondent is invited to "agree strongly", "agree", "neither agree nor disagree", "disagree", or "disagree strongly".

The items are:

Left-right scale

Government should redistribute income from the better-off to those who are less well off. *[Redistrb]*

Big business benefits owners at the expense of workers. *[BigBusnN]*

Ordinary working people do not get their fair share of the nation's wealth. *[Wealth]*[7]

There is one law for the rich and one for the poor. *[RichLaw]*

Management will always try to get the better of employees if it gets the chance. *[Indust4]*

Libertarian-authoritarian scale

Young people today don't have enough respect for traditional British values. *[TradVals]*

People who break the law should be given stiffer sentences. *[StifSent]*

For some crimes, the death penalty is the most appropriate sentence. *[DeathApp]*

Schools should teach children to obey authority. *[Obey]*

The law should always be obeyed, even if a particular law is wrong. *[WrongLaw]*

Censorship of films and magazines is necessary to uphold moral standards. *[Censor]*

Welfarism scale

The welfare state makes people nowadays less willing to look after themselves. *[WelfResp]*

People receiving social security are made to feel like second class citizens. *[WelfStig]*

The welfare state encourages people to stop helping each other. *[WelfHelp]*

The government should spend more money on welfare benefits for the poor, even if it leads to higher taxes. *[MoreWelf]*

Around here, most unemployed people could find a job if they really wanted one. *[UnempJob]*

Many people who get social security don't really deserve any help. *[SocHelp]*

Most people on the dole are fiddling in one way or another. *[DoleFidl]*

If welfare benefits weren't so generous, people would learn to stand on their own two feet. *[WelfFeet]*

In 2000, two additional items were added to the welfarism scale:

Cutting welfare benefits would damage too many people's lives. *[DamLives]*

The creation of the welfare state is one of Britain's proudest achievements. *[ProudWlf]*

These will in future years replace [WelfResp] and [WelfStig].

The indices for the three scales are formed by scoring the leftmost, most libertarian or most pro-welfare position, as 1 and the rightmost, most authoritarian or most anti-welfarist position, as 5. The "neither agree nor disagree" option is scored as 3. The scores to all the questions in each scale are added and then divided by the number of items in the scale giving indices ranging from 1 (leftmost, most libertarian, most pro-welfare) to 5 (rightmost, most authoritarian, most anti-welfare). The scores on the three indices have been placed on the dataset.[8]

The scales have been tested for reliability (as measured by Cronbach's alpha). The Cronbach's alpha (unstandardized item) for the scales in 2000 are 0.83 for the left-right scale, 0.80 for the (original) 'welfarism' scale and 0.75 for the libertarian-authoritarian scale. This level of reliability can be considered "very good" for the left-right scale and "respectable" for the other two scales (DeVellis, 1991: 85).

Other analysis variables

These are taken directly from the questionnaire and to that extent are self-explanatory. The principal ones are:

Sex (Q.35)
Age (Q.36)
Household income (Q.972)
Economic position (Q.328)
Religion (Q.719)

Highest educational qualification
    obtained (Qs.780-842)
Marital status (Q.127)
Benefits received (Qs.926-964)

Sampling errors

No sample precisely reflects the characteristics of the population it represents because of both sampling and non-sampling errors. If a sample were designed as a random sample (if every adult had an equal and independent chance of inclusion in the sample) then we could calculate the sampling error of any percentage, p, using the formula:

$$s.e.\ (p) = \sqrt{\frac{p(100-p)}{n}}$$

where n is the number of respondents on which the percentage is based. Once the sampling error had been calculated, it would be a straightforward exercise to calculate a confidence interval for the true population percentage. For example, a 95 per cent confidence interval would be given by the formula:

$$p \pm 1.96 \times s.e.(p)$$

Clearly, for a simple random sample (srs), the sampling error depends only on the values of p and n. However, simple random sampling is almost never used in practice because of its inefficiency in terms of time and cost.

As noted above, the *British Social Attitudes* sample, like that drawn for most large-scale surveys, was clustered according to a stratified multi-stage design into 200 postcode sectors (or combinations of sectors). With a complex design like this, the sampling error of a percentage giving a particular response is not simply a function of the number of respondents in the sample and the size of the percentage; it also depends on how that percentage response is spread within and between sample points.

The complex design may be assessed relative to simple random sampling by calculating a range of design factors (DEFTs) associated with it, where

$$\text{DEFT} = \sqrt{\frac{\text{Variance of estimator with complex design, sample size n}}{\text{Variance of estimator with srs design, sample size n}}}$$

and represents the multiplying factor to be applied to the simple random sampling error to produce its complex equivalent. A design factor of one means that the complex sample has achieved the same precision as a simple random sample of the same size. A design factor greater than one means the complex sample is less precise than its simple random sample equivalent. If the DEFT for a particular characteristic is known, a 95 per cent confidence interval for a percentage may be calculated using the formula:

$$p \pm 1.96 \times complex\ sampling\ error\ (p)$$

$$= p \pm 1.96 \times \text{DEFT} \times \sqrt{\frac{p(100\text{-}p)}{n}}$$

Calculations of sampling errors and design effects were made using the statistical analysis package STATA.

The following table gives examples of the confidence intervals and DEFTs calculated for a range of different questions: some fielded on all three versions of the questionnaire and some on one only; some asked on the interview questionnaire and some on the self-completion supplement. It shows that most of the questions asked of all sample members have a confidence interval of around plus or minus two to three per cent of the survey proportion. This means that we can be 95 per cent certain that the true population proportion is within two to three per cent (in either direction) of the proportion we report.

It should be noted that the design effects for certain variables (notably those most associated with the area a person lives in) are greater than those for other variables. For example, the question about benefit levels for the unemployed has high design effects, which may reflect differing rates of unemployment across the country. Another case in point is housing tenure as different kinds of tenures (such as council housing, or owner-occupied properties) tend to be concentrated in certain areas; consequently the design effects calculated for these variables in a clustered sample are greater than the design effects calculated for variables less strongly associated with area, such as attitudinal variables.

		% (p)	Complex standard error of p (%)	95 per cent confidence interval	DEFT
Classification variables (Interview)					
DV*	**Party identification**				
	Conservative	27.5	1.2	25.1-30.0	1.63
	Labour	40.2	1.4	37.5-43.0	1.67
	Liberal Democrat	10.3	0.7	8.9-11.7	1.37
DV*	**Housing tenure**				
	Owns	71.2	1.6	68.1-74.2	2.01
	Rents from local authority	14.0	1.2	11.7-16.3	1.99
	Rents privately/HA	13.5	1.2	11.2-15.9	2.03
DV*	**Religion**				
	No religion	39.5	1.2	37.2-41.9	1.42
	Church of England	29.8	1.4	27.0-32.5	1.79
	Roman Catholic	9.2	0.8	7.6-10.8	1.63
Q.779	**Age of completing continuous full-time education**				
	16 or under	60.4	1.6	57.3-63.6	1.95
	17 or 18	18.0	0.8	16.3-19.6	1.27
	19 or over	18.2	1.1	16.1-20.3	1.63
Q.851	**Home internet access**				
	Yes	35.5	1.5	32.6-38.4	1.49
	No	63.8	1.5	60.9-66.8	1.48
Q.621	**Self-rated racial prejudice**				
	Very/a little prejudiced	25.4	1.1	23.2-27.6	1.23
	Not prejudiced at all	73.2	1.1	71.0-75.5	1.24

* DV = Derived variable.

		% (p)	Complex standard error of p (%)	95 per cent confidence interval	DEFT
Attitudinal variables (Interview)					
Q.425	**Benefits for the unemployed are ...**				
	... too low	40.1	1.3	37.6-42.6	1.53
	... too high	36.2	1.2	33.9-38.5	1.45
Q.259	**How much poverty is there in Britain today?**				
	Very little	34.9	1.1	32.8-37.0	1.31
	Quite a lot	62.2	1.1	60.2-64.3	1.27
A.220 B.220	**How comfortable would you be asking to borrow a sink plunger from a neighbour?**				
	Very comfortable	60.4	1.2	58.0-62.8	1.21
	Fairly comfortable	25.5	1.0	23.6-27.3	1.06
	Fairly uncomfortable	7.0	0.6	5.8-8.2	1.16
	Very uncomfortable	6.6	0.7	5.3-7.09	1.26
Attitudinal variables (Self-completion)					
A2.12e B2.12e C2.35e	**Strongly disagree or disagree that run down areas have higher rates of teenage pregnancy**	17.9	0.9	16.2-19.6	1.22
A2.09 B2.09 C2.32	**Cohabiting couples definitely or probably have common law rights**	56.1	1.2	53.7-58.5	1.42
A2.16 B2.16	**Attitudes towards voting in general elections**				
	Not worth voting	11.2	0.8	9.7-12.7	1.08
	Vote if care who wins	24.3	1.0	22.4-26.3	1.03
	Duty to vote	63.5	1.3	61.1-66.0	1.17
C2.10b	**Air pollution from cars is extremely dangerous to family**	18.6	1.2	16.2-20.9	0.96

These calculations are based on the 3,426 respondents to the main questionnaire and 2,968 returning self-completion questionnaires; on the A version respondents (1,159 for the main questionnaire and 1,012 for the self-completion); on the B version respondents (1,134 and 986 respectively); or on the C version respondents (1,133 and 970 respectively). As the examples above show, sampling errors for proportions based only on respondents to just one of the three versions of the questionnaire, or on subgroups within the sample, are somewhat larger than they would have been had the questions been asked of everyone.

Analysis techniques

Regression

Regression analysis aims to summarise the relationship between a 'dependent' variable and one or more 'independent' variables. It shows how well we can estimate a respondent's score on the dependent variable from knowledge of their scores on the independent variables. It is often undertaken to support a claim that the phenomena measured by the independent variables cause the phenomenon measured by the dependent variable. However, the causal ordering, if any, between the variables cannot be verified or falsified by the technique. Causality can only be inferred through special experimental designs or through assumptions made by the analyst.

All regression analysis assumes that the relationship between the dependent and each of the independent variables takes a particular form. In *linear regression*, the most common form of regression analysis, it is assumed that the relationship can be adequately summarised by a straight line. This means that a one point increase in the value of an independent variable is assumed to have the same impact on the value of the dependent variable on average irrespective of the previous values of those variables.

Strictly speaking the technique assumes that both the dependent and the independent variables are measured on an interval level scale, although it may sometimes still be applied even where this is not the case. For example, one can use an ordinal variable (e.g. a Likert scale) as a *dependent* variable if one is willing to assume that there is an underlying interval level scale and the difference between the observed ordinal scale and the underlying interval scale is due to random measurement error. Categorical or nominal data can be used as *independent* variables by converting them into dummy or binary variables; these are variables where the only valid scores are 0 and 1, with 1 signifying membership of a particular category and 0 otherwise.

The assumptions of linear regression can cause particular difficulties where the *dependent* variable is binary. The assumption that the relationship between the dependent and the independent variables is a straight line means that it can produce estimated values for the dependent variable of less than 0 or greater than 1. In this case it may be more appropriate to assume that the relationship between the dependent and the independent variables takes the form of an S-curve, where the impact on the dependent variable of a one-point increase in an independent variable becomes progressively less the closer the value of the dependent variable approaches 0 or 1. *Logistic regression* is an alternative form of regression which fits such an S-curve rather than a straight line. The technique can also be adapted to analyse multinomial non-interval level dependent variables, that is, variables which classify respondents into more than two categories.

The two statistical scores most commonly reported from the results of regression analyses are:

A measure of variance explained: This summarises how well all the independent variables combined can account for the variation in respondent's scores in the dependent variable. The higher the measure, the more accurately we are able in general to estimate the correct value of each respondent's score on the dependent variable from knowledge of their scores on the independent variables.

A parameter estimate: This shows how much the dependent variable will change on average, given a one unit change in the independent variable (while holding all other independent variables in the model constant). The parameter estimate has a positive sign if an increase in the value of the independent variable results in an increase in the value of the dependent variable. It has a negative sign if an increase in the value of the independent variable results in a decrease in the value of the dependent variable. If the parameter estimates are standardised, it is possible to compare the relative impact of different independent variables; those variables with the largest standardised estimates can be said to have the biggest impact on the value of the dependent variable.

Regression also tests for the statistical significance of parameter estimates. A parameter estimate is said to be significant at the five per cent level, if the range of the values encompassed by its 95 per cent confidence interval (see also section on sampling errors) are either all positive or all negative. This means that there is less than a five per cent chance that the association we have found between the dependent variable and the independent variable is simply the result of sampling error and does not reflect a relationship that actually exists in the general population.

Factor analysis

Factor analysis is a statistical technique which aims to identify whether there are one or more apparent sources of commonality to the answers given by respondents to a set of questions. It ascertains the smallest number of *factors* (or dimensions) which can most economically summarise all of the variation found in the set of questions being analysed. Factors are established where respondents who give a particular answer to one question in the set, tend to give the same answer as each other to one or more of the other questions in the set. The technique is most useful when a relatively small number of factors is able to account for a relatively large proportion of the variance in all of the questions in the set.

The technique produces a *factor loading* for each question (or variable) on each factor. Where questions have a high loading on the same factor then it will be the case that respondents who give a particular answer to one of these questions tend to give a similar answer to the other questions. The technique is most commonly used in attitudinal research to try to identify the underlying ideological dimensions which apparently structure attitudes towards the subject in question.

International Social Survey Programme

The *International Social Survey Programme* (*ISSP*) is run by a group of research organisations, each of which undertakes to field annually an agreed module of questions on a chosen topic area. Since 1985, an *International Social Survey Programme* module has been included in one of the *British Social Attitudes* self-completion questionnaires. Each module is chosen for repetition at intervals to allow comparisons both between countries (membership is currently standing at 38) and over time. In 2000, the chosen subject was the Environment, and the module was carried on the C version of the self-completion questionnaire (Qs.1-23).

Notes

1. Until 1991 all *British Social Attitudes* samples were drawn from the Electoral Register (ER). However, following concern that this sampling frame might be deficient in its coverage of certain population subgroups, a 'splicing' experiment was conducted in 1991. We are grateful to the Market Research Development Fund for contributing towards the costs of this experiment. Its purpose was to investigate whether a switch to PAF would disrupt the time-series – for instance, by lowering response rates or affecting the distribution of responses to particular questions. In the event, it was concluded that the change from ER to PAF was unlikely to affect time trends in any noticeable ways, and that no adjustment factors were necessary. Since significant differences in efficiency exist between PAF and ER, and because we considered it untenable to continue to use a frame that is known to be biased, we decided to adopt PAF as the sampling frame for future *British Social Attitudes* surveys. For details of the PAF/ER 'splicing' experiment, see Lynn and Taylor (1995).

2. In 1993 it was decided to mount a split-sample experiment designed to test the applicability of Computer-Assisted Personal Interviewing (CAPI) to the *British Social Attitudes* survey series. CAPI has been used increasingly over the past decade as an alternative to traditional interviewing techniques. As the name implies, CAPI involves the use of lap-top computers during the interview, with interviewers entering responses directly into the computer. One of the advantages of CAPI is that it significantly reduces both the amount of time spent on data processing and the number of coding and editing errors. Over a longer period, there could also be significant cost savings. There was, however, concern that a different interviewing technique might alter the distribution of responses and so affect the year-on-year consistency of *British Social Attitudes* data.

   Following the experiment, it was decided to change over to CAPI completely in 1994 (the self-completion questionnaire still being administered in the conventional way). The results of the experiment are discussed in *The 11th Report* (Lynn and Purdon, 1994).

3. Interview times of less than 20 and more than 150 minutes were excluded as these were likely to be errors.

4. An experiment was conducted on the 1991 *British Social Attitudes* survey, which showed that sending advance letters to sampled addresses before fieldwork begins has very little impact on response rates. However, interviewers do find that an advance letter helps them to introduce the survey on the doorstep, and a majority of respondents have said that they preferred some advance notice. For these reasons, advance letters have been used on the *British Social Attitudes* surveys since 1991.

5. Before 1991, occupational coding was carried out according to the OPCS *Classification of Occupations 1980* (CO80). However, analysts can be confident that the change to SOC does not affect year-on-year comparability of Social Class variables in the *British Social Attitudes* survey. For further details see Appendix I in Jowell *et al.* (1992).

6. Because of methodological experiments on scale development, the exact items detailed in this section have not been asked on all versions of the questionnaire each year.

7. In 1994 only, this item was replaced by: Ordinary people get their fair share of the nation's wealth. *[Wealth1]*

8. In constructing the scale, a decision had to be taken on how to treat missing values ('Don't knows' and 'Refused'/not answered). Respondents who had more than two missing values on the left-right scale and more than three missing values on the libertarian-authoritarian and welfare scale were excluded from that scale. For respondents with just a few missing values, 'Don't knows' were recoded to the midpoint of the scale and not answered or 'Refused' were recoded to the scale mean for that respondent on their valid items.

References

DeVellis, R. F. (1991), 'Scale development: theory and applications', *Applied Social Research Methods Series*, **26**, Newbury Park: Sage.

Jowell, R., Brook, L., Prior, G. and Taylor, B. (1992), *British Social Attitudes: the 9th Report*, Aldershot: Dartmouth.

Lynn, P. and Purdon, S. (1994), 'Time-series and lap-tops: the change to computer-assisted interviewing' in Jowell, R., Curtice, J., Brook, L. and Ahrendt, D. (eds.), *British Social Attitudes: the 11th Report*, Aldershot: Dartmouth.

Lynn, P. and Taylor, B. (1995), 'On the bias and variance of samples of individuals: a comparison of the Electoral Registers and Postcode Address File as sampling frames', *The Statistician*, **44**: 173-194.

Spector, P. E. (1992), 'Summated rating scale construction: an introduction', *Quantitative Applications in the Social Sciences*, **82**, Newbury Park: Sage.

Thomson, K., Park, A., Bryson, C., Jarvis, L. and Bromley, C. (2001), *British Social Attitudes and Young People's Social Attitudes 1998 surveys: Technical Report*, London: National Centre for Social Research.

Appendix II
Notes on the tabulations

1. Figures in the tables are from the 2000 *British Social Attitudes* survey unless otherwise indicated.
2. Tables are percentaged as indicated.
3. In tables, '*' indicates less than 0.5 per cent but greater than zero, and '-' indicates zero.
4. When findings based on the responses of fewer than 100 respondents are reported in the text, reference is generally made to the small base size.
5. Percentages equal to or greater than 0.5 have been rounded up in all tables (e.g. 0.5 per cent = one per cent, 36.5 per cent = 37 per cent).
6. In many tables the proportions of respondents answering "Don't know" or not giving an answer are omitted. This, together with the effects of rounding and weighting, means that percentages will not always add to 100 per cent.
7. The self-completion questionnaire was not completed by all respondents to the main questionnaire (see Appendix I). Percentage responses to the self-completion questionnaire are based on all those who completed it.
8. The bases shown in the tables (the number of respondents who answered the question) are printed in small italics. The bases are unweighted, unless otherwise stated.

Appendix III
The questionnaires

As explained in Appendix I, three different versions of the questionnaire (A, B and C) were administered, each with its own self-completion supplement. The diagram that follows shows the structure of the questionnaires and the topics covered (not all of which are reported on in this volume).

The three interview questionnaires reproduced on the following pages are derived from the Blaise program in which they were written. For ease of reference, each item has been allocated a question number. Gaps in the numbering system indicate items that are essential components of the Blaise program but which are not themselves questions, and so have been omitted. In addition, we have removed the keying codes and inserted instead the percentage distribution of answers to each question. We have also included the SPSS variable name, in square brackets, beside each question. Above the questions we have included filter instructions. A filter instruction should be considered as staying in force until the next filter instruction. Percentages for the core questions are based on the total weighted sample, while those for questions in versions A, B or C are based on the appropriate weighted sub-samples. We reproduce first version A of the interview questionnaire in full; then those parts of version B and version C that differ. The three versions of the self-completion questionnaire follow, with those parts fielded in more than one version reproduced in one version only.

The percentage distributions do not necessarily add up to 100 because of weighting and rounding, or for one or more of the following reasons:

(i)   Some sub-questions are filtered – that is, they are asked of only a proportion of respondents. In these cases the percentages add up (approximately) to the proportions who were asked them. Where, however, a series of questions is filtered, we have indicated the weighted base at the beginning of that series (for example, all employees), and throughout have derived percentages from that base.
(ii)   If fewer than 50 respondents (unweighted) are asked a question, frequencies (the number of people giving each response) are shown, rather than percentages.

(iii)   At a few questions, respondents were invited to give more than one
        answer and so percentages may add to well over 100 per cent. These are
        clearly marked by interviewer instructions on the questionnaires.

As reported in Appendix I, the 2000 *British Social Attitudes* self-completion
questionnaire was not completed by 13 per cent of respondents who were
successfully interviewed. The answers in the supplement have been percentaged
on the base of those respondents who returned it. This means that the
distribution of responses to questions asked in earlier years are comparable with
those given in Appendix III of all earlier reports in this series except in *The
1984 Report*, where the percentages for the self-completion questionnaire need
to be recalculated if comparisons are to be made.

BRITISH SOCIAL ATTITUDES: 2000 SURVEY
Main questionnaire plan

Version A	Version B	Version C
Household grid		
Newspaper readership		
Party identification		
Social Trust		-
Public spending and social welfare		
Attitudes to cohabitation		
Health care		
Employment		
Democracy & participation		Education
Constitutional change		Transport
-	Genetics	
Classification		

Self-completion questionnaire plan

-	-	ISSP (Environment)
Public spending and social welfare		
Health care		
Employment		
Attitudes to cohabitation		
Teenage pregnancies		
Social Trust		Education
Democracy & participation		Transport
Constitutional change		-
-	Genetics	
Attitude scales		

BRITISH SOCIAL ATTITUDES 2000: FACE TO FACE QUESTIONNAIRE

Contents page

VERSION A

Introduction

ASK ALL

Q1 [Serial]
    Serial Number
    Range: 120001 ... 129999

Q8 [StRegion]
%   Standard Region
8.7 Scotland
6.1 Northern
9.9 North West
10.0 Yorkshire and Humberside
8.1 West Midlands
8.7 East Midlands
4.4 East Anglia
8.7 South West
19.2 South East (excluding London)
10.3 Greater London
6.0 Wales

Q25 [ABCVer]
%   Questionnaire version
34.1 A
32.8 B
33.1 C

Household grid

ASK ALL

Q33 [Househld]
     (You have just been telling me about the adults that live in
     this household. Thinking now of **everyone** living in the
     household, **including children**:)
     Including yourself, how many people live here regularly as
     members of this household?
     CHECK INTERVIEWER MANUAL FOR DEFINITION OF HOUSEHOLD IF
     NECESSARY.
     IF YOU DISCOVER THAT YOU WERE GIVEN THE WRONG INFORMATION FOR
     THE RESPONDENT SELECTION ON THE ARF:
     *   **DO NOT** REDO THE ARF SELECTION PRODECURE
     *   **DO** ENTER THE CORRECT INFORMATION HERE
     *   **DO** USE <CTRL + M> TO MAKE A NOTE OF WHAT HAPPENED.
%   **Median: 2 people**
-    (Don't know)
-    (Refusal/Not answered)

HOUSEHOLD GRID: QUESTIONS ASKED ONCE FOR EACH HOUSEHOLD MEMBER

     [Name] **(NOT ON DATA FILE)**
     FOR RESPONDENT: (Can I just check, what is your first name?)
     PLEASE TYPE IN THE FIRST NAME (OR INITIALS) OF RESPONDENT
     FOR OTHER HOUSEHOLD MEMBERS: PLEASE TYPE IN THE FIRST NAME (OR
     INITIALS) OF PERSON NUMBER (number)

     [RSex], [P2Sex] - [P10Sex] (Figures refer to respondent)
     PLEASE CODE SEX OF (name)
%
45.1 Male
54.9 Female
-    (Don't know)
-    (Refusal/Not answered)

     [RAge], [P2Age] - [P10Age]
     FOR RESPONDENT IF ONLY ONE PERSON IN HOUSEHOLD: I would now
     like to ask you a few details about yourself. What was your
     age last birthday?
     FOR RESPONDENT IF SEVERAL PEOPLE IN HOUSEHOLD: I would like to
     ask you a few details about each person in your household.
     Starting with yourself, what was your **age** last birthday?
     FOR OTHER PERSONS IN HOUSEHOLD: What was (name)'s age last
     birthday?
     FOR 97+, CODE 97.
%   **Median: 45 years**
0.0 (Don't know)
0.1 (Refusal/No answered)

IF MORE THAN ONE PERSON IN HOUSEHOLD: FOR PEOPLE OTHER THAN RESPONDENT

N = 3246

[P2Rel3] - [P10Rel3] (Figures refer to second person in household)

PLEASE ENTER RELATIONSHIP OF (name) TO RESPONDENT
%
63.5 Partner/ spouse/ cohabitee
6.0 Son/ daughter (inc step/adopted)
0.1 Grandson/ daughter (inc step/adopted)
7.5 Parent/ parent-in-law
0.3 Grand-parent
1.5 Brother/ sister (inc. in-law)
0.3 Other relative
3.3 Other non-relative
- (Don't know)
- (Refusal/Not answered)

END OF HOUSEHOLD GRID

ASK ALL
Q127 [MarStat2]
CARD A1
Can I just check, which of these applies to you at present?
CODE FIRST TO APPLY
%
55.6 Married
9.2 Living as married
2.2 Separated (after being married)
5.9 Divorced
8.0 Widowed
19.2 Single (never married)
- (Don't know)
- (Refusal/Not answered)

Newspaper readership

N = 3426

ASK ALL
Q134 [ReadPap]
Do you normally read any daily **morning** newspaper at least 3 times a week?
%
57.1 Yes
42.9 No
- (Don't know)
- (Refusal/Not answered)

IF 'yes' AT [ReadPap]
Q135 [WhPaper]
Which one do you normally read?
IF MORE THAN ONE: Which one do you read **most** frequently?
%
4.1 (Scottish) Daily Express
10.7 (Scottish) Daily Mail
10.0 Daily Mirror (/Record)
1.3 Daily Star
13.9 The Sun
4.9 Daily Telegraph
0.4 Financial Times
2.3 The Guardian
1.0 The Independent
3.0 The Times
0.0 Morning Star
5.0 Other Irish/Northern Irish/Scottish regional or local daily **morning** paper (WRITE IN)
0.2 Other (WRITE IN)
0.2 **EDIT ONLY:** More than one paper read with equal frequency
0.0 (Don't know)
- (Refusal/Not answered)

N = 2293

VERSION A AND B: ASK ALL
Q138 [TVHrsWk]
How many **hours** of television do you normally watch on an ordinary **weekday or evening**?
INTERVIEWER: ROUND UP TO NEAREST HOUR
IF DOES NOT WATCH TELEVISION ON WEEKDAYS, CODE 0
IF NEVER WATCHES TELEVISION AT ALL, CODE 97
Median: 3 hours
%
0.1 (Never watches TV)
0.1 (Don't know)
- (Refusal/Not answered)

Party identification

ASK ALL

Q140 *[SupParty]*
Generally speaking, do you think of yourself as a supporter of any one political party?

%
36.8 Yes
63.1 No
0.1 (Don't know)
0.0 (Refusal/Not answered)

IF 'no' OR 'don't know' AT [SupParty]

Q141 *[ClosePty]*
Do you think of yourself as a little closer to one political party than to the others?

%
25.7 Yes
37.4 No
0.1 (Don't know)
0.0 (Refusal/Not answered)

IF 'yes' AT [SupParty] OR 'yes'/'no'/'don't know' AT [ClosePty]

Q143 *[PartyID1]*
IF 'yes' AT [SupParty] OR AT [ClosePty]: Which one?
IF 'no'/'don't know' AT [ClosePty]: If there were a general election tomorrow, which political party do you think you would be most likely to support?
DO NOT PROMPT

%
27.5 Conservative
40.2 Labour
10.3 Liberal Democrat
1.5   Scottish National Party
0.5   Plaid Cymru
0.5   Other party
0.8   Other answer
13.4 None
0.8   Green Party
3.0   (Don't know)
1.4   (Refusal/Not answered)

IF PARTY GIVEN AT [PartyID1]

Q148 *[Idstrng]*
Would you call yourself very strong (party), fairly strong, or not very strong?

%
6.1   Very strong (party)
25.7 Fairly strong
49.3 Not very strong
0.1   (Don't know)
0.1   (Refusal/Not answered)

Q139 *[BkHrsWk]*
How many **hours** do you normally spend reading a book for pleasure in a **whole week**?
INTERVIEWER: ROUND UP TO NEAREST HOUR
IF DOES NOT READ DURING THE WEEK OR NEVER READS, CODE 0
DO **NOT** INCLUDE MAGAZINES
Median: 2 hours

%
- (Don't know)
- (Refusal/Not answered)

VERSIONS A AND B: ASK ALL

Q149 *[Politics]*
How much interest do you generally have in what is going on in politics

%
   ... READ OUT ...
9.7   ... a great deal,
22.5   quite a lot,
32.8   some,
24.1   not very much,
10.8   or, none at all?
0.0   (Don't know)
-   (Refusal/Not answered)

Social Capital

VERSIONS A AND B: ASK ALL

Q151 *[GovTrust]*
CARD B1
How much do you trust British governments of any party to place the needs of the nation above the interests of their own political party?
Please choose a phrase from this card.

Q152 *[PolTrust]*
CARD B1 AGAIN
And how much do you trust British police not to bend the rules in trying to get a conviction?

Q153 *[CSTrust]*
CARD B1 AGAIN
And how much do you trust top civil servants to stand firm against a minister who wants to provide false information to parliament?

Q154 *[MPsTrust]*
CARD B1 AGAIN
And how much do you trust politicians of any party in Britain to tell the truth when they are in a tight corner?

	[GovTrust]	[PolTrust]	[CSTrust]	[MPsTrust]
	%	%	%	%
Just about always	1.3	9.7	6.7	1.3
Most of the time	14.9	49.3	28.6	9.5
Only some of the time	58.5	30.5	39.6	42.4
Almost never	24.4	8.9	16.7	45.5
(Don't know)	1.0	1.6	8.3	1.3
(Refusal/Not answered)	-	-	0.0	-

Q155 *[SocTrust]*
Generally speaking, would you say that most people can be trusted, or that you can't be too careful in dealing with people?
%
44.8   Most people can be trusted
54.4   Can't be too careful in dealing with people
0.8   (Don't know)
0.0   (Refusal/Not answered)

N = 2293

Q156-CARD B2

Q163 Now thinking of MPs, which of the following qualities shown on this card would you say are important for an MP to have?

You may choose more than one, none, or suggest others.

% CODE ALL THAT APPLY
54.0 To be well educated [MPEd]
41.7 To know what being poor means [MPPoor]
27.6 To have business experience [MPBus]
13.9 To have trade union experience [MPUnion]
53.9 To have been brought up in the area he or she represents [MPLocal]
43.1 To be loyal to the party he or she represents [MPLoyal]
55.7 To be independent minded [MPInd]
5.4 **EDIT ONLY:** To be honest [MPOth8]
1.4 **EDIT ONLY:** To be caring / compassionate [MPOth9]
1.8 **EDIT ONLY:** To be loyal to their constituents [MPOOth10]
0.5 **EDIT ONLY:** To be upright / moral [MPOth11]
0.1 **EDIT ONLY:** To be courageous / tough / strong [MPOth12]
1.2 **EDIT ONLY:** To be prepared to listen / to keep in touch [MPOth13]
0.6 None of these qualities [MPNone]
4.2 Other important qualities (PLEASE SPECIFY) [MPOth2]
0.4 (Don't know)
- (Refusal/Not answered)

Q174-CARD B3

Q182 Are you currently a member of any of these?
IF YES: Which ones? PROBE: Which others?
% CODE ALL THAT APPLY
74.6 (None of these) [MemNone]
4.5 Tenants'/residents' association [MemResid]
2.1 Parent-teachers'/ school parents' association [MemPTA]
1.3 Board of school governors/School Board [MemSclGv]
2.6 A political party [MemPlPty]
1.2 Parish, Town or Community council, (**not** English Community Health Councils) [Mem ParCl]
0.9 Neighbourhood council/forum [MemNghCl]
11.1 Neighbourhood Watch Scheme [MemNghWt]
2.2 Local conservation or environmental group [MemEnvir]
5.8 Other local community or voluntary group (PLEASE SPECIFY) [MemComVl]
1.8 **EDIT ONLY:** Voluntary group to help sick / elderly / children / other vulnerable group [MemSikV1]
0.0 (Don't know)
- (Refusal/Not answered)

N = 2293

Q194-CARD B4

Q204 Do you personally belong to any of the groups listed on this card?
% CODE ALL THAT APPLY
9.4 The National Trust [Club1]
4.0 Royal Society for the Protection of Birds [Club2]
0.8 Friends of the Earth [Club6]
2.4 World Wildlife Fund/ Worldwide Fund for Nature [Club7]
1.2 Greenpeace [Club8]
0.3 Council for the Protection of Rural England/ Wales/ Association for the Protection of Rural Scotland [Club9]
1.8 Other wildlife or countryside **protection** group [Club3]
0.7 Ramblers Association [Club10]
2.6 Other countryside sport or **recreation** group [Club4]
0.2 Urban conservation group [Club11]
0.3 Campaign for Nuclear Disarmament [Club12]
82.7 (None of these) [Club5]
- (Don't know)
- (Refusal/Not answered)

Q217 [Clubs]
And are you a member of any kind of local sports club, or of a cultural group such as an art or drama club?
PROBE AS NECESSARY AND CODE ONE ONLY
%
18.2 Yes, sports club(s) only
4.8 Yes, cultural group(s) only
1.9 Yes, both sports club(s) and cultural group(s)
75.0 No
- (Don't know)
- (Refusal/Not answered)

Q218 [NghBrHd]
Can I just check, how long have you lived in your present neighbourhood?
ENTER YEARS. ROUND TO NEAREST YEAR.
PROBE FOR BEST ESTIMATE.
IF LESS THAN ONE YEAR, CODE 0.
% **Median: 14 years**
- (Don't know)
- (Refusal/Not answered)

Q219 [NeigIll]
CARD B5
Suppose that you were in bed ill and needed someone to go to the chemist to collect your prescription while they were doing their shopping.
How comfortable would you be asking a neighbour to do this?

Q220 [NeigSink]
CARD B5 AGAIN
Now suppose you found your sink was blocked, but you did not
have a plunger to unblock it.
How comfortable would you be asking a neighbour to borrow a
plunger?

Q221 [NeigMilk]
CARD B5 AGAIN
Now suppose the milkman called for payment. The bill was £5
but you had no cash.
How comfortable would you be asking a neighbour if you could
borrow £5?

	[NeighIll]	[NeighSink]	[NeighMilk]
	%	%	%
Very comfortable	53.8	60.4	21.6
Fairly comfortable	25.5	25.5	15.5
Fairly uncomfortable	9.6	7.0	16.8
Very uncomfortable	10.6	6.6	45.1
(Don't know)	0.4	0.5	0.9
(Refusal/Not answered)	0.0	0.0	0.1

Q222 [VATCheat]
CARD B6
Using this card, please say what comes closest to what you
think about the following situation.
A householder is having a repair job done by a local plumber.
He is told that if he pays cash, he will not be charged VAT.
So he pays cash.

%
29.0 Nothing wrong
30.2 Bit wrong
27.7 Wrong
8.0 Seriously wrong
4.1 Very seriously wrong
0.9 (Don't know)
0.0 (Refusal/Not answered)

Q223 [VATDo]
Might you do this if the situation came up?
%
70.7 Yes
27.1 No
2.1 (Don't know)
0.2 (Refusal/Not answered)

Q224 [ShopChkp]
CARD B6 AGAIN
Still using this card, what comes closest to what you think
about this situation.
A man gives a £5 note for goods he is buying in a corner shop.
By mistake, he is given change for a £10 note. He notices, but
keeps the change.
%
3.5 Nothing wrong
11.8 Bit wrong
48.3 Wrong
21.3 Seriously wrong
14.9 Very seriously wrong
0.1 (Don't know)
0.0 (Refusal/Not answered)

Q225 [ShopChDo]
Might you do this if the situation came up?
%
16.6 Yes
82.9 No
0.5 (Don't know)
0.0 (Refusal/Not answered)

Q226 [Pay100]
CARD B6 AGAIN
(Still using this card,) what comes closest to what you think
about this situation.
A person in paid work takes on an extra weekend job and is
paid in cash. He does not declare it for tax and so is £100 in
pocket.
%
20.6 Nothing wrong
27.5 Bit wrong
35.9 Wrong
10.1 Seriously wrong
5.0 Very seriously wrong
0.9 (Don't know)
0.1 (Refusal/Not answered)

Q227 [Pay100Do]
Might you do this if the situation came up?
%
48.4 Yes
49.5 No
2.0 (Don't know)
0.1 (Refusal/Not answered)

Q228 [PByLost]
CARD B5 AGAIN
Suppose you are in the middle of a town you do not know very
well. You are trying to find a particular street and have got
a bit lost. How comfortable would you be asking **any** passer-by
for directions?

N = 2293

N = 2293

Q229 [PByPhone]
CARD B5 AGAIN
Again suppose you are in the middle of a town you do not know very well. You need to make an urgent 'phone call from a 'phone box but you only have a £5 note. How comfortable would you be asking any passer-by for the right change?

	[PByLost]	[PByPhone]
	%	%
Very comfortable	51.5	21.0
Fairly comfortable	36.9	35.6
Fairly uncomfortable	8.0	25.5
Very uncomfortable	3.4	17.4
(Don't know)	0.2	0.5
(Refusal/Not answered)	0.0	0.0

Q230 [WmnHelp]
CARD B7
Suppose you are walking down a local street. Ahead of you there is a group of teenagers blocking the pavement, forcing an elderly woman to walk out into a busy road. How likely is it that you would help the woman by asking the young people to move?
Please choose a phrase from this card.

%	
54.0	Definitely help her myself
36.9	Probably help her myself
6.1	Probably not help her, but hope someone else would
2.2	Definitely not help her, but hope someone else would
0.8	(Don't know)
0.0	(Refusal/Not answered)

Public spending and social welfare

VERSIONS A AND C: ASK ALL
Q232 [Spend1]
CARD C1
Here are some items of government spending. Which of them, if any, would be your highest priority for **extra** spending? Please read through the whole list before deciding.
ENTER ONE CODE ONLY FOR HIGHEST PRIORITY

IF NOT None/DK/Ref AT [Spend1]
Q233 [Spend2]
CARD C1 AGAIN
And which next?
ENTER ONE CODE ONLY FOR NEXT HIGHEST

	[Spend1]	[Spend2]
	%	%
Education	25.7	38.5
Defence	1.1	1.7
Health	54.5	26.5
Housing	4.2	7.0
Public transport	3.6	6.2
Roads	2.3	4.0
Police and prisons	3.5	6.4
Social security benefits	2.2	4.8
Help for industry	1.7	3.2
Overseas aid	0.7	0.7
(None of these)	0.2	0.3
(Don't know)	0.3	0.0
(Refusal/Not answered)	-	0.3

ASK ALL
Q234 [SocBen1]
CARD C2
Thinking now only of the government's spending on **social benefits** like those on the card.
Which, if any, of these would be your highest priority for **extra** spending?
ENTER ONE CODE ONLY FOR HIGHEST PRIORITY

IF NOT None/DK/Ref AT [SocBen1]
Q235 [SocBen2]
CARD C2 AGAIN
And which next?
ENTER ONE CODE ONLY FOR NEXT HIGHEST

N = 3426

	[SocBen1]	[SocBen2]
	%	%
Retirement pensions	52.1	21.5
Child benefits	14.0	18.7
Benefits for the unemployed	4.5	8.4
Benefits for disabled people	21.4	39.7
Benefits for single parents	6.7	8.5
(None of these)	0.6	1.6
(Don't know)	0.6	0.2
(Refusal/Not answered)	0.0	0.6

ASK ALL

Q236 [FalseClm]
I will read two statements. For each one please say whether you agree or disagree. Firstly...
Large numbers of people these days **falsely** claim benefits.
IF AGREE OR DISAGREE: Strongly or slightly?

Q237 [FailClm]
And do you agree or disagree that(...)
Large numbers of people who are eligible for benefits these days **fail** to claim them.
IF AGREE OR DISAGREE: Strongly or slightly?

	[FalseClm]	[FailClm]
	%	%
Agree strongly	54.4	45.3
Agree slightly	22.7	33.4
Disagree slightly	10.0	11.8
Disagree strongly	9.6	4.4
(Don't know)	3.4	5.1
(Refusal/Not answered)	-	-

Q238 [Dole]
Opinions differ about the level of benefits for unemployed people.
Which of these two statements comes closest to your own view
... READ OUT ...

%
40.1 ...benefits for unemployed people are **too low** and cause hardship,
36.2 or, benefits for unemployed people are **too high** and discourage them from finding jobs?
14.5 (Neither)
0.1 **EDIT ONLY:** Both: unemployment benefit causes hardship but can't be higher or there would be no incentive to work
0.6 **EDIT ONLY:** Both: unemployment benefit causes hardship to some, while others do well out of it
0.4 **EDIT ONLY:** About right/in between
3.9 Other answer (WRITE IN)
4.3 (Don't know)
- (Refusal/Not answered)

N = 2302

VERSIONS A AND C: ASK ALL

Q240 [TaxSpend]
CARD C3
Suppose the government had to choose between the three options on this card. Which do you think it should choose?

%
4.5 Reduce taxes and spend **less** on health, education and social benefits
40.2 Keep taxes and spending on these services at the **same** level as now
50.1 Increase taxes and spend **more** on health, education and social benefits
4.4 (None)
0.8 (Don't know)
- (Refusal/Not answered)

ASK ALL

N = 3426

Q241 [UB1Poor]
Think of a 25 year-old **unemployed** woman living alone. Her only income comes from state benefits. Would you say that she ...
READ OUT ...

%
3.0 ... has more than enough to live on,
31.0 has enough to live on,
46.3 is hard up,
9.6 or, is really poor?
10.1 (Don't know)
0.0 (Refusal/Not answered)

Q242 [MumPoor]
What about an unemployed single mother with a young child. Their only income comes from state benefits. Would you say that they ... READ OUT ...

%
2.4 ... have more than enough to live on,
23.1 have enough to live on,
50.5 are hard up,
16.8 or, are really poor?
7.3 (Don't know)
0.0 (Refusal/Not answered)

Q243 [PenPoor]
Now think about a pensioner living alone. Her only income comes from the state pension and other benefits specially for pensioners. Would you say that she ... READ OUT ...

%
0.7 ... has more than enough to live on,
19.1 has enough to live on,
56.7 is hard up,
20.1 or, is really poor?
3.4 (Don't know)
- (Refusal/Not answered)

Q244 [UB1On52]   N = 3426
Now thinking again of that 25-year-old unemployed woman living alone. After rent, her income is £52 a week. Would you say that she ... READ OUT ...
%
2.6 ... has more than enough to live on,
28.3 has enough to live on,
54.8 is hard up,
13.2 or, is really poor?
1.0 (Don't know)
0.0 (Refusal/Not answered)

Q245 [MumOn95]
And thinking again about that unemployed single mother with a young child. After rent, their income is £95 a week. Would you say that they ... READ OUT ...
%
4.5 ... have more than enough to live on,
41.2 have enough to live on,
43.0 are hard up,
10.2 or, are really poor?
1.1 (Don't know)
0.0 (Refusal/Not answered)

Q246 [Pen1On82]
And thinking again about that pensioner living alone. After rent, her income is £82 a week. Would you say that she ... READ OUT ...
%
3.8 ... has more than enough to live on,
47.5 has enough to live on,
39.5 is hard up,
8.1 or, is really poor?
1.1 (Don't know)
- (Refusal/Not answered)

Q247 [SavFrRet]
CARD C4
Please tell me, from this card, how much you agree or disagree with the following statement.
The government should encourage people to provide something for their own retirement instead of relying only on the state pension.
%
24.8 Agree strongly
49.3 Agree
10.6 Neither agree nor disagree
11.5 Disagree
3.4 Disagree strongly
0.3 (Don't know)
- (Refusal/Not answered)

Q248 [LonePaWk]   N = 3426
Suppose a lone parent on benefits was asked to visit the job centre every year or so to talk about ways in which they might find work. Which of the following comes closest to what you think should happen to their benefits if they did not go?
READ OUT ...
%
21.5 ... their benefits should not be affected,
45.2 ... their benefits should be reduced a little,
11.8 ... their benefits should be reduced a lot,
18.2 ... or, their benefits should be stopped?
2.3 (Other (PLEASE WRITE IN))
1.0 (Don't know)
- (Refusal/Not answered)

Q250 [SickWk]
Now think about someone on long-term sickness or disability benefits. Which of the following comes closest to what you think should happen to their benefits if they did not go to the job centre to talk about ways in which they might find work?
READ OUT ...
%
42.6 ... their benefits should not be affected,
34.7 ... their benefits should be reduced a little,
7.3 ... their benefits should be reduced a lot,
9.4 ... or, their benefits should be stopped?
4.6 (Other (PLEASE WRITE IN))
1.4 (Don't know)
- (Refusal/Not answered)

Q252 [CarerWk]
And suppose a carer on benefits was asked to visit the job centre every year or so to talk about ways in which they might find work. Which of the following comes closest to what you think should happen to their benefits if they did not go?
READ OUT ...
%
55.5 ... their benefits should not be affected,
27.1 ... their benefits should be reduced a little,
5.0 ... their benefits should be reduced a lot,
8.5 ... or, their benefits should be stopped?
2.5 (Other (PLEASE WRITE IN))
1.5 (Don't know)
0.0 (Refusal/Not answered)

Q254 [MtUnmar1]
Imagine an unmarried couple who split up. They have a child at primary school who remains with the mother. Do you think that the father should always be made to make maintenance payments to support the child?

N = 3426

Q255 [MtUnmar2]
If he **does** make the maintenance payments for the child, should the amount depend on his income, or not?

Q256 [MtUnmar3]
Do you think the amount of maintenance should depend on the **mother's** income, or not?

	[MtUnmar1]	[MtUnmar2]	[MtUnmar3]
	%	%	%
Yes	87.6	88.3	74.2
No	11.1	10.9	24.5
(Don't know)	1.3	0.8	1.2
(Refusal/Not answered)	-	-	0.0

Q257 [MtUnmar4]
Suppose the mother now marries someone else. Should the child's natural father go on paying maintenance for the child, should he stop or should it depend on the step-father's income?

Q258 [MtUnmar5]
Suppose instead the mother does not marry, but the father has another child with someone else. Should he go on paying maintenance for the first child, should he stop or should it depend on his income?

	[MtUnmar4]	[MtUnmar5]
	%	%
Continue	50.3	70.6
Stop	10.5	2.1
Depends	37.8	26.7
(Don't know)	1.4	0.7
(Refusal/Not answered)	-	-

Q259 [MuchPov]
Some people say there is very little **real** poverty in Britain today. Others say there is quite a lot.
Which come closest to **your** view ... READ OUT ...
%
34.9 ... that there is very little real poverty in Britain
62.2 or, that there is quite a lot?
2.8 (Don't know)
0.0 (Refusal/Not answered)

Q260 [PastPov]
Over the last ten years, do you think that poverty in Britain has been increasing, decreasing or staying at about the same level?
%
36.5 Increasing
19.9 Decreasing
38.4 Staying at same level
5.2 (Don't know)
0.0 (Refusal/Not answered)

Q261 [FuturPov]
And over the **next** ten years, do you think that poverty in Britain will
... READ OUT ...
%
40.7 ... increase,
18.2 decrease,
35.3 or, stay at about the same level?
5.8 (Don't know)
0.0 (Refusal/Not answered)

Q262 [Poverty1]
Would you say that someone in Britain **was** or **was not** in poverty if...
... they had enough to buy the things they really needed, but not enough to buy the things most people take for granted?

Q263 [Poverty2]
(Would you say someone in Britain **was** or **was not** in poverty if...)
...they had enough to eat and live, but not enough to buy other things they needed?

Q264 [Poverty3]
(Would you say someone in Britain **was** or **was not** in poverty if...)
..they had not got enough to eat and live without getting into debt?

	[Poverty1]	[Poverty2]	[Poverty3]
	%	%	%
Was in poverty	26.7	59.3	92.8
Was not	70.8	39.2	6.1
(Don't know)	2.4	1.5	1.1
(Refusal/Not answered)	-	-	-

Q265 [WhyNeed]
CARD C5
Why do you think there are people who live in need? Of the four views on this card, which **one** comes closest to your own?
CODE ONE ONLY
%
15.3 Because they have been unlucky
22.8 Because of laziness or lack of willpower
20.5 Because of injustice in our society
34.1 It's an inevitable part of modern life
5.3 (None of these)
2.1 (Don't know)
- (Refusal/Not answered)

Q266 [PovEver]
CARD C6
Looking back over your life, how often have there been times
in your life when you think you have lived in poverty by the
standards of that time?
Please choose a phrase from this card.

```
N = 3426
```

%
50.8 Never
16.7 Rarely
22.6 Occasionally
7.2 Often
2.5 Most of the time
0.1 (Don't know)
- (Refusal/Not answered)

**IF 'rarely', 'occasionally', 'often', 'most of the time' AT
[PovEver]**

Q267 [PovChAd]
%   And was this ... READ OUT ...
12.6 ... as a child,
24.0 or, as an adult?
12.5 (Both)
0.1 (Don't know)
- (Refusal/Not answered)

VERSIONS A AND B: ASK ALL

```
N = 2302
```

[IncomGap]
Q268 Thinking of income levels generally in Britain today, would
you say that the **gap** between those with high incomes and those
with low incomes is ... READ OUT ...

%
82.4 ... too large,
14.3 about right,
1.4 or, too small?
1.9 (Don't know)
- (Refusal/Not answered)

Q269 [SRInc]
%   Among which group would you place yourself ... READ OUT ...
5.0 ... high income,
56.2 middle income,
38.5 or, low income?
0.3 (Don't know)
0.0 (Refusal/Not answered)

Q270 [HIncDiff]
CARD C7
Which of the phrases on this card would you say comes closest
to your feelings about your household's income these days?

```
N = 2302
```

%
42.5 Living comfortably on present income
42.2 Coping on present income
10.7 Finding it difficult on present income
4.4 Finding it very difficult on present income
0.2 (Other answer (WRITE IN))
0.0 (Don't know)
0.0 (Refusal/Not answered)

Cohabitation

ASK ALL

Q273 *[CohbShd1]*

CARD C8

I'd now like you to imagine an unmarried couple with no children who have been living together for ten years. Say their relationship ends. Do you think the woman **should** or **should not** have the same rights to claim for financial support from the man, as she would if they had been married?

%
34.6 Definitely should
27.0 Probably should
19.8 Probably should not
16.9 Definitely should not
1.7 (Don't know)
0.1 (Refusal/Not answered)

Q274 *[CohbDoes1]*

%
And do you think she **does** in fact have ...
38.3 ... the **same** rights as a married woman to claim financial support from the man,
54.1 or, does she have **fewer** rights?
7.7 (Don't know)
- (Refusal/Not answered)

Q275 *[CohbShd2]*

CARD C8 AGAIN

Imagine another unmarried couple without children who have been living together for ten years and live in a house bought in the man's name. Say he dies without making a will. Do you think the woman **should** or **should not** have the same rights to remain in this home as she would if she had been married to the man?

%
70.1 Definitely should
22.3 Probably should
4.1 Probably should not
2.5 Definitely should not
1.0 (Don't know)
- (Refusal/Not answered)

Q276 *[CohbDoes2]*

%
And do you think she **does** in fact have ...
36.5 ... the **same** rights as a married woman to remain in this home,
53.6 or, does she have **fewer** rights?
9.9 (Don't know)
- (Refusal/Not answered)

Q277 *[CohbShd3]*

CARD C8 AGAIN

Now imagine another unmarried couple who have been living together for ten years. They have a child who needs medical treatment. Do you think the father **should** or **should not** have the same rights to make decisions about his child's medical treatment as he would if he was married to the child's mother?

%
86.6 Definitely should
10.7 Probably should
1.4 Probably should not
0.6 Definitely should not
0.7 (Don't know)
- (Refusal/Not answered)

Q278 *[CohbDoes3]*

%
And do you think he **does** in fact have ...
49.8 ... the **same** rights as a married man to make decisions about this medical treatment,
38.2 or, does he have **fewer** rights?
11.9 (Don't know)
- (Refusal/Not answered)

Q279 *[PMS]*

CARD C9

Now I would like to ask you some questions about sexual relationships. If a man and woman have sexual relations before marriage, what would your general opinion be?

Q280 *[YoungSex]*

CARD C9 AGAIN

What if it was a boy and a girl who were both still **under 16**?

Q281 *[ExMS]*

CARD C9 AGAIN

What about a **married person** having sexual relations with someone other than his or her partner?

Q282 *[HomoSex]*

CARD C9 AGAIN

What about sexual relations between two adults of the same sex?

	[PMS]	[YoungSex]	[ExMS]	[HomoSex]
	%	%	%	%
Always wrong	8.6	65.8	60.7	36.8
Mostly wrong	7.7	21.4	24.6	9.3
Sometimes wrong	10.4	7.8	10.3	8.8
Rarely wrong	9.0	1.6	0.9	6.6
Not wrong at all	61.8	1.9	1.4	34.0
(Depends/varies)	1.9	1.0	1.7	2.9
(Don't know)	0.4	0.4	0.3	1.4
(Refusal/Not answered)	0.1	0.1	0.1	0.2

Health

ASK ALL

Q284 [NHSSat]
CARD D1
All in all, how satisfied or dissatisfied would you say you are with the way in which the National Health Service runs nowadays?
Choose a phrase from this card.

Q285 [GPSat]
CARD D1 AGAIN
From your own experience, or from what you have heard, please say how satisfied or dissatisfied you are with the way in which each of these parts of the National Health Service runs nowadays:
First, local doctors or GPs?

Q286 [DentSat]
CARD D1 AGAIN
(And how satisfied or dissatisfied are you with the NHS as regards...)
... National Health Service dentists?

N = 3426

	[NHSSat]	[GPSat]	[DentSat]
	%	%	%
Very satisfied	7.5	29.8	19.0
Quite satisfied	34.5	46.3	42.5
Neither satisfied nor dissatisfied	18.7	8.4	15.4
Quite dissatisfied	25.7	11.6	11.7
Very dissatisfied	13.3	3.7	7.2
(Don't know)	0.3	0.3	4.2
(Refusal/Not answered)	-	-	-

Q287 [InpatSat]
CARD D1 AGAIN
(And how satisfied or dissatisfied are you with the NHS as regards...)
... Being in hospital as an **in**-patient?

Q288 [OutpaSat]
CARD D1 AGAIN
(And how satisfied or dissatisfied are you with the NHS as regards...)
... Attending hospital as an **out**-patient?

Q289 [AESat]
CARD D1 AGAIN
(And how satisfied or dissatisfied are you with the NHS as regards...)
... Accident and emergency departments?

	[InpatSat]	[OutpaSat]	[AESat]
	%	%	%
Very satisfied	17.2	13.8	15.4
Quite satisfied	41.3	44.2	36.4
Neither satisfied nor dissatisfied	15.4	15.0	15.1
Quite dissatisfied	14.6	17.8	18.3
Very dissatisfied	6.7	6.6	10.6
(Don't know)	4.7	2.6	4.2
(Refusal/Not answered)	-	-	-

VERSIONS A AND B: ASK ALL

Q290 [PrivMed]
Are you **yourself** covered by a private health insurance scheme, that is an insurance scheme that allows you to get private medical **treatment**?
ADD IF NECESSARY: 'For example, BUPA or PPP.'
IF INSURANCE COVERS DENTISTRY **ONLY**, CODE 'No'.

IF 'yes' AT [PrivMed]

Q291 [PrivPaid]
Does your employer (or your partner's employer) pay the majority of the cost of membership of this scheme?

N = 2302

	[PrivMed]	[PrivPaid]
	%	%
Yes	19.3	11.1
No	80.4	8.2
(Don't know)	0.3	0.0
(Refusal/Not answered)	-	0.3

ASK ALL

Q292 [NHSLimit]
It has been suggested that the National Health Service should be available **only to those with lower incomes**. This would mean that contributions and taxes could be lower and most people would then take out medical insurance or pay for health care. Do you support or oppose this idea?
IF 'SUPPORT' OR 'OPPOSE': A lot or little?

%
9.1   Support a lot
14.3   Support a little
14.4   Oppose a little
60.0   Oppose a lot
2.2   (Don't know)
-   (Refusal/Not answered)

Q293 [InPat1]
CARD D2
Now, suppose you had to go into a local NHS hospital for observation and maybe an operation. From what you know or have heard, please say whether you think the hospital doctors would tell you all you feel you need to know?

Q294 [InPat2]
CARD D2 AGAIN
(And please say whether you think ...)
...the hospital doctors would take seriously any views you may have on the sorts of treatment available?

Q295 [InPat3]
CARD D2 AGAIN
(And please say whether you think ...)
...the operation would take place on the day it was booked for?

Q296 [InPat4]
CARD D2 AGAIN
(And please say whether you think ...)
...you would be allowed home only when you were really well enough to leave?

Q297 [InPat5]
CARD D2 AGAIN
(And please say whether you think ...)
...the nurses would take seriously any complaints you may have?

Q298 [InPat6]
CARD D2 AGAIN
(And please say whether you think ...)
...the hospital doctors would take seriously any complaints you may have?

Q299 [InPat7]
CARD D2 AGAIN
(And please say whether you think ...)
...there would be a particular nurse responsible for dealing with any problems you may have?

Q300 [OutPat1]
CARD D2 AGAIN
Now suppose you had a back problem and your GP referred you to a hospital out-patients' department. From what you know or have heard, please say whether you think...
...you would get an appointment within three months?

Q301 [OutPat2]
CARD D2 AGAIN
(And please say whether you think ...)
...when you arrived, the doctor would see you within half an hour of your appointment time?

Q302 [OutPat3]
CARD D2 AGAIN
(And please say whether you think ...)
...if you wanted to complain about the treatment you received, you would be able to without any fuss or bother?

Q303 [WhchHosp]
CARD D2 AGAIN
Now suppose you needed to go into hospital for an operation. Do you think you would have a say about which hospital you went to?

	[InPat1]	[InPat2]	[InPat3]
	%	%	%
Definitely would	19.7	12.5	5.4
Probably would	51.6	48.4	42.4
Probably would not	22.1	29.9	40.4
Definitely would not	5.6	6.7	9.8
(Don't know)	0.9	2.5	1.9
(Refusal/Not answered)	0.0	0.0	0.0

	[InPat4]	[InPat5]	[InPat6]
	%	%	%
Definitely would	12.7	18.3	14.3
Probably would	41.8	57.3	56.4
Probably would not	34.4	18.8	23.0
Definitely would not	10.1	3.8	4.4
(Don't know)	1.0	1.8	1.8
(Refusal/Not answered)	0.0	0.0	0.1

N = 3426

	[InPat7]	[OutPat1]	[OutPat2]
	%	%	%
Definitely would	14.0	8.0	4.3
Probably would	40.6	33.2	29.0
Probably would not	33.3	39.4	43.1
Definitely would not	6.8	16.5	22.4
(Don't know)	5.3	3.0	1.2
(Refusal/Not answered)	0.0	0.0	0.0

	[OutPat3]	[WhichHosp]
	%	%
Definitely would	9.9	4.1
Probably would	41.9	17.3
Probably would not	34.7	47.5
Definitely would not	9.6	28.0
(Don't know)	3.8	3.0
(Refusal/Not answered)	0.0	0.0

Q304 [SRHealth]
How is your health in general for someone of your age? Would you say that it is ... READ OUT ...

%
40.0 ... very good,
41.0 fairly good,
13.7 fair,
4.3 bad,
1.0 or, very bad?
- (Don't know)
0.0 (Refusal/Not answered)

Q305 [PrDepres]
Suppose an employee applied for a promotion. He has had repeated periods off work because of depression but this has been under control for a year or so through medication. Do you think he would be ... READ OUT ...

%
8.0 ... just as likely as anyone else to be promoted,
49.6 slightly less likely to be promoted,
40.9 or, much less likely to be promoted?
1.5 (Don't know)
0.0 (Refusal/Not answered)

N = 3426

Q306 [ShdDep]
CARD D3
And what do you think **should** happen? Should his medical history make a difference or not?

%
11.6 Definitely should
33.6 Probably should
31.9 Probably should not
19.7 Definitely should not
0.5 (Other (PLEASE WRITE IN))
1.3 **EDIT ONLY:**Depends on type of work
1.3 (Don't know)
0.0 (Refusal/Not answered)

Q308 [PrSchiz]
And now think about someone who has had repeated periods off work because of schizophrenia but this has been under control for a year or so through medication. Do you think he would be ... READ OUT ...

%
2.8 ... just as likely as anyone else to be promoted,
27.3 slightly less likely to be promoted,
68.0 or, much less likely to be promoted?
1.9 (Don't know)
0.0 (Refusal/Not answered)

Q309 [ShdSchiz]
CARD D3 AGAIN
And what do you think **should** happen? Should his medical history make a difference or not?

%
23.4 Definitely should
36.8 Probably should
25.3 Probably should not
11.0 Definitely should not
0.3 (Other (PLEASE WRITE IN))
1.2 **EDIT ONLY:** Depends on type of work
2.1 (Don't know)
0.0 (Refusal/Not answered)

Q311 [PrDiab]
And now think about someone who has had repeated periods off work because of diabetes but this has been under control for a year or so through medication. Do you think he would be ...
READ OUT ...

%
47.9 ... just as likely as anyone else to be promoted,
43.0 slightly less likely to be promoted,
7.5 or, much less likely to be promoted?
1.6 (Don't know)
0.0 (Not answered)

Q312 [ShdDiab]
CARD D3 AGAIN
And what do you think **should** happen? Should his medical
history make a difference or not?
%
8.7 Definitely should
16.6 Probably should
28.1 Probably should not
44.7 Definitely should not
0.2 (Other (PLEASE WRITE IN))
0.6 **EDIT ONLY:** Depends on type of work
1.0 (Don't know)
0.0 (Refusal/Not answered)

Q314 [MentProb]
Have you, a member of your family or a close friend ever
sought medical help for a mental health problem?
%
28.2 Yes
71.6 No
0.1 (Don't know)
0.0 (Refusal/Not answered)

Economic Activity

ASK ALL

Q328 [REconAct] (Percentages refer to highest answer on the list)
CARD
Which of these descriptions applied to what you were doing
last week, that is the seven days ending last Sunday?
PROBE: Which others? CODE ALL THAT APPLY
%
2.8 In full-time education (not paid for by employer, including on
vacation)
0.2 On government training/ employment programme (e.g. Youth
Training, Training for Work etc)
55.1 In paid work (or away temporarily) for at least 10 hours in
week
0.4 Waiting to take up paid work already accepted
2.5 Unemployed and registered at a benefit office
1.1 Unemployed, **not** registered, but actively looking for a job (of
at least 10 hrs a week)
0.4 Unemployed, wanting a job (of at least 10 hrs a week) but **not**
actively looking for a job
4.9 Permanently sick or disabled
20.8 Wholly retired from work
10.8 Looking after the home
0.9 (Doing something else) (WRITE IN)
–   (Don't know)
0.0 (Refusal/Not answered)

ASK ALL NOT WORKING OR WAITING TO TAKE UP WORK

Q329 [RLastJob]
How long ago did you last have a paid job of at least 10 hours
a ,week?
GOVERNMENT PROGRAMS/SCHEMES DO NOT COUNT AS `PAID JOBS'.
%
16.0 Within past 12 months
21.8 Over 1, up to 5 years ago
18.7 Over 5, up to 10 years ago
23.5 Over 10, up to 20 years ago
14.1 Over 20 years ago
5.7 Never had a paid job of 10+ hours a week
0.1 (Don't know)
0.1 (Refusal/Not answered)

ASK ALL WHO HAVE EVER WORKED (NOT ON DATAFILE)   N = 3339

Q330 [Title] (NOT ON DATAFILE)
IF 'in paid work' AT [REconAct]: Now I want to ask you about your present job. What is your job?
PROBE IF NECESSARY: What is the name or title of the job?
IF 'waiting to take up work' AT [REconAct]: Now I want to ask you about your future job. What is your job?
PROBE IF NECESSARY: What is the name or title of the job?
IF EVER HAD A JOB AT [RLastJob]: Now I want to ask you about your last job. What was your job?
PROBE IF NECESSARY: What was the name or title of the job?
Open Question (Maximum of 80 characters)

Q331 [TypeWk] (NOT ON DATAFILE)
What kind of work (do/will/did) you do most of the time?
IF RELEVANT: What materials/machinery (do/will/did) you use?
Open Question (Maximum of 80 characters)

Q332 [Train] (NOT ON DATAFILE)
What training or qualifications (are/were) needed for that job?
Open Question (Maximum of 80 characters)

Q333 [RSuper2]
(Do/Will/Did) you directly supervise or (are you/will you be/were you) directly responsible for the work of any other people?
%
36.9 Yes
62.9 No
0.1 (Don't know)
0.1 (Refusal/Not answered)

If 'yes' AT [Super2]
Q334 [RMany]
How many?
Median: 5

ASK ALL WHO HAVE EVER WORKED
Q336 [REmployee]
In your (main) job (are you/will you be/were you) ...READ OUT
%
90.0 ... an employee,
9.9 or self-employed?
- (Don't know)
0.1 (Refusal/Not answered)

ASK ALL EMPLOYEES IN CURRENT OR LAST JOB   N = 3008

Q338 [RSupman2]
Can I just check, (are you/will you be/were you) ... READ OUT ...
%
17.8 ...a manager,
15.2 a foreman or supervisor,
66.8 or not?
0.1 (Don't know)
0.1 (Refusal/Not answered)

Q339 [ROcSect2]
CARD
Which of the types of organisation on this card (do you work/will you be working/did you work) for?
%
65.9 PRIVATE SECTOR FIRM OR COMPANY Including, for example, limited companies and PLCs
3.1 NATIONALISED INDUSTRY OR PUBLIC CORPORATION Including, for example, the Post Office and the BBC
28.0 OTHER PUBLIC SECTOR EMPLOYER Incl eg: - Central govt/ Civil Service/ Govt Agency - Local authority/ Local Educ Auth (incl 'opted out' schools) - Universities - Health Authority / NHS hospitals / NHS Trusts/ GP surgeries - Police / Armed forces
2.3 CHARITY/ VOLUNTARY SECTOR Including, for example, charitable companies, churches, trade unions
0.5 Other answer (WRITE IN)
- (Don't know)
0.1 (Refusal/Not answered)

ASK ALL WHO HAVE EVER WORKED (NOT ON DATAFILE)   N = 3339

Q341 [REmpMake]
IF EMPLOYEE: What (does/did) your employer make or do at the place where you (usually work/will usually work/usually worked) (from)?
IF SELF-EMPLOYED: What (do/will/did) you make or do at the place where you (usually work/will usually work/usually worked) (from)?

ASK ALL CURRENTLY SELF-EMPLOYED   N = 233

Q342 [SPartnrs]
In your work or business, do you have any partners or other self-employed colleagues?
NOTE: DOES NOT INCLUDE EMPLOYEES
%
35.0 Yes, has partner(s)
64.1 No
- (Don't know)
0.9 (Refusal/Not answered)

ASK ALL SELF-EMPLOYED IN CURRENT/LAST JOB N = 334

Q344 [SEmpNum]
In your work or business, (do/will/did) you have any employees, or not?
IF YES: How many?
IF 'NO EMPLOYEES', CODE 0.
FOR 500+ EMPLOYEES, CODE 500.
NOTE: FAMILY MEMBERS MAY BE EMPLOYEES ONLY IF THEY RECEIVE A REGULAR WAGE OR SALARY.
Median: 0 employees
%
- (Don't know)
1.2 (Not answered)

ASK ALL WHO HAVE EVER WORKED (for self-employed, coded from [SEmpNm]) N = 3339

Q345 [REmpWork]
Including yourself, how many people (are/were) employed at the place where you usually (work/will work/worked) (from)?
PROBE FOR CORRECT PRECODE.
%
6.1 None
18.9 Under 10
15.0 10-24
22.4 25-99
19.6 100-499
17.3 500 or more
0.6 (Don't know)
0.2 (Refusal/Not answered)

ASK ALL IN PAID WORK N = 1889

Q348 [WkJbTim]
In your present job, are you working ... READ OUT ...
RESPONDENT'S OWN DEFINITION
76.5 ... full-time,
23.2 or, part-time?
- (Don't know)
0.4 (Refusal/Not answered)

Q351 [WkJbHrsI]
How many hours do you normally work a week in your main job - **including** any paid or unpaid overtime?
ROUND TO NEAREST HOUR.
IF RESPONDENT CANNOT ANSWER, ASK ABOUT LAST WEEK.
IF RESPONDENT DOES NOT KNOW EXACTLY, ACCEPT AN ESTIMATE.
FOR 95+ HOURS, CODE 95.
FOR 'VARIES TOO MUCH TO SAY', CODE 96.
Median: 40 hours
%
0.1 (Don't know)
0.5 (Refusal/Not answered)

ASK ALL CURRENT EMPLOYEES N = 1657

Q352 [ExJbHrsX]
What are your **basic or contractual hours** each week in your main job - **excluding** any paid and unpaid overtime?
ROUND TO NEAREST HOUR.
IF RESPONDENT CANNOT ANSWER, ASK ABOUT LAST WEEK.
IF RESPONDENT DOES NOT KNOW EXACTLY, ACCEPT AN ESTIMATE.
FOR 95+ HOURS, CODE 95.
FOR 'VARIES TOO MUCH TO SAY', CODE 96.
Median: 37.00 hours
%
3.1 (Varies too much to say)
1.0 (Don't know)
0.4 (Refusal/Not answered)

ASK ALL WAITING TO TAKE UP WORK OR NOT WORKING BUT HAD A JOB IN THE PAST N = 1450

Q353 [ExPrtFul]
(Will the job be/Was the job) ... READ OUT ...
70.0 ... full-time - that is, 30 or more hours per week,
29.8 or, part-time?
- (Don't know)
0.2 (Refusal/Not answered)

ASK ALL WHO HAVE EVER WORKED N = 3339

Q385 [UnionSA]
(May I just check) are you **now** a member of a trade union or staff association?
CODE FIRST TO APPLY
%
19.2 Yes, trade union
3.3 Yes, staff association
77.3 No
0.1 (Don't know)
0.1 (Refusal/Not answered)

Q386 IF 'no'/DK AT [UnionSA]
[TUSAEver]
Have you **ever** been a member of a trade union or staff association?
CODE FIRST TO APPLY
%
27.9 Yes, trade union
2.2 Yes, staff association
47.1 No
0.1 (Don't know)
0.1 (Refusal/Not answered)

ASK ALL CURRENT EMPLOYEES N = 1657

Q389 [EmploydT]
For how long have you been continuously employed by your present employer?
Median: 60 months
%
- (Don't know)
0.3 (Refusal/Not answered)

N = 1538

ASK ALL NOT IN PAID WORK

Q390 [NPWork10]

In the seven days ending last Sunday, did you have any paid work of less than 10 hours a week?

%
6.0 Yes
93.8 No
- (Don't know)
0.2 (Refusal/Not answered)

N = 1657

ASK ALL CURRENT EMPLOYEES

Q391 [WageNow]

How would you describe the wages or salary you are paid for the job you do - on the low side, reasonable, or on the high side?

IF LOW: Very low or a bit low?

%
12.2 Very low
26.0 A bit low
54.1 Reasonable
7.3 On the high side
0.1 Other answer (WRITE IN)
- (Don't know)
0.3 (Refusal/Not answered)

Q393 [PayGap]
CARD E3

Thinking of the **highest** and the **lowest** paid people at your place of work, how would you describe the **gap** between their pay, as far as you know?

Please choose a phrase from this card.

%
18.9 Much too big a gap
29.4 Too big
42.1 About right
3.2 Too small
0.4 Much too small a gap
5.8 (Don't know)
0.3 (Refusal/Not answered)

Q394 [WageXpct]

If you stay in this job, would you expect your wages or salary over the coming year to ... READ OUT ...

%
22.3 ... rise by more than the cost of living,
45.0 rise by the same as the cost of living,
20.8 rise by less than the cost of living,
9.4 or, not to rise at all?
1.0 (Will not stay in job).
1.1 (Don't know)
0.3 (Refusal/Not answered)

N = 1657

IF 'not rise at all' AT [WageXpct]

Q395 [WageDrop]

Would you expect your wages or salary to stay the same, or in fact to go down?

%
9.0 Stay the same
0.4 Go down
0.1 (Don't know)
1.4 (Refusal/Not answered)

ASK ALL CURRENT EMPLOYEES

Q396 [Numemp]

Over the coming year do you expect your workplace to be ... READ OUT ...

%
30.2 ... increasing its number of employees,
14.7 reducing its number of employees,
53.2 or, will the number of employees stay about the same?
0.5 Other answer (WRITE IN)
1.1 (Don't know)
0.3 (Refusal/Not answered)

Q398 [LeaveJob]

Thinking now about your own job.

How likely or unlikely is it that you will leave this employer over the next year for any reason?

Is it ... READ OUT ...

%
11.6 ... very likely,
15.0 quite likely,
27.9 not very likely,
44.5 or, not at all likely?
0.6 (Don't know)
0.3 (Refusal/Not answered)

IF 'very likely' OR 'quite likely' AT [LeaveJob]

Q399-CARD E4

Q407 Why do you think you will leave? Please choose a phrase from this card or tell me what other reason there is.

CODE ALL THAT APPLY

%
0.8 Firm will close down [WhyGo1]
1.7 I will be declared redundant WhyGo2]
0.7 I will reach normal retirement age [WhyGo3]
1.9 My contract of employment will expire WhyGo4
0.9 I will take early retirement [WhyGo5]
16.2 I will decide to leave and work for another employer [WhyGo6]
1.8 I will decide to leave and work for myself, as self-employed [WhyGo7]
1.3 I will leave to look after home/children/relative [WhyGo10]
0.8 EDIT ONLY: Return to education [WhyGo11]
4.6 Other answer (WRITE IN) [WhyGo8]
0.6 (Don't know)
0.3 (Refusal/Not answered)

IF 'reach normal retirement age' AT [WhyGo3] AND NOT 'early retirement' AT [WhyGo5] N = 1657

Q419 [RetPlcy]
Would your employer allow you to carry on working if you wanted to?

%	
0.6	Yes
0.1	No
-	(Don't know)
0.9	(Refusal/Not answered)

IF 'yes' AT [RetPlcy] OR 'early retirement' AT [WhyGo5]

Q420-CARD E5
Q426 Why do you think you will choose to (retire/take early retirement)?
Please choose a phrase from this card
CODE AS MANY AS APPLY.

%	
0.3	Because of ill health [ERetIll]
-	To look after someone else [ERetCare]
0.5	Because my husband/wife/partner is retired [ERetPrtn]
0.0	It is likely the early retirement package will be attractive [ERetPack]
-	I will lose my job/Instead of being made redundant/My firm will close down [ERetLJob]
0.7	I just want to retire [ERetWant]
0.1	Other answer (WRITE IN) [ERetOth]
	(Don't know)
0.9	(Refusal/Not answered)

ASK ALL CURRENT EMPLOYEES

Q428 [ELookJob]
Suppose you lost your job for one reason or another - would you start looking for another job, would you wait for several months or longer before you started looking, or would you decide **not** to look for another job?

%	
89.4	Start looking
3.8	Wait several months or longer
6.3	Decide not to look
0.2	(Don't know)
0.3	(Refusal/Not answered)

IF 'start looking' AT [ELookJob]

Q431 [EFindJob]
How long do you think it would take you to find an acceptable replacement job?
IF LESS THAN ONE MONTH, CODE AS ONE MONTH
IF 'NEVER' PLEASE CODE 96
ENTER NUMBER. THEN SPECIFY MONTHS OR YEARS
Median: 1 month

%	
1.0	(Never)
6.2	(Don't know)
0.5	(Refusal/Not answered)

IF 3 months or more/never/DK AT [EFindJob] N = 1657

Q432 [ERetrain]
How willing do you think you would be in these circumstances to retrain for a different job ... READ OUT ...

%	
15.2	...very willing,
10.6	quite willing,
5.5	or - not very willing?
0.2	(Don't know)
0.5	(Refusal/Not answered)

ASK ALL CURRENT EMPLOYEES

Q433 [ESelfEm]
For any period during the last five years, have you worked as a **self-employed** person as your main job?

%	
5.7	Yes
94.0	No
-	(Don't know)
0.3	(Refusal/Not answered)

ASK ALL NOT UNEMPLOYED, PERMANENTLY SICK OR RETIRED N = 2406

Q435 [NwUnemp]
During the last **five years** - that is since May 1995 - have you been unemployed and seeking work for any period?

%	
18.0	Yes
81.8	No
0.1	(Don't know)
0.1	(Refusal/Not answered)

ASK ALL WHO ARE CURRENTLY UNEMPLOYED OR 'yes' AT [NwUnemp] N = 438

Q436 [NwUnempT]
For how many **months** in total during the last five years that is, since May 1995, have you been unemployed and seeking work?
INTERVIEWER: IF LESS THAN ONE MONTH, CODE AS 1.
Median: 4 months

%	
0.6	(Don't know)
1.0	(Refusal/Not answered)

ASK ALL UNEMPLOYED N = 141

Q439 [CurUnemp]
How long has this **present** period of unemployment and seeking work lasted so far?
ENTER NUMBER. THEN SPECIFY MONTHS OR YEARS
Median: 6 months

%	
1.2	(Don't know)
1.6	(Refusal/Not answered)

Q440 *[JobQual]*   [N = 141]
How confident are you that you will find a job to match your qualifications ... READ OUT ...
%
20.9 ... very confident,
21.6 quite confident,
32.9 not very confident,
20.7 or, not at all confident?
2.3 (Don't know)
1.6 (Refusal/Not answered)

Q443 *[UFindJob]*
Although it may be difficult to judge, how long **from now** do you think it will be before you find an acceptable job?
ENTER NUMBER. THEN SPECIFY MONTHS OR YEARS
CODE 96 FOR NEVER
Median: 3 months
%
11.3 (Never)
16.4 (Don't know)
1.6 (Refusal/Not answered)

IF 3 months or more/never/DK AT [UFindJob]
Q444 *[URetrain]*
How willing do you think you would be in these circumstances to retrain for a different job ... READ OUT ...

Q445 *[UJobMove]*
How willing would you be to move to a different area to find an acceptable job ... READ OUT ...

Q446 *[UBadJob]*
And how willing do you think you would be in these circumstances to take what you now consider to be an unacceptable job ... READ OUT ...

	[URetrain]	[UJobMove]	[UBadJob]
	%	%	%
... very willing,	24.0	10.7	7.1
quite willing,	21.9	12.1	17.3
or, not very willing?	14.6	40.0	38.5
(Don't know)	3.5	1.2	1.2
(Refusal/Not answered)	1.6	1.6	1.6

ASK ALL UNEMPLOYED
Q447 *[ConMove]*
Have you ever **actually** considered moving to a different area - an area other than the one you live in now - to try to find work?
%
25.6 Yes
72.9 No
- (Don't know)
1.6 (Refusal/Not answered)

Q448 *[UJobChnc]*   [N = 141]
Do you think that there is a real chance nowadays that you will get a job in this area, or is there **no** real chance nowadays?
%
63.9 Real chance
29.8 No real chance
4.7 (Don't know)
1.6 (Refusal/Not answered)

Q449 *[FPtWork]*
Would you prefer full- or part-time work, if you had the choice?
%
65.1 Full-time
29.9 Part-time
3.5 Not looking for work
- (Don't know)
1.6 (Refusal/Not answered)

IF 'part-time' AT [FPtWork]
Q450 *[Parttime]*
About how many hours per week would you like to work?
PROBE FOR BEST ESTIMATE
Median: 20 hours
%
- (Don't know)
1.6 (Refusal/Not answered)

ASK ALL LOOKING AFTER THE HOME   [N = 371]
Q451 *[EverJob]*
Have you, during **the last five years**, ever had a full- or part-time job of 10 hours or more a week?
%
38.1 Yes
61.6 No
0.3 (Don't know)
- (Refusal/Not answered)

IF 'no' AT [EverJob]
Q452 *[FtJobSer]*
How seriously in the past five years have you considered getting a **full-time job**...
PROMPT, IF NECESSARY: Full-time is 30 or more hours a week ... READ OUT ...

IF 'not very seriously', 'not at all seriously' OR DK AT [FtJobSer]
Q453 *[PtJobSer]*
How seriously, in the past five years, have you considered getting a **part-time** job ... READ OUT ...

	[FtJobSer]	[PtJobSer]
	%	%
... very seriously,	3.4	1.8
quite seriously,	2.7	4.6
not very seriously,	8.4	10.4
or, not at all seriously?	46.9	38.6
(Don't know)	-	-
(Refusal/Not answered)	0.4	0.4

ASK ALL CURRENTLY SELF-EMPLOYED

Q454 [SEmplee]
Have you, for any period in the last five years, worked as an employee as your main job rather than as self-employed?

N = 233

%
32.6 Yes
65.7 No
- (Don't know)
1.7 (Refusal/Not answered)

IF 'yes' AT [SEmplee]
Q455 [SEmpleeT]
In total for how many months during the last five years have you been an employee?
ENTER NUMBER OF MONTHS
Median: 30 months

%
0.2 (Don't know)
1.7 (Refusal/Not answered)

IF 'no'/DK AT [SEmplee]
Q456 [SEmplSer]
How seriously in the last five years have you considered getting a job as an **employee** ... READ OUT ...

%
3.8 ... very seriously,
10.6 quite seriously,
9.2 not very seriously,
42.1 or, not at all seriously?
- (Don't know)
1.7 (Refusal/Not answered)

ASK ALL CURRENTLY SELF-EMPLOYED

Q457 [BuslOK]
Compared with **a year ago**, would you say your business is doing ... READ OUT ...

%
12.5 ... very well,
19.6 quite well,
48.5 about the same,
8.3 not very well,
3.5 or, not at all well?
5.2 (Business not in existence then)
0.7 (Don't know)
1.7 (Refusal/Not answered)

Q458 [BuslFut]
And over **the coming year**, do you think your business will do ... READ OUT ...

N = 233

%
36.9 ... better,
47.5 about the same,
9.2 or, worse than this year?
2.1 Other answer (WRITE IN)
2.6 (Don't know)
1.7 (Refusal/Not answered)

ASK ALL CURRENT EMPLOYEES

Q460 [WpUnions]
At your place of work are there unions, staff associations, or groups of unions recognised by the management for negotiating pay and conditions of employment?
IF YES, PROBE FOR UNION OR STAFF ASSOCIATION
IF 'BOTH', CODE '1'

N = 1657

%
43.4 Yes : trade union(s)
4.7 Yes : staff association
48.3 No. none
3.3 (Don't kow)
0.3 (Refusal/Not answered)

IF 'yes, trade unions'/'yes, staff association' AT [WpUnions]
Q461 [WpUnsure]
Can I just check: does management **recognise** these unions or staff associations for the purposes of negotiating **pay** and **conditions of employment?**

Q462 [WpUnionW]
On the whole, do you think (these unions do their/this staff association does its) job well or not?

	[WpUnsure]	[WpUnionW]
	%	%
Yes	45.0	29.9
No	1.5	15.1
(Don't know)	1.6	3.1
(Refusal/Not answered)	3.6	3.6

Q463 [TUShould]
CARD E6
Listed on the card are a number of things trade unions or staff associations can do. Which, if any, do you think is the **most important** thing they should try to do **at your workplace?**

N = 1657

% UNIONS OR STAFF ASSOCIATIONS SHOULD TRY TO:
14.8 Improve working conditions
10.2 Improve pay
12.7 Protect existing jobs
2.1 Have more say over how work is done day-to-day
3.5 Have more say over management's long-term plans
0.8 Work for equal opportunities for women
0.4 Work for equal opportunities for ethnic minorities
2.0 Reduce pay differences at the workplace
1.4 (None of these)
0.4 (Don't know)
3.7 (Refusal/Not answered)

ASK ALL CURRENT EMPLOYEES

Q464 [IndRel]
In general how would you describe relations between management and other employees at your workplace ... READ OUT ...
%
33.4 ... very good,
44.6 quite good,
16.7 not very good,
4.2 or, not at all good?
0.9 (Don't know)
0.3 (Refusal/Not answered)

Q465 [WorkRun]
And in general, would you say your workplace was ... READ OUT ...
%
23.8 ... very well managed,
53.2 quite well managed,
22.2 or, not well managed?
0.3 (Don't know)
0.4 (Refusal/Not answered)

ASK ALL EXCEPT THOSE WHO ARE WHOLLY RETIRED OR PERMANENTLY SICK OR DISABLED

N = 2545

Q466 [NwEmpErn]
IF IN PAID WORK: Now for some more general questions about your work. For some people their job is simply something they do in order to earn a living. For others it means much more than that. On balance, is your present job ... READ OUT ...
IF NOT IN PAID WORK: For some people work is simply something they do in order to earn a living. For others it means much more than that. In general, do you think of work as ... READ OUT ...
%
33.5 ...just a means of earning a living,
65.7 or, does it mean much more to you than that?
0.7 (Don't know)
0.1 (Refusal/Not answered)

IF 'just a means of earning a living' AT [NwEmpErn]
Q467 [NwEmpLiv]
% Is that because ... READ OUT ...
8.3 ...there are no (better/good) jobs around here,
9.1 you don't have the right skills to get a (better/good) job
13.4 or, because you would feel the same about **any** job you had?
2.6 (Don't know)
0.9 (Refusal/Not answered)

ASK ALL IN PAID WORK

N = 1889

Q468-CARD E7
Q476 Now I'd like you to look at the statements on the card and tell me which ones best describe **your own** reasons for working at present.
% PROBE: Which others? CODE ALL THAT APPLY
34.0 Working is the normal thing to do [WkWork1]
66.5 Need money for basic essentials such as food, rent or mortgage [WkWork2]
49.4 To earn money to buy extras [WkWork3]
31.5 To earn money of my own [WkWork4]
29.7 For the company of other people [WkWork5]
56.6 I enjoy working [WkWork6]
28.4 To follow my career [WkWork7]
9.9 For a change from my children or housework [WkWork8]
5.0 Other answer (WRITE IN) [WkWork9]
- (Don't know)
0.4 (Refusal/Not answered)

IF MORE THAN ONE ANSWER GIVEN

N = 1889

Q488 [WkWkMain]
CARD E7 AGAIN
And which one of these would you say is your **main** reason for working?

%
4.8 Working is the normal thing to do
43.9 Need money for basic essentials such as food, rent or mortgage
8.4 To earn money to buy extras
6.8 To earn money of my own
1.3 For the company of other people
10.9 I enjoy working
5.5 To follow my career
0.9 For a change from my children or housework
1.2 Other answer (WRITE IN)
- (Don't know)
0.4 (Refusal/Not answered)

ASK ALL CURRENT EMPLOYEES

N = 1657

Q489 [SayJob]
Suppose there was going to be some decision made at your place of work that changed the way you do your job. Do you think that **you personally** would have any say in the decision about the change, or not?
IF 'DEPENDS': Code as 'Don't know' <CTRL+K>

%
58.1 Yes
39.7 No
1.9 (Don't know)
0.3 (Refusal/Not answered)

IF 'yes' AT [SayJob]

Q490 [MuchSay]
How much say or chance to influence the decision do you think you would have ... READ OUT ...

%
15.4 ...a great deal,
25.0 quite a lot,
17.5 or, just a little?
0.1 (Don't know)
2.2 (Refusal/Not answered)

ASK ALL CURRENT EMPLOYEES

Q491 [MoreSay]
Do you think you should have **more** say in decisions affecting your work, or are you satisfied with the way things are?

%
45.6 Should have more say
53.9 Satisfied with way things are
0.2 (Don't know)
0.3 (Refusal/Not answered)

ASK ALL IN PAID WORK

N = 1889

Q492 [WkPrefJb]
If without having to work, you had what you would regard as a reasonable living income, do you think you would still prefer to (have a paid job/do paid work) or wouldn't you bother?

%
68.1 Still prefer paid (job/work)
28.0 Wouldn't bother
3.2 Other answer (WRITE IN)
0.3 (Don't know)
0.4 (Refusal/Not answered)

ASK ALL CURRENT EMPLOYEES

N = 1657

Q494 [PrefHour]
Thinking about the number of hours you work each week including regular overtime, would you prefer a job where you worked ... READ OUT ...

%
4.7 ...more hours per week,
39.1 fewer hours per week,
55.9 or, are you happy with the number of hours you work at present?
- (Don't know)
0.3 (Refusal/Not answered)

IF 'more hours' AT [PrefHour]

Q495 [MoreHour]
Is the reason why you don't work more hours because ... READ OUT ...

%
3.7 ..your employer can't offer you more hours,
0.8 or, your personal circumstances don't allow it?
0.1 (Both)
- (Don't know)
0.3 (Refusal/Not answered)

IF 'fewer hours' AT [PrefHour]

Q497 [FewHour]
In which of these ways would you like your working hours to be shortened ... READ OUT ...

%
12.5 ... shorter hours each day,
25.6 or, fewer days each week?
1.0 Other answer (WRITE IN)
0.1 (Don't know)
0.3 (Refusal/Not answered)

Q499 [EarnHour]
Would you still like to work fewer hours, if it meant
earning less money as a result?   N = 1657

%
9.8 Yes
27.1 No
2.1 It depends
0.1 (Don't know)
0.3 (Refusal/Not answered)

ASK ALL IN PAID WORK
Q500 [WkWorkHd]
CARD E8
Which of these statements best describes your feelings about
your job?
In my job :   N = 1889
%
6.2 I only work as hard as I have to
41.6 I work hard, but not so that it interferes with the rest of my
life
51.7 I make a point of doing the best I can, even if it sometimes
does interfere with the rest of my life
0.0 (Don't know)
0.4 (Refusal/Not answered)

ASK ALL WHOLLY RETIRED
Q501 [REmplPen]
Do you receive a pension from any past employer?

IF WHOLLY RETIRED AND MARRIED
Q502 [SEmplPen]
Does your (husband/wife) receive a pension from any past
employer?

ASK ALL WHOLLY RETIRED
Q503 [PrPenGet]
And do you receive a pension from any private arrangements you
have made in the past, that is apart from the state pension or
one arranged through an employer?

IF WHOLLY RETIRED AND MARRIED   N = 714
Q504 [SPrPnGet]
And does your (husband/wife) receive a pension from any
private arrangements (he/she) has made in the past, that is
apart from the state pension or one arranged through an
employer?

	[REmplPen]	[SEmplPen]	[PrPenGet]	[SPrPnGet]
	%	%	%	%
Yes	55.0	26.3	11.6	5.7
No	44.8	32.9	88.2	53.5
(Don't know)	0.1	-	-	-
(Refusal/Not answered)	0.2	0.2	0.2	0.2

ASK ALL WHOLLY RETIRED AND OVER STATE
RETIREMENT AGE   N = 590
Q506 [RPension]
On the whole would you say the present state pension is on the
low side, reasonable, or on the high side?
IF `ON THE LOW SIDE': Very low or a bit low?
%
50.9 Very low
31.7 A bit low
15.5 Reasonable
1.1 (Don't know)
0.7 (Refusal/Not answered)

Q507 [RPenInYr]
Do you expect your state pension in a year's time to purchase
more than it does now, less, or about the same?
%
7.8 More
60.9 Less
28.3 About the same
2.2 (Don't know)
0.7 (Refusal/Not answered)

ASK ALL WHOLLY RETIRED   N = 714
Q508 [RetirAg2]
At what age did you retire from work?
NEVER WORKED, CODE: 00
Median: 60 years
%
0.4 (Don't know)
0.4 (Refusal/Not answered)

IF NOT `never worked' AT [RetirAg2]
Q509 [RRetPlcy]
Did you have to retire because of your employer's policy on
retirement age?
%
17.4 Yes
77.8 No
2.5 EDIT ONLY: left work before retirement
0.6 (Don't know)
0.2 (Refusal/Not answered)

IF 'no' AT [RRetPlcy]
Q510-CARD E9
Q516 Why did you retire?
Please choose a phrase from this card.
CODE AS MANY AS APPLY.
%
18.5 I left because of ill health [RRetIll]
7.6 I left to look after someone else [RRetCare]
3.3 I left because my husband/wife/partner retired [RRetPrtn]
6.3 It was made attractive to me to retire early [RRetPack]
10.7 I lost my job/I was made redundant/My firm closed down
[RRetLJob]
30.0 I just wanted to retire [RRetWant]
10.2 Other answer (WRITE IN) [RRetOth]
0.1 (Don't know)
0.8 (Refusal/Not answered)

ASK ALL

Q518 [DisNew]
Do you have any health problems or disabilities that have
% lasted or are expected to last for more than a year?
34.7 Yes
65.2 No
0.1 (Don't know)
0.1 (Refusal/Not answered)

IF 'yes' AT [DisNew]

Q519 [DisWrk]
Does this health problem or disability affect the **kind** of paid
work or the **amount** of paid work that you might do?

Q520 [DisLmt]
And does this health problem or disability limit your ability
to carry out normal day-to-day activities?
If you are receiving medication or treatment please consider
what the situation would be without it.

	[DisWrk]	[DisLmt]
	%	%
Yes	18.9	19.1
No	15.7	15.5
(Don't know)	0.1	0.0
(Refusal/Not answered)	0.2	0.2

ASK ALL

Q521 [DisPrj]
Generally speaking, do you think there is a lot of prejudice
in Britain against people with disabilities, a little, hardly
% any, or none?
35.0 A lot
50.8 A little
9.4 Hardly any
2.9 None
1.8 (Don't know)
0.1 (Refusal/Not answered)

Q522 [DDAEmp]
As far as you know, is it against the law, or not, for an
employer to refuse to take on a person only because they have
a disability?
If you don't know, just say so.

Q523 [DDAShp]
Again, as far as you know, is it against the law, or not, for
someone providing goods and services to refuse to serve a
person only because they have a disability?
Again, if you don't know, just say so.

	[DDAEmp]	[DDAShp]
	%	%
Against the law	72.0	70.9
Not against the law	7.7	11.5
Depends	5.4	3.1
(Don't know)	14.8	14.3
(Refusal/Not answered)	0.1	0.1

Q524 [AgeJob]
When it comes to **getting a job**, do you think there is a lot of
prejudice in Britain against people over 50, a little, hardly
% any, or none?
58.5 A lot
35.4 A little
3.2 Hardly any
1.0 None
1.8 (Don't know)
0.1 (Refusal/Not answered)

Q525 [RetForce]
CARD E10
Some people say that it is wrong to make people retire just
because they have reached a certain age. Others say that older
employees must retire to make way for younger age groups.
What about you? Which of the statements on this card comes
% closest to your view?
67.6 It is wrong to make people retire just because they have
reached a certain age
30.0 Older employees must retire to make way for younger age
groups.
2.3 (Don't know)
0.1 (Refusal/Not answered)

Democracy and participation

VERSIONS A AND B: ASK ALL

Q526 [Lords00]
CARD F1
Which of the statements on this card comes closest to your view about what should happen to the House of Lords.
%
5.4 All or most of its members should be appointed
28.9 All or most of its members should be elected
32.5 It should contain roughly an equal number of appointed and elected members
20.9 It should be abolished
12.0 (Don't know)
0.3 (Refusal/Not answered)

Q527 [Monarchy]
How important or unimportant do you think it is for Britain to continue to have a monarchy ... READ OUT ...
%
30.5 ...very important,
34.0 quite important,
16.6 not very important,
8.0 not at all important,
9.6 or, do you think the monarchy should be abolished?
1.1 (Don't know)
0.3 (Refusal/Not answered)

Q528 [VoteSyst]
Some people say we should change the voting system for general elections to the (UK) House of Commons to allow smaller political parties to get a fairer share of MPs. Others say we should keep the voting system for the House of Commons as it is, to produce effective government.
Which view comes **closer** to your own ... READ OUT ...
IF ASKED YOU CAN SAY, 'This refers to proportional representation.'
%
34.8 ...that we should change the voting system for the^UK House of Commons,
58.6 or, keep it as it is?
6.4 (Don't know)
0.2 (Refusal/Not answered)

Q529 [DefnScrt]
Do you think that the government should have the right to keep its defence plans secret or do you think the public should
%
normally have the right to know what they are?
59.5 Government should have the right to keep them secret
37.3 Public should normally have the right to know what they are
2.9 (Don't know)
0.2 (Refusal/Not answered)

Q530 [EconScrt]
And what about its economic plans? Should the government have the right to keep these secret or should the public normally have the right to know what they are?
%
8.3 Government should have the right to keep them secret
89.4 Public should normally have the right to know what they are
2.1 (Don't know)
0.2 (Refusal/Not answered)

Q531 [GovNoSay]
CARD F2
Please choose a phrase from this card to say how much you agree or disagree with the following statements.
People like me have no say in what the government does.

Q532 [LoseTch]
CARD F2 AGAIN
(Please choose a phrase from this card to say how much you agree or disagree with this statement)
Generally speaking those we elect as MPs lose touch with people pretty quickly.

Q533 [VoteIntr]
CARD F2 AGAIN
(Please choose a phrase from this card to say how much you agree or disagree with this statement)
Parties are only interested in people's votes, not in their opinions.

Q534 [VoteOnly]
CARD F2 AGAIN
(Please choose a phrase from this card to say how much you agree or disagree with this statement)
Voting is the only way people like me can have any say about how the government runs things.

Q535 [GovComp]
CARD F2 AGAIN
(Please choose a phrase from this card to say how much you agree or disagree with this statement)
Sometimes politics and government seem so complicated that a person like me cannot really understand what is going on.

Q536 [PtyNtMat]
CARD F2 AGAIN
(Please choose a phrase from this card to say how much you agree or disagree with this statement)
It doesn't really matter which party is in power, in the end things go on much the same.

Q537 [InfPolit]
CARD F2 AGAIN
(Please choose a phrase from this card to say how much you agree or disagree with this statement)
I think I am better informed than most people about politics and government.

Q538 [MPsCare]
CARD F2 AGAIN
(Please choose a phrase from this card to say how much you agree or disagree with this statement)
MPs don't care much about what people like me think.

	[GovNoSay]	[LoseTch]	[VoteIntr]	[VoteOnly]
	%	%	%	%
Agree strongly	24.9	23.0	25.6	17.2
Agree	42.6	53.8	50.2	53.4
Neither agree nor disagree	9.7	13.0	12.5	9.9
Disagree	19.7	8.3	10.5	16.4
Disagree strongly	2.0	0.4	0.1	1.8
(Don't know)	0.9	1.2	0.8	1.0
(Refusal/Not answered)	0.2	0.2	0.2	0.2

	[GovComp]	[PtyNtMat]	[InfPolit]	[MPsCare]
	%	%	%	%
Agree strongly	17.2	18.8	2.7	13.9
Agree	43.1	52.5	19.9	47.8
Neither agree nor disagree	3.9	5.4	25.5	17.0
Disagree	20.8	19.9	43.7	19.8
Disagree strongly	3.3	2.6	7.2	0.4
(Don't know)	0.6	0.6	0.8	0.9
(Refusal/Not answered)	0.2	0.2	0.2	0.2

Q539 [GovtWork]
CARD F3
Which of these statements best describes your opinion on the present system of governing in Britain?
%
1.8 Works extremely well and could not be improved
33.4 Could be improved in small ways but mainly works well
46.7 Could be improved quite a lot
15.5 Needs a great deal of improvement
2.4 (Don't know)
0.2 (Refusal/Not answered)

Q540 [ImpGHoL]
CARD F4
Do you think that so far **reforming the House of Lords** has improved the way Britain as a whole is governed, made it worse, or has it made no difference?

Q541 [ImpGFOI]
CARD F4 AGAIN
(And has this improved the way Britain as a whole is governed, made it worse, or made no difference...)
Introducing freedom of information

Q542 [ImpGSctP]
CARD F4 AGAIN
(And has this improved the way Britain as a whole is governed, made it worse, or made no difference...)
Creating the Scottish Parliament

Q543 [ImpGWeAs]
CARD F4 AGAIN
(And has this improved the way Britain as a whole is governed, made it worse, or made no difference...)
Creating the Welsh Assembly

	[ImpGHoL]	[ImpGFOI]	[ImpGSctP]	[ImpGWeAs]
	%	%	%	%
Improved it a lot	1.1	2.0	3.1	2.4
Improved it a little	10.1	24.3	16.0	13.3
Made no difference	68.9	58.5	53.5	56.4
Made it a little worse	4.8	2.3	9.0	8.2
Made it a lot worse	3.4	1.1	4.0	3.9
(It is too early to tell)	3.6	2.0	3.7	3.3
(Don't know)	7.8	9.5	10.4	12.3
(Refusal/Not answered)	0.2	0.2	0.2	0.2

N = 2293

Q544-CARD F5

Q551 Suppose a law was being considered by parliament which you thought was really unjust and harmful. Which, if any, of the things on this card do you think you would do?
PROBE Which others?
CODE ALL THAT APPLY

%		[Vot9700]	[VotEU99]

%	
50.0	Contact my MP or MSP [DoMP]
16.8	Speak to an influential person [DoSpk]
14.4	Contact a government department [DoGov]
21.5	Contact radio, TV or a newspaper [DoTV]
68.4	Sign a petition [DoSign]
9.5	Raise the issue in an organisation I already belong to [DoRais]
15.6	Go on a protest or demonstration [DoProt]
6.6	Form a group of like-minded people [DoGrp]
7.2	(None of these) [DoNone]
0.9	(Don't know)
0.3	(Refusal/Not answered)

Q561-CARD F5 AGAIN

Q568 And have you ever done any of the things on this card about a government action which you thought was unjust and harmful? Which ones? Any others?
CODE ALL THAT APPLY

%	
16.4	Contact my MP or MSP [DoneMP]
4.2	Speak to an influential person [DoneSpk]
3.7	Contact a government department [DoneGov]
5.6	Contact radio, TV or a newspaper [DoneTV]
41.6	Sign a petition [DoneSign]
4.6	Raise the issue in an organisation I already belong to [DoneRais]
9.5	Go on a protest or demonstration [DoneProt]
1.9	Form a group of like-minded people [DoneGrp]
47.0	(None of these) [DoneNone]
0.5	(Don't know)
0.3	(Refusal/Not answered)

Q578 [Vot9700]
Talking to people about the last general election to the (UK) House of Commons in 1997, we have found that a lot of people did not manage to vote. How about you - did you manage to vote in the 1997 general election?
IF NECESSARY, SAY: The one where Tony Blair won against John Major
DO NOT PROMPT

Q579 [VotEU99]
Talking to people about the European Elections last year we have found a lot of people did not manage to vote. How about you? Did you manage to vote in the European elections last year?

N = 2293

	[Vot9700]	[VotEU99]
	%	%
Yes	72.3	36.9
No	21.2	56.0
Too young to vote	2.7	1.3
Not eligible/Not on register	2.4	1.6
Can't remember/ Don't know	1.1	3.8
(Don't know)	0.0	0.1
(Refusal/Not answered)	0.3	0.3

Q580 [MyrDone]
CARD F6
It has been suggested every (**city, district or borough council/borough council/local council**) should have a (**mayor/provost**) or leader who is elected by all people in the area and has the power to take some decisions on the council's behalf. Thinking about your area, please use a phrase from this card to say how much you agree or disagree with each of these statements about this idea.
Having an elected (**mayor/provost**) for my (**city, district or borough council/borough council/local council**) would...
...make it easier to get things done

Q581 [MyrPower]
CARD F6 AGAIN
(Having an elected (**mayor/provost**) my (**city, district or borough council/borough council/local council**) would...)
...give too much power to one person

Q582 [MyrSpeak]
CARD F6 AGAIN
(Having an elected (**mayor/provost**) for my (**city, district or borough council/borough council/local council**) would...)
...mean there was someone who could speak up for the whole area

	[MyrDone]	[MyrPower]	[MyrSpeak]
	%	%	%
Agree strongly	8.0	7.0	7.0
Agree	37.7	38.2	61.6
Neither agree nor disagree	25.4	20.6	15.3
Disagree	23.2	31.3	12.9
Disagree strongly	3.6	1.1	1.2
(Don't know)	1.8	1.7	1.7
(Refusal/Not answered)	0.3	0.3	0.3

N = 2293

Q583 [CllrDev1]
CARD F7
Say there was a proposal for a major new building development
in your neighbourhood. Choosing a phrase from this card,
please say how much you would trust the councillors on your
(city, **district or borough** council/ **borough council/local
council**) to come to the best view about the proposal?

Q584 [JuryDev1]
CARD F7 AGAIN
And again choosing a phrase from the card, how much would you
trust a 'jury' of (twelve/fifteen) ordinary local people
chosen at random to come to the best view?

	[CllrDev1]	[JuryDev1]
	%	%
Just about always	2.0	10.3
Most of the time	28.7	54.7
Only some of the time	47.4	27.5
Almost never	20.0	5.3
(Don't know)	1.6	1.9
(Refusal/Not answered)	0.3	0.3

N = 2293

Nations and Regions

VERSIONS A AND B: ASK ALL

Q586 [ScotPar2]
CARD F8

%
Which of these statements comes closest to your view?
7.2 Scotland should become independent, separate from the UK and
the European Union
12.2 Scotland should become independent, separate from the UK but
part of the European Union
44.5 Scotland should remain part of the UK, with its own elected
parliament which has some taxation powers
7.8 Scotland should remain part of the UK, with its own elected
parliament which has no taxation powers
17.4 Scotland should remain part of the UK **without** an elected
parliament
10.4 (Don't know)
0.5 (Refusal/Not answered)

Q587 [WelshAss]
CARD F9

%
Which of these statements comes closest to your view?
6.2 Wales should become independent, separate from the UK and the
European Union
10.0 Wales should become independent, separate from the UK but part
of the European Union
35.2 Wales should remain part of the UK, with its own elected
parliament which has law-making and taxation powers
16.2 Wales should remain part of the UK, with its own elected
assembly which has limited law-making powers only
20.0 Wales should remain part of the UK without an elected assembly
11.9 (Don't know)
0.5 (Refusal/Not answered)

Q588 [EngParGB]
CARD F10
With all the changes going on in the way the different parts
of Great Britain are run, which of the following do you think
would be best for England ...READ OUT...

%
53.9 ...for England to be governed as it is now, with laws made by
the UK parliament,
17.9 for each region of England to have its own assembly that runs
services like health,
19.6 or, for England as a whole to have its own new parliament with
law-making powers?
2.3 (None of these)
5.8 (Don't know)
0.5 (Refusal/Not answered)

Q589 [NIreland]
Do you think the long-term policy for Northern Ireland should be for it
... READ OUT ...

N = 2293

%
25.3 ...to remain part of the United Kingdom
57.0 or, to unify with the rest of Ireland?
0.7 **EDIT ONLY:** Northern Ireland should be an independent state
- **EDIT ONLY:** Northern Ireland should be split up into two
2.8 **EDIT ONLY:** It should be up to the Irish to decide
2.3 Other answer (WRITE IN)
11.4 (Don't know)
0.4 (Refused/Not answered)

Q591 [ECPolicy]
CARD F11
Do you think Britain's long-term policy should be ...READ OUT...
%
17.3 ...to leave the European Union,
38.3 to stay in the EU and try to reduce the EU's powers,
19.5 to leave things as they are,
9.9 to stay in the EU and try to increase the EU's powers,
6.9 or, to work for the formation of a single European government?
7.8 (Don't know)
0.4 (Refusal/Not answered)

Q592 [EuroRef]
If there were a referendum on whether Britain should join the single European currency, the Euro, how do you think you would vote? Would you vote to join the Euro, or not to join the Euro?
IF 'would not vote', PROBE: If you did vote, how would you vote?
IF RESPONDENT INSISTS THEY WOULD NOT VOTE, CODE DON'T KNOW
%
27.3 To join the Euro
63.6 Not to join the Euro
8.8 (Don't know)
0.4 (Refusal/Not answered)

Q593 [ScotGoGB]
If in the future Scotland were to become independent and leave the UK, would you be sorry, pleased, or neither pleased nor sorry?
%
37.7 Sorry
8.7 Pleased
52.3 Neither pleased nor sorry
0.9 (Don't know)
0.4 (Refusal/Not answered)

Q594 [WaleGoGB]
If in the future, Wales were to become independent and leave the UK, would you be sorry, pleased, or neither pleased nor sorry?

N = 2293

%
37.8 Sorry
7.4 Pleased
53.3 Neither pleased nor sorry
1.0 (Don't know)
0.4 (Refusal/Not answered)

Q595 [NIreGoGB]
If in the future, Northern Ireland were to leave the UK, would you be sorry, pleased, or neither pleased nor sorry?
%
20.0 Sorry
28.8 Pleased
49.0 Neither pleased nor sorry
1.7 (Don't know)
0.4 (Refusal/Not answered)

Q596 [SEBenGB]
On the whole, do you think that England's economy benefits more from having Scotland in the UK, or that Scotland's economy benefits more from being part of the UK, or is it about equal?
%
10.7 England benefits more
35.7 Scotland benefits more
39.6 Equal
2.9 (Neither/both lose)
10.7 (Don't know)
0.5 (Refusal/Not answered)

Q597 [UKSpenGB]
CARD F12
Would you say that compared with other parts of the United Kingdom, Scotland gets **pretty much** its fair share of government spending, **more** than its fair share, or **less** than its fair share of government spending?
Please choose your answer from this card.
%
7.3 Much more than its fair share of government spending
12.3 A little more than its fair share of government spending
41.8 Pretty much its fair share of government spending
11.4 A little less than its fair share of government spending
3.6 Much less than its fair share of government spending
23.2 (Don't know)
0.5 (Refusal/Not answered)

Q598 [ScEngCon]
CARD F13
Thinking about the Scots and the English, how serious would you say conflict between them is?

N = 2293

%
4.0 Very serious conflict
16.8 Fairly serious conflict
54.4 Not very serious conflict
20.1 There is no conflict
4.3 (Don't know)
0.4 (Refusal/Not answered)

VERSIONS A AND B: IN ENGLAND: ASK ALL
Q599 [RLvElsE]
Have you ever lived anywhere other than England for more than a year?
IF YES: Where was that? PROBE TO IDENTIFY CORRECT CODE
ELSEWHERE IN UK = SCOTLAND, WALES, N. IRELAND, CHANNEL ISLANDS, ISLE OF MAN

N = 1956

%
73.4 No - have never lived anywhere outside England for more than a year
5.7 Yes - elsewhere in UK
17.0 Yes - outside UK
3.4 Yes - elsewhere in UK and outside UK
0.1 (Don't know)
0.4 (Refusal/Not answered)

Q600 [NatId]
CARD F14
Some people think of themselves first as British. Others may think of themselves first as English.
Which, if any, of the following best describes how you see yourself?

%
18.3 English, not British
13.5 More English than British
33.6 Equally English and British
13.7 More British than English
11.8 British, not English
6.2 Other answer (WRITE IN)
2.3 (None of these)
0.2 (Don't know)
0.4 (Refusal/Not answered)

VERSIONS A AND B: ASK ALL
Q602 [GBPride]
CARD F15
How proud are you of being British or do you not see yourself as British at all?

VERSIONS A AND B: IN ENGLAND: ASK ALL
Q603 [NatPride]
CARD F15 AGAIN
And how proud are you of being English, or do you not see yourself as English at all?

	N = 2293	N = 1956
	[GBPride]	[NatPride]
	%	%
Very proud	42.3	44.3
Somewhat proud	35.2	28.6
Not very proud	8.4	8.9
Not at all proud	2.5	2.5
(Not English)	10.3	14.6
(Don't know)	0.9	0.7
(Refusal/Not answered)	0.4	0.4

Q604 [RBorn]
Were you born in England or somewhere else?
IF 'SOMEWHERE ELSE': Where was that?
PROBE FOR COUNTRY

%
85.8 England
2.3 Scotland
11.5 Somewhere else (WRITE IN)
- (Don't know)
0.4 (Refusal/Not answered)

N = 1956

Q606 [EngLearn]
CARD F16
Please say from this card how much you agree or disagree with each of these statements.
England has a lot to learn from the rest of Britain in running its affairs

Q607 [EngCitzn]
CARD F16 AGAIN
(Please say from this card how much you agree or disagree with each of these statements.)
I would rather live in England than in any other part of Britain

Q608 [EngAshmd]
CARD F16 AGAIN
(Please say from this card how much you agree or disagree with each of these statements.)
There are some things about England today that make me ashamed to be English
IF RESPONDENT SAYS HE/SHE IS NOT ENGLISH: CODE AS 'NEITHER AGREE NOR DISAGREE'

Q609 [EngCrit]
CARD F16 AGAIN
(Please say from this card how much you agree or disagree with each of these statements.)
People in England are too ready to criticise their country

Q610 [EngProud]
CARD F16 AGAIN
(Please say from this card how much you agree or disagree with each of these statements.)
England can only really feel proud of itself if it becomes independent from the rest of Britain

N = 1956

	[EngLearn]	[EngCitzn]	[EngAshmd]
	%	%	%
Strongly agree	3.5	23.2	16.1
Agree	21.9	44.4	53.9
Neither agree nor disagree	36.7	17.2	14.6
Disagree	28.9	12.1	12.9
Strongly disagree	4.4	1.7	1.3
(Don't know)	4.0	1.0	0.8
(Refusal/Not answered)	0.5	0.4	0.4

	[EngCrit]	[EngProud]
	%	%
Strongly agree	9.8	1.1
Agree	55.1	9.5
Neither agree nor disagree	16.1	19.0
Disagree	17.2	55.1
Strongly disagree	0.4	12.4
(Don't know)	1.0	2.4
(Refusal/Not answered)	0.4	0.4

VERSIONS A AND B: ASK ALL

Q611 [NatLearn]
CARD F16 (AGAIN)
Now some questions about **Britain**, again using/ Using) this card please say how much you agree or disagree with each of these statements.
Britain has a lot to learn from other countries in running its affairs.

Q612 [NatCitzn]
CARD F16 AGAIN
(Please say from this card how much you agree or disagree with each of these statements.)
I would rather be a citizen of Britain than of any other country in the world.

N = 2293

Q613 [NatAshmd]
CARD F16 AGAIN
(Please say from this card how much you agree or disagree with each of these statements.)
There are some things about Britain today that make me ashamed to be British.

Q614 [NatCrit]
CARD F16 AGAIN
(Please say from this card how much you agree or disagree with each of these statements.)
People in Britain are too ready to criticise their country.

Q615 [NatState]
CARD F16 AGAIN
(Please say from this card how much you agree or disagree with each of these statements.)
The government should do everything it can to keep all parts of Britain together in a single state.

Q616 [NatCoop]
CARD F16 AGAIN
(Please say from this card how much you agree or disagree with each of these statements.)
Britain should co-operate with other countries, even if it means giving up some independence.

N = 2293

	[NatLearn]	[NatCitzn]	[NatState]	[NatAshmd]
	%	%	%	%
Strongly agree	7.9	24.1	14.9	9.6
Agree	43.8	45.0	43.4	58.5
Neither agree nor disagree	20.0	14.7	19.1	12.2
Disagree	23.0	12.7	19.0	16.9
Strongly disagree	1.8	2.1	1.5	1.8
(Don't know)	0.4	0.9	1.6	0.6
(Refusal/Not answered)	0.4	0.5	0.4	0.5

	[NatCrit]	[NatCoop]
	%	%
Strongly agree	7.1	3.0
Agree	58.9	34.5
Neither agree nor disagree	16.1	16.7
Disagree	15.8	36.0
Strongly disagree	0.6	7.2
(Don't know)	0.9	2.2
(Refusal/Not answered)	0.4	0.4

Q617 [PrejNow]
Do you think there is generally more racial prejudice in Britain now than there was 5 years ago, less, or about the same amount?

N = 2293

%
32.6 More now
23.3 Less now
40.5 About the same
0.5 Other (WRITE IN)
2.7 (Don't know)
0.4 (Refusal/Not answered)

Q619 [PrejFut]
Do you think there will be more, less, or about the same amount of racial prejudice in Britain in 5 years time compared with now?
%
34.8 More in 5 years
23.7 Less
36.8 About the same
0.4 Other (WRITE IN)
3.9 (Don't know)
0.4 (Refusal/Not answered)

Q621 [SRPrej]
%   How would you describe yourself ... READ OUT ...
2.0 ... as very prejudiced against people of other races,
23.4 a little prejudiced,
73.2 or, not prejudiced at all?
0.8 Other (WRITE IN)
0.1 (Don't know)
0.5 (Refusal/Not answered)

Q623 [EqOppBlk]
CARD F17
Please use this card to say whether you think attempts to give equal opportunities to black people and Asians in Britain have gone too far or not gone far enough?
%
8.9 Gone much too far
26.5 Gone too far
36.0 About right
22.9 Not gone far enough
1.8 Not gone nearly far enough
3.3 (Don't know)
0.5 (Refusal/Not answered)

Classification

Housing

N = 3426

ASK ALL
Q712 [HomeType]
CODE FROM OBSERVATION AND CHECK WITH RESPONDENT.
Would I be right in describing this accommodation as a ...
READ OUT ONE YOU THINK APPLIES ...
%
23.4 ...detached house or bungalow
34.8 ...semi-detached house or bungalow
27.4 ...terraced house or bungalow
10.5 ...self-contained, purpose-built flat/maisonette (inc. tenement block)
2.7 ...self-contained converted flat/maisonette
0.4 ...room(s), not self-contained
0.5 Other answer (WRITE IN)
- (Don't know)
0.4 (Refusal/Not answered)

Q714 [HomeEst]
May I just check, is your home part of a housing estate (or scheme)?
NOTE: MAY BE PUBLIC OR PRIVATE, BUT IT IS THE RESPONDENT'S VIEW WE WANT
%
38.0 Yes, part of estate
61.5 No
0.1 (Don't know)
0.4 (Refusal/Not answered)

N = 3426

Q715 [Tenure1]
Does your household own or rent this accommodation?
PROBE IF NECESSARY
IF OWNS: Outright or on a mortgage? IF RENTS: From whom?
%
28.4 Owns outright
42.7 Buying on mortgage
13.5 Rents: local authority
0.5 Rents: New Town Development Corporation
3.7 Rents: Housing Association
1.2 Rents: property company
0.6 Rents: employer
0.9 Rents: other organisation
0.4 Rents: other individual
6.4 Rents: relative
0.3 Rents: Housing Trust
0.3 Rent free, squatting
0.5 Other (WRITE IN)
- (Don't know)
0.4 (Refusal/Not answered)

Q718 [LegalRes]
IF OUTRIGHT OWNER: Are the deeds for the (house/flat) in your name or are they in someone else's?
IF IN RESPONDENT'S NAME: Are they in your name only or jointly with someone else?
IF BUYING ON A MORTGAGE: Is the mortgage in your name or is it in someone else's ?
IF IN RESPONDENT'S NAME: Is it in your name only or jointly with someone else?';
IF RENTING: Is the rent book in your name or is it in someone else's?;
IF IN RESPONDENT'S NAME: Is it in your name only or jointly with someone else?;
IF RENT FREE/SQUATTING/OTHER/DK/REFUSAL: Are you legally responsible for the accommodation or is someone else?
IF LEGALLY RESPONSIBLE: Is that on your own or jointly with someone else?
%
29.3 (Deeds/ Mortgage/ Rent book in respondent's name only/ Yes, respondent solely responsible)
53.2 Jointly with someone else
16.7 (Deeds/ Mortgage/ Rent book in someone else's name/ No responsibility)
0.3 (Don't know)
0.5 (Refusal/Not answered)

N = 3426

Religion, national identity and race

ASK ALL
Q723 [Religion]
Do you regard yourself as belonging to any particular religion?
IF YES: Which?
CODE ONE ONLY - DO NOT PROMPT
%
39.5 No religion
6.3 Christian - no denomination
9.2 Roman Catholic
29.8 Church of England/Anglican
0.9 Baptist
2.5 Methodist
3.4 Presbyterian/Church of Scotland
0.4 Other Christian
1.0 Hindu
0.8 Jewish
2.0 Islam/Muslim
0.4 Sikh
0.1 Buddhist
0.4 Other non-Christian
0.1 Free Presbyterian
- Brethren
0.5 United Reform Church (URC)/Congregational
2.1 Other Protestant
- (Don't know)
0.6 (Refusal/Not answered)

IF NOT REFUSAL AT [Religion]

Q726 [FamRelig]
In what religion, if any, were you brought up?
PROBE IF NECESSARY: What was your family's religion?
CODE ONE ONLY - DO NOT PROMPT
%
11.6 No religion
6.9 Christian - no denomination
13.6 Roman Catholic
47.1 Church of England/Anglican
1.6 Baptist
4.8 Methodist
5.5 Presbyterian/Church of Scotland
0.3 Other Christian
1.1 Hindu
0.9 Jewish
2.0 Islam/Muslim
0.4 Sikh
0.0 Buddhist
0.1 Other non-Christian
0.2 Free Presbyterian
0.1 Brethren
0.7 United Reform Church (URC)/Congregational
2.1 Other Protestant
0.1 (Don't know)
0.4 (Refusal/Not answered)

IF RELIGION GIVEN AT [Religion] OR AT [FamRelig]

Q731 [ChAttend]
Apart from such special occasions as weddings, funerals and
baptisms, how often nowadays do you attend services or
meetings connected with your religion?
PROBE AS NECESSARY.
%
11.4 Once a week or more
2.2 Less often but at least once in two weeks
6.2 Less often but at least once a month
10.2 Less often but at least twice a year
5.3 Less often but at least once a year
3.8 Less often
49.0 Never or practically never
0.5 Varies too much to say
- (Don't know)
0.5 (Refusal/Not answered)

ASK ALL

Q732-CARD L1

Q739 Please say which, if any, of the words on this card describes
the way **you** think of **yourself**. Please choose as many or as few
as apply.
PROBE: Any other?
CODE ALL THAT APPLY
%
64.8 British [NatBrit]
51.5 English [NatEng]
11.1 European [NatEuro]
2.3 Irish [NatIrish]
0.4 Northern Irish [NatNI]
9.2 Scottish [NatScot]
5.6 Welsh [NatWelsh]
3.0 Other answer (WRITE IN) [NatOth]
0.5 (None of these) [NatNone]
1.0 **EDIT ONLY:** Other - Asian mentioned [NatAsia]
0.4 **EDIT ONLY:** Other - African / Caribbean mentioned [NatAfric]
- (Don't know)
0.4 (Refusal/Not answered)

IF MORE THAN ONE ANSWER GIVEN

Q752 [BNation]
CARD L1 AGAIN
And if you had to choose, which one **best** describes the way you
think of yourself?

ASK ALL

Q755 [RaceOri2]
CARD L2
% To which of these groups do you consider you belong?
0.6 BLACK: of African origin
1.2 BLACK: of Caribbean origin
0.0 BLACK: of other origin (WRITE IN)
1.7 ASIAN: of Indian origin
0.2 ASIAN: of Pakistani origin
0.3 ASIAN: of Bangladeshi origin
0.3 ASIAN: of Chinese origin
0.5 ASIAN: of other origin (WRITE IN)
91.7 WHITE: of any European origin
0.8 WHITE: of other origin (WRITE IN)
0.9 MIXED ORIGIN (WRITE IN)
0.6 OTHER (WRITE IN)
0.0 (Don't know)
0.4 (Refusal/Not answered)

Cohabitation

ASK ALL LIVING AS MARRIED

N = 314

Q761 *[MarrEvr]*
Now a few questions about your household. Firstly, have you ever been married in the past?

%
35.9 Yes
64.1 No
- (Refusal/Not answered)

ASK ALL MARRIED

N = 1906

Q762 *[MarrBfre]*
Now a few questions about you and your household. Firstly, have you ever been married before now?

%
18.9 Yes
80.6 No
0.5 (Refusal/Not answered)

ASK ALL NOT CURRENTLY LIVING AS MARRIED

N = 3112

Q763 *[CohabEvr]*
(*Now a few questions about you and your household. Have/ And have)* you and a (*man/ woman)* ever lived together as a couple without being married?

%
26.6 Yes
72.8 No
0 (Don't know)
0.6 (Refusal/Not answered)

ASK ALL CURRENTLY LIVING TOGETHER AS MARRIED OR EVER LIVED TOGETHER AS MARRIED IN THE PAST

N = 1161

Q764 *[CohbLong]*
IF CURRENTLY LIVING TOGETHER AS MARRIED: About how long have you and your partner been living together as a couple?
IF LIVED TOGETHER AS MARRIED IN THE PAST: About how long did you live as a couple for with this (*man/woman)*? If you've lived as couple like this more than once, just tell us about the longest period.
NOTE: ROUND UP/DOWN TO NEAREST YEAR
IF LESS THAN SIX MONTHS, ENTER 0

Median: 3 years

0.1 (Don't know)
1.6 (Not answered)

Q765 *[CohbOwn]*
IF CURRENTLY LIVING TOGETHER AS MARRIED: Do you or your partner own your accommodation?
IF YES: Do you own it jointly or not?
IF LIVED TOGETHER AS MARRIED IN THE PAST: I now want to ask you a few questions about this time when you were living as a couple - again, think of the longest period if you've done this more than once. Firstly, did you or your partner ever own your accommodation while you were living together?
IF YES: Did you own it jointly or not?
IF BOTH OWNED JOINTLY AND NOT JOINTLY DURING PERIOD, CODE AS OWNED JOINTLY

%
27.7 Own - jointly
21.8 Own - not jointly
48.6 (Do/Did) not own
0.1 (Don't know)
1.7 (Refusal/Not answered)

Q766 *[OwnAgree]*
IF 'owned jointly' or 'owned not jointly' AT [CohbOwn]
(*Do/Did)* you have (*then)* any written agreement with your partner other than a will or mortgage about your share in the ownership of your home?

%
4.5 Yes
44.9 No
0.1 (Don't know)
1.8 (Refusal/Not answered)

ASK ALL CURRENTLY LIVING TOGETHER AS MARRIED OR EVER LIVED TOGETHER AS MARRIED IN THE PAST

N = 1161

Q767 *[ChngWill]*
(*Have/ Did)* either you or your partner (*made or changed/ make or change)* a will because you were living together as a couple?

%
10.1 Yes
88.1 No
0.2 (Don't know)
1.6 (Refusal/Not answered)

Q768 [ChldCohb]
I" CURRENTLY LIVING TOGETHER AS MARRIED: And, have you
and your partner any children together?
IF LIVED TOGETHER AS MARRIED IN THE PAST: When you were living
together as a couple with this (man/woman), did you and
(he/she) have any children together? Again, please think of
the partner you lived with for the longest period.
IF ADOPTED/STEP/FOSTER CHILDREN ONLY, CODE AS NO.
%
28.7 Yes
69.7 No
-    (Don't know)
1.6 (Refusal/Not answered)

IF 'yes' AT [ChldCohb]
Q769 [LarResp]
Some people who live together sign parental responsibility
agreements or have parental responsibility orders decided by a
court. Have you taken out these for any of your children by
this partner?
IF YES: Which?
%
1.2 Yes, parental responsibility agreement
0.6 Yes, parental responsibility order
0.2 Yes, both agreement and order
26.8 No
-    (Don't know)
1.6 (Refusal/Not answered)

ASK ALL WHO LIVED TOGETHER AS MARRIED IN THE PAST   N = 847
Q770 [GetMarr]
Did you and this partner ever get married?
%
57.2 Yes
40.6 No
-    (Don't know)
2.2 (Refusal/Not answered)

ASK ALL WHO HAVE NEVER LIVED TOGETHER AS MARRIED   N = 3093
AND THOSE ANSWERING 'no' AT [ChldCohb]
Q771 [Hadchld]
Can I just check, have you ever (fathered a child/ given birth
to a child)?
%
68.0 Yes
31.4 No
-    (Don't know)
0.5 (Refusal/Not answered)

AS ALL WITH CHILDREN   N = 2454
Q772 [AgeBirth]
How old were you when your first child was born?
Median: 25 years
%
0.0 (Don't know)
0.7 (Refusal/Not answered)

Education   N = 3426

ASK ALL
Q773 [RPrivEd]
Have you ever attended a fee-paying, private primary or
secondary school in the United Kingdom?
'PRIVATE' PRIMARY OR SECONDARY SCHOOLS INCLUDE:
*   INDEPENDENT SCHOOLS
*   SCHOLARSHIPS AND ASSISTED PLACES AT FEE-PAYING SCHOOLS
THEY EXCLUDE:
*   DIRECT GRANT SCHOOLS (UNLESS FEE-PAYING)
*   VOLUNTARY-AIDED SCHOOLS
*   GRANT-MAINTAINED ('OPTED OUT') SCHOOLS
*   NURSERY SCHOOLS
%
11.3 Yes
88.3 No
-    (Don't know)
0.5 (Refusal/Not answered)

IF NO CHILDREN IN HOUSEHOLD (AS GIVEN IN HOUSEHOLD GRID)
Q775 [Othchld3]
Have you ever been responsible for bringing up any children of
school age, including stepchildren?
%
35.7 Yes
32.8 No
0.0 (Don't know)
0.4 (Refusal/Not answered)

IF CHILDREN IN HOUSEHOLD (AS GIVEN AT HOUSEHOLD GRID) OR 'yes'
AT [Othchld3]
Q774 [ChPrivEd]
And (have any of your children/ has your child) ever attended
a fee-paying, private primary or secondary school in the
United Kingdom?
'PRIVATE' PRIMARY OR SECONDARY SCHOOLS INCLUDE:
*   INDEPENDENT SCHOOLS
*   SCHOLARSHIPS AND ASSISTED PLACES AT FEE-PAYING SCHOOLS
THEY EXCLUDE:
*   DIRECT GRANT SCHOOLS (UNLESS FEE-PAYING)
*   VOLUNTARY-AIDED SCHOOLS
*   GRANT-MAINTAINED ('OPTED OUT') SCHOOLS
*   NURSERY SCHOOLS
%
7.9 Yes
58.8 No
-    (Don't know)
0.5 (Refusal/Not answered)

N = 1161

ASK ALL   N = 3426

Q777 [TEA2]
How old were you when you completed your continuous full-time education?
PROBE IF NECESSARY
'STILL AT SCHOOL' - CODE 95
'STILL AT COLLEGE OR UNIVERSITY' - CODE 96.
'OTHER ANSWER' - CODE 97 AND WRITE IN
Median: 16 years
%
0.4 (Still at school)
2.2 (Still at university/college)
0.0 (Other)
0.0 (Don't know)
0.4 (Refusal/Not answered)

Q780 [SchQual]
CARD L3
Have you passed any of the examinations on this card?
%
60.8 Yes
38.7 No
0.0 (Don't know)
0.4 (Refusal/Not answered)

IF 'yes' AT [SchQual]
Q781-CARD L3 AGAIN
Q799 Which ones? PROBE: Any others?
% CODE ALL THAT APPLY
28.5 CSE Grades 2-5
     GCE 'O'-level Grades D-E or 7-9
     Scottish (SCE) Ordinary Bands D-E
     Scottish Standard Grades 4-7   [EdQual1]
     GCSE Grades D-G
     CSE Grade 1
     GCE 'O'-level Grades A-C or 1-6
     School Certificate or Matriculation
48.6 Scottish (SCE) Ordinary Bands A-C   [EdQual2]
     Scottish Standard Grades 1-3 or Pass
     Scottish School Leaving Certificate Lower Grade
     SUPE Ordinary
     Northern Ireland Junior Certificate
     GCE 'A'-level/ 'S'-level/ 'AS'-level
21.1 Higher School Certificate   [EdQual3]
     Scottish SCE/SLC/SUPE at Higher Grade
     Northern Ireland Senior Certificate
1.9 Overseas school leaving exam or certificate   [EdQual4]
0.1 (Don't know)
0.4 (Refusal/Not answered)

ASK ALL   N = 3426

Q804 [PSchQual]
CARD L4
And have you passed any of the exams or got any of the qualifications on this card?
%
53.1 Yes
46.4 No
0.0 (Don't know)
0.4 (Refusal/Not answered)

IF 'yes' AT [PSchQual]
Q805-CARD L4 AGAIN
Q822 Which ones? PROBE: Any others?
% CODE ALL THAT APPLY
4.2 Recognised trade apprenticeship **completed** [EdQual5]
7.7 RSA/other clerical, commercial qualification [EdQual6]
7.3 City&Guilds Certif - Part I [EdQual22]
6.5 City&Guilds Certif - Craft/ Intermediate/ Ordinary/ Part II [EdQual23]
3.2 City&Guilds Certif - Advanced/ Final/ Part III [EdQual24]
1.8 City&Guilds Certif - Full Technological/ Part IV [EdQual25]
4.9 BEC/TEC General/Ordinary National Certif (ONC) or Diploma (OND) [EdQual10]
5.2 BEC/TEC Higher/Higher National Certif (HNC) or Diploma (HND) [EdQual11]
3.0 NVQ/SVQ Lev 1/GNVQ Foundation lev [EdQual17]
4.9 NVQ/SVQ Lev 2/GNVQ Intermediate lev [EdQual18]
3.3 NVQ/SVQ Lev 3/GNVQ Advanced lev [EdQual19]
0.5 NVQ/SVQ Lev 4 [EdQual20]
0.3 NVQ/SVQ Lev 5 [EdQual21]
4.9 Teacher training qualification [EdQual12]
3.5 Nursing qualification [EdQual13]
5.0 Other technical or business qualification/certificate [EdQual14]
13.7 Univ/CNAA degree/diploma [EdQual15]
5.4 Other recognised academic or vocational qual (WRITE IN) [EdQual16]
-    (Don't know)
0.4 (Refusal/Not answered)

VERSIONS B AND C: ASK ALL   N = 2258

Q843 [BioQual]
Can I just check, have you ever studied for a qualification in biology or genetics, at school, college or anywhere else?
%
17.4 Yes
82.0 No
0.0 (Don't know)
0.5 (Refusal/Not answered)

IF 'yes' AT   N = 2258

Q844- CARD L5
Q849 Which of these qualifications was it?
CODE ALL THAT APPLY

%
                                                  [BioQOlev]
       O-level/CSE/GCSE/GNVQ Foundation or Intermediate
       NVQ/SVQ levels 1 or 2
13.5 BTEC First or General Diploma
       School Certificate or Matriculation
       SCE/SLC/SUPE ordinary standard
       Northern Ireland Junior Certificate

       A-level/AS-level/S-level   *[BioQAlev]*
       GNVQ Advanced
       NVQ/SVQ level 3
3.1   BTEC National Certificate or Diploma
       Higher School Certificate
       SCE/SLC/SUPE at higher grade
       Northern Ireland Senior Certificate
       ONC/OND

       First degree (BA/BSc/BEd)   *[BioQDegr]*
       BTEC Higher Certificate or Diploma
1.5   HNC/HND
       NVQ/SVQ level 4
0.5   Postgraduate degree (MA/MSc/PhD)   *[BioQPstg]*
       NVQ/SVQ level 5
1.0   Nursing qualification   *[BioQNurs]*
0.9   Other (WRITE IN)   *[BioQOth]*
-      (Don't know)
0.6   (Refusal/Not answered)

VERSIONS A AND B: ASK ALL   N = 2293

Q851 *[Internet]*
Does anyone have access to the Internet or World Wide Web from this address?

Q852 *[WWWUse]*
Do you yourself ever use the Internet or World Wide Web for any reason (other than your work)?

	[Internet]	[WWWUse]
	%	%
Yes	35.5	33.2
No	63.8	66.1
(Don't know)	0.0	0.0
(Refusal/Not answered)	0.6	0.6

If 'yes' AT [WWWUse]   N = 2293

Q853 *[WWWHrsWk]*
How many **hours** a week on average do you spend using the Internet or World Wide Web (other than for your work)?
INTERVIEWER: ROUND UP TO NEAREST HOUR
Median: 2 hours
%
0.2 (Don't know)
0.7 (Not answered)

Partner's job details

ASK ALL MARRIED OR LIVING AS MARRIED   N = 2220

Q866 *[SEconAct]*
CARD
Which of these descriptions applied to what your (husband/wife/partner) was doing last week, that is the seven days ending last Sunday?
PROBE: Which others? CODE ALL THAT APPLY

%
0.8   In full-time education (not paid for by employer, including on vacation)
0.0   On government training/ employment programme (e.g. Youth Training, Training for Work etc)
61.7 In paid work (or away temporarily) for at least 10 hours in week
0.3   Waiting to take up paid work already accepted
1.4   Unemployed and registered at a benefit office
0.6   Unemployed, not registered, but actively looking for a job (of at least 10 hrs a week)
0.2   Unemployed, wanting a job (of at least 10 hrs a week) but not actively looking for a job
3.7   Permanently sick or disabled
19.8 Wholly retired from work
10.4 Looking after the home
0.8   (Doing something else) (WRITE IN)
-      (Don't know)
0.4   (Refusal/Not answered)

ASK ALL WHO ARE MARRIED OR LIVING AS MARRIED AND PARTNER IS NOT WORKING   N = 844

Q867 [SLastJob]
How long ago did (he/she) last have a paid job of at least 10 hours a week?
GOVERNMENT PROGRAMS/SCHEMES DO NOT COUNT AS 'PAID JOBS'.
%
11.7 Within past 12 months
23.5 Over 1, up to 5 years ago
22.6 Over 5, up to 10 years ago
22.9 Over 10, up to 20 years ago
13.5 Over 20 years ago
4.2   Never had a paid job of 10+ hours a week
0.4   (Don't know)
1.1   (Refusal/Not answered)

ASK ALL WHERE PARTNER'S JOB DETAILS ARE BEING COLLECTED[1]   N = 316

Q868 [PTitle] (NOT ON DATAFILE)
IF 'in paid work' AT [SEconAct]: Now I want to ask you about your (husband/ wife/ partner)'s present job. What is (his/her) job?
IF 'waiting to take up work' AT [SEconAct]: Now I want to ask you about your (husband/ wife/ partner)'s future job. What is (his/her) job?
PROBE IF NECESSARY: What is the name or title of the job?
CODE ALL THAT APPLY

Q869 [PTrygewk] (NOT ON DATAFILE)
What kind of work (does/will) (he/she) do most of the time?
IF RELEVANT: What materials/machinery (does/will) (he/she) use?
CODE ALL THAT APPLY

Q870 [Train] (NOT ON DATAFILE)
What training or qualifications are needed for that job?
CODE ALL THAT APPLY

Q871 [PSuper2]
(Does/Will) (he/she) directly supervise or (is/will) (he/she) (be) directly responsible for the work of any other people?
%
41.0 Yes
56.5 No
0.3   (Don't know)
2.1   (Refusal/Not answered)

IF 'yes' AT [PSuper2]   N = 316

Q872 [PMany]
How many?
%
Median: 6 people (of those supervising any)
5.2 (Don't know)
2.4 (Refusal/Not answered)

Q874 [PEmploye]
In your (husband/wife/partner)'s (main) job (is/will) (he/she) (be) ... READ OUT ...
%
73.4 ... an employee,
24.5 or self-employed?
-     (Don't know)
2.1   (Refusal/Not answered)

ASK ALL WHERE PARTNER'S JOB DETAILS ARE BEING COLLECTED AND PARTNER IS EMPLOYEE   N = 239

Q876 [PSupman2]
Can I just check, (are/will) (he/she) (be) ... READ OUT ...
%
23.3 ...a manager,
15.2 a foreman or supervisor,
57.4 or not?
1.4   (Don't know)
2.8   (Refusal/Not answered)

Q877 [POcSect2]
CARD
Which of the types of organisation on this card (does/will) (he/she) work for?
%
71.2 PRIVATE SECTOR FIRM OR COMPANY Including, for example, limited companies and PLCs
2.3   NATIONALISED INDUSTRY OR PUBLIC CORPORATION Including, for example, the Post Office and the BBC
21.9 OTHER PUBLIC SECTOR EMPLOYER
      Incl eg: - Central govt/ Civil Service/ Govt Agency
      - Local authority/ Local Educ Auth (incl 'opted out' schools)
      - Universities
      - Health Authority / NHS hospitals / NHS Trusts/ GP surgeries
      - Police / Armed forces
1.8   CHARITY/ VOLUNTARY SECTOR Including, for example, charitable companies, churches, trade unions
-     Other answer (WRITE IN)
-     (Don't know)
2.8   (Refusal/Not answered)

ASK ALL WHERE PARTNER'S JOB DETAILS ARE BEING COLLECTED   N = 316

Q879 [PEmpMake] (NOT ON DATAFILE)
IF EMPLOYEE: What (does) (his/her) employer make or do at the place where (he/she) (usually works/will usually work) (from)?
IF SELF-EMPLOYED: What (does/will) (he/she) make or do at the place where (he/she) (usually works/will usually work) (from)?

[1] Partner's job details are collected if respondent is not working or waiting to take up work, but partner is working or waiting to take up work.

Q884 [PEmpWork]

IF EMPLOYEE: Including (himself/herself), how many people (are) employed at the place where (he/she) usually (works/will work) (from)?

IF SELF-EMPLOYED: (Does/Will) (he/she) have any employees.

IF YES: PROBE FOR CORRECT PRECODE.

%
13.7 (No employees/ DO NOT USE IF EMPLOYEE)
17.9 Under 10
13.0 10-24
17.9 25-99
16.5 100-499
14.3 500 or more
4.5 (Don't know)
2.1 (Refusal/Not answered)

N = 316

Q896 [PPartFul]

%
(Is/Will) the job (be) ... READ OUT ...
80.5 ... full-time – that is, 30 or more hours per week,
17.4 or, part-time?
-    (Don't know)
2.1 (Refusal/Not answered)

Income

ASK ALL
Q926 [AnyBN2]
CARD L8

Do you (or your husband/wife/partner) receive any of the state benefits on this card at present?

%
63.3 Yes
36.2 No
0.0 (Don't know)
0.5 (Refusal/Not answered)

N = 3426

IF 'yes' AT [AnyBN2]
Q927-CARD L8 AGAIN
Q944 Which ones? PROBE: Any others?
% CODE ALL THAT APPLY
23.1 State retirement pension (National Insurance) [BenefOAP]
1.0 War Pension (War Disablement Pension or War Widows Pension) [BenefWar]
1.0 Widow's Benefits (Widow's Pension and Widowed Mother's Allowance) [BenefWid]
2.4 Jobseeker's Allowance/ Unemployment Benefit / Income Support for the Unemployed [BenefUB]
6.9 Income Support (other than for unemployment) [BenefIS]
29.5 Child Benefit (formerly Family Allowance) [BenefCB]
1.4 One Parent Benefit [BenefOP]
4.2 Working Families Tax Credit/ Family Credit [BenefFC]
8.4 Housing Benefit (Rent Rebate) [BenefHB]
9.9 Council Tax Benefit (or Rebate) [BenefCT]
5.8 Incapacity Benefit / Sickness Benefit / Invalidity Benefit [BenefInc]
0.6 Disability Working Allowance [BenefDWA]
4.1 Disability Living Allowance (for people under 65) [BenefDLA]
2.0 Attendance Allowance (for people aged 65+) [BenefAtA]
1.0 Severe Disablement Allowance [BenefSev]
1.1 Invalid Care Allowance [BenefICA]
0.7 Industrial Injuries Disablement Benefit [BenefInd]
0.5 Other state benefit (WRITE IN) [BenefOth]
0.0 (Don't know)
0.5 (Refusal/Not answered)

N = 3426

ASK ALL

Q965 [MainInc]

CARD L9

Which of these is the **main** source of income for you *(and your husband/wife/partner)* at present?

N = 3426

%
61.4 Earnings from employment (own or spouse / partner's)
9.2 Occupational pension(s) - from previous employer(s)
13.5 State retirement or widow's pension(s)
1.9 Jobseeker's Allowance/ Unemployment benefit
4.7 Income Support
0.7 Family Credit
2.9 Invalidity, sickness or disabled pension or benefit(s)
0.1 Other state benefit (WRITE IN)
1.6 Interest from savings or investments
0.4 Student grant
1.6 Dependent on parents/other relatives
1.2 Other main source (WRITE IN)
0.2 (Don't know)
0.7 (Refusal/Not answered)

ASK ALL WHO ARE NOT RETIRED AND UNDER RETIREMENT AGE

N = 2564

Q968 [PenXpct1]

CARD L10

When you have retired and have stopped doing paid work, where do you think **most** of your income will come from?

INTERVIEWER: IF RESPONDENT SAYS `SPOUSE/ PARTNER'S COMPANY PENSION', CODE AS `A COMPANY PENSION'.

SIMILARLY FOR STATE AND PERSONAL PENSIONS.

%
27.1 State retirement pension
34.6 A company pension
27.0 A personal pension
7.8 Other savings or investments
0.9 From somewhere else (WRITE IN)
0.2 **EDIT ONLY:** Earnings from job / still working
2.1 (Don't know)
0.3 (Refusal/Not answered)

Q970 [PenXpct2]

CARD L10 AGAIN

And which do you think will be your **second most important** source of income?

INTERVIEWER: IF RESPONDENT SAYS `SPOUSE/ PARTNER'S COMPANY PENSION', CODE AS `A COMPANY PENSION'.

SIMILARLY FOR STATE AND PERSONAL PENSIONS.

%
29.9 State retirement pension
12.1 A company pension
15.4 A personal pension
28.1 Other savings or investments
0.9 From somewhere else (WRITE IN)
9.4 (None)
0.7 **EDIT ONLY:** Earnings from job / still working
3.0 (Don't know)
0.4 (Refusal/Not answered)

N = 2564

ASK ALL

Q972 [HHincome]

CARD L11

Which of the letters on this card represents the total income of your household from **all** sources **before tax**?

Please just tell me the letter.

NOTE: INCLUDES INCOME FROM BENEFITS, SAVINGS, ETC.

ASK ALL IN PAID WORK

Q973 [REarn]

CARD L11 AGAIN

Which of the letters on this card represents your **own** gross or total **earnings**, before deduction of income tax and national insurance?

	N = 3426	N = 1889
	[HhIncome]	[REarn]
	%	%
Q (Less than £3,999)	3.5	6.2
T (£4,000 - £5,999)	7.8	7.7
O (£6,000 - £7,999)	6.7	5.9
K (£8,000 - £9,999)	4.9	6.4
L (£10,000 - £11,999)	5.2	9.4
B (£12,000 - £14,999)	6.7	11.8
Z (£15,000 - £17,999)	5.7	9.3
M (£18,000 - £19,999)	3.8	6.0
F (£20,000 - £22,999)	5.0	6.5
J (£23,000 - £25,999)	6.0	7.4
D (£26,000 - £28,999)	3.4	4.2
H (£29,000 - £31,999)	4.0	2.9
C (£32,000 - £34,999)	3.8	2.1
G (£35,000 - £37,999)	3.1	1.6
P (£38,000 - £40,999)	2.9	1.3
N (£41,000 - £43,999)	2.0	0.6
Y (£44,000 - £46,999)	2.2	0.9
S (£37,000 - £49,999)	1.3	0.6
R (£50,000 or more)	8.3	3.4
(Don't know)	6.4	1.1
(Refusal/Not answered)	7.2	4.6

IF 'information given' OR 'information not given' AT   N = 3426
[ComeBac2]

Q978   [CohbCmBk]

On part of this project we are working together with a team
from the universities of Bradford and Aberystwyth. They may
want to do follow up interviews with a few people who have
taken part in this study. If they wanted to contact you, would
it be all right for us to pass on your details to them - by
that, I mean your name and address, and some of the answers
you have given me today?

IF ASKED: They will write to you in advance and if you don't
want to take part then you can just say so. We will not pass
your details on to any organisation other than these
universities.

%
73.0 Yes
20.9 No
0.2 (Don't know)
0.5 (Refusal/Not answered)

N = 3426

Administration

ASK ALL

Q975 *[PhoneX]*
% Is there a telephone in (your part of) this accommodation?
95.7 Yes
3.9 No
– (Don't know)
0.4 (Refusal/Not answered)

IF 'Yes' AT [PhoneX]

Q976 *[PhoneBck]*
A few interviews on any survey are checked by a supervisor to
make sure that people are satisfied with the way the interview
was carried out. In case my supervisor needs to contact you,
it would be helpful if we could have your telephone number.
ADD IF NECESSARY: Your 'phone number will **not** be passed to
anyone outside the National Centre.
IF NUMBER GIVEN, WRITE ON THE ARF
NOTE: YOU WILL BE ASKED TO KEY IN THE NUMBER IN THE ADMIN
BLOCK
%
90.1 Number given
5.6 Number Refusal
– (Don't know)
0.4 (Refusal/Not answered)

ASK ALL

Q977 *[ComeBac2]*
Sometime in the next year, we may be doing a follow up survey
and may wish to contact you again. Could you give us the
address or phone number of someone who knows you well, just in
case we have difficulty in getting in touch with you.
IF NECESSARY, PROMPT: Perhaps a relative or friend who is
unlikely to move?
WRITE IN DETAILS ON ARF
%
46.2 Information given
47.8 Information not given (other than code 3)
5.5 DO NOT PROMPT: Outright refusal ever to take part again
– (Don't know)
0.5 (Refusal/Not answered)

VERSIONS B AND C

Genetics

VERSIONS B AND C: ASK ALL

Q680 *[GenRefin]*
CARD K1
Now some questions on genetic tests.
People can take genetic tests to tell them whether they are
likely to develop a serious genetic condition in the future.
In your opinion, should such tests be used ... by insurance
... by insurance companies to **accept or refuse people** for life
insurance policies?

%
3.2 Definitely should
13.0 Probably should
23.2 Probably should **not**
56.2 Definitely should **not**
0.1 (Other answer (WRITE IN))

Q682 *[GenEmpl]*
CARD K1 AGAIN
Now suppose someone who is applying for a job **has had** such a
genetic test. Should the employer have **the right** to see the
result of this test, or not?

%
4.5 Definitely should
12.8 Probably should
21.6 Probably should **not**
57.1 Definitely should **not**
0.4 (Other answer (WRITE IN))
0.4 **EDIT ONLY:** Depends on the job / depends on the type of work
2.8 (Don't know)
0.5 (Refusal/Not answered)

Q684 *[GenTake?]*
CARD K1 AGAIN
Now suppose the appicant has **never** had such a test. Should
the employer have the right to **make** the applicant have a test?

%
1.3 Definitely should
7.2 Probably should
16.8 Probably should **not**
71.1 Definitely should **not**
0.1 (Other answer (WRITE IN))
0.3 **EDIT ONLY:** Depends on the job / depends on the type of work
2.7 (Don't know)
0.5 (Refusal/Not answered)

Q686 *[GenSens]*
CARD K1 AGAIN
And should the employer have the right to **make** applicants have
a test to see if they are particularly sensitive to chemicals
that may be used in the workplace?

%
28.6 Definitely should
51.8 Probably should
7.7 Probably should **not**
8.5 Definitely should **not**
0.4 (Other answer (WRITE IN))
0.0 **EDIT ONLY:** Depends on the job / depends on the type of work
2.5 (Don't know)
0.5 (Refusal/Not answered)

Q688 *[PregTest]*
CARD K2
Genetic tests can also be taken from unborn babies while still
in the womb, to show if the child is likely to be born with a
serious medical condition, but such tests carry some risks.
Which of the statements on this card comes closest to your
view.

%
43.2 **All pregnant women** should be offered such tests.
48.6 Only women where there is **special reason to suspect a problem**
should be offered such tests.
6.0 Such tests should **not be allowed** at all.
1.8 (Don't know)
0.5 (Refusal/Not answered)

Q689 *[AbMental]*
CARD K3
Now suppose a woman had one of these tests and it showed that
there **was** very likely to be a serious problem with her unborn
child.
Please use this card to say whether you think it would be
right or not for the woman to have a legal abortion...
... if the child was very likely to be born with a serious
mental disability and would never be able to lead an
independent life?

Q690 *[AbPhys]*
CARD K3 AGAIN
(Do you think it would be right or not for the woman to have a
legal abortion...)
... if the child was very likely to be born with a serious
physical disability and would never be able to lead an
independent life?

N = 2258

	[AbMental]	[AbPhys]	[AbDie]	[AbShort]
	%	%	%	%
Never right	8.0	9.9	39.8	51.3
Sometimes right	39.6	45.5	40.7	30.4
Always right	49.4	41.4	15.5	14.0
(Don't know)	2.5	2.8	3.5	3.9
(Refusal/Not answered)	0.5	0.5	0.5	0.5

	[PGDMentl]	[PGDPhys]	[PGDDie]	[PGDShort]
	%	%	%	%
Never right	21.5	20.9	30.2	35.8
Sometimes right	36.2	38.6	38.4	34.6
Always right	37.0	35.1	26.1	23.9
(Don't know)	4.7	4.7	4.8	5.0
(Refusal/Not answered)	0.6	0.6	0.6	0.6

N = 2258

Q691 *[AbDie]*
CARD K3 AGAIN
(Do you think it would be right or not for the woman to have a legal abortion...)
... if the child was very likely to be born with a condition that meant it would live in **good health**, but then would **die in its twenties or thirties**?

Q692 *[AbShort]*
CARD K3 AGAIN
And what if the child would be healthy but would **never grow taller than an eight year old**?
(Do you think it would be right or not for the woman to have a legal abortion?)

Q693 *[PGDMentl]*
CARD K3 AGAIN
There is another way in which couples can try to avoid having a child with a serious medical condition. The woman's eggs are fertilised outside her body with her partner's sperm and genetically tested. Only eggs without the condition are put back, and may then grow into a baby.
Suppose it was likely that a couple would have a child with a serious **mental disability**. Do you think it would be right or not right for them to have this sort of treatment?

Q694 *[PGDPhys]*
CARD K3 AGAIN
Suppose it was likely that a couple would have a child with a serious **physical disability**. Do you think it would be right or not right for **them** to have this sort of treatment?

Q695 *[PGDDie]*
CARD K3 AGAIN
Still thinking about genetically testing eggs outside the woman's body. Suppose a couple were likely to have a child which would live in **good health**, but then would **die in its twenties or thirties**. Do you think it would be right or not right for them to have this sort of treatment?

Q696 *[PGDShort]*
CARD K3 AGAIN
Suppose they would have a child which would be healthy but would **never grow taller than an eight year old**. Do you think it would be right or not right for them to have this sort of treatment?

Q697 *[GenHeigh]*
CARD K4
Some things about a person are caused by their **genes**, which they inherit from their parents. Others may be to do with **the way they are brought up**, or **the way they live**. Some may happen just **by chance**.
Using this card, please say what **you** think decides each of the things that I am going to read out. If you don't know, please just say so.
... a person's height?

Q698 *[GenCleve]*
CARD K4 AGAIN
(Using this card, please say what **you** think decides ...)
... a person's intelligence?
(If you don't know, please just say so).

Q699 *[GenHeart]*
CARD K4 AGAIN
And what do you think decides a person's chances ...
... of getting heart disease?
(If you don't know, please just say so).

Q700 *[GenViol]*
CARD K4 AGAIN
(And what do you think decides a person's chances ...)
... of being aggressive or violent?
(If you don't know, please just say so).

N = 2258

	[GenHeigh]	[GenCleve]
	%	%
All to do with genes	41.0	12.0
Mostly to do with genes	35.9	21.6
Mostly to do with upbringing or lifestyle	1.4	15.1
All to do with upbringing or lifestyle	0.5	4.1
An equal mixture of genes and upbringing/lifestyle	9.4	36.7
Just chance	4.1	3.7
(Don't know)	7.2	6.4
(Refusal/Not answered)	0.5	0.5

	[GenHeart]	[GenViol]
	%	%
All to do with genes	10.8	4.2
Mostly to do with genes	17.8	7.1
Mostly to do with upbringing or lifestyle	14.8	31.3
All to do with upbringing or lifestyle	5.7	15.8
An equal mixture of genes and upbringing/lifestyle	38.6	28.9
Just chance	5.3	4.8
(Don't know)	6.5	7.5
(Refusal/Not answered)	0.5	0.5

Q701 [ChgHeig]
CARD K5
Suppose it was discovered that a person's genes **could** be changed.
Taking your answers from this card, do **you** think this should be allowed or **not** allowed to make a person ...
... taller or shorter?

Q702 [ChgCleve]
CARD K5 AGAIN
(Do **you** think this should be allowed or **not** allowed to make a person ...)
... more intelligent?

Q703 [ChgGay]
CARD K5 AGAIN
(Do **you** think this should be allowed or **not** allowed to make a person ...)
... straight, rather than gay or lesbian?

Q704 [ChgHeart]
CARD K5 AGAIN
And should changing a person's genes be allowed or **not** allowed to...
... reduce a person's chances of getting heart disease?

N = 2258

Q705 [ChgCanc]
CARD K5 AGAIN
(And should changing a person's genes be allowed or **not** allowed to ...)
... reduce a person's chances of getting breast cancer?

Q706 [ChgViol]
CARD K5 AGAIN
(And should changing a person's genes be allowed or **not** allowed to ...)
... make them less aggressive or violent?

Q707 [ChgFat]
CARD K5 AGAIN
(And should changing a person's genes be allowed or **not** allowed to ...)
... make them of average weight, rather than very over-weight?

Q708 [ChgSex]
CARD K5 AGAIN
(And should changing a person's genes be allowed or **not** allowed to ...)
... determine the sex of an unborn baby?

Q709 [ChgBald]
CARD K5 AGAIN
And should changing a person's genes be allowed or **not** allowed to...
... give someone a full head of hair, rather than being bald?

Q710 [ChgSchiz]
CARD K5 AGAIN
(And should changing a person's genes be allowed or **not** allowed to ...)
... stop someone having schizophrenia?

	[ChgHeig]	[ChgCleve]	[ChgGay]	[ChgHeart]
	%	%	%	%
Definitely allowed	4.2	5.1	7.1	23.6
Probably allowed	19.1	14.6	10.5	42.8
Probably **not** allowed	25.3	26.1	23.7	13.2
Definitely **not** allowed	48.0	50.7	53.7	16.8
(Don't know)	3.0	2.8	4.3	3.1
(Refusal/Not answered)	0.5	0.5	0.6	0.5

N = 2258

	[ChgCanc] %	[ChgViol] %	[ChgFat] %
Definitely allowed	36.3	21.2	10.0
Probably allowed	35.9	35.3	27.8
Probably **not** allowed	10.6	19.0	25.5
Definitely **not** allowed	13.5	19.7	32.5
(Don't know)	3.2	4.3	3.7
(Refusal/Not answered)	0.6	0.6	0.5

	[ChgCSex] %	[ChgBald] %	[ChgSchiz] %
Definitely allowed	3.1	6.9	27.7
Probably allowed	12.6	16.0	38.7
Probably **not** allowed	19.3	18.6	12.8
Definitely **not** allowed	62.0	55.2	16.7
(Don't know)	2.6	2.7	3.5
(Refusal/Not answered)	0.5	0.5	0.6

Q711 [GenFamil]
Has a **doctor** ever advised you, or any member of your immediate
family, of a serious genetic condition in your family?
FOR 'NOT SURE', CODE DON'T KNOW.
%
8.3 Yes
90.2 No
1.0 (Don't know)
0.5 (Refusal/Not answered)

VERSION C

Education

VERSION C: ASK ALL

Q625 [EdSpend1]
CARD G1
Now some questions about education.
Which of the groups on this card, if any, would be your
% highest priority for **extra** government spending on education?

IF ANSWER GIVEN AT [EdSpend1]

Q626 [EdSpend2]
CARD G1 AGAIN
And which is your next highest priority?

	[EdSpend1]	[EdSpend2]
	%	%
Nursery or pre-school children	12.6	11.1
Primary school children	21.5	22.2
Secondary school children	28.0	25.2
Less able children with special needs	26.4	22.4
Students at colleges or universities	9.2	15.5
(None of these)	1.3	0.8
(Don't know)	1.1	0.3
(Refusal/Not answered)	-	1.1

VERSION C: ASK ALL

Q627 [PrimImp1]
CARD G2
Here are a number of things that some people think would
improve education in our schools.
Which do you think would be the **most** useful one for improving
the education of children in **primary** schools - aged (5-11/5-
12) years? Please look at the whole list before deciding.
%
1.3 More information available about individual schools
8.7 More links between parents and schools
16.7 More resources for buildings, books and equipment
14.4 Better quality teachers
39.2 Smaller class sizes
1.2 More emphasis on exams and tests
14.4 More emphasis on developing the child's skills and interests
1.6 Better leadership within individual schools
1.6 Other (WRITE IN)
1.2 (Don't know)
-   (Refusal/Not answered)

IF ANSWER GIVEN AT [PrimImp1]

Q629 [PrimImp2]
CARD G2 AGAIN
And which do you think would be the **next** most useful one for
children in **primary** schools?
%
1.5 More information available about individual schools
9.6 More links between parents and schools
22.8 More resources for buildings, books and equipment
15.0 Better quality teachers
21.6 Smaller class sizes
2.7 More emphasis on exams and tests
20.4 More emphasis on developing the child's skills and interests
4.1 Better leadership within individual schools
1.1 Other (WRITE IN)
0.1 (Don't know)
1.2 (Refusal/Not answered)

VERSION C: ASK ALL

Q631 [SecImp1]
CARD G3
And which do you think would be the **most** useful thing for improving the education of children in **secondary** schools – aged (11-18/12-18) years?
%
0.9 More information available about individual schools
5.5 More links between parents and schools
17.0 More resources for buildings, books and equipment
17.6 Better quality teachers
23.5 Smaller class sizes
5.9 More emphasis on exams and tests
13.6 More emphasis on developing the child's skills and interests
11.4 More training and preparation for jobs
1.7 Better leadership within individual schools
1.5 Other (WRITE IN)
1.3 (Don't know)
- (Refusal/Not answered)

IF ANSWER GIVEN AT [SecImp1]
Q633 [SecImp2]
CARD G3 AGAIN
And which do you think would be the **next** most useful one for children in **secondary** schools?
%
0.7 More information available about individual schools
5.1 More links between parents and schools
17.6 More resources for buildings, books and equipment
14.7 Better quality teachers
14.1 Smaller class sizes
7.6 More emphasis on exams and tests
17.2 More emphasis on developing the child's skills and interests
15.5 More training and preparation for jobs
4.9 Better leadership within individual schools
0.8 Other (WRITE IN)
0.4 (Don't know)
1.3 (Refusal/Not answered)

VERSION C: ASK ALL
Q635 [SchSelec]
CARD G4
Which of the following statements comes closest to your views about what kind of **secondary** school children should go to?
%
48.4 Children should go to a different kind of secondary school, according to how well they do at primary school
49.7 All children should go to the same kind of secondary school, no matter how well or badly they do at primary school
1.9 (Don't know)
- (Refusal/Not answered)

Q636 [HEOpp]
Do you feel that opportunities for young people in Britain to go on to **higher education** – to a university or college – should be increased or reduced, or are they at about the right level now?
IF INCREASED OR REDUCED: a lot or a little?
%
26.9 Increased a lot
16.9 Increased a little
48.6 About right
3.1 Reduced a little
1.5 Reduced a lot
3.1 (Don't know)
- (Refusal/Not answered)

Q637 [HEFeeNow]
CARD G5
I'm now going to ask you what you think about university or college students paying towards the costs of their tuition – either while they are studying or after they have finished. Firstly, students and their families paying towards the costs of their tuition **while they are studying**.
Which of the views on this card comes closest to what you think about that?
%
7.5 All students or their families should pay towards their tuition costs while they are studying
61.6 Some students or their families should pay towards their tuition costs while they are studying, depending on their circumstances
30.0 No students or their families should pay towards their tuition costs while they are studying
0.8 (Don't know)
0.0 (Refusal/Not answered)

Q638 [HEFeeAft]
CARD G6
And what about students paying back some of the costs of their tuition **after they have finished studying**?
Which of the views on this card comes closest to what you think about that?
%
17.3 All students should pay back some tuition costs after they have finished studying
50.1 Some students should pay back some tuition costs after they have finished studying, depending on their circumstances
31.3 No students should pay back tuition costs after they have finished studying
1.3 (Don't know)
0.0 (Refusal/Not answered)

N = 1133

N = 1133

Q639 [HEGrant2]

And, at present, some full-time British university students get grants to help cover their **living** costs. Getting a grant depends upon the student's circumstances and those of their family. Do you think that ... READ OUT ...

%
26.5 ...**all** students should get grants to help cover their living costs,
67.1 **some** students should get grants to help cover their living costs,
1.7 or, that no grants should be given to help cover students' living costs?
4.0 (It depends)
0.8 (Don't know)
- (Refusal/Not answered)

Q640 [HELoan]

Many full-time university students are now taking out government loans to help cover their living costs. They have to start repaying these loans when they begin working. Generally speaking, do you think that ... READ OUT ...

%
27.7 ...students **should** be expected to take out loans to help cover their living costs,
58.8 or, students **should not** be expected to take out loans to help cover living costs?
12.0 (It depends)
1.6 (Don't know)
- (Refusal/Not answered)

N = 1133

Drugs

VERSION C: ASK ALL

Q642 [HerLegal]

CARD H1

I'd like to ask you some questions about illegal drug-use in Britain. First, thinking about the drug **heroin**... Which of these statements comes closest to your own view?

%
1.3 Taking heroin should be legal, without restrictions
6.5 Taking heroin should be legal, but it should only be available from licensed shops
91.5 Taking heroin should remain illegal
0.7 (Don't know)
- (Refusal/Not answered)

Q643 [CanCrime]

CARD H2

Now thinking about the drug **cannabis**... How much do you agree or disagree that ... cannabis is a cause of crime and violence?

Q644 [CannabOK]

CARD H2 AGAIN

(How much do you agree or disagree that ...) cannabis isn't nearly as damaging as some people think?

Q645 [CanLegAd]

CARD H2 AGAIN

(How much do you agree or disagree that ...) if you legalise cannabis many more people will become addicts?

Q646 [CanUsePr]

CARD H2 AGAIN

(How much do you agree or disagree that ...) people should **not** be prosecuted for possessing small amounts of cannabis for their own use?

Q647 [CanSelPr]

CARD H2 AGAIN

(How much do you agree or disagree that ...) people who **sell** cannabis should always be prosecuted?

N = 1133

	[CanCrime]	[CannabOK]	[CanLegAd]
	%	%	%
Strongly agree	18.4	8.2	18.9
Agree	25.2	31.1	34.9
Neither agree nor disagree	19.8	19.5	10.3
Disagree	24.7	25.0	28.3
Strongly disagree	10.0	10.3	5.3
(Don't know)	1.9	6.0	2.4
(Refusal/Not answered)	-	-	-

	[CanUsePr]	[CanSelPr]
	%	%
Strongly agree	10.4	39.3
Agree	35.9	33.7
Neither agree nor disagree	12.7	10.3
Disagree	27.0	13.2
Strongly disagree	11.9	2.1
(Don't know)	2.1	1.5
(Refusal/Not answered)	-	-

Q648 *[CanLegal]*
CARD H3
% Which of these statements comes closest to your own view?
5.5 Taking cannabis should be legal, without restrictions
42.9 Taking cannabis should be legal, but it should only be
     available from licensed shops
49.9 Taking cannabis should remain illegal
1.7 (Don't know)
0.0 (Refusal/Not answered)

Transport

N = 1133

VERSION C: ASK ALL
Q650 *[TransCar]*
(May I just check...) ... do you, or does anyone in your
household, own or have the regular use of a car or a van?
IF YES' PROBE FOR WHETHER RESPONDENT, OR OTHER PERSON(S) ONLY,
OR BOTH
%
27.0 Yes, respondent only
14.5 Yes, other(s) only
37.4 Yes, both
21.1 No
- (Don't know)
- (Refusal/Not answered)

IF 'yes' AT [TransCar]
Q651 *[NumbCars]*
% How many vehicles in all?
40.8 One
28.8 Two
6.8 Three
1.7 Four
0.7 Five or more
- (Don't know)
- (Refusal/Not answered)

VERSION C: ASK ALL
Q652 *[TrfPb6u]*
CARD J1
Now thinking about traffic and transport problems, how serious
a problem for you is congestion on motorways?

Q653 *[TrfPb7u]*
CARD J1 AGAIN
(And how serious a problem for you is ...)
..increased traffic on country roads and lanes?

Q654 *[TrfPb8u]*
CARD J1 AGAIN
(And how serious a problem for you is ...)
..traffic congestion at popular places in the countryside?

Q655 *[TrfPb9u]*
CARD J1 AGAIN
(And how serious a problem for you is ...)
..traffic congestion in towns and cities?

Q656 [TrfPb10u]
CARD J1 AGAIN
(And how serious a problem **for you** are ...)
..exhaust fumes from traffic in towns and cities?

	[TrfPb6u]	[TrfPb7u]	[TrfPb8u]
	%	%	%
A very serious problem	13.3	7.1	10.3
A serious problem	21.6	24.7	31.3
Not a very serious problem	33.7	42.3	34.6
Not a problem at all	30.5	25.0	22.5
(Don't know)	0.8	0.8	1.2
(Refusal/Not answered)	-	-	-

	[TrfPb9u]	[TrfPb10u]
	%	%
A very serious problem	32.9	33.3
A serious problem	39.6	40.2
Not a very serious problem	16.5	16.6
Not a problem at all	10.5	9.5
(Don't know)	0.5	0.4
(Refusal/Not answered)	-	-

IF 'yes, respondent', 'yes, both', DK OR REFUSAL AT [TransCar]

Q657 [GetAbb1]
CARD J2
I am going to read out some of the things that might get
people to **cut down** on the number of car journeys they take.
For each one, please tell me what effect, if any, this might
have on how much **you yourself** use the car to get about.
..gradually doubling the cost of petrol over the next ten
years?

Q658 [GetAbb2]
CARD J2 AGAIN
(What effect, if any, might this have on how much you yourself
use the car?)
..greatly improving **long distance** rail and coach services?

Q659 [GetAbb3]
CARD J2 AGAIN
(What effect, if any, might this have on how much you yourself
use the car?)
..greatly improving the reliability of **local** public
transport?

Q660 [GetAbb4]
CARD J2 AGAIN
(What effect, if any, might this have on how much you yourself
use the car?)
..charging all motorists around £2 each time they enter or
drive through a city or town centre at peak times?

Q661 [GetAbb5]
CARD J2 AGAIN
(What effect, if any, might this have on how much you yourself
use the car?)
..charging £1 for every 50 miles motorists travel on
motorways?

Q662 [GetAbb6]
CARD J2 AGAIN
(What effect, if any, might this have on how much you yourself
use the car?)
..making parking penalties and restrictions much more severe?

Q663 [GetAbb7]
CARD J2 AGAIN
(What effect, if any, might this have on how much you yourself
use the car?)
..special cycle lanes on roads around here?

Q664 [GetBoth1]
CARD J3
Now suppose that the two things on this card were done **at the
same time**. What effect, if any, might this have on how much
you yourself use the car?
First, charging motorists £2 for entering town centres at peak
times **but at the same time** greatly improving the reliability
of local public transport?

Q665 [GetBoth2]
CARD J4
And what about charging motorists £1 for every 50 miles on
motorways **but at the same time** greatly improving long distance
rail and coach services?

	[GetAbB1]	[GetAbB2]	[GetAbB3]
	%	%	%
Might use car even more	0.2	0.3	0.1
Might use car a little less	17.3	18.9	17.2
Might use car quite a bit less	16.2	14.8	20.5
Might give up using car	5.6	2.8	3.9
It would make no difference	25.1	27.5	22.5
(Don't know)	0.0	0.1	0.2
(Refusal/Not answered)	-	-	-

	[GetAbB4]	[GetAbB5]	[GetAbB6]
	%	%	%
Might use car even more	-	0.2	0.1
Might use car a little less	16.1	13.1	12.5
Might use car quite a bit less	17.0	10.2	12.8
Might give up using car	5.9	3.3	2.9
It would make no difference	25.4	37.4	35.9
(Don't know)	0.1	0.3	0.3
(Refusal/Not answered)	-	-	-

N = 1133

	[GetAbB7] %	[GetBoth1] %	[GetBcth2] %
Might use car even more	-	0.0	-
Might use car a little less	10.1	19.2	15.1
Might use car quite a bit less	6.5	21.0	14.3
Might give up using car	1.4	6.0	3.7
It would make no difference	46.4	17.9	30.9
(Don't know)	0.0	0.3	0.4
(Refusal/Not answered)	-	-	-

VERSION C: ASK ALL

Q666 [Drive]
May I just check, do you **yourself drive** a car at all these days?

	%
Yes	68.4
No	31.5
(Don't know)	0.1
(Refusal/Not answered)	-

IF 'Yes' AT [Drive]

Q667 [Travel1]
CARD J5
How often nowadays do you **usually** travel
...by car as a driver?

VERSION C: ASK ALL

Q668 [Travel2]
CARD J5 AGAIN
(How often nowadays do you **usually**...)
...travel by car as a passenger?

Q669 [Travel3]
CARD J5 AGAIN
(How often nowadays do you **usually**...)
...travel by local bus?

Q670 [Travel4]
CARD J5 AGAIN
(How often nowadays do you **usually**...)
...travel by train?

Q671 [Travel6]
CARD J5 AGAIN
(How often nowadays do you **usually**...)
...travel by bicycle?

Q672 [Travel19]
CARD J5 AGAIN
(How often nowadays do you **usually**...)
...go somewhere on foot at least 15 minutes' walk away?

N = 1133

	[Travel1] %	[Travel2] %	[Travel3] %
Every day or nearly every day	47.2	9.7	5.8
2-5 days a week	15.5	25.0	11.8
Once a week	3.8	25.9	7.7
Less often but at least once a month	0.8	13.7	9.0
Less often than that	0.6	13.0	13.6
Never nowadays	0.5	12.7	52.1
(Don't know)	-	-	-
(Refusal/Not answered)	0.1	-	-

	[Travel4] %	[Travel16] %	[Travel19] %
Every day or nearly every day	1.9	2.0	32.9
2-5 days a week	2.0	3.5	23.6
Once a week	3.9	4.6	15.7
Less often but at least once a month	12.2	5.3	7.1
Less often than that	31.7	8.2	5.3
Never nowadays	48.3	76.4	15.4
(Don't know)	-	-	-
(Refusal/Not answered)	-	-	-

VERSION C: ASK THOSE WHO HAVE CAR AND TRAVEL EVERY DAY BY CAR AND ODD SERIAL NUMBER

Q673 [CutQrt1]
CARD J6
Suppose you were forced for some reason to cut around a
quarter of your regular car trips?
How inconvenient would you find it?
Please choose your answer from this card

Q674 [CutHalf1]
CARD J6 AGAIN
Suppose you were forced for some reason to cut **as many as a
half** of your regular car trips.
How inconvenient would you find it?
Please choose your answer from this card

VERSION C: ASK THOSE WHO HAVE CAR AND TRAVEL EVERY DAY BY CAR AND EVEN SERIAL NUMBER

Q675 [CutHalf2]
CARD J6
Suppose you were forced for some reason to cut **half** of your
regular car trips.
How inconvenient would you find it?
Please choose your answer from this card

Q676 [CutQrt2]
CARD J6 AGAIN
Suppose you were forced for some reason to cut **only around a quarter** of your regular car trips?
How inconvenient would you find it?
Please choose your answer from this card

	N = 244 [CutQrt1] %	N = 244 [CutHalf1] %	N = 268 [CutHalf2] %	N = 268 [CutQrt2] %
Not at all inconvenient	3.2	0.2	2.1	5.5
Not very inconvenient	12.0	3.4	10.3	15.3
Fairly inconvenient	29.8	18.3	23.5	33.4
Very inconvenient	54.6	78.1	63.8	45.3
(Don't know)	0.5	-	-	-
(Refusal/Not answered)	-	-	0.4	0.4

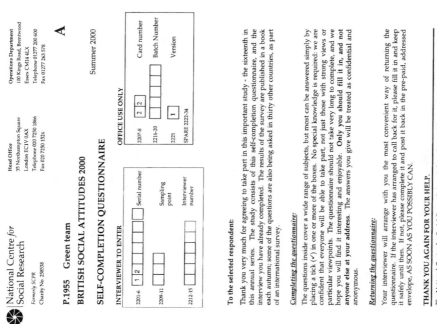

National Centre for Social Research

Formerly SCPR
Charity No 258538

Head Office
35 Northampton Square
London EC1V 0AX
Telephone 020 7250 1866
Fax 020 7250 1524

Operations Department
100 Kings Road, Brentwood
Essex CM14 4LX
Telephone 01277 200 600
Fax 01277 263 578

A

P.1955   Green team

BRITISH SOCIAL ATTITUDES 2000

SELF-COMPLETION QUESTIONNAIRE

Summer 2000

INTERVIEWER TO ENTER

2201-6 | 1 | 2 | Serial number

2209-11 | Sampling point

2212-15 | Interviewer number

OFFICE USE ONLY

2207-8 | 2 | 2 | Card number

2216-20 | Batch Number

2221 | 1 | Version

SPARE 2222-34

To the selected respondent:

Thank you very much for agreeing to take part in this important study - the sixteenth in this annual series. The study consists of this self-completion questionnaire, and the interview you have already completed. The results of the survey are published in a book each autumn; some of the questions are also being asked in thirty other countries, as part of an international survey.

Completing the questionnaire:

The questions inside cover a wide range of subjects, but most can be answered simply by placing a tick (✓) in one or more of the boxes. No special knowledge is required: we are confident that everyone will be able to take part, not just those with strong views or particular viewpoints. The questionnaire should not take very long to complete, and we hope you will find it interesting and enjoyable. **Only you should fill it in, and not anyone else at your address.** The answers you give will be treated as confidential and anonymous.

Returning the questionnaire:

Your interviewer will arrange with you the most convenient way of returning the questionnaire. If the interviewer has arranged to call back for it, please fill it in and keep it safely until then. If not, please complete it and post it back in the pre-paid, addressed envelope, AS SOON AS YOU POSSIBLY CAN.

THANK YOU AGAIN FOR YOUR HELP.

The National Centre for Social Research is an independent social research institute registered as a charitable trust. Its projects are funded by government departments, local authorities, universities and foundations to provide information on social issues in Britain. The British Social Attitudes survey series is funded mainly by the Gatsby Charitable Foundation, one of the Sainsbury Family Charitable Trusts, with contributions also from other grant-giving bodies and government departments. Please contact us if you would like further information.

N = 2991

[TOPUPCHN]
1. Some working couples with children find it hard to make ends meet on low wages. In these circumstances, do you think ...

PLEASE TICK ONE BOX ONLY

	%
... the government should top-up their wages,	61.3
... or, is it up to the couple to look after themselves and their children as best they can?	27.7
Can't choose	9.7
(Refusal/Not answered)	1.4

[TOPUPNCH]
2. And what about working couples without children? If they find it hard to make ends meet on low wages, do you think ...

PLEASE TICK ONE BOX ONLY

	%
... the government should top-up their wages,	26.5
... or, is it up to the couple to look after themselves as best they can?	62.7
Can't choose	9.5
(Refusal/Not answered)	1.3

[TOPUPLPA]
3. And what about working lone parents? If they find it hard to make ends meet on low wages, do you think ...

PLEASE TICK ONE BOX ONLY

	%
... the government should top-up their wages,	71.0
... or, is it up to the parents to look after themselves and their children as best they can?	18.7
Can't choose	8.9
(Refusal/Not answered)	1.4

[HLTHTAX]
4. How much do you agree or disagree with this statement?

"The government should increase income tax by 1p in the pound and spend the extra money on the NHS. (This would mean that every taxpayer would pay about £100 a year extra on average.)"

PLEASE TICK ONE BOX ONLY

	%
Agree strongly	21.7
Agree	34.4
Neither agree nor disagree	16.7
Disagree	17.7
Disagree strongly	5.8
Can't choose	2.5
(Refusal/Not answered)	1.2

N = 2991

5. From what you know or have heard, please tick a box for each of the items below to show whether you think the National Health Service in your area is, on the whole, satisfactory or in need of improvement.

PLEASE TICK ONE BOX ON EACH LINE

		In need of a lot of improvement	In need of some improvement	Satisfactory	Very good	(DK)	(NA)
[HSAREA1] a. GP's appointment systems	%	15.1	36.1	38.1	10.1	-	0.7
[HSAREA2] b. Amount of time GP gives to each patient	%	8.1	25.8	53.0	11.8	-	1.4
[HSAREA5] c. Hospital waiting lists for non-emergency operations	%	34.8	45.8	16.0	1.2	-	2.2
[HSAREA6] d. Waiting time before getting appointments with hospital consultants	%	45.5	40.6	11.5	1.0	-	1.4
[HSAREA16] e. Time spent waiting in out-patient departments	%	33.6	44.8	19.1	1.0	-	1.4
[HSAREA17] f. Time spent waiting in accident and emergency departments before being seen by a doctor	%	39.8	37.9	18.3	1.9	-	2.1
[HSAREA18] g. Time spent waiting for an ambulance after a 999 call	%	9.2	34.0	44.5	8.4	-	3.8

6. In the last twelve months, have you or a close family member ...

PLEASE TICK ONE BOX ON EACH LINE

		Yes, just me	Yes, not me but close family member	Yes, both	No, neither	(DK)	(NA)
[GPUSESC] a. ... visited an NHS GP?	%	22.2	15.5	55.2	5.4	-	1.7
[OUTPUSSC] b. ... been an out-patient in an NHS hospital?	%	22.8	25.3	14.2	34.9	-	2.8
[INPUSSC] c. ... been an in-patient in an NHS hospital?	%	11.2	19.4	3.4	60.3	-	5.7
[VISTUSSC] d. ... visited a patient in an NHS hospital?	%	19.0	11.5	25.6	40.0	-	3.9
[PRIVUSSC] e. ... had any medical treatment as a private patient?	%	5.5	7.1	1.8	82.5	-	3.0

N = 2991

7. Please tick one box for each statement to show how much you agree or disagree with it.

PLEASE TICK ONE BOX ON EACH LINE	Agree strongly	Agree	Neither agree nor disagree	Disagree	Disagree strongly	Can't choose	(NA)
[MENTHOUS] a. I would worry if housing were provided near my home for people with mental health problems leaving hospital	% 14.4	28.7	29.3	17.5	4.5	5.0	0.6
[MENTFAM] b. Serious mental health problems are just as likely to affect my family as anyone else's	% 17.0	54.6	16.1	6.9	1.4	3.2	0.9

8. Please tick a box for each statement to show how you feel about disabled people.

PLEASE TICK ONE BOX ON EACH LINE	Agree strongly	Agree	Neither agree nor disagree	Disagree	Disagree strongly	Can't choose	(NA)
[DISNTEFF] a. In general, people with disabilities cannot be as effective at work as people without disabilities	% 3.4	21.0	19.3	41.1	11.8	2.9	0.6
[DISPREJD] b. The main problem faced by disabled people at work is other people's prejudice, not their own lack of ability	% 16.6	58.3	14.3	7.4	0.9	2.0	0.6
[DISNOALL] c. Employers should not make special allowances for people with disabilities	% 3.0	14.8	17.5	50.0	12.0	2.0	0.7
[DISFORCD] d. Employers should be forced to employ more people with disabilities, even if it leads to extra costs	% 7.0	32.7	26.6	25.7	3.9	3.6	0.4
[DISSHOPS] e. Shops and banks should be forced to make themselves easier for people with disabilities to use, even if this leads to higher prices	% 19.5	54.7	16.4	6.3	1.0	1.8	0.4
[DISSERVS] f. Services run by government or local authorities should be forced to make themselves easier for people with disabilities to use, even if this leads to higher taxes	% 17.7	50.8	19.3	7.8	1.4	2.6	0.4

N = 2991

[COMMLAW]

9. As far as you know, do unmarried couples who live together for some time have a 'common law marriage' which gives them the same legal rights as married couples?

PLEASE TICK ONE BOX ONLY

	%
Definitely do	17.0
Probably do	39.1
Probably do not	23.9
Definitely do not	13.9
Can't choose	5.7
(Refusal/Not answered)	0.4

10. Please tick one box to show how much you agree or disagree with each of these statements.

PLEASE TICK ONE BOX ON EACH LINE	Agree strongly	Agree	Neither agree nor disagree	Disagree	Disagree strongly	Can't choose	(NA)
[MARVIEWS] a. People who want children ought to get married	% 20.8	32.6	19.1	19.8	5.9	0.8	0.9
[MARVIE11] b. It is all right for a couple to live together without intending to get married	% 16.9	50.4	16.5	9.7	4.2	1.4	0.8
[MARVIE12] c. It is a good idea for a couple who intend to get married to live together first	% 14.7	41.0	27.2	10.7	3.8	1.9	0.7

11. And please tick one box to show how much you agree or disagree with each of these statements.

PLEASE TICK ONE BOX ON EACH LINE	Agree strongly	Agree	Neither agree nor disagree	Disagree	Disagree strongly	Can't choose	(NA)
[MARRY1] a. Married couples make better parents than unmarried ones	% 10.3	16.7	28.2	31.8	10.9	1.9	0.3
[MARRY2] b. Too many people just drift into marriage without really thinking about it	% 10.9	58.0	19.2	9.7	0.4	1.4	0.5
[MARRY3] c. Even though it might not work out for some people, marriage is still the best kind of relationship	% 15.4	43.1	20.3	16.7	3.2	1.0	0.3
[MARRY4] d. Many people who live together without getting married are just scared of commitment	% 4.7	30.9	27.8	28.0	5.6	2.3	0.6
[MARRY5] e. Marriage gives couples more financial security than living together	% 8.4	39.9	21.9	24.8	2.7	1.6	0.6
[MARRY6] f. There is no point getting married - it's only a piece of paper	% 2.4	6.9	16.2	50.0	22.6	1.5	0.4

12. Please tick one box to show how much you agree or disagree with each of these statements.

N = 2991

PLEASE TICK **ONE BOX** ON EACH LINE	Agree strongly	Agree	Neither agree nor disagree	Disagree	Disagree strongly	Can't choose	(NA)
[PREGTN1] a. Teenage girls who want to get on in life don't usually become teenage mothers %	17.3	54.4	14.6	10.3	1.2	1.6	0.7
[PREGTN2] b. Many teenage mothers simply have babies because they want someone to love %	2.9	24.1	28.5	36.3	4.7	3.0	0.6
[PREGTN3] c. One of the main causes of teenage pregnancy is the lack of morals among young people %	12.6	42.5	19.1	21.2	2.7	1.2	0.6
[PREGTN4] d. People in Britain are far too tolerant of teenage pregnancies %	12.7	41.1	24.6	17.0	1.8	2.0	0.7
[PREGTN5] e. Teenage girls living in run down areas are more likely than others to become teenage mothers %	11.4	50.6	17.0	16.0	1.9	2.4	0.7
[PREGTN6] f. If a teenage couple aged 16 or older are in a stable relationship, there's nothing wrong with them having a child %	1.7	17.8	20.3	45.9	11.7	1.8	0.8
[PREGTN7] g. Teenage pregnancy isn't really that much of a problem in Britain %	1.1	3.8	10.5	55.9	25.9	1.9	0.9
[PREGTN8] h. A teenager can be just as good a parent as someone who is older %	2.5	36.3	23.9	28.6	6.3	1.6	0.8
[PREGTN9] i. There would be fewer teenage pregnancies if sex education at school gave more advice about sex, relationships and contraception %	14.3	40.2	18.9	20.6	3.6	1.8	0.6

13. Please tick one box to show how much you agree or disagree with each of these statements.

N = 2991

PLEASE TICK **ONE BOX** ON EACH LINE	Agree strongly	Agree	Neither agree nor disagree	Disagree	Disagree strongly	Can't choose	(NA)
[PREGTN10] a. Teenage girls who have children often do so to jump the housing queue %	10.2	35.4	25.9	22.2	2.9	2.9	0.4
[PREGTN11] b. Contraception should be more easily available to teenagers, even if they are under 16 %	13.3	51.3	11.8	17.9	3.8	1.3	0.6
[PREGTN12] c. There would be fewer teenage pregnancies if more parents talked to their children about sex, relationships and contraception %	17.9	56.6	14.4	9.3	0.4	0.9	0.4
[PREGTN13] d. All too often Britain's welfare system rewards teenage mothers %	12.4	42.9	25.2	14.0	1.8	2.7	1.0
[PREGTN14] e. Giving teenagers lessons at school about sex and contraception encourages them to have sex too early %	4.2	18.2	25.6	43.6	5.6	2.2	0.7
[PREGTN15] f. Pregnant teenagers should be encouraged to consider having an abortion %	3.7	17.1	27.9	34.3	12.2	4.1	0.6
[PREGTN16] g. Television and advertising put teenagers under too much pressure to have sex before they are ready %	16.2	45.5	18.0	16.7	1.8	1.3	0.6
[PREGTN17] h. Bringing up a child is simply too hard for most teenage girls to do alone %	20.0	62.9	10.1	5.0	0.5	1.0	0.5
[PREGTN18] i. Bringing up a child is simply too hard for a woman of any age to do alone %	5.5	35.6	23.8	30.2	3.1	1.3	0.6

[BRPRIOR1]

14a. Looking at the list below, please tick the box next to the one thing you think should be Britain's highest priority, the most important thing it should do.

PLEASE TICK ONE BOX ONLY

Britain should …

	%
Maintain order in the nation	37.0
Give people more say in government decisions	29.3
Fight rising prices	15.1
Protect freedom of speech	8.5
Can't choose	8.2
(Refusal/Not answered)	2.0

[BRPRIOR2]

b. And which one do you think should be Britain's next highest priority, the second most important thing it should do?

PLEASE TICK ONE BOX ONLY

Britain should …

	%
Maintain order in the nation	20.1
Give people more say in government decisions	24.1
Fight rising prices	26.3
Protect freedom of speech	16.6
Can't choose	10.9
(Refusal/Not answered)	2.0

N = 2991

15. Please tick one box to show how much you agree or disagree with each of these statements.

N = 2015

PLEASE TICK ONE BOX ON EACH LINE	Agree strongly	Agree	Neither agree nor disagree	Disagree	Disagree strongly	Can't choose	(NA)
[GOVRUN] a. Between elections, the government should get on with running the country rather than bothering about public opinion	% 10.3	32.6	12.9	32.4	7.2	3.7	0.8
[NOTGOVIN] b. Even if I had the chance I would not be interested in having more government decisions	% 2.0	19.0	19.7	42.0	12.7	3.8	0.7
[WESTLOTH] c. Now that Scotland has its own parliament, Scottish MPs should no longer be allowed to vote in the House of Commons on laws that only affect England	% 17.2	45.1	19.2	9.6	0.7	7.4	0.6
[PROPREP] d. Britain should introduce proportional representation, so that the number of MPs in the House of Commons each party gets matches more closely the number of votes each party gets	% 11.2	37.1	22.8	11.7	4.1	12.3	0.7

[VOTEDUTY]

16. Which of these statements comes closest to your view about general elections?

PLEASE TICK ONE BOX ONLY

In a general election …

	%
It's not really worth voting	11.2
People should vote only if they care who wins	24.3
It's everyone's duty to vote	63.5
(Don't know)	-
(Refusal/Not answered)	1.0

17. On the whole, do you think it should or should not be the government's responsibility to …

N = 2015

PLEASE TICK ONE BOX ON EACH LINE	Definitely should be	Probably should be	Probably should not be	Definitely should not be	Can't choose	(NA)
[GOVRESP1] a. Provide a job for everyone who wants one	% 39.3	36.5	11.9	5.9	5.1	1.4
[GOVRESP2] b. Keep prices under control	% 63.7	30.8	1.8	0.8	1.2	1.6
[GOVRESP3] c. Provide health care for the sick	% 87.2	10.8	0.1	0.2	0.7	1.0
[GOVRESP4] d. Provide a decent standard of living for the old	% 80.3	16.3	0.8	0.4	0.7	1.4

18. Do you think it is easy or difficult these days for any government, irrespective of party, to ensure the following?

PLEASE TICK ONE BOX ONLY	Very easy	Fairly easy	Neither easy nor difficult	Fairly difficult	Very difficult	Can't choose	(NA)
[GOVCAN1] a. That everyone who wants a job has one	% 3.0	12.4	14.4	46.5	19.8	2.0	2.0
[GOVCAN2] b. That prices are kept under control	% 7.3	22.0	17.7	39.1	9.5	2.1	2.3
[GOVCAN3] c. That everyone has good access to adequate health care	% 12.2	28.6	14.9	30.9	10.0	1.5	1.8
[GOVCAN4] d. That all old people have a decent standard of living	% 17.3	28.3	13.4	27.9	9.5	1.6	2.0

N = 2015

[PEOPADVT]
19. How often do you think that people would try to take advantage of you if they got the chance and how often would they try to be fair?

PLEASE TICK **ONE** BOX ONLY

	%
Try to take advantage almost all of the time	7.1
Try to take advantage most of the time	27.8
Try to be fair most of the time	47.2
Try to be fair almost all of the time	8.3
Can't choose	7.8
(Refusal/Not answered)	1.8

[DEPTALK]
20. Suppose you felt just a bit down or depressed, and wanted to talk about it. Apart from your husband, wife or partner if you have one, who would you turn to first for help?

PLEASE TICK **ONE** BOX ONLY

	%
A friend who lives nearby	39.3
A friend who lives further away	10.6
A relative (including in-laws)	32.3
A work colleague	6.1
No-one	7.7
Someone else (PLEASE WRITE IN WHO)	2.6
(EDIT ONLY: Religious support)	0.7
(Don't know)	-
(Refusal/Not answered)	0.8

[MOTTALK]
21. And suppose you needed some advice about an important change in your life – for example about a job, or moving to another part of the country. Apart from your husband, wife or partner if you have one, who would you turn to first for help?

PLEASE TICK **ONE** BOX ONLY

	%
A friend who lives nearby	30.0
A friend who lives further away	8.4
A relative (including in-laws)	43.7
A work colleague	6.6
No-one	8.2
Someone else (PLEASE WRITE IN WHO)	1.4
(EDIT ONLY: Religious support)	0.5
(Don't know)	-
(Refusal/Not answered)	1.2

N = 2015

22. Have you done any voluntary activity in the past 12 months in any of the following areas? Voluntary activity is unpaid work, not just belonging to an organisation or group. It should be of service or benefit to other people or the community and not only to one's family or personal friends.

During the last 12 months did you do volunteer work in any of the following areas?

PLEASE TICK **ONE** BOX ON EACH LINE

		No	Yes, once or twice	Yes, 3-5 times	Yes, 6 or more times	(NA)
[VOLACTG1]						
a. Political activities (helping political parties, political movements, election campaigns, etc.)	%	86.7	2.6	0.3	0.7	9.6
[VOLACT2]						
b. Charitable activities (helping the sick, elderly, poor, etc.)	%	71.4	11.3	2.9	6.3	8.2
[VOLACT3]						
c. Religious and church-related activities (helping churches and religious groups	%	76.7	5.7	2.3	5.7	9.7
[VOLACT4]						
d. Any other kind of voluntary activities	%	74.2	8.0	2.9	7.7	7.2

If the same voluntary activity falls under two or more of the categories listed above, please report it only once under the first relevant category. For example, if you were involved in political campaigning for a candidate endorsed by a church or religious group, you would report it under **a. Political activities** not under **c. Religious and church-related activities**.

N = 2991

23. Do you personally think it is wrong or not wrong for a woman to have an abortion ...

PLEASE TICK **ONE** BOX ON EACH LINE

		Always wrong	Almost always wrong	Wrong only sometimes	Not wrong at all	Can't choose	(NA)
[ABORWRGA]							
a. ...if there is a strong chance of a serious defect in the baby?	%	7.8	5.8	21.9	57.7	5.8	1.1
[ABORWRGB]							
b. ...if the family has a very low income and cannot afford any more children?	%	20.9	16.4	19.4	30.9	10.0	2.5

N = 2291

24. Please tick one box for each statement to show how much you agree or disagree with it.

PLEASE TICK ONE BOX ON EACH LINE		Agree strongly	Agree	Neither agree nor disagree	Disagree	Disagree strongly	(Don't know)	(NA)
a.	[WELFRESP] The welfare state makes people nowadays less willing to look after themselves	% 9.4	41.5	22.9	23.5	1.4	-	1.3
b.	[WELFSTIG] People receiving social security are made to feel like second class citizens	% 6.2	36.5	26.1	28.5	1.4	-	1.2
c.	[WELFHELP] The welfare state encourages people to stop helping each other	% 4.3	30.8	31.7	29.8	2.0	-	1.4
d.	[MOREWELF] The government should spend more money on welfare benefits for the poor, even if it leads to higher taxes	% 6.6	31.7	31.1	26.6	3.0	-	0.9
e.	[UNEMPJOB] Around here, most unemployed people could find a job if they really wanted one	% 13.2	47.2	18.9	17.4	1.9	-	1.3
f.	[SOCHELP] Many people who get social security don't really deserve any help	% 5.3	25.9	30.0	33.6	3.8	-	1.4
g.	[DOLEFIDL] Most people on the dole are fiddling in way way or another	% 8.5	31.7	31.0	24.7	2.8	-	1.3
h.	[WELFFEET] If welfare benefits weren't so generous, people would learn to stand on their own two feet	% 7.3	30.9	25.3	30.8	4.4	-	1.3
i.	[DAMLIVES] Cutting welfare benefits would damage too many people's lives	% 9.9	48.7	24.3	14.3	1.6	-	1.1
j.	[PROUDWLF] The creation of the welfare state is one of Britain's proudest achievements	% 17.9	38.5	29.9	10.4	2.2	-	1.1

N = 2291

25. Please tick one box for each statement below to show how much you agree or disagree with it.

PLEASE TICK ONE BOX ON EACH LINE		Agree strongly	Agree	Neither agree nor disagree	Disagree	Disagree strongly	(Don't know)	(NA)
a.	[REDISTRB] Government should redistribute income from the better-off to those who are less well off	% 9.6	29.2	24.0	30.4	5.7	-	1.1
b.	[BIGBUSNN] Big business benefits owners at the expense of workers	% 12.3	42.7	25.8	15.5	2.0	-	1.6
c.	[WEALTH] Ordinary working people do not get their fair share of the nation's wealth	% 13.0	49.3	23.0	12.2	1.0	-	1.6
d.	[RICHLAW] There is one law for the rich and one for the poor	% 20.4	44.0	18.1	15.0	1.5	-	1.1
e.	[INDUST4] Management will always try to get the better of employees if it gets the chance	% 15.1	45.0	21.9	15.7	1.1	-	1.1

N = 2291

26. Please tick one box for each statement below to show how much you agree or disagree with it.

PLEASE TICK ONE BOX ON EACH LINE	Agree strongly	Agree	Neither agree nor disagree	Disagree	Disagree strongly	(Don't know)	(NA)
[TRADVALS]							
a. Young people today don't have enough respect for traditional British values %	18.8	51.7	19.9	8.0	0.4	-	1.2
[STIFSENT]							
b. People who break the law should be given stiffer sentences %	29.9	50.0	14.1	4.4	0.4	-	1.3
[DEATHAPP]							
c. For some crimes, the death penalty is the most appropriate sentence %	28.2	30.2	13.5	17.4	9.6	-	1.1
[OBEY]							
d. Schools should teach children to obey authority %	28.0	55.6	10.6	4.0	0.6	-	1.3
[WRONGLAW]							
e. The law should always be obeyed, even if a particular law is wrong %	7.1	32.0	30.7	25.7	3.3	-	1.2
[CENSOR]							
f. Censorship of films and magazines is necessary to uphold moral standards %	18.9	46.9	15.8	13.8	3.4	-	1.2

N = 2291

[QTIME]

27a. To help us plan better in future, please tell us about how long it took you to complete this questionnaire.

PLEASE TICK ONE BOX ONLY   %

Less than 15 minutes	16.7
Between 15 and 20 minutes	35.8
Between 21 and 30 minutes	27.0
Between 31 and 45 minutes	12.7
Between 46 and 60 minutes	3.8
Over one hour	3.1
(Don't know)	-
(Refusal/Not answered)	1.0

b. And on what date did you fill in the questionnaire?

PLEASE WRITE IN: ☐☐ DATE   ☐☐ MONTH   2000

28. And lastly just a few details about yourself.

a. Are you ....

Male

Female

b. What was your age last birthday?

PLEASE WRITE IN: ☐☐ YEARS

Thank you very much for your help

Please keep the completed questionnaire for the interviewer if he or she has arranged to call for it. Otherwise, please post it as soon as possible in the pre-paid envelope provided.

National Centre *for*
Social Research

Formerly SCPR
Charity No. 258538

Head Office
35 Northampton Square
London EC1V 0AX
Telephone 020 7250 1866
Fax 020 7250 1524

Operations Department
100 Kings Road, Brentwood
Essex CM14 4LX
Telephone 01277 200 600
Fax 01277 263 578

B

P.1955 Green team

BRITISH SOCIAL ATTITUDES 2000

Summer 2000

SELF-COMPLETION QUESTIONNAIRE

INTERVIEWER TO ENTER

| 2201-6 | 1 | 2 | | | | Serial number |

2209-11   Sampling point

2212-15   Interviewer number

OFFICE USE ONLY

2207-8	2	2	Card number
2216-20			Batch Number
2221	2		Version
SPARE 2222-34			

To the selected respondent:

Thank you very much for agreeing to take part in this important study - the sixteenth in this annual series. The study consists of this self-completion questionnaire, and the interview you have already completed. The results of the survey are published in a book each autumn; some of the questions are also being asked in thirty other countries, as part of an international survey.

Completing the questionnaire:

The questions inside cover a wide range of subjects, but most can be answered simply by placing a tick (✓) in one or more of the boxes. No special knowledge is required: we are confident that everyone will be able to take part, not just those with strong views or particular viewpoints. The questionnaire should not take very long to complete, and we hope you will find it interesting and enjoyable. **Only you should fill it in, and not anyone else at your address.** The answers you give will be treated as confidential and anonymous.

Returning the questionnaire:

Your interviewer will arrange with you the most convenient way of returning the questionnaire. If the interviewer has arranged to call back for it, please fill it in and keep it safely until then. If not, please complete it and post it back in the pre-paid, addressed envelope, AS SOON AS YOU POSSIBLY CAN.

THANK YOU AGAIN FOR YOUR HELP.

The National Centre for Social Research is an independent social research institute registered as a charitable trust. Its projects are funded by government departments, local authorities, universities and foundations to provide information on social issues in Britain. The British Social Attitudes survey series is funded mainly by the Gatsby Charitable Foundation, one of the Sainsbury Family Charitable Trusts, with contributions also from other grant-giving bodies and government departments. Please contact us if you would like further information.

Note: B1-B22 are the same as questions A1 to A22 of Version A of the questionnaire

N = 1966

23. How much do you agree or disagree with each of these statements?

PLEASE TICK ONE BOX ON EACH LINE

	Agree strongly	Agree	Neither agree nor disagree	Disagree	Disagree strongly	Can't choose	(NA)
[SCIEBELF] a. We believe too often in science, and not enough in feelings and faith	% 9.9	38.1	28.7	15.7	2.8	3.3	1.5
[SCIEHARM] b. Overall, modern science does more harm than good	% 4.1	16.6	27.3	39.0	7.9	2.9	2.2

[GENRESCH]
24. Now some questions on research into human genes. Do you think that ...

PLEASE TICK ONE BOX ONLY

	%
... scientists should **not** be allowed to carry out *any* research into human genes,	7.6
or, that the only genetic research that should be allowed is to help detect, prevent and cure diseases,	78.2
or, that scientists should be allowed to carry out whatever genetic research they choose to do?	7.5
Can't choose	5.5
(Refusal/Not answered)	1.2

N = 1966

25. Please tick one box for each statement to show how much you agree or disagree with it.

PLEASE TICK ONE BOX ON EACH LINE

	Agree strongly	Agree	Neither agree nor disagree	Disagree	Disagree strongly	Can't choose	(NA)
[GENNOCHD] a. People at risk of having a child with a serious genetic disorder should not start a family	% 11.3	30.6	25.9	22.1	3.3	5.7	1.0
[GENHARM] b. Research into human genes will do more harm than good	% 3.6	14.8	24.2	42.8	6.6	5.6	2.5

[GENHOPE]
26. How hopeful or worried for the future do you feel about discoveries into human genes and what these may lead to?

PLEASE TICK ONE BOX ONLY

	%
Very hopeful about the future	11.9
Fairly hopeful	13.7
Hopeful about some things, worried about others	49.0
Fairly worried	7.8
Very worried about the future	5.1
Haven't really thought about it	7.1
Can't choose	4.4
(Refusal/Not answered)	0.9

27. How likely or unlikely do you think it is within the next 25 years that genetic information will be used to judge a person's suitability for getting ...

PLEASE TICK ONE BOX ON EACH LINE

	Very likely	Quite likely	Not very likely	Not at all likely	Can't choose	(NA)
[DNAINSUR] a. ... health or life insurance?	% 28.3	48.2	12.7	2.8	6.4	1.7
[DNAJOB] b. ... a job they've applied for?	% 16.5	41.2	26.7	4.6	7.4	3.6
[DNACREDT] c. ... credit at the bank?	% 14.4	27.9	35.0	11.2	8.3	3.3

[GENPATNT]
28. Please say which of these two statements comes closest to your view.

PLEASE TICK ONE BOX ONLY

	%
If a company paid to discover a human gene, it should be allowed to patent or copyright it to make a profit from it	3.6
OR	
Human genes are part of everyone and not something that should be patented or copyrighted	81.9
Can't choose	12.9
(Refusal/Not answered)	1.6

Note: questions B29 to B34 are the same as questions A23 to A26 of Version A of the questionnaire

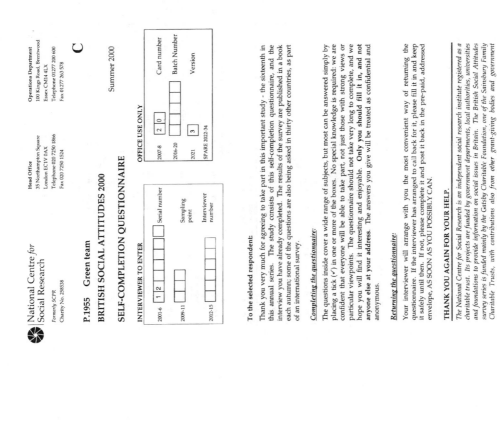

National Centre *for* **Social Research**

Formerly SCPR
Charity No. 258538

Head Office
35 Northampton Square
London EC1V 0AX
Telephone 020 7250 1866
Fax 020 7250 1524

Operations Department
100 Kings Road, Brentwood
Essex CM14 4LX
Telephone 01277 200 600
Fax 01277 263 578

C

P.1955   Green team

BRITISH SOCIAL ATTITUDES 2000   Summer 2000

SELF-COMPLETION QUESTIONNAIRE

INTERVIEWER TO ENTER

| 2001-6 | 1 | 2 | | | | Serial number |

2009-11 Sampling point

2012-15 Interviewer number

OFFICE USE ONLY

2007-8   2   0   Card number

2016-20   Batch Number

2021   3   Version

SPARE 2022-34

To the selected respondent:

Thank you very much for agreeing to take part in this important study - the sixteenth in this annual series. The study consists of this self-completion questionnaire, and the interview you have already completed. The results of the survey are published in a book each autumn; some of the questions are also being asked in thirty other countries, as part of an international survey.

Completing the questionnaire:

The questions inside cover a wide range of subjects, but most can be answered simply by placing a tick (✓) in one or more of the boxes. No special knowledge is required: we are confident that everyone will be able to take part, not just those with strong views or particular viewpoints. The questionnaire should not take very long to complete, and we hope you will find it interesting and enjoyable. **Only you should fill it in, and not anyone else at your address.** The answers you give will be treated as confidential and anonymous.

Returning the questionnaire:

Your interviewer will arrange with you the most convenient way of returning the questionnaire. If the interviewer has arranged to call back for it, please fill it in and keep it safely until then. If not, please complete it and post it back in the pre-paid, addressed envelope, AS SOON AS YOU POSSIBLY CAN.

THANK YOU AGAIN FOR YOUR HELP.

The National Centre for Social Research is an independent social research institute registered as a charitable trust. Its projects are funded by government departments, local authorities, universities and foundations to provide information on social issues in Britain. The British Social Attitudes survey series is funded mainly by the Gatsby Charitable Foundation, one of the Sainsbury Family Charitable Trusts, with contributions also from other grant-giving bodies and government departments. Please contact us if you would like further information.

1. How much do you agree or disagree with each of these statements?

N = 976

PLEASE TICK ONE BOX ON EACH LINE	Agree strongly	Agree	Neither agree nor disagree	Disagree	Disagree strongly	Can't choose	(NA)
[PRIVENT] a. Private enterprise is the best way to solve Britain's economic problems	% 7.7	26.8	32.3	15.1	2.7	5.1	10.3
[INCDIFF] b. It is the responsibility of the government to reduce the differences in income between people with high incomes and those with low incomes	% 18.2	39.3	15.9	15.3	4.0	1.9	5.5

Note: C2 is the same as question A14 on Version A of the questionnaire.
C3a and C3b are the same as questions B23a and B23b of Version B of the questionnaire

3. How much do you agree or disagree with each of these statements?

N = 976

PLEASE TICK ONE BOX ON EACH LINE	Agree strongly	Agree	Neither agree nor disagree	Disagree	Disagree strongly	Can't choose	(NA)
[SCIESOLV] c. Modern science will solve our environmental problems with little change to our way of life	% 2.6	19.3	28.1	37.0	8.2	2.5	2.3

4. And how much do you agree or disagree with each of these statements?

PLEASE TICK ONE BOX ON EACH LINE	Agree strongly	Agree	Neither agree nor disagree	Disagree	Disagree strongly	Can't choose	(NA)
[FUTENVIR] a. We worry too much about the future of the environment and not enough about prices and jobs today	% 7.3	28.0	12.8	40.7	8.9	0.7	1.5
[HARMEVIR] b. Almost everything we do in modern life harms the environment	% 7.6	40.7	21.2	26.5	1.5	0.9	1.7
[HARMV/RW] c. People worry too much about human progress harming the environment	% 3.7	24.2	22.1	39.8	6.0	1.9	2.4

5. And please tick one box for each of these statements to show how much you agree or disagree with it.

PLEASE TICK ONE BOX ON EACH LINE	Agree strongly	Agree	Neither agree nor disagree	Disagree	Disagree strongly	Can't choose	(NA)
[ENVIRECG] a. In order to protect the environment Britain needs economic growth	% 5.3	36.6	26.7	22.6	1.8	5.1	1.9
[MEDTEST2] b. It is right to use animals for medical testing if it might save human lives	% 7.2	42.8	15.8	19.2	10.4	2.8	1.7
[GROWHARM] c. Economic growth always harms the environment	% 2.0	13.9	32.9	43.1	2.2	4.1	1.9
[POPGROW] d. The earth simply cannot continue to support population growth at its present rate	% 14.8	46.7	20.2	12.5	1.0	3.2	1.5

[NATVIEW]
6. Please tick one box to show which statement is closest to your views.

PLEASE TICK ONE BOX ONLY

	%
Nature is sacred because it is created by God	21.7
Nature is spiritual or sacred in itself	18.1
Nature is important, but not spiritual or sacred	49.0
Can't choose	9.9
(Refusal/Not answered)	1.2

[PRENVIR]
7a. How willing would you be to pay **much higher prices** in order to protect the environment?

PLEASE TICK ONE BOX ONLY

	%
Very willing	6.3
Fairly willing	36.4
Neither willing nor unwilling	30.4
Fairly unwilling	16.4
Very unwilling	7.8
Can't choose	2.3
(Refusal/Not answered)	0.5

[TAXENVIR]
7b. And how willing would you be to pay **much higher taxes** in order to protect the environment?

PLEASE TICK ONE BOX ONLY

	%
Very willing	5.1
Fairly willing	26.2
Neither willing nor unwilling	25.7
Fairly unwilling	22.5
Very unwilling	17.1
Can't choose	2.8
(Refusal/Not answered)	0.6

[CUTENVIR]
7c. And how willing would you be to **accept cuts in your standard of living** in order to protect the environment?

PLEASE TICK ONE BOX ONLY

	%
Very willing	3.3
Fairly willing	22.5
Neither willing nor unwilling	23.9
Fairly unwilling	27.1
Very unwilling	21.0
Can't choose	1.9
(Refusal/Not answered)	0.3

8. How much do you agree or disagree with each of these statements?

PLEASE TICK ONE BOX ON EACH LINE

		Agree strongly	Agree	Neither agree nor disagree	Disagree	Disagree strongly	Can't choose	(NA)
a.	[ENVIRDIF] It is just too difficult for someone like me to do much about the environment	% 5.1	23.1	16.8	46.6	5.0	2.1	1.3
b.	[ENVIRRGT] I do what is right for the environment, even when it costs more money or takes more time	% 4.2	38.3	31.8	19.4	1.5	3.1	1.7
c.	[MORIMPEN] There are more important things to do in life than protect the environment	% 2.2	18.5	28.3	38.3	9.0	1.9	1.9
d.	[NOPTENV] There is no point in doing what I can for the environment unless others do the same	% 7.4	35.5	11.5	38.9	4.6	0.8	1.4
e.	[EXAGENV] Many of the claims about environmental threats are exaggerated	% 3.0	20.7	24.9	35.1	10.4	4.1	1.7

9. For each statement below, just tick the box that comes closest to your opinion of how true it is.

PLEASE TICK ONE BOX ON EACH LINE

In your opinion, how true is this?

		Definitely true	Probably true	Probably not true	Definitely not true	Can't choose	(NA)
a.	[ANTIBIOT] 'Antibiotics can kill bacteria but not viruses'	% 36.2	42.4	8.5	3.3	8.1	1.5
b.	[ORIGMAN] 'Human beings developed from earlier species of animals'	% 29.9	43.7	11.0	8.7	5.8	0.9
c.	[CHEMEAT] 'All man-made chemicals can cause cancer if you eat enough of them'	% 5.0	29.6	39.4	13.7	11.0	1.4
d.	[RADIODIE] 'If someone is exposed to any amount of radioactivity, they are certain to die as a result'	% 7.7	21.9	34.9	29.4	4.9	1.2
e.	[GRHSEFF] 'The greenhouse effect is caused by a hole in the earth's atmosphere'	% 29.8	41.7	7.8	13.3	5.9	1.5
f.	[GRHSEFF1] 'Every time we use coal or oil or gas, we contribute to the greenhouse effect'	% 34.6	45.6	10.1	2.4	6.4	1.0

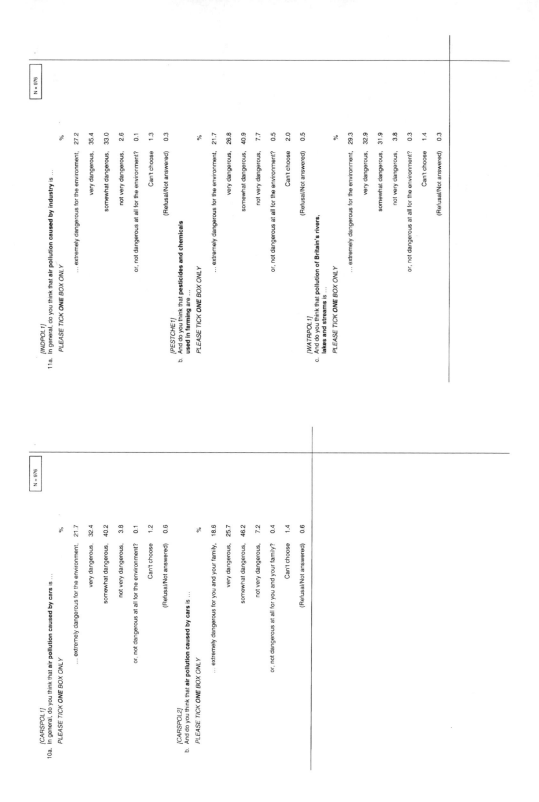

[CARSPOL1]
10a. In general, do you think that **air pollution caused by cars** is ...

PLEASE TICK ONE BOX ONLY

	%
...extremely dangerous for the environment,	21.7
very dangerous,	32.4
somewhat dangerous,	40.2
not very dangerous,	3.8
or, not dangerous at all for the environment?	0.1
Can't choose	1.2
(Refusal/Not answered)	0.6

[CARSPOL2]
b. And do you think that **air pollution caused by cars** is ...

PLEASE TICK ONE BOX ONLY

	%
...extremely dangerous for you and your family,	18.6
very dangerous,	25.7
somewhat dangerous,	46.2
not very dangerous,	7.2
or, not dangerous at all for you and your family?	0.4
Can't choose	1.4
(Refusal/Not answered)	0.6

[INDPOL1]
11a. In general, do you think that **air pollution caused by industry** is ...

PLEASE TICK ONE BOX ONLY

	%
...extremely dangerous for the environment,	27.2
very dangerous,	35.4
somewhat dangerous,	33.0
not very dangerous,	2.6
or, not dangerous at all for the environment?	0.1
Can't choose	1.3
(Refusal/Not answered)	0.3

[PESTCHE1]
b. And do you think that **pesticides and chemicals used in farming** are ...

PLEASE TICK ONE BOX ONLY

	%
...extremely dangerous for the environment,	21.7
very dangerous,	26.8
somewhat dangerous,	40.9
not very dangerous,	7.7
or, not dangerous at all for the environment?	0.5
Can't choose	2.0
(Refusal/Not answered)	0.5

[WATRPOL1]
c. And do you think that **pollution of Britain's rivers, lakes and streams** is ...

PLEASE TICK ONE BOX ONLY

	%
...extremely dangerous for the environment,	29.3
very dangerous,	32.9
somewhat dangerous,	31.9
not very dangerous,	3.8
or, not dangerous at all for the environment?	0.3
Can't choose	1.4
(Refusal/Not answered)	0.3

[GRHSEFF2]
12a. In general, do you think that **a rise in the world's temperature caused by the 'greenhouse effect'** is ...

PLEASE TICK ONE BOX ONLY

	%
... extremely dangerous for the environment,	22.7
very dangerous,	27.4
somewhat dangerous,	37.3
not very dangerous,	6.4
or, not dangerous at all for the environment?	0.4
Can't choose	5.0
(Refusal/Not answered)	0.8

[GMCROPS]
b. And do you think that **modifying the genes of certain crops** is ...

PLEASE TICK ONE BOX ONLY

	%
... extremely dangerous for the environment,	17.3
very dangerous,	21.4
somewhat dangerous,	35.3
not very dangerous,	13.3
or, not dangerous at all for the environment?	1.5
Can't choose	10.6
(Refusal/Not answered)	0.6

[PROTENVP]
13a. If you had to choose, which **one** of the following would be closest to your views?

PLEASE TICK ONE BOX ONLY

	%
Government should let **ordinary people** decide for themselves how to protect the environment, even if it means they don't always do the right thing	26.9

OR

Government should pass laws to make **ordinary people** protect the environment, even if it interferes with people's rights to make their own decisions	53.0
Can't choose	18.7
(Refusal/Not answered)	1.4

[PROTENVB]
b. And which **one** of the following would be closest to your views?

PLEASE TICK ONE BOX ONLY

	%
Government should let **businesses** decide for themselves how to protect the environment, even if it means they don't always do the right thing	8.1

OR

Government should pass laws to make **businesses** protect the environment, even if it interferes with businesses' rights to make their own decisions	81.5
Can't choose	9.4
(Refusal/Not answered)	1.1

[CTRYEFEN]
14. Some countries are doing more to protect the world environment than other countries are. In general, do you think that Britain is doing ....

PLEASE TICK ONE BOX ONLY

	%
.... more than enough,	5.4
about the right amount,	36.5
or, too little?	50.0
Can't choose	7.6
(Refusal/Not answered)	0.5

[ENVEFF1]
15a. On balance, which of these two do you think is making more effort to look after the environment...

PLEASE TICK ONE BOX ONLY

	%
.... business and industry,	12.3
or people in general?	46.6
Both equally	20.4
Can't choose	20.1
(Refusal/Not answered)	0.6

[ENVEFF2]
b. And which of these two groups do you think is making more effort to look after the environment...

PLEASE TICK ONE BOX ONLY

	%
.... government,	30.1
or business and industry?	14.1
Both equally	21.3
Can't choose	33.8
(Refusal/Not answered)	0.6

[ENVEFF3]
c. And which of these two groups is making more effort to look after the environment...

PLEASE TICK ONE BOX ONLY

	%
.... people in general,	39.4
or government?	15.9
Both equally	21.4
Can't choose	22.2
(Refusal/Not answered)	1.1

N = 976

16. How much do you agree or disagree with each of these statements?

PLEASE TICK ONE BOX ON EACH LINE		Agree strongly	Agree	Neither agree nor disagree	Disagree	Disagree strongly	Can't choose	(NA)
[INTAGENV] a. For environmental problems, there should be international agreements that Britain and other countries should be made to follow	%	32.9	54.1	7.4	1.5	0.1	3.4	0.6
[POORLESS] b. Poorer countries should be expected to make less effort than richer countries to protect the environment	%	2.0	18.3	14.5	48.0	12.3	2.8	2.1
[ECPSLOW] c. Economic progress in Britain will slow down unless we look after the environment better	%	6.4	32.3	32.1	16.6	2.5	7.8	2.3

[NUCACCID]
17. Within the next five years, how likely is it that an accident at a nuclear power station will cause long-term environmental damage across many countries?

PLEASE TICK ONE BOX ONLY

	%
Very likely	18.8
Likely	41.1
Unlikely	24.5
Very unlikely	5.5
Can't choose	9.4
(Refusal/Not answered)	0.7

N = 976

18. How much trust do you have in each of the following groups to give you correct information about causes of pollution?

N = 976

PLEASE TICK ONE BOX ON EACH LINE	A great deal of trust	Quite a lot of trust	Some trust	Not much trust	Hardly any trust	Can't choose	(NA)
[POLLINF1] a. Business and industry ... %	0.8	4.7	32.1	40.1	14.7	2.6	4.9
[POLLINF2] b. Environmental groups ... %	15.2	38.3	31.4	7.7	1.7	2.1	3.5
[POLLINF3] c. Government departments ... %	1.5	11.5	46.7	24.0	9.0	2.3	5.0
[POLLINF4] d. Newspapers ... %	1.6	11.9	38.5	26.7	14.0	2.6	4.7
[POLLINF5] e. Radio or TV programmes ... %	3.9	24.1	44.8	15.5	5.4	1.8	4.7
[POLLINF6] f. University research centres ... %	18.2	45.3	24.9	4.0	1.1	2.5	4.0

[RECYCLE]
19a. How often do you make a special effort to sort glass or tins or plastic or newspapers and so on for recycling?

PLEASE TICK ONE BOX ONLY

	%
Always	29.6
Often	21.1
Sometimes	26.9
Never	16.3
(Recycling not available where I live)	5.1
(Refusal/Not answered)	1.1

[LESSDRIV]
b. And how often do you cut back on driving a car for environmental reasons?

PLEASE TICK ONE BOX ONLY

	%
Always	3.3
Often	10.3
Sometimes	28.6
Never	37.7
(I do not have or cannot drive a car)	19.2
(Refusal/Not answered)	0.8

[MEMBENV]
20. Are you a member of any group whose main aim is to preserve or protect the environment?

PLEASE TICK ONE BOX ONLY

	%
Yes	5.6
No	92.6
(Refusal/Not answered)	1.9

21. In the last five years, have you ...
PLEASE TICK ONE BOX ON EACH LINE

N = 976

	Yes I have	No I have not	(NA)
[PETITENV] a. ... signed a petition about an environmental issue? %	29.9	67.4	2.7
[MONEYENV] b. ... given money to an environmental group? %	23.1	73.1	3.8
[DEMOENV] c. ... taken part in a protest or demonstration about an environmental issue? %	2.9	92.8	4.3

[GODBELF1]
22. Please tick one box below to show which statement comes closest to expressing what you believe about God.

PLEASE TICK ONE BOX ONLY

	%
I don't believe in God	12.3
I don't know whether there is a God and I don't believe there is any way to find out	14.7
I don't believe in a personal God, but I do believe in a Higher Power of some kind	12.3
I find myself believing in God some of the time, but not at others	13.1
While I have doubts, I feel that I do believe in God	23.5
I know God really exists and I have no doubts about it	21.2
Can't choose	2.2
(Refusal/Not answered)	0.8

[RESPRES]
23. Would you describe the place where you live as ...

PLEASE TICK ONE BOX ONLY

	%
... a big city,	9.7
the suburbs or outskirts of a big city,	18.8
a small city or town,	51.5
a country village,	16.6
or, a farm or home in the country?	2.5
(Refusal/Not answered)	0.8

Note: C24-37 are the same as questions A1-13 on Version A of the questionnaire

37. From what you know or have heard, please tick one box on each line to show how well you think state secondary schools nowadays ...

PLEASE TICK ONE BOX ON EACH LINE

N = 976

	Very well	Quite well	Disagree	Not very well	Not at all well	(Don't know)	(NA)
[STATSEC1] a. ...prepare young people for work?	% 5.0	49.6		38.8	4.7	-	2.0
[STATSEC2] b. ...teach young people basic skills such as reading, writing and maths?	% 16.4	58.9		20.2	3.0	-	1.5
[STATSEC3] c. ...bring out young people's natural abilities?	% 7.4	43.9		40.9	6.0	-	1.9

38. Please tick one box to show how much you agree or disagree with each of these statements?

PLEASE TICK ONE BOX ON EACH LINE

	Agree strongly	Agree	Neither agree nor disagree	Disagree	Disagree strongly	I never travel by car	Can't choose	(NA)
[CARWALK] a. Many of the short journeys I now make by car I could just as easily walk	% 7.3	33.8	10.8	28.0	6.5	9.5	3.2	1.0
[CARBUS] b. Many of the short journeys I now make by car I could just as easily go by bus	% 4.0	25.7	8.3	38.4	12.2	7.8	2.2	1.5
[CARBIKE] c. Many of the short journeys I now make by car I could just as easily cycle, if I had a bike	% 6.3	35.1	8.6	27.9	10.3	6.9	3.4	1.6

39. Please tick one box for each statement to show how much you agree or disagree.

PLEASE TICK ONE BOX ON EACH LINE

N = 976

	Agree strongly	Agree	Neither agree nor disagree	Disagree	Disagree strongly	Can't choose	(NA)
[CARTAXHI] a. For the sake of the environment, car users should pay higher taxes	% 2.4	11.4	16.9	49.7	16.8	2.0	0.9
[MOTORWAY] b. The government should build more motorways to reduce traffic congestion	% 5.4	27.4	26.6	30.3	6.0	3.4	1.0
[BUILDTRA] c. Building more roads just encourages more traffic	% 7.3	35.4	21.1	28.3	4.4	2.2	1.2
[CARALLOW] d. People should be allowed to use their cars as much as they like, even if it causes damage to the environment	% 2.5	17.1	33.5	33.5	8.7	3.4	1.2

40a. [CUTCARS] How important do you think it is to cut down the number of cars on Britain's roads?

PLEASE TICK ONE BOX ONLY

	%
Very important	26.1
Fairly important	48.6
Not very important	15.8
Not at all important	2.4
Can't choose	6.0
(Refusal/Not answered)	1.1

b. [PTIMPRIM] And how important is it to improve public transport in Britain?

PLEASE TICK ONE BOX ONLY

	%
Very important	76.3
Fairly important	17.8
Not very important	3.2
Not at all important	0.3
Can't choose	1.3
(Refusal/Not answered)	1.0

41. Many people feel that public transport should be improved. Here are some ways of finding the money to do it. How much would you support or oppose each one, as a way of raising money to improve public transport?

N = 976

PLEASE TICK ONE BOX ON EACH LINE	Strongly support	Support	Neither support nor oppose	Oppose	Strongly oppose	Can't choose	(NA)
[PTIMPR1] a. Gradually doubling the cost of petrol over the next ten years	% 1.1	5.4	8.4	40.5	40.0	2.7	1.9
[PTIMPR2] b. Charging all motorists around £2 each time they enter or drive through a city or town centre at peak times	% 4.2	24.3	13.8	30.7	22.2	2.9	1.9
[PTIMPR3] c. Cutting in half spending on new roads	% 3.0	16.2	25.4	31.2	17.1	4.7	2.4
[PTIMPR4] d. Cutting in half spending on maintenance of the roads we have already	% 1.1	4.2	13.3	46.0	29.1	3.8	2.5
[PTIMPR5] e. Charging £1 for every 50 miles motorists travel on motorways	% 2.8	22.2	16.0	32.5	20.7	3.2	2.5
[PTIMPR6] f. Increasing taxes like VAT that we all pay on goods and services	% 0.6	6.4	14.4	42.9	30.3	2.7	2.7
[PTIMPR7] g. Increasing road tax for all vehicles	% 1.5	13.3	11.0	38.9	29.5	2.8	2.8
[PTIMPR8] h. Taxing employers for each car parking space they provide for their employees	% 3.7	20.1	17.0	32.4	21.3	3.6	1.9

42. Please tick one box for each of these statements below to show how much you agree or disagree with it.

N = 976

PLEASE TICK ONE BOX ON EACH LINE	Agree strongly	Agree	Neither agree nor disagree	Disagree	Disagree strongly	Can't choose	(NA)
[BUSPRIOR] a. Buses should be given more priority in towns and cities, even if this makes things more difficult for car drivers	% 17.5	44.4	18.0	15.1	2.6	1.2	1.1
[CYCPEDPR] b. Cyclists and pedestrians should be given more priority in towns and cities even if this makes things more difficult for other road users	% 21.4	46.7	16.0	11.0	2.5	1.2	1.2

43. Here are some things that could be done about traffic in residential streets that are not main roads. Please tick one box for each to show whether you would be in favour or not in favour.

PLEASE TICK ONE BOX ON EACH LINE	Strongly in favour	In favour	Neither in favour nor against	Against	Strongly against	Can't choose	(NA)
[RESCLOSE] a. Closing residential streets to through traffic	% 10.1	41.4	21.6	19.5	2.9	2.4	2.1
[RES20MPH] b. Having speed limits of 20 miles per hour in residential streets	% 22.9	55.6	10.4	6.7	2.1	0.7	1.6
[RESCROSS] c. Making cars stop for people to cross residential streets even if they are not at a pedestrian crossing	% 9.3	25.4	21.1	35.7	5.4	1.5	1.7
[RESBUMPS] d. Having speed bumps to slow down traffic in residential streets	% 16.1	43.6	14.0	18.8	5.1	0.8	1.6

Note: C44-48 are the same questions as B24-28 on Version B of the questionnaire
C49-54 are the same questions as A23-28 on Version A of the questionnaire

Subject index